THE Minority and Women's COMPLETE SCHOLARSHIP BOOK

Student Services, L.L.C.

Property of Library
Cape Fear Comm. College
Wilmington, N.C.

Sourcebooks, Inc.

Naperville, IL

Copyright © 1998 by Student Services, L.L.C.
Cover design copyright © 1998 by Sourcebooks, Inc.

All rights reserved. No part of this book may be reproduced in any form or by any electronic or mechanical means including information storage and retrieval systems—except in the case of brief quotations embodied in critical articles or reviews, or in the case of the exercises in this book solely for the personal use of the purchaser—without permission in writing from its publisher, Sourcebooks, Inc.

Published by: **Sourcebooks, Inc.**
P.O. Box 372, Naperville, Illinois 60566
(630) 961-3900
FAX: 630-961-2168

This publication is designed to provide accurate and authoritative information in regard to the subject matter covered. It is sold with the understanding that the publisher is not engaged in rendering legal, accounting, or other professional service. If legal advice or other expert assistance is required, the services of a competent professional person should be sought.

From a Declaration of Principles Jointly Adopted by a Committee of the American Bar Association and a Committee of Publishers and Associations

Every effort has been made to provide you with the best, most up-to-date information on private sector financial aid. However, if you discover an award in this book is listed incorrectly, please contact our research department by mail at: Research Department, Student Services, L.L.C., 2550 Commonwealth Avenue, North Chicago, IL 60064.

Disclaimer

Care has been taken in collecting and presenting the material contained in this book; however, Student Services, L.L.C., and Sourcebooks, Inc., do not guarantee its accuracy.

Student Services, L.L.C., and Sourcebooks, Inc., are private corporations and are not affiliated in any way with the U.S. Department of Education or any other government agency.

Library of Congress Cataloging-in-Publication Data
The minority and women's complete scholarship book / Student Services, L.L.C.
        p.   cm.
   Includes index.
   ISBN 1-57071-193-3
     1. Scholarships—United States—Directories. 2. Minority college students—Scholarships, fellowships, etc.—United States—Directories. 3. Women college students—Scholarships, fellowships, etc.—United States—Directories. 4. Student aid—United States.
    I. Student Services, L.L.C.
   LB2338.M56   1998
   378.3'4—dc21   97-32078
                                             CIP

Printed and bound in the United States of America.

Paperback — 10 9 8 7 6 5 4 3 2 1

Read This First

Congratulations! You hold in your hands one of the most thoroughly researched publications ever produced on the subject of non-government college financial aid for women, minorities, and people with disabilities. This book lists more than twelve hundred sources of college financial aid, representing over thirty thousand college scholarships, fellowships, grants, and low-interest loans from private organizations.

College financial aid from non-government organizations is provided by philanthropic foundations, corporations, employers, professional societies and associations, clubs, religious organizations, and civic service groups. About half of the non-government financial aid opportunities listed in this book are college-specific; i.e., you would have to attend a particular college to receive the award. The other half of the opportunities listed in this book are independent of any specific college; i.e., you could receive the financial aid no matter which accredited school you attended.

Eligibility Requirements

The scholarships in this book are based on who you are, rather than solely on your academic record or your financial need. That means that your background and personal circumstances—your heritage, your religion, any physical disabilities you may have—could open the door to a wide array of sources of college money.

To promote cultural diversity and understanding, many colleges offer special financial aid opportunities to ethnic and racial minorities. If just one of your parents or grandparents was a member of a 'minority' group, that might improve your financial aid package. In addition, many organizations focus on people in other "special circumstances"—the blind, for example, or women—and offer scholarships based on such circumstances.

In a very real sense, women, minorities, and people with disabilities have an advantage in the search for financial aid because they can apply for all general scholarships, as well as the scholarships designated for their specific groups. Overall, there are thousands of financial aid opportunities for African-Americans alone—and thousands more for everyone from Hindus, Jews, and Armenians to people with dyslexia or epilepsy.

Today, you can find college money that is earmarked for a tremendous range of special circumstances. In fact, in terms of qualifying for college aid, almost all of us are a 'minority' in some way.

There are scholarships for people with *disabilities* such as:

- Arthritis
- Asthma
- Blindness
- Cancer
- Epilepsy
- Hearing Impairments
- Hemophilia
- Learning Disabilities
- Neurological Disorders
- Respiratory Problems
- Speech Impairments

There are scholarships for people whose *ethnic* background is:

- African
- Aleut
- Armenian
- Australian
- Black/African-American
- Cambodian
- Caribbean
- Creole
- Cuban
- Danish
- Dutch
- East Indian
- English
- Eskimo
- Finnish
- French
- German
- Greek
- Haitian
- Hawaiian
- Hebrew
- Hispanic
- Hungarian
- Indian
- Iranian
- Irish
- Italian
- Latin-American
- Lebanese
- Lithuanian
- Mongolian
- Native Alaskan
- Norwegian
- Pacific Islander
- Pakistan
- Polish
- Portuguese
- Puerto Rican
- Russian
- Scottish
- Serbian
- Swedish
- Swiss
- Syrian
- Welsh

And there are scholarships for people whose *religious background* is:

- Baptist
- Catholic
- Christian
- Christian Science
- Church of Brethren
- Church of Christ
- Eastern Orthodox
- Episcopal
- Free Will Baptist
- Greek Orthodox
- Hindu
- Islam
- Jehovah's Witness
- Jewish
- Lutheran
- Mennonite
- Mormon
- Pentecostal
- Presbyterian
- Protestant
- Quaker
- Roman Catholic
- Seventh Day Adventist
- Unitarian
- United Church of Christ
- United Methodist

In short, your background and circumstances can be a powerful asset in the search for college financing—but it is up to you to put that asset to work.

Types of Assistance

Financial aid for college is offered in three basic forms:

➤ grants and scholarships;
➤ fellowships and internships;
➤ loans designed especially for students (and parents of students).

Grants and scholarships, sometimes referred to as gift assistance, do not have to be repaid.

Fellowships and internships are monetary awards paid to the student in return for research or work performed according to the guidelines set forth by the sponsor of the award. Fellowships and internships are usually awarded to a student so that he or she may gain experience in a particular field of interest.

Student loans, and loans to parents of students, must be repaid. Generally, these loans feature favorable rates of interest and/or deferred payment options.

Where Financial Aid Comes From

Each year, billions of dollars are made available to college students in the form of financial aid.

By far, the greatest source of this funding is the federal government, which offers awards through grant, work-study, and loan programs. In addition to general aid, the federal government offers financial aid programs that target students with disabilities.

The next biggest source of scholarships and loans, involving several billion dollars, comes from the colleges themselves. Depending on the college, some of these awards will be based on financial need, while other awards will be merit-based (not based on financial need). Many colleges and universities have specific funding programs for minorities, women, and the disabled.

Depending on where you live and where you will attend college, you may also be eligible to receive financial aid from the few billion dollars contributed by state governments. Again, many states operate their own programs for students in special circumstances.

To find out more, contact the career center or guidance counseling office at your high school, or the financial aid office at the college(s) that interests you.

Beyond these traditional opportunities for college financial aid, another important source is philanthropic foundations, religious organizations, employers, clubs, local governments, corporations, and civic service organizations that offer millions of dollars in financial aid. Most of the sources of private-sector funding available exclusively to women, minorities, and people with disabilities are listed in this book.

However, do not rely on the opportunities listed in this book as your only potential sources of financial aid. It is always wise to pursue several options, including government and college-sponsored programs.

How to Request Applications for College Financial Aid from Private Donors

To save time and effort, we suggest that you use a standard form letter when requesting applications and additional information from private donors. Here is a standard form letter that works well:

<Date>

<Contact Name at Donor Organization>
<Name of Donor Organization>
<Donor's Street Address>
<Donor's City, State Zip>

Dear Sir or Madam:

Please forward an application and any additional information concerning your financial aid program for post-secondary education.

Sincerely,

<Your Name>
<Your Address>
<Your City, State Zip>

Be sure to enclose a self-addressed, stamped envelope with your form letter.

How to Use This Book

This book lists over twelve hundred different sources of college financial aid from private organizations. Many donors target their money toward a specific type of student, often based on prospective majors, academic interests, skills, and personal background.

To help you quickly and easily find the awards that are most appropriate to you, *The Minority and Women's Complete Scholarship Book* provides you with two ways to find your most likely private sector donors:

- Extensive indexes at the end of the book, identifying awards available by school, major, or career objective, ethnic background, gender, religion, marital status, military background of you or your parents, disability, and intercollegiate athletics.

- An icon system that allows you to scan the sources quickly.

The Icon System

The icons in this book will allow you to visually identify scholarships that may be appropriate for you based on majors and special criteria.

Majors/Career Objective

College majors have been grouped into nine categories to guide you to general fields of study. The following list includes the most common majors within each category and the icon that will identify them.

 Business
Accounting
Advertising/Public Relations
Banking/Finance/Insurance
Business Administration
Economics
Human Resources
Management
Marketing
Sales
Transportation

 Education
Childhood Development
Early Childhood Education
Education (General)
Education Administration
Elementary Education
Middle-Level Education
Post-Secondary Education

 Engineering
Aerospace Engineering
Architecture
Aviation
Civil Engineering/Construction
Computer Science
Engineering (General)
Material Science
Surveying/Cartography
Telecommunications

 Fine Arts
Art
Filmmaking
Fine Arts (General)
Graphic Design
Music (General)
Performing Arts
Photography

 Humanities
Broadcasting/Communications
Classical Studies
English/Literature
Foreign Languages
Humanities (General)
Journalism
Library/Information Sciences
Philosophy
Religion

 Medicine
Dentistry
Healthcare Management
Medicine/Medical (General)
Nursing
Pharmacy/Pharmacology/Pharmaceutical
Public Health
Therapy (General)
Veterinary Medicine

Science

Agriculture
Animal Science
Biology
Chemistry
Ecology/Environmental Science
Energy-Related Studies
Geology
Land Management/Design
Marine Sciences
Mathematics
Meteorology
Physics
Science (General)

Social Sciences

Anthropology
Archaeology
Ethnic Studies
Foreign Studies
Geography
Government
History
International Relations
Law
Military Science
Political Science
Psychology
Social Sciences (General)
Sociology
Women's Studies

Vocational

Automotive
Court Reporting
Data Processing
Food Services
Funeral Services
Heating/Plumbing/Cooling Industry
Hotel/Motel Management/Administration
Manufacturing
Real Estate
Textiles
Travel and Tourism
Vocational (General)

Special Criteria

The following categories are the most common criteria on which private sector scholarship awards are based. Look for these icons to help find awards for which you may qualify.

Athletics

Almost all athletic scholarships are talent-based. Primarily, these scholarships will only be appropriate for you if you plan to compete at the intercollegiate level or major in physical education.

Disability

Many scholarships are available to individuals who are challenged with a mental or physical disability. Awards marked with this icon include those for the blind, hearing impaired, learning disabled, and physically challenged, in addition to several other disabilities.

Ethnic

This category includes scholarships awarded based on race and heritage. The most common are for African-American, Asian-American, Hispanic, and Native American students, but the range of available awards is truly global and can get very specific. Consider your family background, and be sure to check with the scholarship provider if you are not sure whether you fit its requirements.

Grade Point Average (GPA)

Three cutoffs have been established for the GPA icons—at 2.5+, 3.0+, and 3.5+. Some scholarships' actual requirements may be somewhere between these numbers, so be sure to read the complete listing for the exact GPA criteria.

Military

Scholarships marked with this icon most often require that either you or one of your parents serve or served in the armed forces. Many of these awards are available to veterans or children of veterans of particular military actions or branches of the service. Also, many scholarships are for students whose parents were disabled or killed in military action. Items marked with this icon may also denote a major in military science or a related field.

Religion

Religious groups and organizations offer scholarships to students who are involved in religious or church-related activities, attending or coming from a religious school, or are interested in professional religious study.

Women

This icon identifies scholarships that are available to women only. Please note that many other scholarships are not for women only, but will often give preference to women.

Reading the Listings

Each scholarship listing includes the following information:

- Scholarship name
- Dollar amount of the available award or awards
- Deadline for submission of application materials
- Fields/Majors of intended study
- Further information you may need in order to apply
- The award sponsor's address to write for application forms and additional information

Identifying the Icons

Major/Career Objective

Business

Education

Engineering

Fine Arts

Humanities

Medicine

Science

Social Sciences

Vocational

Special Criteria

Athletics

Disability

Ethnic

Military

Religion

Women

GPA 2.5+

GPA 3.0+

GPA 3.5+

Powerful Cash-for-College Tips for Women, Minorities, and People with Disabilities

Tip 1 Submit a FAFSA[1], Even if You Do Not Think You Will Be Eligible for Federal Financial Aid

To be considered for federal financial aid for college, you must submit a FAFSA form.

Even if you think you will not be eligible for federal financial aid, submit a FAFSA anyway. This is important for four reasons:

1. You might be pleasantly surprised by the results; many middle-class people are eligible for federal financial aid (typically, loans with favorable interest rates and deferred-payment options).

2. Even if you do not qualify for federal loans with deferred-payment options, you might still qualify for loans with favorable interest rates.

3. Submitting a FAFSA is often a prerequisite for many non-federal financial aid programs.

4. Being rejected for financial aid from the government is sometimes a pre-condition for private sector awards.

Tip 2 Take a Good Look at Yourself

Although we often think of ourselves as part of one group—as being a woman, for example, or Italian or Lutheran or African-American—you may actually belong to several groups. A woman, for example, may also be Hispanic, Catholic, and hearing impaired—or have any number of other "minority" attributes. In other words, taking a broader look at your background may reveal aspects that make you eligible for a wider variety of specialized scholarships.

Tip 3 Take Advantage of Your Personal History and Experience

Many scholarships for women, minorities, and people with disabilities focus on certain areas of interest, as well as your heritage. There are, for example, scholarships for people of Japanese ancestry who are interested in agriculture, Native Americans who are studying in

[1] A 'FAFSA' is a 'Free Application for Federal Student Aid'

health-related fields, and disabled people who want to pursue a degree in electronics. So look for financial aid that reflects your interests. Consider factors such as:

➤ *Your activities and work experience.* Your hobbies, your involvement in sports, and your participation in organizations such as scouts and church groups may help you qualify for certain scholarships. For example, there are scholarships for people who have worked as golf caddies or who have been Boy Scouts or 4-H Club members—and athletic scholarships for everything from football and tennis to bowling and rodeo.

➤ *Your career interests and goals.* Many people know about the aid opportunities in engineering and medicine, but you can find scholarships for virtually any career interest. For example, do you want to be a weather forecaster? The American Meteorological Society has scholarships for minorities. Or, maybe your interest in flight puts you in the running for a Karen Janice Maloney Scholarship, which gives money to first-year women in the flight operations program at Daniel Webster College.

➤ *Your academic performance.* The minimum requirement for many private awards is a GPA of 3.0; if yours is that—or better—you will have a broader range of options to consider.

Tip 4 Look for Organizations That Have Your Interests in Mind

Many organizations are interested in advancing the causes of women, minorities, and people with disabilities. Consider:

➤ *Corporations that want to be socially responsible.* For instance, the General Motors Scholarship Program offers scholarships to minorities through several colleges. Xerox Scholarships are offered to Hispanic students who are majoring in engineering.

➤ *Associations that wish to support their members.* For instance, the American Medical Women's Association provides up to $4,000 in loans to women enrolled in accredited U.S. medical or osteopathic medical schools and offers a $500 award to a student member of the Association who submits the best original research paper.

➤ *Minority-based professional associations.* For example, organizations such as the National Association of Black Journalists, the National Association of Black Women Attorneys, and the Society of Women Engineers offer scholarships to people in their respective groups.

➤ *Organizations that want to promote participation from women and minorities in certain activities or sports.* For instance, Gloria Fecht Memorial Scholarships are available to female southern California residents who are enrolled in a four-year university and have a demonstrated interest in golf.

➤ *Organizations that support Women's Studies.* For example, the Illinois chapter of the National Women's Studies Association offers a $1000 prize and publication at University of Illinois Press for the best book-length manuscript in women's studies. Also, the University at Albany Center for Women in Government awards a Fellowship on Women and Public Policy to female graduate students to encourage greater participation among women in the public-policy process and encourage state policies that recognize the needs of women and families.

➤ *Organizations that wish to support single mothers and/or women who have had their college education interrupted.* The Association for Women Geoscientists Foundation awards $750 Chrysalis Scholarships to women who are candidates for an advanced degree in a geoscience field and have had their education interrupted for at least one year. Women of the Evangelical Lutheran Church in America provide Women of the ELCA Scholarships up to $2,000 to female members of their congregation who have experienced an interruption in their schooling of at least two years since high school.

➤ *Organizations that wish to support women and minorities who are pursuing majors in careers in which they have been traditionally underrepresented.* For instance, the Association for Women in Science Education Foundation provides scholarship aid and incentive awards to women who are actively working towards a Ph.D. degree in Engineering, Mathematics, Physical Sciences, Life Sciences, or Behavioral Sciences. Similarly, the Howard Rock Foundation Scholarship program provides scholarships to Native American students studying economics, education, business, or public administration.

➤ *Religious or ethnic organizations that wish to support women and minorities who share their religion or ethnicity.* For instance, the Presbyterian Church offers seminary scholarships to church members who are African, Asian, Hispanic, Native Americans, or Alaskan Natives.

Tip 5   Don't Forget to Look Close to Home

There are a number of financial aid opportunities to be found at the local level, through community civic groups, churches, and corporations. For example, the Jewish Vocational Service offers a number of awards for Jewish men and women living in the Chicago metropolitan area. Or, students of Swiss citizenship residing within a 150 mile radius of San Francisco City Hall can apply for a Clement and Frieda Amstutz award offered through the Swiss Benevolent Society.

Tip 6   Ensure that 'Cost of Attendance' Calculations Accurately Reflect Your Circumstances

Ensure that your Financial Aid Administrator(s) includes all reasonable costs in your Cost of Attendance calculation. Cost of Attendance includes not only tuition and fees, but also other costs associated with going to school. Women, minorities, and people with disabilities may have some expenses that typically would not be incurred by other students. For instance:

➤ If you have a disability, you may be able to include costs for necessary equipment and services—such as Telecommunications Devices for the Deaf (TDDs) or readers—in your Cost of Attendance calculation. Remember, however, that any such expenses covered by another agency won't be covered by college financial aid.

➤ If you have children, you may be able to include childcare expenses in the Cost of Attendance calculation.

Tip 7   Find Out What Worked Before

If you are interested in applying for a specific award, find out the qualities of last year's winner. Where there are similarities between you and last year's winner, emphasize those aspects in your application. Where important deficiencies exist, consider upgrading your credentials in those areas.

Tip 8 Choose a Major in an Area where Demand for Graduating Students Exceeds Supply

Competitive on-campus recruiting motivates employers to offer incentives to students who pursue majors in high demand areas. For instance, if you notice that graduating engineering and computer science students are receiving a large number of job offers, that is a good indication that employer-paid scholarships and high paying summer jobs may also be available. To learn more, check with your campus recruiting office.

Tip 9 If You Are a Woman, Consider a "Non-Traditional" Career

There are many scholarships designed to bring more women into the work force in areas such as science and engineering, where women have traditionally been underrepresented. For example:

➤ The American Council of Independent Laboratories, Inc. provides scholarships to women who begin majors in physics, chemistry, engineering, geology, and biology at the University of New Mexico.

➤ The Esther Carter Ogle Memorial Scholarship is awarded to first-year women mathematics majors at Fort Hays State University.

➤ Purdue University offers the Carol A. Thiele Scholarship for female students who intend to pursue careers related to agriculture.

➤ The Society of Women Engineers offers Bertha Lamme Westinghouse Scholarships to first-year women majoring in engineering.

➤ The Zonta International Foundation awards dozens of $6,000 Amelia Earhart Fellowships annually to women who wish to pursue graduate work in aerospace sciences.

➤ The National Physical Science Consortium offers up to $15,000 Graduate Fellowships for Minorities and Women in the Physical Sciences.

➤ The Landscape Architecture Foundation provides Harriett Barnhart Wimmer Scholarships to female undergraduates in their last year of studying landscape architecture.

Tip 10 Learn All You Can about the College Financial Aid Process

It took twelve years for you to learn enough to be eligible for a college education. With that in mind,

please do not be disconcerted if it takes a few weeks to learn how to best finance a college education.

For most parents and students, paying for college is one of the largest investments they will ever make. Yet, despite the importance, many parents and students stumble confused through the college financial aid process. That is unfortunate for them, but fortunate for you, since you can gain a tremendous advantage by learning thoroughly about college financial aid.

Such knowledge can help you to:

➤ not miss deadlines;

➤ position yourself to get a better financial aid package.

Good sources of information include:

➤ *Parent Page*, located on the Internet at *http://www.fastweb.com/parents.html*. Parent Page is an ideal place for parents to meet financial experts, talk with other parents about their financial aid experiences, and learn more on how to help their children obtain scholarships, fellowships, grants, and loans. (Note: even though Parent Page is designed for parents, this site is a tremendous resource for students as well.)

➤ *The Student Guide: Financial Aid from the US Department of Education*[2];

➤ the career center or guidance counseling office at your high school;

➤ the financial aid office at the college(s) to which you will apply;

➤ *Don't Miss Out: The Ambitious Student's Guide to Financial Aid*;

➤ financial planners, if they are reputable and specialize in college financing.

Several sites on the Internet offer information about college financial aid. However, be discerning, since the quality of the information available varies. Links to the plethora of financial aid information available on the Internet can be found by accessing: *http://www.fastweb.com*

[2]To order this free guide from the Federal Student Aid Information Center, call 1-800-4-FED-AID, or access an electronic version through the Internet at *http://www.ed.gov*

Tip 11 If You Are Classified as a 'Dependent' Student, but have 'Unusual Circumstances,' Ask Your Financial Aid Administrator to Change Your Status to 'Independent'

Students are classified as either 'dependent' or 'independent' because federal student aid programs are based on the idea that students (and their parents, or spouse, if applicable) have the primary responsibility for paying for post-secondary education. According to the federal government, students who have access to parental support (dependent students) should not receive as much need-based federal funds as students who do not have such access to parental support (independent students).

Based on the federal government's methodology for determining Expected Family Contribution, it is generally in your best interest to be considered 'independent' from your parents, rather than 'dependent' on them.

If you are considered dependent, then the income and assets owned by you and your parents will be considered in determining your Expected Family Contribution. If you are considered independent, then only the income and assets owned by you (and your spouse, if married) will be considered.

Declaring yourself to be independent can be advantageous, especially if your parents are wealthy. You are automatically considered to be an independent student if at least one of the following applies to you:

➤ you will be at least twenty-four years of age on or before December 31st of the year in which you receive the financial aid;

➤ you are married;

➤ you are enrolled in a graduate or professional education program;

➤ you are an orphan or a ward of the court (or were a ward of the court until age eighteen);

➤ you are a veteran of the United States Armed Forces.

Otherwise, you will have to convince the Financial Aid Administrator at your college that 'unusual circumstances' make your situation similar to an independent student. 'Unusual circumstances' include situations that cause your parents to be absolutely unable to help pay for your college education.

If you think that unusual circumstances make you independent, ask a Financial Aid Administrator at your college to change your status. But remember, the Financial Aid Administrator will not automatically do this. That decision is based on his or her judgment, and it is final—you cannot appeal to the U.S. Department of Education.

Tip 12 Find Out Whether Your Parents' Employer(s) Offer College Scholarships

Many big corporations offer college scholarships and tuition reimbursement programs to children of employees. Often, top marks are not a requirement. Refer questions about availability and eligibility requirements to the human resources department at your parents' employer(s).

Tip 13 Investigate Company-Sponsored Tuition Plans

If you are already employed, some employers will subsidize the cost of your college tuition if, in return, you promise to work for the employer for a certain number of years upon graduation. In some cases, the employer will grant a leave of absence so that you can attend college full-time. More often, however, employers prefer participants to attend college part-time while maintaining a full-time schedule at work.

Generally, participation in company-sponsored tuition plans is based on the quality of work performance rather than previous grades.

As long as you like the employer and the job opportunity, company-sponsored tuition plans can be a great deal. You get substantial tuition subsidies and 'guaranteed' employment upon graduation.

Tip 14 Investigate Cooperative Education Opportunities

Cooperative education opportunities combine traditional classroom teaching with off-campus work experience related to your major. In practice, this could mean that you would:

➤ attend classes in the morning and work in the afternoon (or vice versa);

- or -

➤ work during the day and attend classes during the evenings;

- or -

➤ attend classes for a semester, then work for a semester, then attend classes for a semester, then work for a semester, etc.

The biggest disadvantage of cooperative education is that it lengthens the time required to earn a college degree.

The biggest advantages of cooperative education include:

➤ earning money while you're learning;

➤ the opportunity to build a strong relationship with a prospective full-time employer, based on work performance rather than grades;

➤ graduating from college with more practical experience than students who did not attend a cooperative education program.

Opportunities for cooperative education vary considerably by college. To learn more, contact the colleges that interest you, or refer to *A College Guide to Cooperative Education* published by Oryx Press.

Tip 15 Try to Establish Residency in the State Where You Will Attend College

Publicly-funded colleges charge in-state students substantially less tuition than out-of-state students for identical educational programs.

If you plan to attend a public college, an easy way to save several thousand dollars is to attend a public college that is located in the state where you have already satisfied residency requirements.

Alternatively, if you have strong reasons to attend an out-of-state public college, you can try to establish new state residency, wherever the college you attend happens to be located.

Guidelines for establishing residency vary, so check with each of the public colleges that interest you. Generally, some of the factors considered include:

➤ Do you and/or your parents own property in the state?

➤ Have you and/or your parents lived primarily in that state during the previous two years?

➤ Do you possess a driver's license in the state?

➤ Did you earn a significant portion of your income in the state in the year prior to attending college? Did you file an income tax return for that state?

Tip 16 Consider Attending a Lower-Priced College, Particularly if Your 'Expected Family Contribution' Is High

In general, a wealthy student will have to pay most or all of the cost of college tuition without the benefit of government grants. Therefore, the easiest way for a wealthy student to reduce his or her college debt burden is to attend a lower-priced college.

On the other hand, if your family's income and assets are more modest, the difference in the Cost of Attendance between a low-priced and high-priced college may be negated, in whole or in part, by grants and work-study programs, especially if a particular high-priced college is committed to meeting your financial need with an attractive financial aid package.

If you are considering a variety of colleges at which your out-of-pocket costs would be substantially different, your decision can be assisted by comparing graduation rates, job placement rates, graduate school admission rates, and any other factors which you value. At many colleges, career counselors can tell you the percentage of students that find jobs within their chosen fields within six months of graduation. Average salary statistics and graduate school admission rates may also be available. Comparing statistics such as these can help you determine whether or not the extra tuition charged by more expensive colleges is worth it.

Keep in mind, highly motivated students can get a great education at almost any accredited college in the United States, no matter how inexpensive; whereas, unmotivated students will get a lousy education even at the most expensive private colleges.

Tip 17 Do Not Absorb More Debt Than You Can Handle

To put college debt in perspective, suppose that after graduation you could afford to pay a maximum of $600 a month towards a total of $70,000 in loans with an average interest rate of 10%. Paying off that debt would take over thirty-three years!

Here's another example: It would take over ten years to pay back $20,000 in loans at 10% interest, if the most you could afford to pay off is $250 a month.

A high debt burden can take a staggering toll on the quality of your life. During the time that every cent is diverted to paying back college loans, you may have to forgo: buying a car, saving for a house, going on vacation, and perhaps even starting a family.

Be especially wary of building up too much debt on high-interest credit cards.

Tip 18 Consider Attending a Community College for the First Two Years of Post-Secondary Education

If you cannot afford the full cost of a four-year college, consider enrolling in a two-year community college for the first two years of your post-secondary education. Community colleges tend to charge annual tuition that is substantially less than tuition charged by four-year colleges.

If you earn good grades at a community college, you may be able to transfer, as a junior, to a four year college. Upon graduation from the four-year college, you would enjoy the best of both worlds:

➤ you would have the prestige of a degree from the four-year college;

➤ you would have paid less tuition, in total, than your classmates at the four-year college.

Tip 19 Consider Attending a College in an Area Where the Cost of Living Is Lower

Tuition is only one component of the Cost of Attendance. Other major costs include food and rent—both of which are affected by the local cost of living. For instance, a hamburger at a fast food chain in Boston, Massachusetts might cost $1.79 whereas the same hamburger from the same fast food chain might cost only $1.29 in Little Rock, Arkansas. For similar accommodations, rent can also vary considerably from city to city.

In fact, you can save hundreds or thousands of dollars per year by attending a college in an area where the cost of living is lower.

Tip 20 Consider Joining the Military

Ignore this idea if you dislike hierarchy, rebel against authority, or conscientiously object to the activities of the military. However, if you would consider it an honor to serve your country as a member of the armed services, the military can be a tremendous source of college financial aid.

In return for military service, the U.S. armed forces provides several options that help students defray or eliminate their college costs. ROTC programs are especially popular among undergraduate students.

➤ For more information on Army ROTC programs, contact 800-USA-ROTC.

➤ For more information on Navy ROTC programs, contact 800-NAV-ROTC.

➤ For more information on Marine Corps ROTC programs, contact 800-NAV-ROTC.

➤ For more information on Air Force ROTC programs, contact 800-423-USAF.

Tip 21 Maintain Your Eligibility for Renewable Awards

If you receive an award that can be renewed, ensure that you understand, and do, whatever it takes to maintain eligibility for future years. For instance, many renewable awards will expect you to maintain a predetermined grade point average. Sometimes the criteria for renewal will be very creative, such as remaining a non-smoker or doing a certain number of hours of volunteer work.

Tip 22 Check into Residence Hall Counselor Scholarships

Many colleges with on-campus housing need students to serve as counselors for their residence halls, in return for a scholarship that is sometimes worth as much as the value of room and board. Most often, colleges do not announce the availability of these scholarships publicly, so you may have to approach people who are in-charge of on-campus residences and dormitories. Generally, Residence Hall Counselors are chosen based on personal character and leadership rather than grades.

Tip 23 Establish a Relationship with Your Financial Aid Administrator

Theoretically, establishing a relationship with your Financial Aid Administrator is not supposed to give you an advantage, since financial aid calculations are based on pre-defined rules and mathematical formulas. However, when borderline situations or unusual circumstances occur, a Financial Aid Administrator is allowed to use discretion. In such situations, the Financial Aid Administrator's decision could mean the difference between receiving $2,000 in loans versus $2,000 in grants. Therefore, the Financial Aid Administrator is an important person to know. Be a face, not just a name.

In Summary...

You cannot receive financial aid for any of the awards in this book if you do not apply. A great number of students 'kick the tires' of the financial aid process without following up. These passive students seem to get overwhelmed by the process, or lose interest, or both. Whatever the reason, their loss can be your gain.

Be an informed, educated, and assertive consumer of higher education services and resources. Do not leave your financial aid eligibility to chance. Conduct research on as many resources as possible. Read and understand your rights, responsibilities, and opportunities. Be persistent in talking to all of the people who could either help you or direct you to the right resources for help, including high school counselors, members of local civic, women's, and minority organizations, and clergy—and, of course, your Financial Aid Administrator.

Admittedly, the process is not always easy or simple—in fact, it can be quite time-consuming, and you will probably have to work to keep yourself motivated. But the effort can be worth it for the short-term benefit of having more money for college, and for the long-term opportunities to be found through higher education.

Awards

1

A.T. Anderson Memorial Scholarship

AMOUNT: $1000-$2000
DEADLINE: Jun 15
FIELDS/MAJORS: Medicine, Natural Resources, Math/Science Secondary Education, Engineering, Sciences, Business

Open to students who are 1/4 American Indian or recognized as a member of a tribe. Must be a member of AISES and enrolled full-time at an accredited institution. $1000 award for undergraduates, and $2000 award for graduates. May reapply each year. Contact the address below for further information.

American Indian Science and Engineering Society
Scholarship Coordinator
5661 Airport Blvd.
Boulder, CO   80301-2339

2

AAAA Minority Advertising Intern Program

AMOUNT: $3000   DEADLINE: Jan 30
FIELDS/MAJORS: Advertising, Communications, Liberal Arts, Marketing

Summer internship program for minority students beyond their junior year of undergraduate work or in graduate school. Must be a U.S. citizen or permanent resident and have a GPA of at least 3.0. Write to the address below for more information.

American Association of Advertising Agencies, Inc.
AAAA Minority Advertising Intern Program
405 Lexington Ave. 18th Floor
New York, NY   10174-1801

3

AACP-AFPE First-Year Graduate Scholarship Program

AMOUNT: $5000   DEADLINE: May 1
FIELDS/MAJORS: Pharmacy, Pharmacology

Scholarships for students in a pharmacy college. Created to encourage students to pursue Ph.D. Degree after undergraduate studies. Must be a participant in the AACP undergraduate research participation program for minorities or the Merck undergraduate research scholar program. For U.S. citizens or permanent residents. Information may be available in your school or department of pharmacy. If not, write to the address below.

American Foundation for Pharmaceutical Education
One Church Street
Suite 202
Rockville, MD   20850

4

AAUW Centennial Scholarship Fund

AMOUNT: $1200   DEADLINE: Mar 15
FIELDS/MAJORS: All Areas of Study

This fund will provide college assistance to area high school females who demonstrate financial need, are in the top 10% of their class, and have work experience and are involved in community activities. Contact your high school counselor for further information.

Greater Kansas City Community Foundation and Affiliated Trusts
1055 Broadway
Suite 130
Kansas City, MO   64105

5

AAUW Grants

AMOUNT: $1000   DEADLINE: May 15
FIELDS/MAJORS: All Areas of Study

Scholarships for female graduate students from the Norwalk-Westport area or for women (in the same area) who are furthering their education or who are changing careers. Must be a resident of Norwalk, Westport, Wilton, Weston, or Darien. One award is offered annually. Please enclose a SASE with your request for an application. Write to Willadean Hart, chair, at the address below.

American Association of University Women, Norwalk-Westport Branch
Chair, Student Grant Committee
36 Colony Road
Westport, CT   06880

6

AAUW Scholarship for Cody Women

AMOUNT: None Specified   DEADLINE: Mar 1
FIELDS/MAJORS: All Areas of Study

Scholarships are available at UNC for full-time female juniors, seniors, or graduate students from Cody, Wyoming, who demonstrate academic ability and financial need. Write to the address below for information.

University of Northern Colorado—AAUW
American Assoc. of University Women
PO Box 1531
Cody, WY   82414

7 AAUW, Walnut Creek Scholarships

AMOUNT: None Specified DEADLINE: Mar 1
FIELDS/MAJORS: All Areas of Study

Open to women who are U.S. citizens, residents of Contra Costa, and are at least thirty years of age. Must be enrolling as a junior or senior, have a minimum GPA of 2.6, and be able to demonstrate financial need. Contact the address below for further information.

American Association of University Women—Walnut Creek
Local Scholarship Fund
PO Box 3009
Walnut Creek, CA 94598

8 Abbott Memorial Scholarship

AMOUNT: None Specified DEADLINE: Mar 15
FIELDS/MAJORS: All Areas of Study

Scholarships are available to Osage Indian students. Write to the address listed for more details.

Kansas Wesleyan University
Office of Financial Assistance
100 E. Claflin
Salina, KS 67401

9 Abe and Esther Hagiwara Student Aid Award

AMOUNT: None Specified DEADLINE: Apr 1
FIELDS/MAJORS: All Areas of Study

Open to members who can demonstrate severe financial need. Applications and information may be obtained from local JACL chapters, district offices, and national headquarters at the address below. Please indicate your level of study and be certain to include a legal-sized SASE.

Japanese American Citizens League
National Scholarship and Award Program
1765 Sutter St.
San Francisco, CA 94115

10 Abigail Associates Research Grants

AMOUNT: $1000-$3000 DEADLINE: Apr 17
FIELDS/MAJORS: Women's Studies

Awards are available at from the College of St. Catherine for preparation and presentation of publishable quality research in women's studies. Grants are awarded in two categories—contribution of women from the Catholic tradition to public policy and/or services, and self-esteem among women and girls. For female researchers. Does not require residency at the center. Write to Sharon Doherty at the address below for information.

College of St. Catherine
Abigail Quigley McCarthy Center
2004 Randolph Avenue
St. Paul, MN 55105

11 Abraham Lincoln Mitchell Memorial Scholarships

AMOUNT: None Specified DEADLINE: Mar 1
FIELDS/MAJORS: All Areas of Study

Awards are available at the University of New Mexico for African-American students. Write to the address below for more information.

University of New Mexico, Albuquerque
Office of Financial Aid
Albuquerque, NM 87131

12 Abram Leftkowitz Scholarship

AMOUNT: None Specified DEADLINE: Mar 1
FIELDS/MAJORS: All Areas of Study

Scholarships are available at the University of Central Florida for full-time entering freshman who are Jewish and graduates of high schools in Seminole, Orange, Brevard, or Osceola Counties. Must be a Florida resident. Write to the address below for information.

University of Central Florida
Student Financial Assistance Office
Administration Building, Room 120
Orlando, FL 32816

13 ABWA Scholarship

AMOUNT: None Specified DEADLINE: May 9
FIELDS/MAJORS: All Areas of Study

Scholarships are available for female New Hampshire residents, in good scholastic standing, seeking a business or professional career and showing financial need. Write to the address below for information.

American Business Women's Association—New Hampshire
Charter Chapter
Melissa R. Giboney and Sandra L. Cox
PO Box 3795
Manchester, NH 03105

14 Academic Opportunity Program Scholarship

AMOUNT: Maximum: $1200
DEADLINE: Jan 31
FIELDS/MAJORS: All Areas of Study

Award for African-American high school seniors. Must have a minimum GPA of 3.0 and a recommendation from a counselor or faculty member. Renewable by maintaining a minimum GPA of 2.5. Write to address below for information and application.

Florida International University
Office of Minority Student Services
University Park
Miami, FL 33199

15 Academic Scholarship

AMOUNT: $300-$800
DEADLINE: None Specified
Fields/Majors: All Areas of Study

Awards for high school seniors with a GPA of at least 3.5 and a minimum SAT of 1020 or ACT of 21. Transfer students are also eligible if they meet the high school GPA requirement and they have a college GPA of at least 3.3. Renewable with continued academic success. Write to the address below for more information.

California Baptist College
8432 Magnolia Ave.
Riverside, CA   92504

16 ACB of Colorado Scholarships

AMOUNT: $1500   DEADLINE: Mar 1
FIELDS/MAJORS: All Areas of Study

Scholarships are available to legally blind students who are residents of Colorado. Write to the address below for details.

American Council of the Blind
Scholarship Coordinator
1155 15th St., NW, Suite 720
Washington, D.C.   20005

17 Actuarial Scholarships for Minority Students

AMOUNT: None Specified   DEADLINE: May 1
FIELDS/MAJORS: Actuarial Science

Scholarships for students who are African-American, Hispanic-American, or Native American. Must be enrolled/accepted in a program in Actuarial Science. Applicants must demonstrate financial need and be U.S. citizens. Write to the address below for details.

Society of Actuaries
Minority Scholarship Coordinator
475 N. Martingale Rd. #800
Schaumburg, IL   60173

18 Adele Kagan Scholarship

AMOUNT: None Specified
DEADLINE: Mar 1
FIELDS/MAJORS: Mathematics, Engineering, and Other Sciences

Scholarships for Jewish men and women living in the Chicago Metro area who are identified as having promise for significant contributions in their chosen careers and are in need of financial assistance. For full-time juniors through graduate level. Write to the address below after Dec 1 for details.

Jewish Vocational Service
Attn: Academic Scholarship Program
One South Franklin Street
Chicago, IL   60606

19 Adolph Van Pelt, Inc. Scholarship

AMOUNT: $500-$800   DEADLINE: Jun 1
Fields/Majors: All Areas of Study

Open to American Indian or Alaskan natives. Must have tribal affiliation, proof of enrollment, and be at least 25% Native American/Alaskan. Recipients are eligible to reapply in subsequent years. Write to the address below for complete details.

Association on American Indian Affairs, Inc.
Box 268
Sisseton, SD   57262

20 Advanced Opportunity Fellowships

AMOUNT: Maximum: $17500   DEADLINE: Jan 15
FIELDS/MAJORS: All Areas of Study

Fellowships available for qualified minority students enrolled at any level in a graduate program. Applicants must be U.S. citizens or permanent residents. See your department and the AOF Fact Sheet at the Office of Fellowships and Minority Programs for specific eligibility requirements and application procedures. Contact your department office for details. For additional information, visit the Office of Fellowships and Minority Programs.

University of Wisconsin, Madison
Graduate School Fellowships Office
217 Bascom Hall, 500 Lincoln Drive
Madison, WI   53706

21 Advocacy Diversity Award

AMOUNT: Maximum: $1000
DEADLINE: Mar 21
FIELDS/MAJORS: All Areas of Study

Scholarships for ethnically underrepresented, women, adult, and students with disabilities at Colorado State University. Must be Colorado residents, U.S. citizens, have a minimum GPA of 2.0, and pursuing a first bachelor's degree. Based on grades, contribution to multicultural awareness. May be renewed if recipients maintain pre-set standards. Write to the address below for details.

Colorado State University
Financial Aid Office
108 Student Services
Fort Collins, CO   80523

22 African Dissertation Internship Awards

AMOUNT: $20000   DEADLINE: Mar 2
FIELDS/MAJORS: Agriculture, Education, Health, Humanities, Population

Doctoral dissertation internships are available for African doctoral candidates currently enrolled in U.S. or Canadian institutions to travel to Africa for twelve to eighteen months of supervised doctoral research. U.S. citizens, permanent residents, and Canadian landed immigrants are not eligible. Please write to the address listed for complete information.

Rockefeller Foundation
Fellowship Office
420 Fifth Ave.
New York, NY   10018

23 African-American Achievement Scholarship

AMOUNT: Maximum: $3500   DEADLINE: Mar 15
FIELDS/MAJORS: All Areas of Study

Scholarships are available for African-American undergraduate students pursuing a four-year degree, who reside in Hampden, Hampshire, or Franklin County in Massachusetts. Write to the address below for information.

Community Foundation of Western Massachusetts
PO Box 15769
1500 Main Street
Springfield, MA   01115

24 African-American Scholarships

AMOUNT: $500-$1500   DEADLINE: Dec 13
FIELDS/MAJORS: All Areas of Study

Scholarships awarded to African-American incoming freshmen and transfer students who have a minimum GPA of 3.0. Contact the office of admissions for details.

Appalachian State University
Office of Admissions
Scholarship Section
Boone, NC   28608

25 AGBU Education Loan Program

AMOUNT: $5000-$7500
DEADLINE: May 15
FIELDS/MAJORS: Communication, Education, or Public Administration, Armenian Studies, International Relations

Loans for students of Armenian heritage pursuing master's degrees in the fields listed above, doctoral degrees in Armenian studies, or professional degrees in law or medicine. Applicants must have an undergraduate GPA of at least 3.5. Loan repayments begin after graduation at an interest rate of 3%. Write to the address below for more information.

Armenian General Benevolent Union
Education Department
31 West 52nd St.
New York, NY   10019

26 Agricultural Women-in-Network Scholarship

AMOUNT: None Specified   DEADLINE: Mar 1
FIELDS/MAJORS: Agriculture

Award open to women juniors and seniors majoring in Agriculture. Must be an Oregon resident and a U.S. citizen or permanent resident. May be used at four-year schools in any of the following three states: Oregon, Washington, or Idaho. Contact the address below for further information.

Oregon State Scholarship Commission
Valley River Office Park
1500 Valley River Dr. #100
Eugene, OR   97401

27 Ahora Scholarship Award

AMOUNT: $300   DEADLINE: Mar 1
FIELDS/MAJORS: Liberal Art, Science

Student must be Hispanic and complete 12 hours per semester. Financial need will be a determining factor. One award per year. Renewable if recipient maintains a pre-set GPA. Write to the address below for more information.

Eastern New Mexico University
College of Liberal Arts and Sciences
Station 19
Portales, NM   88130

28 AICPA Minority Scholarships/ Fellowships

AMOUNT: Maximum: $5000   DEADLINE: Jul 1
FIELDS/MAJORS: Accounting

Scholarships and fellowships for minority students who are attending school full-time. May be renewed if recipients maintain pre-set standards. Approximately four hundred awards are offered annually. Write to the address below for details.

American Institute of Certified Public Accountants
Manager, Minority Recruitment
1211 Avenue of the Americas
New York, NY   10036-8775

29

AICPA Scholarships for Minority Accounting Students

AMOUNT: Maximum: $5000
DEADLINE: Jul 1
FIELDS/MAJORS: Accounting

For U.S. citizens or permanent residents. Must be full-time undergraduate or master level minority students with a GPA of at least 3.0. Must demonstrate financial need and academic achievement. Applicants must have completed 30 semester hours, with at least 6 in accounting. Write to the address below for details.

American Institute of Certified Public Accountants
AICPA Order Dept. Product #870110
PO Box 2209
Jersey City, NJ   07303-2209

30

Aid to Blind Students

AMOUNT: Maximum: $800   DEADLINE: None Specified
FIELDS/MAJORS: All Areas of Study

Scholarship program for legally blind undergraduate students in Washington state to help offset the cost of equipment required because of their visual impairment. Must attend a Washington post-secondary institution. Write to the address below for information.

Washington Higher Education Coordinating Board
917 Lakeridge Way
PO Box 43430
Olympia, WA   98504

31

Aiko Susanna Tashiro Hiratsuka Memorial Scholarship

AMOUNT: None Specified   DEADLINE: Apr 1
FIELDS/MAJORS: Performing Arts

Applicants must be undergraduates of Japanese ancestry and majoring in the performing arts. Must also be members of the JACL.

Applications and information may be obtained from local JACL chapters, district offices, and the national headquarters at the address below. Please indicate your level of study and be certain to include a legal-sized SASE.

Japanese American Citizens League
National Scholarship and Award Program
1765 Sutter St.
San Francisco, CA   94115

32

Al Qoyawayma Award

AMOUNT: $2000   DEADLINE: Jun 15
FIELDS/MAJORS: Engineering, Science

Scholarships are available for Native Americans enrolled in a science or engineering program who also show interest or skill in one of the arts (Art, Music, Dance). Must have a GPA of 2.0 or better. Write to the address below for information.

American Indian Science and Engineering Society
Scholarship Coordinator
5661 Airport Blvd.
Boulder, CO   80301-2339

33

Alana Leadership Merit Award

AMOUNT: $7335   DEADLINE: Mar 2
FIELDS/MAJORS: All Areas of Study

Scholarships are awarded to entering freshmen African-American, Hispanic, Asian, and Native American students who demonstrate academic excellence, leadership, and participation in school and community activities. Write to the address below for more information.

Dominican College of San Rafael
Office of Admissions
50 Acacia Avenue
San Rafael, CA   94901

34

Alaska Native and American Indian Award at APU

AMOUNT: $2563   DEADLINE: Mar 1
FIELDS/MAJORS: All Areas of Study

Open to students who will/are attending Alaska Pacific University and are Native Alaskan or Native Americans and have high levels of academic achievement. Contact the financial aid office and your department for further information.

Alaska Pacific University
APU Scholarships
4101 University Drive
Anchorage, AK   99508

35

Alaska Visitors Association/Gomar Scholarship

AMOUNT: None Specified   DEADLINE: None Specified
FIELDS/MAJORS: Travel and Tourism

Applicants must be enrolled in programs of study emphasizing travel and tourism at any campus in the University of Alaska system. Preference will be given to students of Latin-American descent. Write to the address below for more information.

University of Alaska Southeast (Juneau Campus)
Financial Aid Office
11120 Glacier Highway
Juneau, AK   99801

36

Albert Baker Fund Student Loans

AMOUNT: $2800-$3200   DEADLINE: Aug 1
FIELDS/MAJORS: All Areas of Study

Applicants must be members of the Mother Church, the First Church of Christ Scientist, Boston, Massachusetts, and be currently active as Christian Scientists. Open to undergraduates, graduates, and Christian Science nurses in training. The $2800 awards are for freshmen and sophomores, and the $3200 awards are for juniors and seniors. Write to the address below for details.

Albert Baker Fund
5 Third St., Suite 717
San Francisco, CA   94103

37 Albert W. Dent Scholarship

AMOUNT: $3000   DEADLINE: Mar 31
FIELDS/MAJORS: Hospital/Healthcare Management

Varying number of scholarships for students in an accredited graduate program in healthcare management. Must be a student associate of the American College of Healthcare Executives. Financial need is considered. Must be U.S. or Canadian citizen. Previous scholarship recipients ineligible. Goal of scholarship is to increase enrollment of minority students. Write to address below for details.

Foundation of the American College of Healthcare Executives
1 North Franklin Street, Suite 1700
Chicago, IL   60606

38 Alexander Graham Bell College Award

AMOUNT: None Specified   DEADLINE: Mar 1
FIELDS/MAJORS: All Areas of Study

Applicants must be born deaf or deaf before acquiring language, must use speech/residual hearing or lip-reading as primary communication. Must be a graduating high school senior attending a college or university for hearing students. Write to address below for details.

Alexander Graham Bell Association for the Deaf
Miss America Starts Program
3417 Volta Place, NW
Washington, D.C.   20007

39 Alfred and Jane Dewey Scholarship

AMOUNT: $500-$1500   DEADLINE: Apr 17
FIELDS/MAJORS: All Areas of Study

Open to high school seniors who are Manchester residents. Must be able to demonstrate financial need. Preference given to minorities. Contact the address listed for further information.

Manchester Scholarship Foundation, Inc.
Kathleen F. Hedlund, President
20 Hartford Rd.
Manchester, CT   06040

40 Alice Allen Everett American Indian Scholarship

AMOUNT: $1000   DEADLINE: Apr 30
FIELDS/MAJORS: Arts and Sciences

Student must be an incoming Native American freshman at the University of Oklahoma-Norman. Student must be on the roll of a recognized Indian tribe or be a descendant of a relative who is on the roll. Student must have a GPA of 3.5 or better, with preference given to those students entering the medical field. One award offered annually. Write to the address below for information.

University of Oklahoma, Norman
College of Arts and Sciences
601 Elm, Room 429
Norman, OK   73019

41 Alice E. Smith Fellowship

AMOUNT: Maximum: $2000
DEADLINE: Jul 15
FIELDS/MAJORS: American History

An outright grant for any woman doing research in American history. Preference given to graduate research on the history of the middle west or Wisconsin. Applicants should submit four copies of a two-page, single-spaced letter of application describing her training in historical research and summarizing her current project. Write to the address below for details.

State Historical Society of Wisconsin
State Historian
816 State St.
Madison, WI   53706

42 Alice Freeman Palmer Fellowship

AMOUNT: Maximum: $4000   DEADLINE: Dec 16
FIELDS/MAJORS: All Areas of Study

Fellowships are available at Wellesley for study or research abroad and in the United States. The holder must be no more than twenty-six years of age at the time of her appointment and unmarried throughout the whole of her tenure. Write to the address below for information.

Wellesley College
Committee on Graduate Fellowships
106 Central Street, Career Center
Wellesley, MA   02181

43
Alice Lockmiller Endowed Scholarship

AMOUNT: None Specified   DEADLINE: None Specified
FIELDS/MAJORS: All Areas of Study

Open to undergraduates, with preference given to active members of the United Methodist Church. Based on financial need. Contact the address below for further information.

Alaska Pacific University
Office of Financial Aid
4101 University Dr.
Anchorage, AK   99508

44
Alice V. Rivas Memorial Scholarship

AMOUNT: None Specified   DEADLINE: Mar 1
FIELDS/MAJORS: All Areas of Study

For a female freshman with serious financial need and a minimum GPA of 2.5. Write to the address below for more information.

New Mexico State University
Office of Student Financial Aid
Box 30001, Dept. 5100
Las Cruces, NM   88003

45
Alison H. Atkins Vocal Scholarship

AMOUNT: None Specified
DEADLINE: Jan 15
FIELDS/MAJORS: Vocal Music, Music Education, Vocal Performance

Award open to women sopranos or mezzo-sopranos. Must have a minimum GPA of 3.0 and at least a 3.5 in the major. Contact the address below for further information.

Fort Hays State University
Office of Student Financial Aid
600 Park St.
Hays, KS   67601

46
Alma College Religious Leadership Award

AMOUNT: Maximum: $1000
DEADLINE: None Specified
FIELDS/MAJORS: All Areas of Study

This award is for membership in any religious denomination. Based on financial need, recommendations, and essay. Renewable based on a "B" average at Alma. Students must be accepted at Alma to be eligible. Contact the address below for further information.

Alma College
Office of Admissions
Alma, MI   48801

47
Alpha Delta Kappa Scholarship

AMOUNT: $400   DEADLINE: Apr 15
FIELDS/MAJORS: Education

Awards are available for female students who are planning to enter the field of education. Must have financial need and a GPA of at least 3.0. Applicants must be residents of one of the following Ohio counties: Fairfield, Franklin, Hocking, Licking, Perry, or Pickaway. Scholarships will be awarded by Jun 1. Write to the address below for more information.

Alpha Delta Kappa Educational Sorority, Beta Gamma Chapter
ADK Scholarship Committee
1917 Yorktown Court
Lancaster, OH   43130

48
Alpha Phi Endowed Scholarship

AMOUNT: None Specified   DEADLINE: None Specified
FIELDS/MAJORS: All Areas of Study

Scholarship is given to a junior or senior sorority sister in good standing who has shown excellent leadership qualities, high ideals, good scholarship, and outstanding contribution to Alpha Phi and Ashland University. Write to the address below for more information.

Ashland University
401 College Ave.
Ashland, OH   44805

49
Alphonso Deal Scholarship Award

AMOUNT: None Specified   DEADLINE: Jun 1
FIELDS/MAJORS: Law Enforcement, Criminal Justice

Scholarships for graduating high school seniors who plan to attend a two-year college or a university and study law enforcement or a related field. Must be a U.S. citizen. Based on character, transcripts, and recommendation. Write to the address below for details.

National Black Police Association
NBPA Scholarship Award
3251 Mt. Pleasant Street, NW
Washington, D.C.   20010

50
Altar (Augie J.) Scholarship

AMOUNT: $500
DEADLINE: May 31
FIELDS/MAJORS: Medical, Psychology, Agricultural, and Horticultural Fields

Scholarship for undergraduate students of Lithuanian descent from Illinois. Must have at least a 2.0 GPA. Must be enrolled or accepted to an accredited college or university. Financial need is a major consideration. Write to the address below and include a SASE for details. Requests for applications must be mailed by Apr 8.

Augie J. Altar Scholarship
7115 W. 91st St.
Bridgeview, IL   60455

51
Alumni Association Minority Scholarship

AMOUNT: None Specified   DEADLINE: None Specified
FIELDS/MAJORS: All Areas of Study

Awards for minority juniors at UMass for use during their senior year of study. Must demonstrate a high level of motivation and potential for leadership. Contact the Alumni Relations Office, not the address below, for more information.

University of Massachusetts, Amherst
Office of Financial Aid Services
255 Whitmore Administration Bldg., Box 38230
Amherst, MA   01003

52
Alvah Rock Memorial Scholarship

AMOUNT: None Specified   DEADLINE: Mar 15
FIELDS/MAJORS: All Areas of Study

Scholarships are available to any member of the United Methodist Church of Hope, Kansas, or a Methodist from Dickinson County, Kansas, who desires to attend Kansas Wesleyan University. Write to the address listed for more details.

Kansas Wesleyan University
Office of Financial Assistance
100 E. Claflin
Salina, KS   67401

53
Alvin B. Wood Scholarship Fund

AMOUNT: None Specified   DEADLINE: None Specified
FIELDS/MAJORS: All Areas of Study

Awarded to a minority student with a minimum 24 credits completed and demonstrated leadership and service to Central Connecticut State University. Write to the address below for complete details.

Central Connecticut State University
CCSU Foundation, Inc.
PO Box 612
New Britain, CT   06050

54
Alvin G. Burton Memorial Scholarship and Rooney Elvin Buford Memorial Trust

AMOUNT: None Specified   DEADLINE: Mar 15
FIELDS/MAJORS: United Methodist Ministry

Scholarships are available to junior or senior men entering the United Methodist ministry. Write to the address below for more details.

Kansas Wesleyan University
Office of Financial Assistance
100 E. Claflin
Salina, KS   67401

55
Amelia Earhart Fellowship Awards

AMOUNT: $6000   DEADLINE: Nov 1
FIELDS/MAJORS: Aerospace Engineering and Related Sciences

Graduate fellowships for women. Must have a bachelor's degree in science as preparation for graduate work in aerospace sciences. Must be women of exceptional ability and character. Approximately thirty fellowships per year. Renewable once (or twice in exceptional cases). Completion of one year of graduate school or well-defined research on a specific project is required. Write to the address below for details.

Zonta International Foundation
Amelia Earhart Fellowships
557 W Randolph Street
Chicago, IL   60661

56
America's Junior Miss National Scholarship Awards

AMOUNT: $1000-$30000   DEADLINE: None Specified
FIELDS/MAJORS: All Areas of Study

Scholarships are available for the winner, finalists, and other select contestants in the America's Junior Miss Competition. Applicants must be high school seniors who demonstrate scholastic excellence and future potential for outstanding contribution to society. Applicants must never have been married and must be U.S. citizens. Write to the address below for information.

America's Junior Miss Program
PO Box 2786
Mobile, AL   36652

57
American Association of University Women

AMOUNT: None Specified   DEADLINE: None Specified
FIELDS/MAJORS: All Areas of Study

Available to a female adult re-entry program student. Contact the address listed for further information.

Columbus State University
Financial Aid Office
4225 University Ave.
Columbus, GA   31907

58
American Association of University Women Scholarship

AMOUNT: $150-$500   DEADLINE: Feb 1
FIELDS/MAJORS: Arts and Sciences

Scholarships are available at the University of Hawaii, Hilo for full-time female students in the College of Arts and Sciences who are of junior status or higher. Write to the address below for information.

University of Hawaii at Hilo
Financial Aid Office
200 West Kawili Street
Hilo, HI   96720

59 American Business Women's Assoc. (Santa Fe Trail Chapter) Scholarship

AMOUNT: None Specified   DEADLINE: Mar 1
FIELDS/MAJORS: Business

Scholarships are available at the University of New Mexico for full-time undergraduate female business majors who reside in the Santa Fe area. Write to the address below for information.

University of New Mexico, Albuquerque
Department of Student Financial Aid
Mesa Vista Hall North
Albuquerque, NM   87131

60 American Business Women's Association Scholarships

AMOUNT: None Specified   DEADLINE: Mar 1
FIELDS/MAJORS: Business

Scholarships are available at the University of New Mexico for full-time female business majors. Both the Albuquerque and LA Luz chapters offer awards. Write to the address below for information.

University of New Mexico, Albuquerque
Department of Student Financial Aid
Mesa Vista Hall North
Albuquerque, NM   87131

61 American Business Women's Association, Nani' O Hilo Scholarship

AMOUNT: None Specified   DEADLINE: Feb 1
FIELDS/MAJORS: All Areas of Study

Scholarships are available at the University of Hawaii, Hilo for full-time female students at the junior, senior, or graduate level of study. Write to the address below for information.

University of Hawaii at Hilo
Ms. Bernadette V. Baker, ABWA
134 Kimo Place
Hilo, HI   96720

62 American Cancer Society Scholarships

AMOUNT: $2250   DEADLINE: Apr 10
FIELDS/MAJORS: All Areas of Study

Awards for Florida residents who are U.S. citizens and have had a diagnosis of cancer before age twenty-one. Must demonstrate financial need. Applicants must be under twenty-one years of age at time of application. For undergraduate study in any accredited school in Florida. Write to the address below for more information.

American Cancer Society—Florida Division, Inc.
Scholarship Coordinator
3709 W. Jelton Ave.
Tampa, FL   33629

63 American Chemical Society Minority Scholars Program

AMOUNT: $2500-$5000   DEADLINE: Feb 28
FIELDS/MAJORS: Chemistry, Biochemistry, Chemical Engineering

Scholarships are open to African-Americans, Hispanic-Americans, and Native Americans who are high school seniors or in college at the freshman through junior levels. Must be planning a career in a chemically related field. Must be U.S. citizens or permanent residents. Approximately fifty to one hundred awards are made annually. Write to the address below for more information.

American Chemical Society
1155 16th St., NW
Washington, D.C.   20036

64 American Council of Independent Laboratories, Inc. Scholarships

AMOUNT: None Specified   DEADLINE: Mar 1
FIELDS/MAJORS: Physics, Chemistry, Engineering, Geology, Biology

Awards are available at the University of New Mexico for women in their junior year of study in one of the fields listed above. Contact: 11665 Sunset Loop, Bainbridge Island, WA 98110, for more details.

University of New Mexico, Albuquerque
Office of Financial Aid
Albuquerque, NM   87131

65 American Council of the Blind Scholarships

AMOUNT: $1000-$3000   DEADLINE: Mar 1
FIELDS/MAJORS: All Areas of Study

Open to full-time enrolled students who are legally blind. Write to the address below for details.

Loras College
Office of Financial Planning
1450 Alta Vista St., P.O. Box 178
Dubuque, IA   52004

66 American Fellowships— Postdoctoral or Dissertation

AMOUNT: $5000-$25000   DEADLINE: Nov 15
FIELDS/MAJORS: All Areas of Study

Fellowships for postdoctoral or dissertation research for female scholars. Must be a citizen or permanent resident of the United

States. Available for the summer, as well as the school year. One-year fellowships and summer programs start Jun 1. Write to the address below for complete details.

American Association of University Women Educational Foundation
2201 N. Dodge Street
Iowa City, IA   52243

67 American Indian Emergency Aid Fund

AMOUNT: Maximum: $200   DEADLINE: None Specified
FIELDS/MAJORS: All Areas of Study

Award available at Portland State University for undergraduates of American Indian descent. Applicants must have the UISHE faculty advisor or student coordinator endorse the application. Emergency needs include the cost of books and materials for specific courses and other course related expenses. Write to the address below for more information.

Portland State University
Educational Equity Programs and Services
120 Smith Memorial Center
Portland, OR   97207

68 American Indian Endowed Scholarship

AMOUNT: Maximum: $1000   DEADLINE: None Specified
FIELDS/MAJORS: All Areas of Study

Scholarship program for undergraduate Native American students who reside in Washington state and are enrolled in a Washington state schools. Write to the address below for information.

Washington Higher Education Coordinating Board
917 Lakeridge Way
PO Box 43430
Olympia, WA   98504

69 American Indian Graduate Program

AMOUNT: None Specified
DEADLINE: None Specified
FIELDS/MAJORS: Public Health

American Indian or Alaskan native graduate students in public health. Consideration is given to past experience and academics and also to goals of working with Indian communities. Write for complete details.

University of California, Berkeley
School of Public Health
American Indian Graduate Program
Berkeley, CA   94720

70 American Indian MBA Scholarship

AMOUNT: None Specified   DEADLINE: Mar 1
FIELDS/MAJORS: Business

Scholarships are available at the University of New Mexico for full-time American Indian graduate students in an MBA program. Write to the address below for information.

University of New Mexico, Albuquerque
Department of Student Financial Aid
Mesa Vista Hall North
Albuquerque, NM   87131

71 American Indian Scholarship

AMOUNT: None Specified   DEADLINE: Jul 1
FIELDS/MAJORS: All Areas of Study

Awards available for Native American students at the undergraduate or graduate level. Applicants must have a GPA of at least 2.75, have proof of Indian blood as indicated in letters or proof papers, and have financial need. Send a SASE to the address below for additional information.

National Society Daughters of the American Revolution
American Indians Committee
3738 South Mission Dr.
Lake Havasu City, AZ   86406

72 American Indian Scholarship

AMOUNT: None Specified   DEADLINE: May 1
FIELDS/MAJORS: All Areas of Study

Awards for incoming freshmen who are at least 25% Native American and demonstrate financial need. Contact the address below for further information.

Iowa State University—Special Population Unit
Office of Student Financial Aid
12 Beardshear Hall
Ames, IA   50011

73 American Indian Scholarships

AMOUNT: None Specified
DEADLINE: None Specified
FIELDS/MAJORS: Archaeology

Scholarships are available to American Indian students to participate in one of the center's summer field schools. The awards will cover the full cost of tuition, travel, room and board, and will include a weekly stipend. All applicants must be high school students who are members of a federally or state recognized tribe. Write to the address below for more information.

Center for American Archaeology
Admissions Office, Attn: Ms. Brenda Nord
PO Box 366
Kempsville, IL   62053

74 American Legion Auxiliary Memorial Scholarships

AMOUNT: $500   DEADLINE: Mar 15
FIELDS/MAJORS: All Areas of Study

Scholarships available for Michigan residents who will be or are attending a college or university in Michigan. Applicants must be citizens of the U.S. and daughters of veterans. Write to the address below for additional information.

American Legion Auxiliary—Department of Michigan
212 North Verlinden
Lansing, MI   48915

75
American Medical Women's Association Medical Education Loans

AMOUNT: $2000   DEADLINE: Apr 30
FIELDS/MAJORS: Medicine, (Medical and Osteopathic)

Loans for women who are members of the American Medical Women's Association. Must be U.S. citizen or permanent resident enrolled in accredited U.S. medical or osteopathic medicine school. Additional loans may be made to a maximum of $4000. Payment and interest deferred until graduation. Write to the address below (or call (703) 838-0500) for details.

American Medical Women's Association Foundation
Student Loan Fund
801 N. Fairfax Street, Suite 400
Alexandria, VA   22314

76
American Meteorological Society Minority Scholarships

AMOUNT: $3000   DEADLINE: Jan 31
FIELDS/MAJORS: Meteorology, Atmospheric Science, Hydrology, Oceanic Science

Awards for minority students who will be entering their freshman year of college and are planning to study in one of the areas listed above. Write to the address below for more information.

American Meteorological Society
Attn: Fellowship/Scholarship
45 Beacon St.
Boston, MA   02108

77
American Research Institute in Turkey

AMOUNT: Maximum: $30000
DEADLINE: Nov 15
FIELDS/MAJORS: Humanities, Social Sciences

Scholarships are available for graduate students engaged in research in ancient, medieval, or modern times in Turkey, in any field of the humanities and social sciences. Applicants must be of Czech, Hungarian, Polish, or Slovak heritage. Two to three awards offered annually. Write to the address below for more information.

University of Pennsylvania Museum
33rd and Spruce Streets
Philadelphia, PA   19104

78
American Scandinavian Foundation Scholarships

AMOUNT: None Specified   DEADLINE: Mar 15
FIELDS/MAJORS: Business, Art, Science, Music

Scholarships are available for juniors, seniors, and graduate students studying in one of the fields listed above. Applicants must be enrolled in a college or university in the Los Angeles area and demonstrate interest in Scandinavia. Write to the address below for information.

American Scandinavian Foundation of Los Angeles
Ellissa Della Rocca
42 Paloma Avenue
Venice, CA   90291

79
Amoco Accounting Scholarships

AMOUNT: $750   DEADLINE: Feb 7
FIELDS/MAJORS: Accounting

Scholarships are available at the University of Oklahoma, Norman for full-time juniors or senior minority accounting majors. Two awards offered annually. Write to the address below for information.

University of Oklahoma, Norman
School of Accounting
200 Adams Hall
Norman, OK   73019

80
Amoco Minority Chemical Engineering Scholarship

AMOUNT: None Specified   DEADLINE: None Specified
FIELDS/MAJORS: Chemical Engineering

Open to students who are ethnic minorities majoring in chemical engineering. Recipients chosen by the school. Write to the address listed for further information.

Georgia Institute of Technology
Financial Aid Office
225 North Ave.
Atlanta, GA   30332

81
Amy Reiss Blind Student Scholarship

AMOUNT: None Specified   DEADLINE: Feb 1
FIELDS/MAJORS: Law

Scholarship for a blind student admitted or matriculated in the Fordham University School of Law (studying toward JD). Award is based on financial need. Write to the address below for details.

Morrison, Cohen, Singer & Weinstein
Amy Reiss
750 Lexington Ave.
New York, NY   10022

82 Anderson Publishing Company Minority Scholarship

AMOUNT: $2500   DEADLINE: Feb 1
FIELDS/MAJORS: Law

Awards for minority law students who are residents of the greater Cincinnati area. Contact the assistant dean, Chase College of Law, for further information.

Northern Kentucky University
Chase College of Law
Office of Admissions
Highland Heights, KY   41099

83 Anheuser-Busch Foundation

AMOUNT: $500-$800   DEADLINE: Jul 15
FIELDS/MAJORS: All Areas of Study

Available for male or female minority students who are heads of households and currently enrolled in Harold Washington College. Write to the address below for more information.

Chicago Urban League
Gina Blake, Scholarship Specialist
4510 South Michigan Ave.
Chicago, IL   60653

84 Ann August Moser Scholarship

AMOUNT: $1000   DEADLINE: Mar 1
FIELDS/MAJORS: All Areas of Study

Scholarships are available at the University of Oklahoma, Norman for female students demonstrating financial need. Applicant must have a GPA of at least 3.25 to qualify. Three or four awards are offered annually. Write to the address below for information.

University of Oklahoma, Norman
Office of Financial Aid Services
731 Elm
Norman, OK   73019

85 Ann Livingston Memorial Scholarship

AMOUNT: None Specified
DEADLINE: None Specified
FIELDS/MAJORS: Physical Education

Scholarships are available at CSU for female undergraduate students with preference given to graduates of Poudre R-1 school district. Applicant must be a U.S. citizen. Write to the office of the dean at the address below for details.

Colorado State University
Applied Human Sciences
104 Gibbons
Fort Collins, CO   80523

86 Anna & Pietro Dapolonia Trust

AMOUNT: $2558   DEADLINE: None Specified
FIELDS/MAJORS: All Areas of Study

Scholarships are available at the University of Iowa for undergraduate students who are descendants of Italian immigrants who came to Iowa prior to Jan 1, 1929. Applicant must have a GPA of at least 3.0. Write to the address below for information.

University of Iowa
Office of Student Financial Aid
208 Calvin Hall
Iowa City, IA   52242

87 Anna M. Nielsen Scholarship

AMOUNT: None Specified   DEADLINE: Feb 1
FIELDS/MAJORS: Music

Open to music majors who are of Danish descent and residents of Cedar Falls, Iowa. Contact the address below for further information.

University of Northern Iowa
Dr. Alan Schmitz, Associate Director
110 Russell Hall
Cedar Falls, IA   50614

88 Anne Gilliland Memorial Scholarship

AMOUNT: None Specified   DEADLINE: Mar 1
FIELDS/MAJORS: All Areas of Study

Scholarships are available at the University of New Mexico for full-time female students who will be participating in the intercollegiate track and field program. Contact the scholarship office or the athletic department for more details.

University of New Mexico, Albuquerque
Department of Student Financial Aid
Mesa Vista Hall North
Albuquerque, NM   87131

89 Annette Mumma Nation Scholarship

AMOUNT: None Specified   DEADLINE: Mar 1
FIELDS/MAJORS: All Areas of Study

Awarded to outstanding Elizabethtown College women who have balanced academics with their extracurricular activities and contributions to college life. Contact the address listed for further information.

Elizabethtown College
M. Clarke Paine, Dir. of Financial Aid
One Alpha Dr.
Elizabethtown, PA   17022

90 APA Fellowships

AMOUNT: $2000-$4000   DEADLINE: May 15
FIELDS/MAJORS: Urban Planning

Applicants must be minority graduate students enrolled in an accredited planning program. Must be able to document need for financial assistance. Must be a United States citizen. Minority groups eligible for this program are African-American, Hispanic, and Native Americans. Contact your department, or write to "APA Planning Fellowships" at the address below for further information and application forms.

American Planning Association
Attn: Asst. for Div. and Student Services
1776 Massachusetts Avenue, NW
Washington, D.C.   20036

91 Appalachian Scholarship

AMOUNT: $100-$1000   DEADLINE: None Specified
FIELDS/MAJORS: All Areas of Study

Scholarships for undergraduate students who are residents of Appalachia, U.S. citizens, or permanent residents, and members of the Presbyterian Church (U.S.A.). Must be able to demonstrate financial need. Write to the address below for information and an application.

Presbyterian Church (U.S.A.)
Office of Financial Aid for Studies
100 Witherspoon Street
Louisville, KY   40202

92 Applied Human Sciences Scholarships

AMOUNT: $800   DEADLINE: None Specified
FIELDS/MAJORS: All Areas of Study

Scholarships are available at CSU for undergraduate students from underrepresented populations (minority, disabled, etc.) Write to the address below for details.

Colorado State University
Applied Human Sciences
104 Gibbons
Fort Collins, CO   80523

93 APS Minorities Scholarship Program

AMOUNT: $2000   DEADLINE: Feb 2
FIELDS/MAJORS: Physics

The American Physical Society has organized this scholarship program for minority freshmen and sophomores majoring in physics. Must be African-American, Native American, or Hispanic-American, as well as a U.S. citizen. Renewable. Contact address below between Nov and Feb for complete details. If already in college, check with your physics department, a description of this program may be posted.

American Physical Society
One Physics Ellipse
College Park, MD   20740

94 Arab Women's Scholarship

AMOUNT: None Specified   DEADLINE: Mar 1
FIELDS/MAJORS: All Areas of Study

Awards are available at the University of New Mexico for students of Arab descent. Write to the address below for more information.

University of New Mexico, Albuquerque
Office of Financial Aid
Albuquerque, NM   87131

95 Archdiocesan Scholarships

AMOUNT: $15062   DEADLINE: Feb 15
FIELDS/MAJORS: All Areas of Study

Scholarships are available at the Catholic University of America for Catholic members of high school graduating classes. Based on aptitude and achievement. Not restricted to Catholic high schools. Write to the address below for details.

Catholic University of America
Office of Admissions and Financial Aid
Washington, D.C.   20064

96 Arco Aspen Scholarship

AMOUNT: None Specified
DEADLINE: Mar 1   FIELDS/MAJORS: Accounting

Scholarships are available at the University of New Mexico for full-time minority or female accounting majors. Write to the address below for information.

University of New Mexico, Albuquerque
Department of Student Financial Aid
Mesa Vista Hall North
Albuquerque, NM   87131

97 Armenian Bible College Scholarships

AMOUNT: Maximum: $2000   DEADLINE: Jun 30
FIELDS/MAJORS: All Areas of Study

Scholarships for students attending Armenian Bible College in any area of study who have pledged to work as a minister, evangelist, missionary, or youth director after graduation. Write to the address below for more details.

Armenian Bible College
Dr. Yeghia Babikian, Director
1605 E. Elizabeth St.
Pasadena, CA   91104

98

Armenian Professional Society of the Bay Area Scholarships

AMOUNT: $1000   DEADLINE: Nov 15
FIELDS/MAJORS: Armenian Studies, Music, Fine Arts, Literature, Journalism, Cinematography

Scholarships for students at the junior level or higher who are enrolled full-time at an accredited four-year college or university and are in need of financial assistance. Applicants must maintain a GPA of 3.2 or higher, be California residents, and be able to demonstrate a substantial involvement in Armenian affairs. Write to the address below for details.

Armenian Professional Society of the Bay Area
Dr. John Missirian
839 Marina Boulevard
San Francisco, CA   94123

99

Armstrong World Industries Scholarship

AMOUNT: None Specified   DEADLINE: Mar 1
FIELDS/MAJORS: All Areas of Study

Awarded to minority students demonstrating financial need, with preference given to students from Lancaster, York, and Harrisburg. Contact the address listed for further information.

Elizabethtown College
M. Clarke Paine, Dir. of Financial Aid
One Alpha Dr.
Elizabethtown, PA   17022

100

Arnold & Bess Ungerman Charitable Trust Scholarship

AMOUNT: None Specified   DEADLINE: None Specified
FIELDS/MAJORS: Medicine

Scholarships are available at the University of Oklahoma for medical students who are of African-American or Native American heritage. Four awards offered annually. Write to the address below for information.

University of Oklahoma, Norman
Director, Office of Financial Aid
OUHSC, P.O. Box 73190
Oklahoma City, OK   73190

101

Arnold Ostwald Memorial Science Scholarship

AMOUNT: $2000   DEADLINE: Mar 1
FIELDS/MAJORS: Science

Scholarships are available to legally blind entering freshmen majoring in science. Based on academic ability. Write to the address below for details.

American Council of the Blind
Scholarship Coordinator
1155 15th St., NW, Suite 720
Washington, D.C.   20005

102

ASA Minority Fellowship Program

AMOUNT: $10000   DEADLINE: Dec 31
FIELDS/MAJORS: Sociology, Mental Health

Applicants must be minority graduate students who have an interest and can express a commitment to the sociological aspects of mental health issues relevant to ethnic and racial minorities. Write to the address below for details.

American Sociological Association
Minority Fellowship Program
1722 N Street, NW
Washington, D.C.   20036

103

Ashland University Faculty Women's Club Memorial Scholarship

AMOUNT: $400   DEADLINE: None Specified
FIELDS/MAJORS: All Areas of Study

Awarded to a woman at the end of her sophomore year. The recipient must be superior in leadership, character, promise, and scholastic ability. Write to the address below for more information.

Ashland University
401 College Ave.
Ashland, OH   44805

104

Asian American Journalists Association Scholarships

AMOUNT: $250-$2000   DEADLINE: Apr 15
FIELDS/MAJORS: Print Journalism, Photojournalism, Broadcast Journalism

Applicants must be Asian-Americans who are pursuing careers in journalism (print, photo, or broadcast). Based on academics and financial need. Enclose a SASE with your request for information to the address below for details.

Asian American Journalists Association
Scholarship Committee
1765 Sutter St. Suite 1000
San Francisco, CA   94115

105

Asian Pacific American Support Group Scholarships

AMOUNT: None Specified   DEADLINE: Mar 21
FIELDS/MAJORS: All Areas of Study

Scholarships for Asian Pacific American students at the University of Southern California. Based on academic achievement, personal merit, and financial need. Must be U.S. citizens or permanent residents enrolled in full-time study and have a GPA of 3.0 or better. Write to the address below for details.

Asian Pacific American Support Group Scholarship Committee
University of Southern California
Student Union 410, University Park
Los Angeles, CA   90089

106 ASM Faculty Fellowship Program

AMOUNT: $4000   DEADLINE: Feb 1
FIELDS/MAJORS: Microbiological Sciences

One to two month fellowship for full-time minority undergraduates in the field of microbiological sciences. Applicants must be ASM members and U.S. citizens or permanent residents. This is a joint application with an ASM member faculty mentor. Write to the address below for additional information.

American Society for Microbiology
Office of Education and Training
1325 Massachusetts Ave., NW
Washington, D.C.   20005

107 Assembly of God 50% Tuition Discount

AMOUNT: $3650   DEADLINE: Feb 15
FIELDS/MAJORS: All Areas of Study

Scholarships are available at Evangel for full-time students who are legal dependents of nationally appointed full-time Assemblies of God foreign or home missionaries, active duty chaplains, Assembly of God College faculty members, or employees of General Council of the Assemblies of God. Write to the address below for information.

Evangel College
Office of Enrollment
1111 N. Glenstone
Springfield, MO   65802

108 Assistantships for Minority and Women Graduate Students

AMOUNT: $2005   DEADLINE: None Specified
FIELDS/MAJORS: All Areas of Study

Scholarships are available to graduate minority students in all fields and to women who are pursuing doctorate degrees in academic fields. Must be U.S. citizens or permanent residents. Write to the address below for more information.

University of Wyoming
Office Specialist
Graduate School Rm. 109; Knight Hall
Laramie, WY   82071

109 Associated Press Minority Summer Internships

AMOUNT: None Specified   DEADLINE: None Specified
FIELDS/MAJORS: Print Editorial, Broadcasting, Photojournalism, Graphic Communications

Minority internship program for full-time upperclassmen or graduate students enrolled in a four-year college or university in the U.S. Selection based on a testing process that takes place in an AP bureau or designated testing site. There is no application form. Check the Editor and Publisher International Yearbook at your local library, or contact the address below for the location of the nearest AP bureau.

Associated Press
Director of Recruiting
50 Rockefeller Plaza
New York, NY   10020

110 Association for Women Veterinarians Scholarship

AMOUNT: $1500   DEADLINE: Feb 18
FIELDS/MAJORS: Veterinary Medicine

Awarded to current second or third year veterinary medical students who are attending a college or school of veterinary medicine in the U.S. or Canada. Four awards offered annually. Write to the address below for more information.

Association for Women Veterinarians
Sherrilyn Wainwright, DVM
3201 Henderson Mill Rd. #27C
Atlanta, GA   30341

111 Asthma Athlete Scholarship Program

AMOUNT: $1000-$10000   DEADLINE: Mar 31
FIELDS/MAJORS: All Areas of Study

Scholarships for high school senior athletes who have asthma and will graduate in the current school year. Must be accepted to a regionally accredited U.S. college and plan to attain a bachelor's degree. Ten awards offered annually. Contact your guidance counselor for further information.

Schering-Key Foundation
Schering Asthma Athlete Scholarship
PO Box 328
Omaha, NE   68164

112 Astrid G. Cates Scholarship Fund

AMOUNT: $500-$750   DEADLINE: Mar 1
FIELDS/MAJORS: All Areas of Study

Open to undergraduates between the ages of seventeen and twenty-two who are members of Sons of Norway or children or grandchildren of Sons of Norway members. Based on financial need, academics, and career goals. Write to the address below for details.

Sons of Norway Foundation
1455 W. Lake St.
Minneapolis, MN   55408

113 ASWA Scholarship

AMOUNT: None Specified
DEADLINE: Mar 1
FIELDS/MAJORS: Accounting

Open to juniors and seniors who have a minimum GPA of 3.0. Preference given to women. Information and applications available Jan 1 through Mar 1 in the Advising Center of the College.

New Mexico State University
College of Business Administration and Economics
Box 30001 Dept. 3AD
Las Cruces, NM   88003-8001

114 ASWA Scholarship

AMOUNT: None Specified
DEADLINE: Mar 1
FIELDS/MAJORS: Accounting

One or more scholarships awarded to female junior or seniors majoring in accounting. Applicants must have a cumulative GPA of 3.0. Write to the address below for details.

New Mexico State University
College of Business Administration and Economics
Box 30001, Dept. 3AD
Las Cruces, NM   88003

115 AT&T Achievement Award for Minority Engineering Students

AMOUNT: $2500   DEADLINE: Mar 1
FIELDS/MAJORS: Engineering

Awards for college sophomores enrolled in the College of Engineering who demonstrate superior academic achievement, potential for leadership, and an unwavering goal of obtaining a degree in engineering. Contact the director of the minority engineering program for more information.

University of Massachusetts, Amherst
Director
Minority Engineering Program
Amherst, MA   01003

116 AT&T Computer Science Scholarship

AMOUNT: None Specified
DEADLINE: Mar 1
FIELDS/MAJORS: Computer Science

Open to sophomores, juniors, seniors, and first year graduate students who are of Hispanic descent. Must have a minimum GPA of 3.0. Contact the address below for further information.

New Mexico State University
College of Arts and Sciences
Box 30001 Dept. 3335
Las Cruces, NM   88003-8001

117 AT&T Engineering Scholarship

AMOUNT: Maximum: $500
DEADLINE: Mar 1
FIELDS/MAJORS: Engineering Technology, Electrical Engineering

Open to minority students who have completed their sophomore year with a minimum GPA of 3.0. Contact the address below for further information.

New Mexico State University
College of Engineering
Box 30001 Dept. 3449
Las Cruces, NM   88003-8001

118 Athletic Scholarship

AMOUNT: None Specified
DEADLINE: None Specified
FIELDS/MAJORS: All Areas of Study

Awards are available in the following sports: basketball, baseball, cross country/track, golf, soccer, tennis, softball, volleyball, and cheerleading. Write to the address below for more information.

California Baptist College
8432 Magnolia Ave.
Riverside, CA   92504

119 Aura E. Severinghaus Award

AMOUNT: $2000   DEADLINE: Aug 31
FIELDS/MAJORS: Medicine

For senior minority medical students attending Columbia University, College of Physicians and Surgeons. Must be U.S. citizen. Minorities are defined as African-American, Mexican-American, mainland Puerto Rican, and American Indian. Based on academics and leadership. One award is presented annually. Send a SASE to the address below for additional information.

National Medical Fellowships, Inc.
110 West 32nd St. 8th Floor
New York, NY   10001

120 Austrian Cultural Institute Grants

AMOUNT: $740-$810   DEADLINE: Jan 31
FIELDS/MAJORS: Music, Art

Grants are for foreign students for studies at academies of music and dramatic art or at art academies in Austria. Applicants for the program must be advanced students and between twenty and thirty-five years old. Write to the address below for more information.

Austrian Cultural Institute
950 Third Ave., 20th Flr.
New York, NY   10022

121 Avon Foundation for Women in Business Studies

AMOUNT: $1000   DEADLINE: Apr 15
FIELDS/MAJORS: Business

Women twenty-five or older seeking the necessary education for a career in a business related field. Must be within twenty-four months of graduation. Must demonstrate need and be a U.S. citizen. The pre-application screening form is only available between Oct 1 and Apr 1. Up to one hundred scholarships are available. Not for doctoral, correspondence, or non-degreed programs. Write to the address below for information, and enclose a business-size (#10), self-addressed, double stamped envelope.

Business and Professional Women's Foundation
Scholarships
2012 Massachusetts Avenue, NW
Washington, D.C.   20036

122 AWIS Predoctoral Awards

AMOUNT: $500   DEADLINE: Jan 15
FIELDS/MAJORS: Engineering, Mathematics, Physical, Life, and Behavioral Sciences

Scholarship aid and incentive awards for women who are working actively toward a Ph.D. in the above fields. For U.S. citizens who are studying in the U.S.A. or abroad, or for foreign citizens studying in the U.S. Usually awarded to a student at dissertation level. Four awards per year. (AWIS also publishes a directory of financial aid) Write to the address below for details.

Association for Women in Science Educational Foundation
AWIS National Headquarters
1200 New York Ave. NW #650
Washington, D.C.   20005

123 B'Nai Brith Women of Greater Hartford Scholarship

AMOUNT: $200-$500   DEADLINE: MAR 1
FIELDS/MAJORS: All Areas of Study

Open to Jewish graduating seniors who are residents of the greater Hartford area with average academics. Preference given to relatives of B'nai Brith members. Contact the address listed for further information.

Endowment Foundation of the Jewish Federation of Greater
   Hartford, Inc
Mrs. Harriet Rosenblit
333 Bloomfield Ave.
West Hartford, CT   06117

124 B.C. Scholarship, Marcella H. Brown Medical Scholarship

AMOUNT: None Specified   DEADLINE: None Specified
FIELDS/MAJORS: Medicine

Scholarships are available at the University of Oklahoma for female medical students. Write to the address below for information.

University of Oklahoma, Norman
Director, Office of Financial Aid
OUHSC, P.O. Box 73190
Oklahoma City, OK   73190

125 B.M. Woltman Foundations Scholarship Program

AMOUNT: $200-$3000   DEADLINE: Jun 1
FIELDS/MAJORS: Theology, Religious Studies

Scholarship grants are available for Texas residents who will be attending Concordia Theological Seminary (Fort Wayne, In), Concordia Seminary (St. Louis), or Concordia Lutheran College (Austin, TX). Must be members of the Lutheran Church—Missouri Synod. Contact the financial aid office at your school for information.

Lutheran Church—Missouri Synod, Texas District
B.M. Woltman Foundation
7900 E. Highway 290
Austin, TX   78724

126 Barbara Jones Ameduri Memorial Scholarship

AMOUNT: $1000   DEADLINE: None Specified
FIELDS/MAJORS: Track and Field Sports

Student must be a member of the SMSU women's track and field team. Preference is given to a minority student who demonstrates financial need. Consideration is also given to students majoring in wildlife. Write to the address below for more information.

Southwest Missouri State University
Office of Financial Aid
901 South National Ave.
Springfield, MO   65804

127 Barbara MacCaulley Endowment Scholarship Fund for Archaeology

AMOUNT: None Specified   DEADLINE: Mar 1
FIELDS/MAJORS: Archaeology

Scholarships are available at the University of New Mexico for full-time female senior archaeology majors with a GPA of at least 3.0. Write to the address below for information.

University of New Mexico, Albuquerque
Anthropology Department
Albuquerque, NM   87131

128 Barbara McDermott Scholarship

AMOUNT: Maximum: $900   DEADLINE: Mar 15
FIELDS/MAJORS: All Areas of Study

Open to full-time female undergraduates who can demonstrate financial need. Contact the address below for further information.

Arizona State University
Scholarship Office Main Campus
PO Box 870412
Tempe, AZ   85287

129 Basselin Scholarships

AMOUNT: None Specified
DEADLINE: None Specified
FIELDS/MAJORS: Theology

Scholarships are available at the Catholic University of America for full-time juniors who are preparing for the priesthood. Contact the financial aid office at the address below for details.

Catholic University of America / Basselin Foundation
Office of Admissions and Financial Aid
Washington, D.C.   20064

130 Bates Scholarships

AMOUNT: Maximum: $2200   DEADLINE: May 1
FIELDS/MAJORS: All Areas of Study

Scholarships are available to minority high school seniors from Arkansas who are pursuing study at an Arkansas college or university. Application forms are available from your high school guidance counselor.

Southwestern Bell Telephone
Bates Scholarships
PO Box 1611, Room 1096
Little Rock, AR   72203

131 Bay State Council of the Blind Scholarships

AMOUNT: $1500   DEADLINE: Mar 1
FIELDS/MAJORS: All Areas of Study

Scholarships are available to legally blind students who are residents of Massachusetts. Write to the address below for details.

American Council of the Blind
Scholarship Coordinator
1155 15th St., NW, Suite 720
Washington, D.C.   20005

132 Bazard Award

AMOUNT: None Specified   DEADLINE: Mar 1
FIELDS/MAJORS: Architecture

Scholarships are available at the University of New Mexico for full-time architecture students who are of Native American heritage. Write to the address below for information.

University of New Mexico, Albuquerque
School of Architecture
Office of the Dean
Albuquerque, NM   87131

133 Bella Vista Christian Church Scholarship

AMOUNT: None Specified   DEADLINE: None Specified
FIELDS/MAJORS: All Areas of Study

Awards available to Disciple students who demonstrate financial need and academic commitment. Also includes the First Christian Church of Huntington Park Scholarship and Hollydale Christian Church Scholarship. Contact the address below for information.

Chapman University
333 N. Glassell
Orange, CA   92866

134 Belle P. Kilhefner Scholarship

AMOUNT: None Specified   DEADLINE: None Specified
FIELDS/MAJORS: All Areas of Study

Awarded annually to a worthy female student who is attending Ashland University. Write to the address below for more information.

Ashland University
401 College Ave.
Ashland, OH   44805

135 Bement Scholarship Program

AMOUNT: Maximum: $750   DEADLINE: Feb 15
FIELDS/MAJORS: All Areas of Study

Scholarships for worshippers in churches in the Diocese of western Massachusetts. Write to the address below for details.

Episcopal Diocese of Western Massachusetts
37 Chestnut St.
Springfield, MA   01103

136 Beneficiary Grants

AMOUNT: Maximum: $3000   DEADLINE: Feb 1
FIELDS/MAJORS: All Areas of Study

Open to dependents of United Methodist clergy. Grants are renewable annually if recipients maintain pre-set standards. Contact the address below for further information.

Southwestern University
Office of Admissions
PO Box 770
Georgetown, TX   78627-0770

137 Berger Memorial Scholarship

AMOUNT: $1000 DEADLINE: Mar 1
FIELDS/MAJORS: Engineering, Business

Scholarships are available to Native American students at Montana State University in the fields of engineering or business. One award is given to first-year students, one award is given to transfer students from a tribally controlled community college, and one award is given to a first-year graduate student. Write to the address below for information.

Montana State University
Center for Native American Studies
2-152 Wilson Hall
Bozeman, MT   59717

138 Bertha B. Hollis and Louise E. Johnson Scholarships

AMOUNT: None Specified DEADLINE: Mar 1
FIELDS/MAJORS: All Areas of Study

Awards are available at the University of New Mexico for American Indian students. Write to the address below for more information.

University of New Mexico, Albuquerque
Office of Financial Aid
Albuquerque, NM   87131

139 Bertha Lamme Westinghouse Scholarships

AMOUNT: $1000 DEADLINE: May 15
FIELDS/MAJORS: Engineering

Applicants must be incoming female freshmen who are pursuing an engineering degree. Three awards per year. Must be U.S. citizens or permanent residents and have a GPA of at least 3.5. Contact the address below for further information. Be certain to enclose a SASE.

Society of Women Engineers
120 Wall Street, 11th Floor
New York, NY   10005

140 Bertha Margaret Diaz Health Services Scholarship Fund

AMOUNT: $1500 DEADLINE: Mar 5
FIELDS/MAJORS: Health Service Administration

Scholarship is available to a deserving health services administration graduate student who maintains a 3.1 GPA or better and is of Hispanic descent. Write to the address below for more information.

Florida International University
College of Urban and Public Affairs
Office of the Dean—AC1 200
North Miami, FL   33181

141 Bess Zeldich Ungerman Scholarship

AMOUNT: $1500 DEADLINE: Sep 1
FIELDS/MAJORS: Law

Scholarships are available at the University of Oklahoma, Norman for full-time third year minority law students. Write to the address below for information.

University of Oklahoma, Norman
Admissions and Records, Law Center
Room 22, 300 Timberdell Road
Norman, OK   73019

142 Bessie Coleman Scholarship Award

AMOUNT: Maximum: $5000 DEADLINE: Nov 14
FIELDS/MAJORS: All Areas of Study

Scholarships are available for African-American graduating high school seniors who reside in Dallas or Tarrant County in Texas and plan to attend a historically black college or university. Family members of *Dallas Weekly* or American Airline employees are not eligible. Write to the address below for information.

Dallas Weekly
3101 Martin Luther King, Jr. Blvd.
Anthony T. Davis Building
Dallas, TX   75215

143 Beta Sigma Phi-Xi Upsilon Chi Chapter

AMOUNT: $200 DEADLINE: May 1
FIELDS/MAJORS: All Areas of Study

Scholarships for female freshman who attend the College of the Siskiyous full-time and are residents of Siskiyou County. Applicants must demonstrate financial need, have a minimum GPA of 3.0, and have graduated from a Siskiyou County high school. One award is given annually. Write to the address below for details.

College of the Siskiyous
Financial Aid Office
800 College Ave.
Weed, CA   96094

144 Betty Everhart Scholarship

AMOUNT: None Specified   DEADLINE: Mar 1
FIELDS/MAJORS: All Areas of Study

Award open to female undergraduates who are U.S. citizens. Contact the address below for further information.

University of North Carolina, Greensboro
Financial Aid Office
723 Kenilworth St.
Greensboro, NC   27412

145 Beulah Harriss Memorial Scholarships

AMOUNT: $500-$1000   DEADLINE: Mar 31
FIELDS/MAJORS: Health Related, Physical Education

Awards open to undergraduate women majoring in a health related field or physical education. Must have a minimum GPA of 3.0. Contact the address below for further information.

University of North Texas
Scholarship Office
Marquis Hall #218
Denton, TX   76203

146 Biery (Guy and Marie Paul) Memorial Scholarship

AMOUNT: None Specified   DEADLINE: None Specified
FIELDS/MAJORS: All Areas of Study

Awards for needy Ohio County, West Virginia, residents with preference to Central Catholic students. Write to the address below for more information.

Wheeling Jesuit College
Student Financial Planning
316 Washington Ave.
Wheeling, WV   26003

147 Bishop Maher Catholic Leadership Scholarships

AMOUNT: $2000-$3000   DEADLINE: Feb 20
FIELDS/MAJORS: All Areas of Study

Scholarships are available at the University of San Diego for undergraduate Catholic students who demonstrate academic excellence, parish leadership, and campus and community service. Write to the address below for information.

University of San Diego
Office of Financial Aid
5998 Alcala Park
San Diego, CA   92110

148 Bishop W. Bertrand Stevens Foundation Grants and Loans

AMOUNT: None Specified   DEADLINE: May 15
FIELDS/MAJORS: All Areas of Study

Grants of part gift and part loan for residents of the (Episcopal) diocese of Los Angeles (Los Angeles, Orange, Ventura, Santa Barbara, and parts of San Bernadino and Riverside Counties). Interview required. 0% interest, repay after graduation. Membership in the Episcopal church is not a requirement. Some preference is given to students planning to attend a seminary. Students in all fields of study are encouraged to apply. Write for details.

Bishop W. Bertrand Stevens Foundation
PO Box 80251
San Marino, CA   91118

149 Black Achievers Scholarship

AMOUNT: None Specified   DEADLINE: Jan 1
FIELDS/MAJORS: All Areas of Study

Applicants must be African-American students who are outstanding participants in the YMCA's Black Achievers Program. Based on academic accomplishment. Renewable if recipients maintain pre-set standards. Awards are one half tuition. Write to the address listed for details.

Denison University
Financial Aid Office
Box M
Granville, OH   43023

150 Black Scholarship Fund

AMOUNT: None Specified   DEADLINE: None Specified
FIELDS/MAJORS: All Areas of Study

Scholarships are available to African-American students from Kansas City area high schools who will be attending UMKC. Contact Joe Seabrooks, UMKC, (816) 235-6013 for further information.

Greater Kansas City Community Foundation and Affiliated Trusts
1055 Broadway #130
Kansas City, MO   64105

151 Blackfeet Higher Education Program

AMOUNT: None Specified   DEADLINE: Mar 3
FIELDS/MAJORS: All Areas of Study

Scholarships are available for members of the Blackfeet Tribe who are actively pursuing an undergraduate degree in any area of study. Special awards are also available for adult students. Write to the address below for more information.

Blackfeet Tribe
PO Box 850
Browning, MT   59417

152

Blanche Fischer Foundation

AMOUNT: $500   DEADLINE: None Specified
FIELDS/MAJORS: All Areas of Study

Open to disabled or physically handicapped persons (excluding mental problems) residing within the state of Oregon. Must demonstrate financial need, and medical confirmation of disability is required. Write to the address below for more information.

Blanche Fischer Foundation
7912 SW 35th Avenue, Ste. 7
Portland, OR   97219

153

Blanche Honaker Brakebill Scholarship

AMOUNT: $500-$1000   DEADLINE: Feb 7
FIELDS/MAJORS: Elementary Education

Scholarships are available at the University of Oklahoma, Norman for full-time elementary education majors. Applicant must be a female and plan to work in a public school setting upon graduation. For sophomore level and above. one to two awards offered annually. Write to the address below for information.

University of Oklahoma, Norman
College of Education, Student Services
Room 137, ECH
Norman, OK   73019

154

Blind and Deaf Students Scholarship

AMOUNT: None Specified   DEADLINE: None Specified
FIELDS/MAJORS: All Areas of Study

Exemption of tuition and fees to blind and deaf students at public colleges and universities in Texas. Student must present certification of deafness or blindness from the appropriate state vocational rehabilitation agency and have a high school diploma or its equivalent. Write to the address below for details.

Texas Higher Education Coordinating Board
PO Box 12788
Austin, TX   78711

155

Blind Service Association Scholarship Grant Program

AMOUNT: $200-$2500   DEADLINE: Mar 31
FIELDS/MAJORS: All Areas of Study

Scholarships for legally blind students. For study at college, university, professional, or vocational educational program. Applicants must reside in the six-county Chicago metropolitan area. Applications are available after Jan 1 by writing to the address below. You must be legally blind to qualify for these awards.

Blind Service Association, Inc.
22 W. Monroe St.
Chicago, IL   60603

156

Bobby Foster Scholarship

AMOUNT: None Specified   DEADLINE: Mar 1
FIELDS/MAJORS: All Areas of Study

Awards are available at the University of New Mexico for minority juniors or seniors with financial need and a GPA of at least 2.0. Write to the address below for more information.

University of New Mexico, Albuquerque
Office of Financial Aid
Albuquerque, NM   87131

157

Boeing Scholarship

AMOUNT: Maximum: $2000
DEADLINE: Mar 1
FIELDS/MAJORS: Electrical, Mechanical Engineering

Open to sophomore, junior, and senior minorities who are U.S. citizens and have a minimum GPA of 3.0. Contact the address below for further information.

New Mexico State University
College of Engineering
Box 30001 Dept. 3449
Las Cruces, NM   88003-8001

158

Boy Brotherhood, Carrie Hoff Baer Memorial Award and Bell-Walker Scholarship

AMOUNT: None Specified   DEADLINE: None Specified
FIELDS/MAJORS: Pre-seminary or Seminary

Scholarship awarded to a pre-seminary or seminary student of the Ashland-based Brethren Church. Write to the address below for more information.

Ashland University
401 College Ave.
Ashland, OH   44805

159

BPW Loan Fund for Women in Engineering Studies

AMOUNT: Maximum: $5000   DEADLINE: Apr 15
FIELDS/MAJORS: Engineering

Loans for women in the final two years of an accredited engineering program. Based on need. Renewable. Must be U.S. citizen. Write to the address below for details.

Business and Professional Women's Foundation
Loan Programs
2012 Massachusetts Ave., NW
Washington, D.C.   20036

160
BPW/Sears-Roebuck Loan Fund for Women in Graduate Business Studies

AMOUNT: Maximum: $2500   DEADLINE: Apr 15
FIELDS/MAJORS: Business Administration

Loans to encourage women to enter programs in business administration. Must demonstrate financial need. May apply annually for additional loans totalling $2500. Must be U.S. citizen and enrolled in accredited MBA program. BPW Foundation and Sears-Roebuck Foundation employees are not eligible. Write to address below for details.

Business and Professional Women's Foundation
Loan Programs
2012 Massachusetts Ave., NW
Washington, D.C.   20036

161
Brasfield-Gorrie Architectural Scholarship

AMOUNT: None Specified   DEADLINE: None Specified
FIELDS/MAJORS: Architecture

Open to African-American students majoring in architecture. Recipient is selected by the scholarship committee of the College of Architecture. Write to the address listed for further information.

Georgia Institute of Technology
Financial Aid Office
225 North Ave.
Atlanta, GA   30332

162
Brethren Grant

AMOUNT: $1000   DEADLINE: None Specified
FIELDS/MAJORS: All Areas of Study

Students who are members of the Ashland-based Brethren Church are eligible for this grant. A letter verifying membership is required from the student's minister. Write to the address below for more information.

Ashland University
401 College Ave.
Ashland, OH   44805

163
Brewer Scholarship

AMOUNT: Maximum: $1000   DEADLINE: None Specified
FIELDS/MAJORS: All Areas of Study

Recipient must exemplify Christian values in lifestyle and commitment, be a resident of Lancaster, Kershaw, or Chesterfield Counties of South Carolina or other deserving students. Must be enrolled a minimum of 12 semester hours and have a GPA of at least 2.0. Contact the address listed for further information.

Charleston Southern University
PO Box 118087
Charleston, SC   29423

164
Brian M. Day Scholarships

AMOUNT: $3000   DEADLINE: Mar 1
FIELDS/MAJORS: All Areas of Study

Awards open to Seattle area gay men of color. Must be able to demonstrate significant financial need and activism in the gay/lesbian community. Approximately three awards offered annually. Contact the address below for further information.

Greater Seattle Business Association and Pride Foundation
2033 6th Ave. #804
Seattle, WA   98121

165
Brigham Young University Multicultural Program

AMOUNT: None Specified   DEADLINE: None Specified
FIELDS/MAJORS: All Areas of Study

Scholarships available at Brigham Young University for undergraduates who are African-American, Latino, Asian, Polynesian, and Native American. Applicants must be at least 1/4 of one of the listed ethnicities. Write to the address below for information.

Brigham Young University
199 Ernest L. Wilkinson Center
PO Box 27908
Provo, UT   84602

166
Bureau of Indian Affairs (BIA) Grant

AMOUNT: None Specified   DEADLINE: Feb 1
FIELDS/MAJORS: All Areas of Study

Scholarships for students who are at least one-quarter American Indian, Eskimo, or Aleut. Contact your tribal agency for more information.

California State University at Fresno
Financial Aid Office
5150 North Maple Ave.
Fresno, CA   93740

167
Burlington Northern Santa Fe Pacific Foundation Scholarships

AMOUNT: $2500   DEADLINE: Mar 31
FIELDS/MAJORS: Science, Business, Education, Health Administration

This scholarship is made available to American Indian high school seniors who reside in states serviced by the Burlington Northern and Santa Fe Pacific Corporation and its affiliated companies: AZ, CO, KS, MN, MT, NM, ND, OK, SD, WA, and CA. Applicants must be 1/4 American Indian or recognized as a member of a tribe. Contact the address below, and specify you are interested in the Santa Fe Pacific awards.

American Indian Science and Engineering Society
Scholarship Coordinator
5661 Airport Blvd.
Boulder, CO   80301

168 Business Reporting Internship Program for Minorities

AMOUNT: $1000   DEADLINE: Nov 15
FIELDS/MAJORS: Journalism

Internships consist of summer paid jobs as reporters for business sections of daily newspapers. Includes one week free pre-intern training seminar. $1000 scholarships to successful interns who return to college in the fall. Open to college sophomores and juniors who are U.S. citizens. Write to the address below for further information.

Dow Jones Newspaper Fund
PO Box 300
Princeton, NJ   08543

169 Byzantine Rite Scholarships

AMOUNT: $500-$4000   DEADLINE: Jan 1
FIELDS/MAJORS: All Areas of Study

Awards for students who live in West Virginia, Pennsylvania, or Ohio and attend Byzantine parishes. Recipients must be nominated by their pastor in order to be considered for this award. Write to the address below for more information.

Wheeling Jesuit College
Student Financial Planning
316 Washington Ave.
Wheeling, WV   26003

170 C. Helene Hansen Scholarships

AMOUNT: None Specified   DEADLINE: Feb 15
FIELDS/MAJORS: Physical Education

Awards for female students at UW, Platteville in the area of physical education. Two awards are offered annually. Write to the address below for more information.

University of Wisconsin, Platteville
Office of Enrollment and Admissions
Platteville, WI   53818

171 C. Pauline Spencer Excellence Scholarship

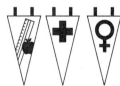

AMOUNT: $1952   DEADLINE: None Specified
FIELDS/MAJORS: Health, Physical Education, Leisure, Recreation, Sports Studies

Scholarships are available at the University of Iowa for full-time female undergraduate students studying in one of the above fields. One award is offered. Write to the address below for information.

University of Iowa
Dept. of Sport, Health, Leisure, and Phys.
E102 Field House
Iowa City, IA   52240

172 C.B. Mashburn Scholarship

AMOUNT: None Specified   DEADLINE: Mar 15
FIELDS/MAJORS: Religion

Open to students majoring in religion, with preference given to members of Disciples of Christ. Selection made by Department of Religion and Philosophy, Chaplain of the College and Office of Financial Aid. Contact the address below for further information.

Barton College
Financial Aid Office
Wilson, NC   27893

173 C.F.W. Walther Grant

AMOUNT: Maximum: $1000
DEADLINE: None Specified
FIELDS/MAJORS: Religion, Theology

Awards for Concordia students who are children of full-time LCMS church professionals in the areas of parish pastor, directors of Christian education and evangelism, missionaries, or social workers in a church-sponsored agency. Must have GPAs of 2.5, be U.S. citizens, and have financial need. Write to the address below for more information.

Concordia University, Irvine
Financial Aid Office
1530 Concordia West
Irvine, CA   92715

174 C.M. Lee Distinguished Scholar Award

AMOUNT: None Specified   DEADLINE: None Specified
FIELDS/MAJORS: All Areas of Study

Two scholarships available for incoming freshmen at Geneva College. Based upon grades, test scores, a written essay, an interview, and commitment to the Christian religion. Contact the office of admissions for further information.

Geneva College
Office of Admissions
Beaver Falls, PA   15010

175 CAMFT—Ronald D. Lunceford Scholarship

AMOUNT: $1000   DEADLINE: Feb 26
FIELDS/MAJORS: Counseling (Marriage, Family, Child Counseling)

Scholarship for a member of an underrepresented minority group studying toward a MA, MS, or Ph.D. and qualifying for licensure as a marriage, family, and child counselor. Write to the address below for details.

California Association of Marriage and Family Therapists
Educational Foundation
7901 Raytheon Road
San Diego, CA   92111

176 Career Advancement Scholarship Program

AMOUNT: $500-$1000 DEADLINE: Apr 15
FIELDS/MAJORS: Computer Science,
Education, Paralegal, Engineering, or Science

Up to one hundred scholarships for women
twenty-five or older. Criteria: within twenty-
four months of completing an accredited course
of study in the U.S.A. Should lead to entry or advancement in the
work force. Must be U.S. citizens. The pre-application screening
form is only available between Oct 1 and Apr 1. Not for doctoral
study, correspondence schools, or non-degreed programs. Write to
address below for details.

Business and Professional Women's Foundation
    Scholarships
2012 Massachusetts Avenue, NW
Washington, D.C.   20036

177 Career Development Grants

AMOUNT: $1000-$5000 DEADLINE: Jan 3
FIELDS/MAJORS: All Areas of Study

Grants to prepare for re-entry into work force or training for a
career change. Special consideration is given to qualified AAUW
members, minorities, women pursuing their first terminal degrees,
and women pursuing degrees in non-traditional fields. Must be a
U.S. citizen or permanent resident and have earned your last
degree at least five years previously. Write to the address below for
details.

American Association of University Women Educational
    Foundation
2201 N. Dodge Street
Iowa City, IA   52243

178 Carole A. Thiele Scholarship

AMOUNT: None Specified
DEADLINE: Nov 1
FIELDS/MAJORS: Soil/Water Conservation, Agriculture,
Agricultural Engineering

Open to full or part-time women students. Based on academics
and financial need. Usually one award is offered annually. Contact
the address below for further information.

Purdue University—School of Agriculture
Karla Hay, School of Agriculture
1140 Agricultural Administration Bldg. #121
West Lafayette, IN   47907

179 Carolyn Love Sparks Scholarship

AMOUNT: None Specified
DEADLINE: None Specified
FIELDS/MAJORS: Women Sports

Student must be full-time and a member of a women's athletic
team. Contact the Women's Athletics Office for more information.

Southwest Missouri State University
Office of Financial Aid
901 South National Ave.
Springfield, MO   65804

180 Carrie E. Smith Schuyler Scholarships

AMOUNT: Maximum: $400 DEADLINE: Apr 1
FIELDS/MAJORS: Business, Music

Open to female students who are enrolled in
business or music. Contact the address listed for
further information.

Northwestern Michigan College
Financial Aid Office, Administration Bldg. #142
1701 E. Front St.
Traverse City, MI   49684

181 Carrie Schaeffer Scholarships

AMOUNT: None Specified DEADLINE: Mar 1
FIELDS/MAJORS: All Areas of Study

Awards are available at the University of New Mexico for African-
American students demonstrating academic merit. Write to the
address below for more information.

University of New Mexico, Albuquerque
Office of Financial Aid
Albuquerque, NM   87131

182 Carroll Donner Commemorative Scholarship in Music

AMOUNT: $5000 DEADLINE: Feb 1
FIELDS/MAJORS: Music

Scholarship for first-year woman or undergraduate
transfer student who has demonstrated superior musical
talent. Applicants must audition in person or on tape.
Renewable with a 3.2 GPA and full-time enrollment.
Write to the address below for more information.

Mills College
Office of Financial Aid
5000 MacArthur Blvd.
Oakland, CA   94613

183 Carroll L. Birch Award

AMOUNT: $500 DEADLINE: Jun 30
FIELDS/MAJORS: Medicine

This award is presented to an AMWA student member for the
best original research paper. Write to the address below for details.

American Medical Women's Association
Carroll L. Birch Award
801 N. Fairfax Street, Suite 400
Alexandria, VA   22314

184
Catherine L. Gates Scholarship

AMOUNT: None Specified   DEADLINE: Mar 1
FIELDS/MAJORS: All Areas of Study

Award for a promising female sophomore to be used in her junior year. One award is offered annually. Write to the address below for more information.

Lake Erie College
Financial Aid Office
391 W. Washington St.
Painesville, OH   44077

185
Catherine S. Eberly Center for Women Scholarship

AMOUNT: $500   DEADLINE: None Specified
FIELDS/MAJORS: All Areas of Study

Open to women undergraduates (who already hold an associate's, bachelor's, or master's) or graduates returning to school to pursue an additional degree or update an existing degree. Contact the address below for further information.

University of Toledo—Center for Women
Dianne Mills/Lora Beckwith
Tucker Hall #0168
Toledo, OH   43606

186
Catholic Graduates Club Scholarship

AMOUNT: Maximum: $1000   DEADLINE: Mar 15
FIELDS/MAJORS: All Areas of Study

Open to Catholic graduating seniors who are residents of Hartford County, CT. For use at a four-year institution. Selections based on strong academics, financial need, extracurricular and community activities. Contact the address listed for further information.

Catholic Graduates Club of Greater Hartford
Bob Mittica, Scholarship Chairman
PO Box 1501
Hartford, CT   06144

187
Cay Drachnik Minorities Fund

AMOUNT: None Specified
DEADLINE: Jun 15
FIELDS/MAJORS: Art Therapy

Scholarships for minority students who are enrolled in an AATA approved art therapy program. Applicants must demonstrate financial need. This award is designed primarily for the purchase of books. Write to the address below for complete details.

American Art Therapy Association, Inc.
Scholarship Committee
1202 Allanson Road
Mundelein, IL   60060

188
CBS Scholarship of the Westinghouse Foundation

AMOUNT: $1000-$2000   DEADLINE: Sep 26
FIELDS/MAJORS: Broadcast Communications, Engineering, Film, English, Journalism, Computer Science

Open to minority juniors who are preparing for careers in broadcast communications at any one of the twenty-six ACI member schools. Contact your financial aid office for further information after Aug 15. The school offices will have the information. DO NOT WRITE TO THE LISTED ADDRESS, they CANNOT provide any additional information or forms.

Associated Colleges of Illinois
ACI Program Administration
1735 N. Paulina Loft 301
Chicago, IL   60622

189
Celebrate Women Scholarship

AMOUNT: None Specified   DEADLINE: Feb 15
FIELDS/MAJORS: All Areas of Study

Scholarships are awarded to women who are nontraditional, full-time sophomore, junior, senior, or graduate students with a GPA of 3.0 or better. Write to the address below for more information.

Murray State University
Office of University Scholarships
Ordway Hall, P.O. Box 9
Murray, KY   42071

190
Celine Davis Raff Endowed Scholarship

AMOUNT: None Specified   DEADLINE: Mar 1
FIELDS/MAJORS: Latin-American Studies

Awards are available at the University of New Mexico for graduate students in a Latin-American studies program. Applicant must exhibit financial need and academic achievement. Must be a female resident of New Mexico. Write to the address below for more information.

University of New Mexico, Albuquerque
Office of Financial Aid
Albuquerque, NM   87131

191
Center for Global Education Scholarships for Students of Color

AMOUNT: Maximum: $2500   DEADLINE: Oct 15
FIELDS/MAJORS: Foreign Study

Scholarships are available to enable students of color, who otherwise may not have sufficient funding, to participate in semester abroad programs. Priority will be given to U.S. citizens and permanent residents. Must be currently enrolled as an undergraduate.

The second deadline date is May 15 for the Fall program. Write to the address below for more information.

Center for Global Education at Augsburg College
2211 Riverside Ave.
Minneapolis, MN   55454

192
Central College Christian Leadership Scholarships

AMOUNT: $4000   DEADLINE: None Specified
FIELDS/MAJORS: All Areas of Study

Open to Christian high school seniors who display leadership qualities that reflect the philosophy of Central College. Must have a minimum of 14 on the composite ACT or 600 on the SAT. Must have a minimum GPA of 3.5. Write to the address below for additional information.

Central College
Financial Aid Office
1200 S. Main St.
McPherson, KS   67460

193
CERT Scholarship Program

AMOUNT: $1000
DEADLINE: None Specified
FIELDS/MAJORS: Business, Engineering, Science, Energy, or Environmental-Related Fields

Scholarships are available for American Indian students pursuing degrees in one of the above fields. Applicant must have a GPA of at least 2.5, and have successfully completed either a CERT pre-college summer program or the CERT ten-week summer internship. Write to the address below for information.

Council of Energy Resource Tribes
CERT Comprehensive Education Program
1999 Broadway, Suite 2600
Denver, CO   80202

194
CERT Summer Tribal Internship Program

AMOUNT: None Specified   DEADLINE: Mar 15
FIELDS/MAJORS: Conservation, Ecology, Energy Resource Development, Etc.

Summer internship program for Indian students. Provides training and practical experience in scientific, technical and policy areas relating to energy and economic resource development of tribal lands. Write to the address below for details.

Council of Energy Resource Tribes
711 Stewarts Ferry Pike, Suite 100
Denver, CO   80202

195
Cesar E. Chavez Scholarship Endowment Fund

AMOUNT: Maximum: $1000   DEADLINE: None Specified
FIELDS/MAJORS: All Areas of Study

Open to children of agricultural and migrant workers who are full-time daytime students at a college or university. Students may be attending a junior college with the intention of transferring to a four-year institution. Must have completed a minimum of 15 college credits before applying. Must also be a U.S. citizen or permanent resident. Contact the address below for further information. Be sure to include a SASE.

United Farm Workers of America—National Hispanic
   Scholarship Fund
Ernest Z. Robles, Executive Director
PO Box 728
Novato, CA   94948

196
Challenge Scholarships

AMOUNT: Maximum: $4000   DEADLINE: Jan 15
FIELDS/MAJORS: All Areas of Study

Scholarships of $1000 to $4000 are available to African-American entering freshmen. Based on high school academics, college entrance examination, and financial need. Renewable up to four years, provided student maintains satisfactory academic progress. More than forty awards offered annually. Write to the address below for details.

University of Pittsburgh
Office of Admissions and Financial Aid
Bruce Hall, Second Floor
Pittsburgh, PA   15260

197
Champlain Valley Business and Professional Women's Club Scholarships

AMOUNT: None Specified   DEADLINE: None Specified
FIELDS/MAJORS: All Areas of Study

Scholarships for Champlain Valley area (Clinton County, NY) women who are twenty-five years old or older and returning to college. Must have a GPA of 2.5 or better, be enrolled for a minimum of 12 credit hours, and be pursuing a bachelor's or master's degree at SUNY-Plattsburgh. Must be able to demonstrate financial need. Write to the address below for more details.

Business and Professional Women's Club of Champlain Valley
Scholarship Selection Committee
PO Box 925
Plattsburgh, NY   12901

198
Chancellor's Graduate Fellowship Program

AMOUNT: $19291   DEADLINE: Jan 15
FIELDS/MAJORS: College or University Education

Fellowships for African-American graduate students at Washington University in St. Louis who plan to pursue a career teaching on the college level. Contact Mrs. Joyce Edwards at the address below for further information.

Washington University
Graduate School of Arts and Sciences
Campus Box 1187, One Brookings Drive
St. Louis, MO   63130

199 Chapter VV of P.E.O. Scholarship

AMOUNT: $600   DEADLINE: None Specified
FIELDS/MAJORS: All Areas of Study

Scholarships are available for female students over age eighteen from Siskiyou County who currently attend the College of the Siskiyous. For undergraduate study, not intended for freshmen. Must have a GPA of at least a 3.0. Write to the address below for additional information.

College of the Siskiyous
Office of Financial Aid
800 College Ave
Weed, CA   96094

200 Charlene Thomas Dale Memorial Scholarship

AMOUNT: None Specified   DEADLINE: Mar 1
FIELDS/MAJORS: Pre-Professional

Award open to female juniors and seniors who are U.S. citizens majoring in pre-professional areas. Contact the address below for further information.

University of North Carolina, Greensboro
Financial Aid Office
723 Kenilworth St.
Greensboro, NC   27412

201 Charles A. Eastman Dissertation Fellowship for Native American Scholars

AMOUNT: $25000   DEADLINE: Mar 15
FIELDS/MAJORS: Arts and Sciences

Fellowships are available for U.S. citizens of Native American descent who plan careers in college or university teaching. Write to the address below for information.

Dartmouth College
Office of Graduate Studies
6062 Clement, Room 305
Hanover, NH   03755

202 Charles and Edith Getz Memorial Scholarship

AMOUNT: Maximum: $450   DEADLINE: Mar 15
FIELDS/MAJORS: All Areas of Study

Open to incoming freshmen who are Arizona residents and graduates from Arizona high schools. Must be able to demonstrate financial need. Preference given to students of the Jewish faith. Renewable if recipient maintains full-time status with a minimum GPA of 3.0. Contact the address below for further information.

Arizona State University
Scholarship Office Main Campus
PO Box 870412
Tempe, AZ   85287

203 Charles and Louise Rosenbaum Student Loan Fund

AMOUNT: None Specified   DEADLINE: Mar 29
FIELDS/MAJORS: All Areas of Study

Interest free loans for Jewish graduating high school seniors from Colorado who will be entering their freshmen year of college. Write to the address below for details.

Endowment Fund of the Allied Jewish Federation
300 Dahlia St.
Denver, CO   80222

204 Charles and Phyllis Kates Living Scholarship

AMOUNT: None Specified   DEADLINE: None Specified
FIELDS/MAJORS: All Areas of Study

Awarded each year to worthy students who have special needs. Write to the address below for more information.

Ashland University
401 College Ave.
Ashland, OH   44805

205 Charles F. Gould Endowment Scholarship

AMOUNT: None Specified   DEADLINE: None Specified
FIELDS/MAJORS: All Areas of Study

Applicant must be an Alaskan Native, preferably Eskimo, with a minimum GPA of 2.0. Write to the address below for more information.

University of Alaska Southeast (Juneau Campus)
Financial Aid Office
11120 Glacier Highway
Juneau, AK   99801

206 Charles Gregory Forgan Scholarship

AMOUNT: $1000   DEADLINE: MAR 1
FIELDS/MAJORS: All Areas of Study

Scholarships are available at the University of Oklahoma, Norman for students of American Indian heritage. Requires a GPA of at least 3.25. One to two awards annually. Write to the address below for information.

University of Oklahoma, Norman
Office of Financial Aid Services
731 Elm
Norman, OK   73019

207 Charlotte B. Flagg Scholarship

AMOUNT: None Specified **DEADLINE:** May 1
FIELDS/MAJORS: Nursing

Open to worthy young women in nursing. Contact the address listed for further information.

Walker College
Financial Aid Office
1411 Indiana Ave.
Jasper, AL   35501-4967

208 Chase Manhattan Scholarship

AMOUNT: $1200 **DEADLINE:** Mar 15
FIELDS/MAJORS: All Areas of Study

Awards open for full-time minority students who will graduate from a Connecticut high school with a GPA of 2.5. Must be able to demonstrate leadership and academics. Renewable if student maintains a 2.5 GPA and remains a full-time student. Write to the address below for more information.

Teikyo Post University
Office of Financial Aid
800 Country Club Road
Waterbury, CT   06723

209 Chase Minority Educational Opportunity Tuition Award

AMOUNT: $1410 **DEADLINE:** Feb 1
FIELDS/MAJORS: Law

Awards for minority students who have been admitted to Chase College of Law. Contact the assistant dean, Chase College of Law, for further information.

Northern Kentucky University
Chase College of Law
Office of Admissions
Highland Heights, KY   41099

210 Cherokee Nation Higher Education Undergraduate Grant Program

AMOUNT: None Specified **DEADLINE:** Apr 1
FIELDS/MAJORS: All Areas of Study

Scholarships are available for undergraduate students who are members of the Cherokee nation. Must be enrolled in a two or four-year accredited school and be able to demonstrate financial need. Write to the address below for information.

Cherokee Nation
PO Box 948
Tahlequah, OK   74465

211 Chi Omega Golden Anniversary Scholarship

AMOUNT: None Specified **DEADLINE:** Mar 1
FIELDS/MAJORS: All Areas of Study

Awarded to a female student who is a junior and a member of the Pi Delta of Chi Omega chapter. Student must be a U.S. citizen with a minimum 3.0 cumulative GPA. Recipient should be a well-rounded individual, as evidenced by her participation in a variety of quality campus and community service activities, career development goals, and high personal standards. Write to the address below for details.

New Mexico State University
Student Financial Aid Office
Box 30001, Dept 5100
Las Cruces, NM   88003

212 Chicanos for Creative Medicine Scholarships

AMOUNT: $200-$1500 **DEADLINE:** Apr 1
FIELDS/MAJORS: Medicine

Awards for students of Chicano/Latino/Hispanic ancestry who are high school students at a school in East Los Angeles or for students at East Los Angeles College who have completed at least 24 units. Based on academics, financial need, recommendations, and personal statements. Fifteen awards are offered annually. Write to the address below for more information.

Chicanos for Creative Medicine
1301 Avenida Cesar Chavez
Monterey Park, CA   91754

213 Children of Unitarian Universalist Ministers

AMOUNT: None Specified **DEADLINE:** None Specified
FIELDS/MAJORS: All Areas of Studies

Awards for children of Unitarian Universalist ministers. Limited funding is available. Write to the address below for more information.

Unitarian Universalist Association of Congregations
Office of Church Staff Finances
25 Beacon St.
Boston, MA   02108

214 Chinese-American Citizens Alliance Scholarships

AMOUNT: None Specified **DEADLINE:** Mar 1
FIELDS/MAJORS: All Areas of Study

Awards are available at the University of New Mexico for juniors or seniors of Chinese-American descent who exhibit financial need and good citizenship. Write to the address below for more information.

University of New Mexico, Albuquerque
Office of Financial Aid
Albuquerque, NM   87131

215 Chinese-American Medical Society Scholarships

AMOUNT: $1500   DEADLINE: Mar 31
FIELDS/MAJORS: Medicine, Dentistry

Awards for medical and dental students of Chinese heritage for completion of their studies in the U.S. Must be able to demonstrate financial need. One award offered annually. Contact the address below for further information.

Chinese American Medical Society
Dr. H.H. Wang, Executive Director
281 Edgewood Ave.
Teaneck, NJ   07666

216 Chinese Association of Greater Toledo Memorial Scholarships

AMOUNT: None Specified   DEADLINE: None Specified
FIELDS/MAJORS: Political Science

Awards open to full-time international graduate students with an ethnic Chinese background. Contact the address below for further information.

University of Toledo
Dr. Harold H. Lee, Dept. of Biology
1025 Bowman-Oddy
Toledo, OH   43606

217 Chinese Professional Club Scholarship

AMOUNT: $500-$1500   DEADLINE: Nov 15
FIELDS/MAJORS: All Areas of Study

Scholarships are available to graduating high school seniors who are residents of Houston and of Chinese descent. Applicant must be planning to enroll on a full-time basis in any accredited college or university in the U.S. A minimum of thirteen awards offered annually. Write to the address below for information. Applications will not be available until June.

Chinese Professional Club Scholarship Committee
Susannah Wong, Chair
2915 Carnegie
Houston, TX   77005

218 Chiyoko and Thomas Tomotsu Shimazaki Memorial Scholarship

AMOUNT: None Specified   DEADLINE: Apr 1
FIELDS/MAJORS: Oncological Research, Medicine

Applicants must be graduate students of Japanese ancestry who are pursuing cancer research. Must be a member of the JACL to apply. Applications and information may be obtained from local JACL chapters, district offices, and the national headquarters at the address below. Please indicate your level of study, and be certain to include a legal-sized SASE.

Japanese American Citizens League
National Scholarship and Award Program
1765 Sutter St.
San Francisco, CA   94115

219 Choctaw Nation Higher Education Scholarships

AMOUNT: None Specified   DEADLINE: Mar 15
FIELDS/MAJORS: All Areas of Study

Awards open to Choctaw undergraduates. Must provide copies of certificate of degree of Indian blood, tribal membership cards, and verification of college enrollment. For any accredited two or four-year school. Contact the address below for further information.

Choctaw Nation Higher Education Program
Drawer 1210
Durant, OK   74702

220 Christ College Grant

AMOUNT: $1000-$3000
DEADLINE: None Specified
FIELDS/MAJORS: Religion, Theology

Awards for Concordia students who intend to enter full-time church careers in the Lutheran Church—Missouri Synod. Must have GPAs of at least 2.5 and be U.S. citizens. Renewable. Write to the address below for more information.

Concordia University, Irvine
Financial Aid Office
1530 Concordia West
Irvine, CA   92715

221 Christian Church (Disciples of Christ) Awards

AMOUNT: None Specified   DEADLINE: None Specified
FIELDS/MAJORS: All Areas of Study

Awards are available to full-time students who are members of the Christian Church (Disciples of Christ). Contact the address below for further information.

Chapman University
333 N. Glassell
Orange, CA   92866

222 Christian Leadership Scholarship

AMOUNT: None Specified   DEADLINE: Mar 15
FIELDS/MAJORS: All Areas of Study

Awarded to new students who have demonstrated exceptional Christian character and leadership abilities, as well as proven academic skills. Awarded to students who have demonstrated servant-leadership by giving their lives to serving God and His people. To remain in good standing for the scholarship, the student must live on campus, maintain at least a 2.5 GPA, enroll as a full-time student, complete the Christian Leadership Course during the first year of enrollment, be involved in a volunteer or service activity on campus, have a positive influence on the Dallas Baptist University campus, submit an annual renewal form, and complete the Free Application for Federal Student Aid and all other required financial aid applications. Contact the address listed for further information.

Dallas Baptist University
3000 Mountain Creek Pkwy.
Dallas, TX   75211-9299

223
Christian Record Services Scholarships

AMOUNT: Maximum: $500   DEADLINE: Apr 1
FIELDS/MAJORS: All Areas of Study

Scholarships for legally blind, undergraduate students. Awards are to assist students in becoming more independent and self-supportive. Write to the address shown for details.

Christian Record Services
4444 S. 52nd St.
Box 6097
Lincoln, NE   68506

224
Christine A. Ponquinette Memorial Minority Scholarship

AMOUNT: $1000   DEADLINE: Feb 28
FIELDS/MAJORS: Social Work

Scholarships for Hispanic or African-American students in their junior or senior year at Aurora University, working toward a bachelor or master of social work degree. Contact the address below or Aurora University's financial aid office.

Aurora Foundation
111 W. Downer Place, Suite 312
Aurora, IL   60506

225
Chrysalis Scholarship

AMOUNT: $750   DEADLINE: Mar 1
FIELDS/MAJORS: Geoscience Fields

Scholarships available to women who are candidates for an advanced degree in a geoscience field. Applicants must have had their education interrupted for at least one year. Applicant must be completing her thesis during the current academic year. Awards will be made by Mar 31. Write to the address below for further details.

Association for Women Geoscientists Foundation
G & H Production Company
518 17th St. #930
Denver, CO   80202

226
Church and Campus Scholarships

AMOUNT: Maximum: $7000   DEADLINE: Mar 1
FIELDS/MAJORS: All Areas of Study

Renewable scholarships for Presbyterian freshmen at Eckerd College who show promise for a career in Christian service (either as a lay person or as a minister). Requires nomination by your pastor. Fifty awards per year. Write to the address below for details.

Eckerd College
Director of Financial Aid
PO Box 12560
St. Petersburg, FL   33733

227
Church-Related Vocation (CRV) Scholarship

AMOUNT: Maximum: $1000   DEADLINE: None Specified
FIELDS/MAJORS: Christian Vocation

Southern Baptist student preparing for vocational ministry as a Minister of Education, Music, Children, or Youth; Pastor, Missionary or Denominational Minister through the Southern Baptist Convention. Recommendation by a faculty member of the Division of Religion and satisfactory church attendance is required. Write to the address below or contact the division of religion for more information.

California Baptist College
8432 Magnolia Ave.
Riverside, CA   92504

228
Ciba-Geigy for Minorities in Agriculture

AMOUNT: $1000   DEADLINE: Mar 2
FIELDS/MAJORS: Crop Science

Awards open to minority students with special interest in obtaining a pest control license. Must have a minimum GPA of 2.5. Contact the address below for further information.

California Polytechnic State University
Financial Aid Office
212 Administration Bldg.
San Luis Obispo, CA   93407

229
Cindy Barr Memorial Scholarship

AMOUNT: $1000   DEADLINE: None Specified
FIELDS/MAJORS: All Areas of Study

Awarded to a female freshmen athlete at Ashland University. Write to the address below for more information.

Ashland University
401 College Ave.
Ashland, OH   44805

230
Claddagh Club of Enfield Scholarship

AMOUNT: Maximum: $500   DEADLINE: Apr 30
FIELDS/MAJORS: All Areas of Study

Open to high school seniors and undergraduates who are of Irish heritage and residents of any of the following towns in Connecticut: Enfield, East Windsor, Ellington, Suffield, and Windsor Locks. May be used for two and four-year institutions. Must be able to demonstrate financial need. Contact the address below for further information.

Claddagh Club of Enfield, Inc.
John Reardon
45 Skyridge Dr.
Somers, CT   06071

231 Class of 1943 Disabled Student Scholarship

AMOUNT: None Specified   **DEADLINE:** None Specified
FIELDS/MAJORS: All Areas of Study

Awards for disabled undergraduates at UMass in an approved course of study. Applicants must demonstrate financial need. Contact the director of disability services, not the address below, for more information.

University of Massachusetts, Amherst
Office of Financial Aid Services
255 Whitmore Administration Bldg., Box 38230
Amherst, MA   01003

232 Class of 1968 Scholarship

AMOUNT: None Specified   **DEADLINE:** Mar 1
FIELDS/MAJORS: All Areas of Study

Awards for Massachusetts residents at UMass. Applicants must be children affected by the Vietnam War or children of Southeast Asian descent. Must have financial need. Students must file a FAFSA as soon as possible after Jan 1 and before the Mar 1 financial aid priority consideration date. You will automatically be considered for this scholarship if you are enrolled at the University and apply for financial aid. Separate applications, requests, or inquiries are not required and cannot be honored.

University of Massachusetts, Amherst
Office of Financial Aid Services
255 Whitmore Administration Bldg., Box 38230
Amherst, MA   01003

233 Claude M. Gladdin Minority Scholarships

AMOUNT: $1500   **DEADLINE:** Mar 1
FIELDS/MAJORS: Forestry, Natural Resources

Open to incoming minority freshmen admitted to forestry and natural resources. Based on academics in high school and professional potential. Two awards offered annually. Contact the address below for further information.

Purdue University—Dept. of Forestry and Natural Resources
Professor Douglas M. Knudson
West Lafayette, IN   47907

234 Claver Scholarships and Grants

AMOUNT: None Specified   **DEADLINE:** Jan 15
FIELDS/MAJORS: All Areas of Study

Awards for full-time African-American Loyola undergraduate students. Based on academic potential, community service, or financial need. Write to the address below for additional information.

Loyola College in Maryland
Director of Financial Aid
4501 North Charles St.
Baltimore, MD   21210

235 Clayton, Jackson, McGhie African-American Scholarship

AMOUNT: $300   **DEADLINE:** None Specified
FIELDS/MAJORS: All Areas of Study

Awards open to African-American incoming freshmen. Based on academics, community involvement, and financial need. Contact the address below for further information.

University of Minnesota, Duluth
Ken Foxworth
138 Library
Duluth, MN   55812

236 Clearwood Scholarship

AMOUNT: $350   **DEADLINE:** Feb 3
FIELDS/MAJORS: All Areas of Study

Offered to a currently enrolled student of color attending Evergreen full-time who can demonstrate a commitment to enhancing multiculturalism at the college. Student must demonstrate financial need. Contact the address listed for further information.

Evergreen State College
Office of the Dean of Enrollment Service
2700 Evergreen Parkway
Olympia, WA   98505-0002

237 Clement and Frieda Amstutz Fund

AMOUNT: None Specified   **DEADLINE:** May 15
FIELDS/MAJORS: All Areas of Study

Awards for students of Swiss citizenship who live within a 150 mile radius of San Francisco City Hall. Applicants must have a GPA of 3.0 or better and have completed at least two years of college. Send a SASE to the address below for more details.

Swiss Benevolent Society
c/o Swiss Consulate General
456 Montgomery St. #1500
San Francisco, CA   94104

238 Cleo Zoukis Ploussis Scholarship

AMOUNT: None Specified
DEADLINE: None Specified
FIELDS/MAJORS: English

Awards for students entering their sophomore, junior, or senior year at UMass in the field of English. Preference is given to women with financial need. Contact the Chair of the English Department, not the address below, for more information.

University of Massachusetts, Amherst
Office of Financial Aid Services
255 Whitmore Administration Bldg., Box 38230
Amherst, MA   01003

239 Clergy Grants

AMOUNT: Maximum: $1000   DEADLINE: Mar 15
FIELDS/MAJORS: All Areas of Study

Open to children of ordained Presbyterian Church, U.S.A. ministers engaged in full-time Church work. Contact the address below for further information.

Muskingum College
Office of Financial Aid
New Concord, OH   43762

240 Cliff Bearden Memorial Scholarship

AMOUNT: $125   DEADLINE: None Specified
FIELDS/MAJORS: All Areas of Study

Scholarships are available for African-American students of Siskiyou County to attend the College of the Siskiyous. For undergraduate study. Write to the address below for additional information.

College of the Siskiyous
Office of Financial Aid
800 College Ave
Weed, CA   96094

241 Clinical Training Fellowship

AMOUNT: Maximum: $8340
DEADLINE: Jan 15
FIELDS/MAJORS: Psychology, Clinical

Fellowships for minority doctoral students of psychology who are specializing in clinical training. Must be a U.S. citizen or permanent resident enrolled in a full-time academic program. Fellowships are usually awarded for ten months, with a monthly stipend of $834. Write to the address below for more information.

American Psychological Association
750 First Street, NE
Washington, D.C.   20002

242 Colgate "Bright Smiles, Bright Futures" Minority Scholarships

AMOUNT: None Specified   DEADLINE: Apr 1
FIELDS/MAJORS: Dental Hygiene

Awarded to members of a minority group(s) currently underrepresented in dental hygiene programs. Two awards per year. Write to the address below for more information.

American Dental Hygienists' Association Institute for Oral Health
444 North Michigan Ave., Ste 3400
Chicago, IL   60611

243 College of Agriculture and Home Economics Multicultural Scholarship

AMOUNT: None Specified   DEADLINE: Feb 1
FIELDS/MAJORS: Agriculture, Home Economics

Award open to minority incoming freshmen and transfer students. Must have a minimum GPA of 3.0. Contact the address below for further information.

Washington State University—Scholarship Committee
College of Agriculture and Home Economics
423 Hulbert Hall
Pullman, WA   99164

244 College of Business Administration Minority/ Non-Traditional Scholarship

AMOUNT: $500   DEADLINE: Feb 7
FIELDS/MAJORS: Business

Students must be COBA majors who show promise of academic success and have financial need. African-Americans, Hispanics, and Native Americans are encouraged to apply. Preference is given to entering freshmen. Two awards are offered annually. Contact the COBA office for more information.

Southwest Missouri State University
Office of Financial Aid
901 South National Ave.
Springfield, MO   65804

245 College of Design Minority Scholarships

AMOUNT: $1000   DEADLINE: Apr 1
FIELDS/MAJORS: Design

Awards for entering freshmen of African-American, Asian-American, Hispanic-American, Native American, or Alaskan descent. Based on academic achievement, high school records, and statements of interests and abilities. Open to majors in a College of Design curriculum. Contact the address below for further information.

Iowa State University
Michael Chinn, Interim Assistant Dean
134 College of Design
Ames, IA   50011

246 College of Law First Year Minority Scholarships

AMOUNT: $1000-$4000   DEADLINE: Sep 1
FIELDS/MAJORS: Law

Scholarships are available at the University of Oklahoma, Norman for full-time, first year minority law students. Includes the Sequoyah scholarship, the ADA Lois Sipuel Fisher scholarship, and the Oklahoma state regents professional study grants. Six to seven awards offered annually. Write to the address below for information.

University of Oklahoma, Norman
Admissions and Records, Law Center
Room 22, 300 Timberdell Road
Norman, OK   73019

247 Collegiate Achievement Award for Transfer Students

AMOUNT: $1500   DEADLINE: Mar 1
FIELDS/MAJORS: All Areas of Study

Open to African-American or Hispanic-American transfer students who have received an associate degree or have completed a minimum of 60 credit hours at another accredited college or university. Must be U.S. citizens or permanent residents and have a GPA of at least 3.0. Write to the address below for details.

Texas A & M University
Office of Honors Programs and Acad. Schol.
College Station, TX   77843

248 Colonel Hayden W. Wagner Memorial Scholarship

AMOUNT: $1000   DEADLINE: Mar 31
FIELDS/MAJORS: All Areas of Study

Scholarships for daughters or granddaughters of Commissioned Officers or Warrant Officers in the U.S. Army who are on active duty, died while on active duty, or retired after at least twenty years of service. For undergraduate study. Renewable. Write to the address below for details. Specify the officers name, rank, social security number, and dates of active duty when requesting an application. Be sure to include a SASE.

Society of Daughters of the U.S. Army
Janet B. Otto, Scholarship Chairman
7717 Rockledge Court
West Springfield, VA   22152

249 Commonwealth Council of the Blind Scholarships

AMOUNT: $2000   DEADLINE: Mar 1
FIELDS/MAJORS: All Areas of Study

Scholarships are available to legally blind undergraduates who are residents of Virginia, attending a college or university in Virginia. Two awards per year. Write to the address below for details.

American Council of the Blind
Scholarship Coordinator
1155 15th St., NW, Suite 720
Washington, D.C.   20005

250 Connecticut Association of Latin Americans in Higher Education Scholarship

AMOUNT: Maximum: $500   DEADLINE: Mar 10
FIELDS/MAJORS: All Areas of Study

Open to high school seniors and undergraduates who are Connecticut residents, have a Latino background, and have a minimum GPA of 3.0. Based on academic success, community service, and financial need. Contact the address listed for further information.

Connecticut Association of Latin Americans in Higher
    Education, Inc.
Wilson Luna, Ed D.
Box 2415
Hartford, CT   06146

251 Connecticut Education Association Minority Scholarship

AMOUNT: Maximum: $500   DEADLINE: May 1
FIELDS/MAJORS: Teaching

Open to high school seniors and college students who are Connecticut residents and entering a teacher preparation program. For use at two or four-year schools. Applicants must be members of minority groups, have a minimum GPA of 2.75, and be able to demonstrate financial need. Contact the address listed for further information.

Connecticut Education Foundation, Inc.
President
21 Oak St. #500
Hartford, CT   06106-8001

252 Consortium for Graduate Study in Management

AMOUNT: None Specified   DEADLINE: Feb 1
FIELDS/MAJORS: Business, Economics

Graduate fellowships for minorities. U.S. citizenship required. Must have received a bachelor's degree from an accredited institution and must submit GMAT scores. Each fellow undertakes the regular MBA curriculum at one of the eleven consortium graduate schools of business. Must be a member of one of the following minority groups: Native American, African-American, or Hispanic. Write to the address below for details.

Consortium for Graduate Study in Management
200 S. Hanley Rd., Suite 1102
St. Louis, MO   63105

253 Constance L. Lloyd, FACMPE Scholarship

AMOUNT: Maximum: $1500   DEADLINE: Jun 1
FIELDS/MAJORS: Health Administration, Clinical Healthcare

One award for female students attending school in the state of Georgia who are pursuing either an administrative or clinically related degree in the healthcare field. Write to the address listed for more information.

American College of Medical Practice Executives
Attn: Ms. Laurie J. Draizen
104 Inverness Terrace East
Englewood, CO   80112

254 Constantinople Armenian Relief Society (C.A.R.S.) Scholarship

AMOUNT: $400-$600   DEADLINE: Jul 15
FIELDS/MAJORS: All Areas of Study

Awards for Armenian students enrolled in an accredited college or university at the sophomore level or above. Based mainly on merit and financial need. Write to the address below for more information.

Constantinople Armenian Relief Society
Mr. Berc Araz
66 Stephenville Parkway
Edison, NJ   08820

255 Continental Society Daughters of Indian Wars Scholarship

AMOUNT: $500   DEADLINE: Jun 15
FIELDS/MAJORS: Education, Social Service

Scholarships are available to certified tribal members enrolled in one of the areas of study listed above who plan to work on a reservation upon graduation. Preference will be given to juniors. Must have a GPA of at least 3.0. Write to the address below for information.

Continental Society Daughters of Indian Wars
Miss Eunice T. Connally
206 Springdale Drive
La Grange, GA   30240

256 Continuing Education Grant

AMOUNT: $500   DEADLINE: None Specified
FIELDS/MAJORS: All Areas of study

Scholarships are awarded to female students attending the UAS Ketchikan campus with plans to enroll in the spring. Applicants must indicate motivation, as well as academic and employment potential in the selected field. Write to the address below for more information.

University of Alaska Southeast (Ketchikan Campus)
2600 7th Ave.
Ketchikan, AK   99901-5798

257 Cooper, Mitch, Crawford, Kuykendall & Whatley Minority Scholarship

AMOUNT: $1500   DEADLINE: Feb 15
FIELDS/MAJORS: Speech Communication, Forensics

Awards for minority undergraduates participating in forensics and graduate students who serve as forensics assistants. Also available to undergraduates and graduates who are majoring in speech communications. Write to the address below for further information and an application.

University of Alabama
College of Communications
PO Box 870172
Tuscaloosa, AL   35487

258 Cora Smith King Scholarship Endowment

AMOUNT: None Specified   DEADLINE: Apr 15
FIELDS/MAJORS: Medicine

Awards for female students enrolled in the School of Medicine. Contact the address below for further information or the financial aid office at your school's location.

University of North Dakota—School of Medicine
Sandra Elshaug, Financial Aid Office
PO Box 9037—501 N. Columbia Rd.
Grand Forks, ND   58202

259 Courage Center Scholarship for People with Disabilities

AMOUNT: Maximum: $1000   DEADLINE: May 31
FIELDS/MAJORS: All Areas of Study

Award open to students with sensory impairments or physical disabilities who want to pursue educational goals or gain technical expertise beyond high school. Based on intentions and achievements. Must be U.S. citizens, residents of Minnesota, already enrolled full-time in accredited institutions, and able to demonstrate financial need. Scholarships are awarded in Jul. Contact the address below for further information.

Courage Center/United Way
Courage Center Scholarship Committee
3915 Golden Valley Rd.
Golden Valley, MN   55422

260 Cox Enterprises Scholarship

AMOUNT: None Specified   DEADLINE: Feb 28
FIELDS/MAJORS: Journalism

Open to high school seniors, undergraduates, or graduate students pursuing a career in journalism. Based on academics and financial need. Write to the address below for details.

National Association of Hispanic Journalists
529 14th Street, NW
1193 National Press Bldg.
Washington, D.C.   20045

261 Crazy Horse Memorial— Book Scholarships

AMOUNT: $300   DEADLINE: Feb 15
FIELDS/MAJORS: All Areas of Study

Four scholarships for Native American students at Black Hills State University who are sophomores and demonstrate financial need. Write to the address below for more information.

Black Hills State University
1200 University St.
Spearfish, SD   57783

262 Crazy Horse Memorial—Jonas Scholarships

AMOUNT: $1000   DEADLINE: Feb 15
FIELDS/MAJORS: All Areas of Study

One scholarship for a Native American student at Black Hills State University who has a GPA of 3.0 or better and is in the third or fourth year of study. Write to the address below for more information.

Black Hills State University
1200 University St.
Spearfish, SD   57783

263 Crowley Maritime Scholarship

AMOUNT: None Specified   DEADLINE: None Specified
FIELDS/MAJORS: Business, International Trade

Applicants must have at least two years remaining in school and be a business major. Must have a cumulative GPA of 3.5. Preference will be given to students with an emphasis in international trade and commerce, students who are Alaska native, and students who are Alaska residents. Applicants must be willing to explore working in the maritime industry. Write to the address below for more information.

University of Alaska Southeast (Juneau Campus)
Financial Aid Office
11120 Glacier Highway
Juneau, AK   99801

264 Cultural Diversity Scholarship

AMOUNT: None Specified   DEADLINE: Feb 3
FIELDS/MAJORS: All Areas of Study

Offered to a new or currently enrolled students attending Evergreen at least half time who are from different ethnic backgrounds and/or can demonstrate the capacity to assist the college in achieving its commitment to cultural diversity. Contact the address listed for further information.

Evergreen State College
Office of the Dean of Enrollment Service
2700 Evergreen Parkway
Olympia, WA   98505-0002

265 Cultural Diversity Scholarships

AMOUNT: Maximum: $1500   DEADLINE: Apr 15
FIELDS/MAJORS: All Areas of Study

Awards for incoming freshmen and minority students who attend Baker. Must be a U.S. citizen or permanent resident to apply. Recipients of Kansas minority scholarship are not eligible. Renewable with a GPA of at least 2.0. Write to the address below for more information.

Baker University
Office of Financial Aid
PO Box 65
Baldwin City, KS   66006

266
Curry Awards for Girls and Young Women

AMOUNT: $500   DEADLINE: Apr 15
FIELDS/MAJORS: All Areas of Study

Scholarships are available for young women, age sixteen to twenty-six, who are residents of San Mateo County and have experienced undue hardship in attempting to complete their education. Three awards are offered annually. Write to the address below for additional information.

Peninsula Community Foundation
1700 South El Camino Real, Suite 300
San Mateo, CA   94402

267
Curtis Wilson Scholarship for New Freshmen

AMOUNT: $1000   DEADLINE: May 1
FIELDS/MAJORS: All Areas of Study

Recipient must be a Cleveland or East Cleveland high school graduate of African-American descent. Applicants must demonstrate financial need and have a 2.5 GPA or higher. Contact the address listed for further information.

Cleveland State University
Office of Student Financial Assistance
2344 Euclid Ave.
Cleveland, OH   44115

268
Cyrus B. Krall Memorial Scholarship

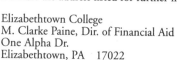

AMOUNT: None Specified   DEADLINE: Mar 1
FIELDS/MAJORS: Religion, Philosophy, or Education

Awarded to students who are members of the Church of the Brethren and who are preparing for a career in the fields of religion and philosophy or education. Contact the address listed for further information.

Elizabethtown College
M. Clarke Paine, Dir. of Financial Aid
One Alpha Dr.
Elizabethtown, PA   17022

269
DAAD Fellowships in German-Jewish History and Culture

AMOUNT: $2000   DEADLINE: Nov 1
FIELDS/MAJORS: Jewish Studies

Research fellowships available at the Leo Baeck Institute for postdoctoral scholars who are studying the social, communal, and intellectual history of German-speaking Jewry. Applicants must be less than thirty-six years of age and citizens of the U.S. Write to the address below for information.

Leo Baeck Institute
Fellowship Programs
129 East 73rd Street
New York, NY   10021

270
Dale Wood Memorial Scholarship Fund

AMOUNT: None Specified   DEADLINE: Apr 15
FIELDS/MAJORS: Mathematics or Science

Scholarships are available to graduating females from Linn County R-4 High School pursuing a degree in math or science. Contact Laurie Hardy, High School Counselor for further information.

Greater Kansas City Community Foundation and Affiliated Trusts
1055 Broadway
Suite 130
Kansas City, MO   64105

271
Daniel E. Mayers Memorial Scholarship

AMOUNT: Maximum: $300   DEADLINE: Mar 1
FIELDS/MAJORS: All Areas of Study

Open to juniors and seniors who have performed service to the African-American community and are able to demonstrate academic merit. Contact the address listed for further information.

Brooklyn College
Office of the V.P. for Student Life
2113 Boylan Hall
Brooklyn, NY   11210

272
Daniel J. Steiner Scholarship

AMOUNT: $1000   DEADLINE: Apr 1
FIELDS/MAJORS: Nursing

Scholarship available for female students in nursing at Kent State, who were graduates of either New Philadelphia High School or Tuscarawas Central Catholic High School. Applicant must demonstrate financial need. Contact the financial aid office for details.

Kent State University, Tuscarawas Campus
Financial Aid Office
University Drive, NE
New Philadelphia, OH   44663

273
Daniel Memorial Fund Endowed Scholarships

AMOUNT: None Specified   DEADLINE: Mar 1
FIELDS/MAJORS: All Areas of Study

Scholarship for entering minority freshmen. Two awards given. Renewable for three years. Contact the financial aid office at the address below for details.

Clemson University
Financial Aid Office
G01 Sikes Hall
Clemson, SC   29634

274
Daniella Altfeld-Moreno Scholarships

AMOUNT: $3000   DEADLINE: Mar 1
FIELDS/MAJORS: All Areas of Study

Awards open to Latino/Latina youth (under twenty-one), self-identified gay/lesbian or children of gay/lesbian families. Preference given to students involved in athletics. Approximately three awards offered annually. Contact the address below for further information.

Greater Seattle Business Association and Pride Foundation
2033 6th Ave. #804
Seattle, WA   98121

275
Danny Lee Wing Scholarship

AMOUNT: $1000   DEADLINE: None Specified
FIELDS/MAJORS: Management

Awards for Asian-American School of Management students in their sophomore, junior, or senior year from an urban area who have good academic standing and are in financial need. Applications for School of Management scholarships will be available in the SOM Development Office, Room 206.

University of Massachusetts, Amherst
School of Management
SOM Development Office, Room 206
Amherst, MA   01003

276
Daryl Damon Memorial Scholarship

AMOUNT: $500   DEADLINE: Mar 2
FIELDS/MAJORS: Business Administration

Award open to juniors and seniors with a concentration in management information systems. Must have a minimum GPA of 2.5. Preference given to disabled students. Contact the address below for further information.

California Polytechnic State University
Financial Aid Office
212 Administration Bldg.
San Luis Obispo, CA   93407

277
Daughters of Penelope National Scholarship Awards (graduate)

AMOUNT: $750-$1500   DEADLINE: Jun 20
FIELDS/MAJORS: All Areas of Study

Scholarships for women who are currently enrolled in a post-graduate degree program (MA, Ph.D., MD, etc.) who are immediate family members (or members themselves) of Daughters of Penelope, order of AHEPA, or maids of Athena. Must be enrolled for a minimum of 9 credits a year. Not renewable. Nine award programs are offered each year. Write to the address below for details.

Daughters of Penelope National Headquarters
National Scholarship Awards
1909 Q St., NW, Suite 500
Washington, D.C.   20009

278
Daughters of Penelope National Scholarship Awards (undergraduate)

AMOUNT: $750-$1500   DEADLINE: Jun 20
FIELDS/MAJORS: All Areas of Study

Scholarships for women who are or will be attending college or university as an undergraduate and who are immediate family members (or members themselves) of daughters of Penelope, order of AHEPA, or maids of Athena. Nine award programs offered each year. Write to the address below for details.

Daughters of Penelope National Headquarters
National Scholarship Awards
1909 Q St., NW, Suite 500
Washington, D.C.   20009

279
Daughters of Penelope Scholarship

AMOUNT: $500   DEADLINE: Apr 1
FIELDS/MAJORS: All Areas of Study

Awards for full-time, degree-seeking students with a GPA of 3.0 or higher and financial need. Preference is given to females. Write to the address below for more information.

Christopher Newport University
Office of Financial Aid
50 Shoe Lane
Newport News, VA   23606

280
Daughters of the Cincinnati Scholarships

AMOUNT: None Specified   DEADLINE: Mar 15
FIELDS/MAJORS: All Areas of Study

Open to high school senior daughters of commissioned regular active or retired officers in U.S. Army, Navy, Air Force, Marine Corps, or Coast Guard. Based on need and merit. Renewable. The award is only for daughters of commissioned officers. Also, please be certain to put your name, address, parent's rank, and parent's branch of service on your letter (not just on the outside of the envelope).

Daughters of the Cincinnati
Attn: Scholarship Administrator
122 East 58th Street
New York, NY   10022

281 David B. and May Umstead Roberts Scholarship

AMOUNT: None Specified   DEADLINE: MAR 1
FIELDS/MAJORS: All Areas of Study

Award open to female undergraduates who are U.S. citizens.
Preference given to residents of Durham County, North Carolina.
Contact the address below for further information.

University of North Carolina, Greensboro
Financial Aid Office
723 Kenilworth St.
Greensboro, NC   27412

282 David Baumgardt Memorial Fellowships

AMOUNT: $3000   DEADLINE: Nov 1
FIELDS/MAJORS: Jewish Studies

Fellowships are available for research at the Leo Baeck
Institute for current predoctoral scholars who are
studying the social, communal, and intellectual history
of German-speaking Jewry. Applicants must be U.S.
citizens. Write to the address below for information.

Leo Baeck Institute
Fellowship Programs
129 East 73rd Street
New York, NY   10021

283 David Hall Scholarship

AMOUNT: $200   DEADLINE: Sep 1
FIELDS/MAJORS: Law

Scholarships are available at the University of Oklahoma, Norman
for full-time first year African-American law students who earned
at least a B+ in Contracts I. Write to the address below for information.

University of Oklahoma, Norman
Admissions and Records, Law Center
Room 22, 300 Timberdell Road
Norman, OK   73019

284 David Spurgeon, Wincy Julette Black and Fannie Sumner Scholarship

AMOUNT: None Specified   DEADLINE: Mar 1
FIELDS/MAJORS: Liberal Arts

Award open to undergraduate females who are U.S. citizens and
residents of Randolph County, North Carolina. Contact the
address below for further information.

University of North Carolina, Greensboro
Financial Aid Office
723 Kenilworth St.
Greensboro, NC   27412

285 David Tamotsu Kagiwada Memorial Scholarship

AMOUNT: None Specified   DEADLINE: Mar 15
FIELDS/MAJORS: Theology

Applicants must be Asian-American members of the
Christian Church (Disciples of Christ) who are preparing
for the ordained ministry. For full-time study. Financial
need is considered. Must have at least a "C+" grade average.
Write to the address below for details.

Christian Church (Disciples of Christ)
Attn: Scholarships
PO Box 1986
Indianapolis, IN   46206

286 Dean's Scholarship

AMOUNT: $8600-$13000   DEADLINE: Feb 1
FIELDS/MAJORS: All Areas of Study

Awards for entering African-American students with outstanding
academic achievement. Write to the address below for more information.

Rhodes College
Office of Admissions
2000 North Parkway
Memphis, TN   38112

287 Debra Levy Neimark Memorial Scholarship

AMOUNT: Maximum: $1500
DEADLINE: Apr 1
FIELDS/MAJORS: All Areas of Study

One award open to women for vocational education assistance
and one award for traditional higher education. Must attend an
accredited Florida school. Awards are to help promote higher education and economic self-sufficiency. Contact the address below
for further information.

Debra Levy Neimark Scholarship Foundation
Selection Committee
800 Corporate Dr. #602
Ft. Lauderdale, FL   33334

288 Delaney MFA Fellowship Fund Scholarship

AMOUNT: None Specified
DEADLINE: None Specified
FIELDS/MAJORS: Fiction Writing

Awards for non-traditional students at UMass pursuing a MFA in
fiction. Preference is given to women thirty years of age or above.
Contact the Chair of the English Department, not the address
below for more information.

University of Massachusetts, Amherst
Office of Financial Aid Services
255 Whitmore Administration Bldg., Box 38230
Amherst, MA   01003

289 Delbert K. Aman Memorial Scholarships

AMOUNT: $500   DEADLINE: Mar 1
FIELDS/MAJORS: All Areas of Study

Scholarships are available to legally blind students who are residents of South Dakota or attending a South Dakota college or university. For undergraduate study. Write to the address below for details.

American Council of the Blind
Scholarship Coordinator
1155 15th St., NW, Suite 720
Washington, D.C.   20005

290 Delores Auzenne Fellowship

AMOUNT: $5000   DEADLINE: Feb 1
FIELDS/MAJORS: All Areas of Study

Fellowships available for African-American graduate students attending school full-time. Must have a minimum GPA of 3.0 and be U.S. citizens or permanent residents. Write to the address below for more information.

Florida International University
Equal Opportunity Program, PC 215
University Park
Miami, FL   33199

291 Delta Gamma Foundation Florence Margaret Harvey Memorial Scholarship

AMOUNT: $1000   DEADLINE: Apr 1
FIELDS/MAJORS: Rehabilitation, Education of Visually Impaired or Blind Persons

Open to legally blind undergraduates and graduates in the field of rehabilitation or education of the visually impaired or blind. Must be U.S. citizens. Write to the address below for complete details.

American Foundation for the Blind
Scholarship Committee
11 Penn Plaza, Suite 300
New York, NY   10001

292 Delta Kappa Gamma Grant

AMOUNT: None Specified   DEADLINE: Mar 1
FIELDS/MAJORS: Education

Award open to female seniors who are U.S. citizens. Contact the address below for further information.

University of North Carolina, Greensboro
Financial Aid Office
723 Kenilworth St.
Greensboro, NC   27412

293 Delta Kappa Gamma International Scholarships

AMOUNT: $1000   DEADLINE: May 15
FIELDS/MAJORS: Education, Child Development

Scholarships are available for female juniors and seniors who are residents of Sarasota County, Florida and attending school full-time in Florida. Must be majoring in education or child development. Write to the address below for information.

Delta Kappa Gamma International—Gamma Upsilon
c/o Dr. Laura Wiggins
130 Ogden Street
Sarasota, FL   34242

294 Delta Kappa Gamma Scholarship

AMOUNT: $300   DEADLINE: Mar 31
FIELDS/MAJORS: Elementary Education, Secondary Education

Student must be a female elementary or secondary education major with a GPA of 3.0 or above. Must be a junior or senior admitted to the teacher education program and have demonstrated leadership. Three awards are offered annually. Contact the address below for details.

Southwest Missouri State University
Office of Financial Aid
901 South National Ave.
Springfield, MO   65804

295 Delta Kappa Gamma Scholarship

AMOUNT: $500   DEADLINE: Mar 1
FIELDS/MAJORS: Education

Awarded to a female junior or senior majoring in the field of education who exhibits financial need, has an academic GPA of 3.0, and exhibits high moral character. Write to the address below for more information.

New Mexico State University
College of Education
PO Box 30001, Dept. 3AC
Las Cruces, NM   88003

296 Delta Kappa Gamma Scholarship

AMOUNT: $500   DEADLINE: Mar 1
FIELDS/MAJORS: Education

Scholarships for women who graduated from a Geauga County, Ohio, high school. Must be at least juniors in college. Write to the address below for details.

Delta Kappa Gamma—Omega Chapter
Shirley Haueter, Scholarship Chair
PO Box 865
Chardon, OH   44024

297
Delta Kappa Gamma Society International Scholarship

AMOUNT: $500   DEADLINE: None Specified
FIELDS/MAJORS: Education

Scholarships are available at the University of Oklahoma, Norman for full-time female education majors of junior level or higher. Recipients must be residents of Tulsa County, Oklahoma, or daughters of Delta Kappa Gamma members of a chapter in Tulsa County. Write to the address below for information.

University of Oklahoma, Norman
College of Education, Student Services
Room 137, ECH
Norman, OK   73019

298
Delta Sigma Theta Hartford Alumnae Scholarship

AMOUNT: $500-$1000   DEADLINE: Apr 1
FIELDS/MAJORS: All Areas of Study

Open to African-American female high school seniors from Hartford, Bloomfield, and Windsor who plan on attending a four-year school. Must be in the top 25% of class and be able to demonstrate leadership, citizenship, and financial need. Contact the address below for further information.

Delta Sigma Theta Sorority, Inc.
Chairperson, Hartford Alumnae Chapter
PO Box 320079
Hartford, CT   06132

299
Des Moines Chapter Iowa Council of the United Blind

AMOUNT: $1000-$1500   DEADLINE: Apr 15
FIELDS/MAJORS: All Areas of Study

Open to full-time enrolled students who are legally blind. Write to the address below for details.

Loras College
Office of Financial Planning
1450 Alta Vista St., P.O. Box 178
Dubuque, IA   52004

300
Des Moines Women's Club Memorial Scholarship

AMOUNT: Maximum: $1000   DEADLINE: Feb 1
FIELDS/MAJORS: Education, Health

Open to female students who are residents of any of the following Iowa counties: Polk, Boone, Dallas, Jasper, Madison, Marion, Story, or Warren. Contact the address listed for more information.

Loras College
Office of Financial Planning
1450 Alta Vista St., P.O. Box 178
Dubuque, IA   52004

301
Dial Corporation Scholarship for Black Students

AMOUNT: None Specified   DEADLINE: Mar 1
FIELDS/MAJORS: All Areas of Study

Awarded to an African-American incoming freshman who exhibits financial need. Contact the address listed for further information.

Elizabethtown College
M. Clarke Paine, Dir. of Financial Aid
One Alpha Dr.
Elizabethtown, PA   17022

302
Disciple Chaplains' Scholarship

AMOUNT: None Specified   DEADLINE: Mar 15
FIELDS/MAJORS: Theology

Applicants must be members of the Christian Church (Disciples of Christ) who are entering their first year in seminary. For full-time study. Financial need is considered. Must have better than a "C+" grade average. Write to the address below for details.

Christian Church (Disciples of Christ)
Attn: Scholarships
PO Box 1986
Indianapolis, IN   46206

303
Disciples Fellowship Award

AMOUNT: $2000   DEADLINE: None Specified
FIELDS/MAJORS: All Areas of Study

Awards are available to students who are members of the Christian Church (Disciples of Christ) with GPAs of 3.0 or higher. Contact the address listed for further information.

Chapman University
333 N. Glassell
Orange, CA   92866

304
Dissertation Fellowships

AMOUNT: Maximum: $14500   DEADLINE: Nov 15
FIELDS/MAJORS: All Areas of Study

Fellowships for women in the final year of writing their dissertations. Applicants must have completed all course work, passed all preliminary exams, and have their dissertation research proposal (or plan) approved by Nov 15. Must be a United States citizen or permanent resident. Awards are for one year, beginning Jul 1. The fellow is expected to devote full-time to the project for the fellowship year. Scholars may apply up to two times for a dissertation fellowship on the same topic. Write for complete details.

American Association of University Women
2401 Virginia Avenue, NW
Washington, D.C.   20037

305
Distinguished Achievement Award

AMOUNT: $1500   DEADLINE: May 1
FIELDS/MAJORS: Any Area of Study

Open to African-American and Hispanic-American students currently enrolled at Texas A & M who have completed 30 or more credit hours. Based on academic achievement, extracurricular activities, and student leadership. Must not concurrently hold any other multi-year scholarship valued at more than $1000. Must have a minimum GPA of 2.75 and be U.S. citizens or permanent residents. For more information, contact the address below.

Texas A & M University
Student Financial Aid Department
College Station, TX   77843

306
Distinguished Scholar Award

AMOUNT: $1200   DEADLINE: Mar 31
FIELDS/MAJORS: All Areas of Study

Award open to legally blind students who are residents of Illinois and enrolled full-time in school. Contact the address below for further information.

National Federation of the Blind of Illinois
Deborah Kent Stein, Chairman
5817 N. Nina
Chicago, IL   60631

307
Diversity Grants

AMOUNT: $2000   DEADLINE: Feb 20
FIELDS/MAJORS: All Areas of Study

Scholarships are available at the University of San Diego for undergraduate minority students. Write to the address below for information.

University of San Diego
Office of Financial Aid
5998 Alcala Park
San Diego, CA   92110

308
Diversity Tuition Waiver Program

AMOUNT: None Specified   DEADLINE: Apr 15
FIELDS/MAJORS: Medicine

Awards for Native Americans and Alaskans and economically disadvantaged students. Emphasis is given to American Indian medical students from the twenty-four tribes of North/South Dakota, Montana, Nebraska, and Wyoming. Contact the address below or the financial aid office at your school for further information.

University of North Dakota—School of Medicine
Sandra Elshaug, Financial Aid Office
PO Box 9037—501 N. Columbia Rd.
Grand Forks, ND   58202

309
Doris C. Stout Memorial Scholarship

AMOUNT: None Specified
DEADLINE: None Specified
FIELDS/MAJORS: All Areas of Study

Awarded annually to a Brethren female student on the basis of financial need, scholastic achievement, and promise. Write to the address below for more information.

Ashland University
401 College Ave.
Ashland, OH   44805

310
Dorothy Campbell Memorial Scholarships

AMOUNT: None Specified   DEADLINE: Mar 1
FIELDS/MAJORS: All Areas of Study

Open to female Oregon high school graduates with a minimum GPA of 2.75. A strong and continuing interest in golf will be a factor in the selection process. May be used at any four-year Oregon college. For undergraduate study. Must be an Oregon resident and a U.S. citizen or permanent resident. Contact the address below for further information.

Oregon State Scholarship Commission
Private Awards
1500 Valley River Dr. #100
Eugene, OR   97401-2130

311
Dorothy Hatch Scholarship

AMOUNT: None Specified   DEADLINE: Mar 1
FIELDS/MAJORS: All Areas of Study

Awards are available at the University of New Mexico for American Indian students. Write to the address below for more information.

University of New Mexico, Albuquerque
Office of Financial Aid
Albuquerque, NM   87131

312
Dorothy Klindt Memorial Scholarship

AMOUNT: $1000   DEADLINE: Dec 1
FIELDS/MAJORS: Agriculture, Consumer Science

Awards for incoming freshmen in the Colleges of Agriculture or Family and Consumer Sciences. Based on above average academics and involvement in school/community/work activities. Preference to female students from rural areas and small towns in the Iowa counties of: Scott, Cedar, Clinton, or Muscatine. Four awards offered annually. Contact the address below for further information.

Iowa State University
M. Porter, Alumni Suite, Memorial Union
2229 W. Lincoln Way
Ames, IA   50014

313
Dow Chemical Scholarships

AMOUNT: None Specified   DEADLINE: Mar 1
FIELDS/MAJORS: Engineering

Awards are available at the University of New Mexico for minority undergraduates who have demonstrated high proficiency in math and science. Selection based on scholastic performance and extracurricular activities. Write to the address below for more information.

University of New Mexico, Albuquerque
Office of Financial Aid
Albuquerque, NM   87131

314
Dow Elanco Minority Scholarship

AMOUNT: $1000   DEADLINE: Feb 1
FIELDS/MAJORS: Agriculture, Related Areas

Open to minority sophomores, (who have completed 30 hours at P.U. or V.U.), juniors, (who have completed 60 hours at P.U. or V.U.) or seniors, (who have completed 90 hours at P.U. or V.U.). One award offered annually. Write to the address below for more information.

Purdue University—School of Agriculture
Thomas W. Atkinson
1140 Agricultural Administration Bldg. #121
West Lafayette, IN   47907

315
Dr. Agnes Logan Braganza Scholarship

AMOUNT: None Specified   DEADLINE: Apr 1
FIELDS/MAJORS: All Areas of Study

Awards for students who are sophomores or higher with a GPA of at least 2.0 and 30 or more credit hours earned. Applicants must be females who are age thirty or above. Write to the address below for more information.

Christopher Newport University
Office of Financial Aid
50 Shoe Lane
Newport News, VA   23606

316
Dr. Alonzo Atencio Medical Scholarship

AMOUNT: None Specified   DEADLINE: Mar 1
FIELDS/MAJORS: Medicine

Awards are available at the University of New Mexico for minority medical students who demonstrate financial need and academic achievement. Must be enrolled full-time and be a resident of New Mexico. Write to the address below for more information.

University of New Mexico, Albuquerque
Office of Financial Aid
Albuquerque, NM   87131

317
Dr. Gombojab Hangin Scholarship

AMOUNT: Maximum: $2500   DEADLINE: Jan 1
FIELDS/MAJORS: All Areas of Study

Scholarships are available for students of Mongolian heritage. Preference given to citizens of Mongolia, People's Republic of China, or the former Soviet Union. Write to the address below for information.

Mongolia Society, Inc.
Hangin Scholarship Committee
322 Goodbody Hall, Indiana University
Bloomington, IN   47405

318
Dr. Irvin E. Hendryson Scholarship Fund

AMOUNT: None Specified   DEADLINE: Mar 1
FIELDS/MAJORS: Medicine

Awards are available at the University of New Mexico for Native American medical students. Write to the address below for more information.

University of New Mexico, Albuquerque
Office of Financial Aid
Albuquerque, NM   87131

319
Dr. James L. Gutman Family Scholarship

AMOUNT: None Specified   DEADLINE: None Specified
FIELDS/MAJORS: Dentistry

Open to full-time dental students of Native American descent. Amounts vary depending upon fund availability. Contact the address below for further information.

Marquette University
Office of Admissions
1217 W. Wisconsin Ave.
Milwaukee, WI   53233

320 Dr. Kiyoshi Sonoda Memorial Scholarship

AMOUNT: None Specified   DEADLINE: Apr 1
FIELDS/MAJORS: Dentistry

Applicants must be of Japanese ancestry, majoring in dentistry, and a member of the JACL. Applications and information may be obtained from local JACL chapters, district offices, and the national headquarters at the address below. Please indicate your level of study, and be certain to include a legal-sized SASE.

Japanese American Citizens League
National Scholarship and Award Program
1765 Sutter St.
San Francisco, CA   94115

321 Dr. Mae Davidow Memorial Scholarship

AMOUNT: $1000   DEADLINE: Mar 1
FIELDS/MAJORS: All Areas of Study

Applicants must be legally blind graduate students who demonstrate outstanding academic achievement. Write to the address below for details.

American Council of the Blind
Scholarship Coordinator
1155 15th St., NW, Suite 720
Washington, D.C.   20005

322 Dr. Martin Luther King Scholarships

AMOUNT: Maximum: $1500
DEADLINE: None Specified
FIELDS/MAJORS: All Areas of Study

Awards open to multicultural students who are U.S. citizens and at sophomore standing. Contact the address below for further information.

University of Toledo
Office of Student Financial Aid
4023 Gillham Hall
Toledo, OH   43606

323 Dr. William L. Ullom Memorial Scholarship

AMOUNT: None Specified   DEADLINE: Mar 1
FIELDS/MAJORS: All Areas of Study

Awards are available at the University of New Mexico for physically handicapped students with financial need who are enrolled for full-time study. Write to the address below for more complete details.

University of New Mexico, Albuquerque
Office of Financial Aid
Albuquerque, NM   87131

324 Drama Scholarship

AMOUNT: $500-$1500
DEADLINE: None Specified
FIELDS/MAJORS: Drama

Recipient must be selected by the drama department for participation in the Drama Ministry Team or as an assistant to the director. Recipient must sign a participation agreement with the college. Write to the address below or contact the drama department for more information.

California Baptist College
8432 Magnolia Ave.
Riverside, CA   92504

325 Drs. Sara & Daniel Susmano Scholarships

AMOUNT: $1000   DEADLINE: Feb 28
FIELDS/MAJORS: Health Related (etc.)

For graduating Hispanic high school seniors from schools in the Aurora area who will be entering vocational fields (not necessarily limited to healthcare). Schools are East Aurora, West Aurora, and Waubonsie Valley high schools. Renewable. Applications are made through high school counselors; it is not necessary to specify scholarship category. Contact your counselor for details, or call the Aurora Foundation at (708) 896-7600.

Aurora Foundation
111 W. Downer Place, Suite 312
Aurora, IL   60506

326 Duchesne Scholarship Program

AMOUNT: None Specified   DEADLINE: Feb 20
FIELDS/MAJORS: Elementary and Secondary Education

Scholarships available at the University of San Diego for minority undergraduates. Freshmen must have a minimum high school GPA of 3.0, and transfer students must have a minimum GPA of 2.8 and at least 24 completed semester hours. Write to the address below for information.

University of San Diego
Office of Financial Aid
5998 Alcala Park
San Diego, CA   92110

327 DuPont Minority Academic Achievement Award

AMOUNT: None Specified   DEADLINE: None Specified
FIELDS/MAJORS: All Areas of Study

Open to deserving minority undergraduates majoring in any field. Awards are given by the DuPont Committee for Educational Grants and Scholarships. Write to the address listed for further information.

Georgia Institute of Technology
Financial Aid Office
225 North Ave.
Atlanta, GA   30332

328
Duracell/National Urban League Scholarship

AMOUNT: $10000   DEADLINE: Apr 15
FIELDS/MAJORS: Engineering, Marketing, Finance, Sales, Manufacturing Operations

Scholarships for minority students in their junior year of college. Must be in top 25% of class and have a strong interest in summer employment with Duracell. Contact your local Urban League or write to the address below for details.

National Urban League
500 E. 62nd St.
New York, NY   10021

329
E.K. Wise Loan Program

AMOUNT: None Specified
DEADLINE: None Specified
FIELDS/MAJORS: Occupational Therapy

Applicants must be female students who already hold a bachelor's degree and are members of AOTA. Must be U.S. citizen or permanent resident. Write to the address below for details.

American Occupational Therapy Association
1383 Piccard Dr., Ste. 300
Rockville, MD   20850

330
E.U. Parker Scholarship

AMOUNT: Maximum: $3000   DEADLINE: Mar 31
FIELDS/MAJORS: All Areas of Study

Open to full-time students who are legally blind. Contact the address below for further information.

National Federation of the Blind
Mrs. Peggy Elliott, Chairman
814 Fifth Ave.
Grinnell, IA   50112

331
Earl Warren Legal Training Program General Scholarships

AMOUNT: $3000-$4500   DEADLINE: Mar 15
FIELDS/MAJORS: Law

Scholarships for entering African-American law students. Preference is given to applicants who express an interest in civil rights or in public interest litigation. Must be a U.S. citizen. Applications are available after Nov 15. Twenty to twenty-five awards are offered annually. Write to the address below for further information.

Earl Warren Legal Training Program, Inc.
99 Hudson Street, Suite 1600
New York, NY   10013

332
Eastern Orthodox Scouting Scholarship

AMOUNT: $500-$1000   DEADLINE: Mar 15
FIELDS/MAJORS: All Areas of Study

Scholarships for Eagle Scouts who are members of the Eastern Orthodox Church. Applicants must have received the Alpha Omega Religious Reward and have demonstrated practical citizenship in their church, school, scouting unit, and community. Awarded to high school seniors. Write to the address below for more details.

Eastern Orthodox Committee on Scouting
Scholarship Chairman
862 Guy Lombardo Ave.
Freeport, NY   11520

333
Ed Bradley and Carole Simpson Scholarships

AMOUNT: $2000-$5000   DEADLINE: MAR 1
FIELDS/MAJORS: Broadcast or Electronic Journalism

Must be a minority undergraduate seeking a career in broadcast journalism. Based on examples of reporting and/or photographic skills. Thirteen awards are offered per year. Write to the address below for details.

Radio and Television News Directors Foundation, Inc.
RTNDF Scholarships
1000 Connecticut Ave., NW, Suite 615
Washington, D.C.   20036

334
Ed E. and Gladys Hurley Foundation Grants

AMOUNT: Maximum: $1000   DEADLINE: Mar 31
FIELDS/MAJORS: Religion/Theology

Grants available to students who wish to study toward the ministry or other aspects of Protestantism. To support students who, along with their families, are unable to afford such an education. For use at participating schools listed below. Application forms are available between Jan 15 and Mar 31 (only) from Criswell College of Biblical Studies, Dallas Theological, Episcopal Theology Seminary of the Southwest, Houston Graduate School of Theology, South West Baptist Theology Seminary, Texas Bible College. If attending another school, write to the below address. Indicate the school you will be attending.

Ed E. and Gladys Hurley Foundation
Nationsbank Trust Division
100 North Main
Corsicana, TX   75110

335
Edgar A. & Ida M. Alekna Scholarship

AMOUNT: $1500   DEADLINE: None Specified
FIELDS/MAJORS: All Areas of Study

Four awards are available to female students with high unmet financial need and GPAs of 3.0 or higher. Contact the address listed for further information.

Broome Community College
Financial Aid Office
PO Box 1017
Binghamton, NY   13902

336
Edna Yelland Memorial Scholarship

AMOUNT: $2000   DEADLINE: May 31
FIELDS/MAJORS: Library Science

Applicants must be a member of an ethnic minority group and pursuing a graduate library degree in library or information sciences. Must be a U.S. citizen or permanent resident and California resident. For study in a master's program at a California library school. Must be able to demonstrate financial need. Request an application form and further information from the address below.

California Library Association
Scholarship Committee
717 K St., Suite 300
Sacramento, CA   95814

337
Education Grant Program for Native Alaskans

AMOUNT: Maximum: $1200   DEADLINE: Jul 1
FIELDS/MAJORS: Technical

Grant program for Alaska Natives who qualify under the1971 Alaska Native Claims Settlement Act to promote preparation for successful careers in a specialized technical skills field. Applicants must be high school graduates and have a GPA of at least 2.5. Availability of employment upon completion of training must be demonstrated. Write to the address below for more information.

CIRI Foundation
2600 Cordova St. #206
Anchorage, AK   99503

338
Educational Advancement Foundation Scholarships

AMOUNT: $1000-$1500   DEADLINE: Feb 15
FIELDS/MAJORS: All Areas of Study

Available to African-American college students with sophomore status or higher who demonstrate exceptional academic achievement. Applicants must be full-time students planning on completing degree requirements. Includes the merit scholarship ($1000), based upon academic ability, and the financial assistance scholarship ($1500), based upon demonstrated financial need. Write to the address below for details.

Alpha Kappa Alpha
5656 S. Stony Island Ave.
Chicago, IL   60637

339
Edward D. Stone Jr. and Associates Minority Scholarship

AMOUNT: $1000   DEADLINE: Mar 31
FIELDS/MAJORS: Landscape Architecture/Design

Applicants must be minority students in the last two years of undergraduate study. Must submit a five hundred-word essay and photo or slide examples of design work. Two awards per year. Financial need is considered. Write to the address below for details.

Landscape Architecture Foundation
4401 Connecticut Ave., NW, Suite 500
Washington, D.C.   20008

340
Edward E. Hood Scholarships

AMOUNT: $3500   DEADLINE: Mar 1
FIELDS/MAJORS: Science and Engineering

Awards for African-American or Native American freshman who have demonstrated academic performance and leadership potential. Applicants must be from North Carolina and majoring in science or engineering. Two awards offered per year. Write to the address below for more details.

North Carolina State University
Financial Aid Office
Box 7302
Raleigh, NC   27695

341
Edward N. Reynolds Graduate Diversity Scholarship

AMOUNT: None Specified   DEADLINE: Mar 2
FIELDS/MAJORS: All Areas of Study

For first-time and continuing full-time domestic traditionally underrepresented ethnic minority graduate students. Must demonstrate academic achievement and/or promise, and financial need. Awarded on a competitive basis. Priority consideration given to those filing their university admissions application by May 1st. Write to the address below for more information.

United States International University
Financial Aid Office
10455 Pomerado Rd.
San Diego, CA   92131

342
Edwin G. and Lauretta M. Michael Scholarship

AMOUNT: None Specified   DEADLINE: Mar 15
FIELDS/MAJORS: All Areas of Study

Open to minister's wives who are members of the Christian Church (Disciples of Christ). Must have at least a 2.3 GPA. Award is for full-time study. Write to the address below for details.

Christian Church (Disciples of Christ)
Attn: Scholarships
PO Box 1986
Indianapolis, IN   46206

343
Edwin T. Pratt Memorial Scholarship

AMOUNT: None Specified   DEADLINE: None Specified
FIELDS/MAJORS: All Areas of Study

Open to African-Americans who reside in King County and have a high school diploma (or equivalent). Must be planning to enroll, or currently enrolled in a vocational, two or four-year college in Washington state. Applications available after Feb 1. Contact the address below for further information. Must include a SASE for a reply.

Urban League of Metropolitan Seattle
Ms. Terry Marsh
105 Fourteenth Ave.
Seattle, WA   98122

344
EIF Scholarship Program for Students with Disabilities

AMOUNT: $5000   DEADLINE: Feb 1
FIELDS/MAJORS: Technical and Electronic Related Studies

Scholarships for students with disabilities, as defined by the 1990 Americans with disabilities act, pursuing technical and electronics degrees. Must be accepted or enrolled in a program. For undergraduate or graduate study. Must be a U.S. citizen. Write to the address below for details.

Electronic Industries Foundation
Scholarship Program Coordinator
2500 Wilson Blvd. #210
Arlington, VA   22201

345
Eiichi Matsushita Memorial Scholarship

AMOUNT: None Specified   DEADLINE: Oct 15
FIELDS/MAJORS: Christian Service, Religion, Theology

Scholarships for students of Asian backgrounds who intend to pursue careers in leadership positions in the Lutheran Church, Asian Ministry. Based on need. Write to the address below for details.

Pacific Lutheran Theological Seminary
Eiichi Matsushita Memorial Scholarship
2770 Marin Ave.
Berkeley, CA   94708

346
Eileen M. Hutchison Scholarship Fund

AMOUNT: None Specified   DEADLINE: Mar 10
FIELDS/MAJORS: Medicine, Dental Health, Related Fields

Scholarships available to female residents of Stevens County, Washington, pursuing training/education in the above fields. Primary factors for consideration include: academics, financial need, and good personal character. May reapply in subsequent years. Write to the address below for more information.

Citizens' Scholarship Foundation of America, Inc.
Foundation Northwest Scholarship Funds
PO Box 297
St. Peter, MN   56082

347
El Paso Natural Gas MBA Fellowship

AMOUNT: None Specified   DEADLINE: Mar 1
FIELDS/MAJORS: Business

Open to minority students pursuing an MBA. Based on academics and financial need. Contact the address below for further information.

New Mexico State University
College of Business Admin. and Economics
Box 30001 Dept. 3AD
Las Cruces, NM   88003-8001

348
Elaine J. Hudson Memorial Medical Scholarship

AMOUNT: None Specified   DEADLINE: Mar 1
FIELDS/MAJORS: Medicine

Awards are available at the University of New Mexico for female students enrolled in the UNM School of Medicine. Write to the address below for more information.

University of New Mexico, Albuquerque
Office of Financial Aid
Albuquerque, NM   87131

349
Electronic Data Systems Vision of Success Scholarship

AMOUNT: None Specified   DEADLINE: Mar 1
FIELDS/MAJORS: Engineering

Awards for minority juniors enrolled full time in the College of Engineering. Must have a GPA of 3.0 or better and an interest in software development. Contact the director of the Minority Engineering Program for more information.

University of Massachusetts, Amherst
Director
Minority Engineering Program
Amherst, MA   01003

350
Elisabeth Maxwell Memorial Scholarship

AMOUNT: None Specified   DEADLINE: Feb 15
FIELDS/MAJORS: All Areas of Study

Scholarships are awarded to a female classified as a single parent, head of household, who is entering her junior or senior year or who is entering graduate school with a GPA of 3.0 or better. Preference will be given to students pursuing a course of study leading to a career in veterinary science or who have a major in the department of biological sciences. Write to the address below for more information.

Murray State University
Office of University Scholarships
Ordway Hall, P.O. Box 9
Murray, KY   42071

351
Elizabeth B. Corbett Memorial

AMOUNT: None Specified   DEADLINE: Mar 1
FIELDS/MAJORS: Chemistry

Scholarship for a female student who is a junior or senior chemistry major with a GPA of 3.0 or greater. Write to the address below for details.

New Mexico State University
College of Arts and Sciences
Box 30001, Dept. 3335
Las Cruces, NM   88003

352
Elizabeth R. Hanson Endowed Scholarship

AMOUNT: None Specified   DEADLINE: Mar 1
FIELDS/MAJORS: All Areas of Study

Awards for full-time undergraduate or graduate students with a disability that might cause difficulty in pursuing academic study. First consideration given to those having health or visual problems. Contact the address below for further information.

Iowa State University
Office of Student Financial Aid
12 Beardshear Hall
Ames, IA   50011

353
Ella Schulz Lynn Scholarship

AMOUNT: $3000   DEADLINE: Mar 1
FIELDS/MAJORS: Liberal Arts

Awards for freshmen females at Lake Erie College who plan to major in a discipline within the liberal arts. Applicants must be citizens of the United States and demonstrate financial need. Write to the address below for more information.

Lake Erie College
Financial Aid Office
391 W. Washington St.
Painesville, OH   44077

354
Ellen Setterfield Memorial Scholarship

AMOUNT: $3000-$10000   DEADLINE: Mar 31
FIELDS/MAJORS: Social Sciences

Open to legally blind students studying any of the social sciences on the graduate level. Write to the address below for complete details.

National Federation of the Blind
Mrs. Peggy Elliott, Chairman
814 Fifth Ave., Suite 200
Grinnell, IA   50112

355
Eloise Campbell Scholarship

AMOUNT: None Specified   DEADLINE: None Specified
FIELDS/MAJORS: All Areas of Study

Awards for female students from Bowie County, Texas, or Miller County, Arkansas. Must be a member or dependent of a member of the United Daughters of the Confederacy or the Children of the Confederacy. Contact your local chapter of the UDC or write to the address below for more information.

United Daughters of the Confederacy
Education Committee
328 North Ave.
Richmond, VA   23220

356
Elva Benson Memorial Scholarship

AMOUNT: None Specified   DEADLINE: Mar 1
FIELDS/MAJORS: All Areas of Study

Awards are available at the University of New Mexico for Native American students who are full time and demonstrate financial need. Write to the address below for more information.

University of New Mexico, Albuquerque
Office of Financial Aid
Albuquerque, NM   87131

357
Emergency Aid and Health Professions Scholarships

AMOUNT: $50-$300   DEADLINE: None Specified
FIELDS/MAJORS: All Areas of Study

Scholarships are available for undergraduate Native American or Alaskan Indian students who require funds for emergency needs. Write to the address below for details. Application allowed only after classes begin.

Association on American Indian Affairs, Inc.
Box 268
Sisseton, SD   57262

358
Emilia Polak Scholarship

AMOUNT: Maximum: $500
DEADLINE: Feb 15
FIELDS/MAJORS: Agriculture, Roman Catholic Divinity

Four awards for Rhode Island students of Polish-American descent studying agriculture or planning to enroll in Roman Catholic Divinity School. Write to the address listed or call (401) 831-7177 for more information.

Rhode Island Polonia Scholarship Foundation
Foundation Office
866 Atwells Ave.
Providence, RI   02909

359
Emma May Olson Memorial Scholarship in Education

AMOUNT: None Specified   DEADLINE: Mar 1
FIELDS/MAJORS: Education

Awards are available at the University of New Mexico for students enrolled full time in the College of Education with demonstrated academic performance. First preference given to Native Americans. Write to the address below for more information.

University of New Mexico, Albuquerque
Office of Financial Aid
Albuquerque, NM   87131

360
Emma May Olson Scholarship

AMOUNT: None Specified   DEADLINE: Mar 1
FIELDS/MAJORS: Nursing

Awards are available at the University of New Mexico for junior or senior Native American nursing students with financial need and the qualities of mind and spirit necessary to become a nurse. A GPA of 2.25 is required. Write to the address below or contact the School of Nursing for more details.

University of New Mexico, Albuquerque
Office of Financial Aid
Albuquerque, NM   87131

361
Emma McAllister Novel Scholarships

AMOUNT: $1000   DEADLINE: Feb 1
FIELDS/MAJORS: Studio Art

Scholarships are available for undergraduate or graduate minority students with an interest in studio art. Two awards per year. Write to the address below for more information.

University of Iowa
School of Art and Art History
Iowa City, IA   52242

362
Endowment Grants

AMOUNT: None Specified
DEADLINE: None Specified
FIELDS/MAJORS: Theology, Religion

Awards for Concordia students preparing for full-time church careers in the LCMS and/or as specified by the donor. Must have GPAs of at least 2.5 and be enrolled in full-time study. For U.S. citizens. Write to the address below for more information.

Concordia University, Irvine
Financial Aid Office
1530 Concordia West
Irvine, CA   92715

363
Engineering Dissertation Fellowships

AMOUNT: $14500   DEADLINE: Nov 15
FIELDS/MAJORS: Engineering

Fellowships are available to those women who have successfully completed all required course work and exams by Nov 15. Awards are to be used for the final year of doctoral work. Fellowships cannot cover tuition for additional coursework. Degree should be received at the end of the award year. Fellow is expected to devote full time to the project during the award year. Write for details.

American Association of University Women Educational Foundation
2201 N. Dodge Street
Iowa City, IA   52243

364
Engineering Merit Scholarship

AMOUNT: None Specified
DEADLINE: None Specified
FIELDS/MAJORS: Chemical, Mechanical, Civil Engineering

Open to minority students who complete their freshman, sophomore, or junior year. Awards based on financial need and merit. Write to the address listed for further information.

Georgia Institute of Technology
Financial Aid Office
225 North Ave.
Atlanta, GA   30332

365
Engineering Scholarships for Minority High School Seniors

AMOUNT: $500-$1000   DEADLINE: Mar 1
FIELDS/MAJORS: Engineering

Scholarships are for Hispanic-American and African-American high school seniors who are in the top 25% of their class and have at least a 3.0 GPA. Must be U.S. citizens and plan to study engineering. Contact the address below for further information.

National Society of Professional Engineers Education Foundation
1420 King Street
Alexandria, VA   22314

366
Ernest and Young Scholarship

AMOUNT: None Specified
DEADLINE: None Specified
FIELDS/MAJORS: Accounting

Awards for minority students in the Department of Accounting in recognition of academic excellence. For students in their sophomore, junior, or senior year. Contact the Department of Accounting and Information Services for more details and an application.

University of Massachusetts, Amherst
Department of Accounting
Information Service
Amherst, MA   01003

367
Ernest I. & Eurice Miller Bass Scholarship

AMOUNT: None Specified   DEADLINE: Jun 1
FIELDS/MAJORS: Theology, Religious Studies

Scholarships are available for Methodist students planning to enter the ministry or another full-time religious vocation. Applicants should have above average grades and be U.S. citizens. Must be active full members of the United Methodist Church for at least one year prior to application. Write to the address below for information.

General Board of Higher Education and Ministry
Office of Loans and Scholarships
PO Box 871
Nashville, TN   37202

368
Esperanza, Inc. Scholarship

AMOUNT: $500   DEADLINE: Feb 28
FIELDS/MAJORS: All Areas of Study

Awards open to Hispanic residents of Cuyahoga County, Ohio, who are full-time students. May be enrolled in colleges, trade programs, or technical institutes. Must be able to demonstrate financial need. Contact the address below for further information.

Esperanza, Inc.
4115 Bridge Ave.
Cleveland, OH   44113

369
Esther Carter Ogle Memorial Scholarships

AMOUNT: None Specified   DEADLINE: Jan 15
FIELDS/MAJORS: Mathematics

Award open to first semester freshman female mathematics major. Contact the address below for further information.

Fort Hays State University
Office of Student Financial Aid
600 Park St.
Hays, KS   67601

370
Esther Tuttle Scholarship

AMOUNT: $500   DEADLINE: None Specified
FIELDS/MAJORS: Ceramic Engineering

For incoming freshmen women who are entering the ceramics engineering program as full-time students. Renewable with a GPA of at least 2.75. Write to the address below for details.

Alfred University
Student Financial Aid Office
26 N. Main St.
Alfred, NY   14802

371
Ethel J. Viles Scholarship Fund

AMOUNT: None Specified   DEADLINE: None Specified
FIELDS/MAJORS: All Areas of Study

Awards for female graduating seniors from Cony High School who plan to attend a college or university in Maine. Based on character and academic achievement. Contact the Cony High School guidance office for more information.

Maine Community Fund
PO Box 148
Ellsworth, ME   04605

372
Ethel MacPhail Scholarship

AMOUNT: $2000   DEADLINE: Feb 3
FIELDS/MAJORS: Business Management, Business Administration, Management Science, or Economics

Offered to an upper-division (junior or senior) female student who is attending full time, with strong academic standing concentrating in a field related to business management (business administration, management science, economics, etc.), and with demonstrated financial need. Contact the address listed for further information.

Evergreen State College
Office of the Dean of Enrollment Service
2700 Evergreen Parkway
Olympia, WA   98505-0002

373
Ethel Tingley Scholarship

AMOUNT: $1410   DEADLINE: Feb 1
FIELDS/MAJORS: Law

Award for entering female law student. Must demonstrate financial need. Renewable for three academic years for full-time students and four academic years for part-time students. Contact the assistant dean, Chase College of Law, for further information.

Northern Kentucky University
Chase College of Law
Admissions Office
Highland Heights, KY   41099

374
Ethel V. Artman Scholarship

AMOUNT: None Specified   DEADLINE: Jan 15
FIELDS/MAJORS: All Areas of Study

Scholarships available for female sophomores who can demonstrate financial need. Write to the address below for information.

Fort Hays State University
Office of Student Financial Aid
600 Park St.
Hays, KS   67601

375
Ethnic Diversity Scholarships

AMOUNT: $750   DEADLINE: Mar 1
FIELDS/MAJORS: Accounting

Open to minority Colorado residents who are high school seniors. Must have a minimum GPA of 3.0 and plan to attend a Colorado school. Write to the address below for details.

Colorado Society of Certified Public Accountants
Educational Foundation
7979 E. Tufts Avenue, #500
Denver, CO   80237

376
Ethnic Minority and Women's Enhancement Programs

AMOUNT: $1400   DEADLINE: Feb 15
FIELDS/MAJORS: Intercollegiate Athletics Administration

Postgraduate scholarships, internships, and curricula Vitae bank for women and minorities who intend to pursue careers in coaching, officiating, or athletic administration. Ten awards for women and ten for minorities. Contact the athletic director of the financial aid office at an NCAA member institution for details, or write to the director of personal development at the address below for details.

National Collegiate Athletic Association
6201 College Blvd.
Overland Park, KS   66211

377
Ethnic Minority Fellowship Program

AMOUNT: $11946   DEADLINE: Jan 15
FIELDS/MAJORS: Nursing, Behavioral Sciences, Clinical Research, Biomedical Research, Mental Health

Fellowships for minorities with a commitment to a career in nursing related to minority mental health; and/or the research training program for careers in behavioral science or the clinical training program for careers in psychiatric nursing. For pre or postdoctoral study. Must be a U.S. citizen or permanent resident and a R.N. Write to the address below for more information.

American Nurse's Association, Inc.
Minority Fellowships Office
600 Maryland Ave., SW, Suite 100 West
Washington, D.C.   20024

378
Ethnic Minority Scholarship, Hana Scholarship

AMOUNT: None Specified   DEADLINE: May 1
FIELDS/MAJORS: All Areas of Study

Scholarships are available for minority Methodist students who have been members of the Methodist church for at least one year and are U.S. citizens. For students of African-American, Asian, Hispanic, or Native American heritage with a GPA of at least 2.3. Write to the address below for information.

General Board of Higher Education and Ministry
Office of Loans and Scholarships
PO Box 871
Nashville, TN   37202

379
Eugenia Bradford Roberts Memorial Scholarship

AMOUNT: $1000   DEADLINE: Mar 31
FIELDS/MAJORS: All Areas of Study

Scholarships for daughters or granddaughters of Career Commissioned Officers (including Warrant) currently active in the U.S. Army, retired after twenty years, or deceased while on duty. Preference given to student best qualified academically and most deserving of financial assistance. Eight renewable scholarships per year. Write to the address below for details. Please include name, rank, and social security number of qualifying parent when requesting application. Be certain to include a SASE.

Society of Daughters of the U.S. Army
Janet B. Otto, Scholarship Chairman
7717 Rockledge Court
West Springfield, VA   22152

380
Euola Cox Scholarship for Minorities

AMOUNT: $125   DEADLINE: Mar 1
FIELDS/MAJORS: Education

Award for minority students who are pursuing a teaching career. Financial need is a major consideration. One award per year. Write to the address below for more information.

Eastern New Mexico University
College of Education and Technology
Station 25
Portales, NM   88130

381
Eve Drewelowe Scholarship Fund

AMOUNT: $450   DEADLINE: Mar 1
FIELDS/MAJORS: Painting

Scholarships are available for female undergraduate students with an interest in painting. One award per year. Write to the address below for more information.

University of Iowa
School of Art and Art History, E100AB
Iowa City, IA   52242

382
Excel Scholarship

AMOUNT: None Specified
DEADLINE: None Specified
FIELDS/MAJORS: Business Administration

Open to minority students enrolled in the College of Business Administration. Must be able to demonstrate financial need. Contact the address below for further information.

University of Northern Iowa
Elizabeth Peterson
204 Business
Cedar Falls, IA   50614

383 F.W.J. Sylwester—Church Work Family Award

AMOUNT: Maximum: $1500   **DEADLINE:** None Specified
FIELDS/MAJORS: All Areas of Study

Awards for students at Concordia University, Oregon, who are either married to or children of professional church workers in the Lutheran Church—Missouri Synod. Write to the address listed for more information.

Concordia University, Oregon
Office of Admissions
2811 NE Holman St.
Portland, OR   97211

384 Faculty Minority Scholarship

AMOUNT: None Specified   **DEADLINE:** Mar 1
FIELDS/MAJORS: All Areas of Study

Awarded to black students who would otherwise not be able to matriculate at Elizabethtown College because of financial need. Contact the address listed for further information.

Elizabethtown College
M. Clarke Paine, Dir. of Financial Aid
One Alpha Dr.
Elizabethtown, PA   17022

385 Faculty/Administrators Development

AMOUNT: None Specified   **DEADLINE:** Jun 1
FIELDS/MAJORS: Education

Available to minority American teachers or administrators at, or alumni of, sponsoring Arkansas public colleges or universities who have been admitted as full time, in-residence, doctoral program students. Write to the address below for more information.

Arkansas Department of Higher Education
Financial Aid Division
114 East Capitol
Little Rock, AR   72201

386 Falmouth Institute Scholarships

AMOUNT: Maximum: $1000   **DEADLINE:** May 1
FIELDS/MAJORS: All Areas of Study

Scholarships are available for American Indian graduating high school seniors. One award is offered annually. Write to the address below for information.

Falmouth Institute
3918 Prosperity, Suite 302
Fairfax, VA   22031

387 Fellowship of United Methodists in Music and Worship Arts

AMOUNT: None Specified   **DEADLINE:** Mar 1
FIELDS/MAJORS: Church Music, Worship Arts

Open to a full-time music degree candidate either entering as a freshman or already in an accredited university, college, school of theology, or doing special education in worship or the arts related to worship. Generally, four awards are offered annually. Write to the address below for more information.

Fellowship of United Methodists in Music and Worship Arts
PO Box 24787
Nashville, TN   37202

388 Fellowship on Women and Public Policy

AMOUNT: None Specified   **DEADLINE:** May 30
FIELDS/MAJORS: All Areas of Study

Fellowships are available to encourage greater participation of women in the public policy process, to develop public policy leaders, and to encourage the formulation of state policy that recognizes and responds to the needs of women and families. Applicants must be female graduate students with at least 12 credit hours completed in an accredited New York University and planning to continue education in New York. Write to the address below for information.

University at Albany, Center for Women in Government
Joeanna Hurston Brown, Director
135 Western Ave, Draper Hall, Room 302
Albany, NY   12222

389 Fellowship Program in Academic Medicine

AMOUNT: $6000   **DEADLINE:** Aug 31
FIELDS/MAJORS: Biomedical Research and Academic Medicine

Scholarships, fellowships, and awards for minority medical students. Minorities are defined here as African-American, Mexican-American, mainland Puerto Rican, and American Indian. Must be a U.S. citizen. Thirty-five awards are presented annually. Send a SASE to the address below for additional information.

National Medical Fellowships, Inc.
110 West 32nd St. 8th Floor
New York, NY   10001

390 Ferdinand Torres AFB Scholarship

AMOUNT: $1000   **DEADLINE:** None Specified
FIELDS/MAJORS: All Areas of Study

Open to undergraduates in the New York metropolitan area or new immigrants to the United States who are legally blind. Applicants must demonstrate financial need. Write to the address below for more information.

American Foundation for the Blind
11 Penn Plaza
Suite 300
New York, NY   10001

391
Fifth Third Bank/Lions Tip Off Tournament Scholarship

AMOUNT: None Specified   DEADLINE: Feb 1
FIELDS/MAJORS: All Areas of Study

Student must be enrolled at least 12 credit hours. Priority given to applicants who are visually impaired. Contact the address below for further information.

Northern Kentucky University
Financial Aid Office-Nunn Dr.
Administrative Center #416
Highland Heights, KY   41099

392
Fine Fellowship Program

AMOUNT: $7000-$10000
DEADLINE: None Specified
FIELDS/MAJORS: Education

Scholarships are available at the University of Oklahoma, Norman for full-time master's or doctoral level graduate students who are of Native American heritage. Write to the address below for information.

University of Oklahoma, Norman
College of Education
Room 105, ECH
Norman, OK   73019

393
First Baptist Church of Findlay, Ohio, Scholarship Fund

AMOUNT: None Specified   DEADLINE: None Specified
FIELDS/MAJORS: All Areas of Study

Awards are available for students at Cedarville College who are from the First Baptist Church in Findlay, Ohio. Must have a GPA of at least 2.0. Write to the address below for more information.

Cedarville College
Financial Aid Office
PO Box 601
Cedarville, OH   45314

394
First Peoples' Scholarship

AMOUNT: None Specified
DEADLINE: Feb 3
FIELDS/MAJORS: Music, Art, Journalism, or Science

Offered to a new student of color (Asian, Black, Hispanic, Native American) entering Evergreen in the fall quarter as a full-time undergraduate student. Scholarships are awarded to students who have distinguished themselves in a wide range of areas, e.g., high academic achievement, community service, music, art, journalism, science, etc. Contact the address listed for further information.

Evergreen State College
Office of the Dean of Enrollment Service
2700 Evergreen Parkway
Olympia, WA   98505-0002

395
Fisher College Scholarship

AMOUNT: $600   DEADLINE: Mar 1
FIELDS/MAJORS: All Areas of Study

Applicants must be young women high school graduates with credits acceptable to an admittance committee, as well as indication of financial need. For study at Fisher College. Not renewable. Write to the address below for details, be sure to include a SASE.

General Federation of Women's Clubs of Massachusetts
118 Beacon St.
Boston, MA   02116

396
Five College Fellowship Program for Minority Scholars

AMOUNT: $25000   DEADLINE: None Specified
FIELDS/MAJORS: All Areas of Study

Program for minority graduate students in the final phase of the doctoral degree. While the emphasis is on completing the dissertation, fellows may be expected to teach a single one-semester course within the hosting department. Applicants must attend Amherst, Hampshire, Mount Holyoke, or Smith Colleges or the University of Massachusetts. Write to the address below for more information. Award also includes office space, housing assistance, and library privileges at the five colleges.

Five Colleges, Inc.
Fellowship Program Committee
97 Spring St.
Amherst, MA   01002

397
Fleet Scholars Work/ Study Scholarship

AMOUNT: $1000   DEADLINE: Apr 30
FIELDS/MAJORS: All Areas of Study, but Preference Given to Business

Open to minority graduating high school seniors who are residents of Hartford and surrounding towns. For use at a four-year school. Must be able to demonstrate academic success and financial need. Each of the scholarships include $1000 and summer/vacation employment. Contact the address listed for further information.

Fleet Bank NA
Ms. Maxine R. Deanat
1 Constitution Plaza
Hartford, CT   06115-1600

398
Fleeta Davis Endowed Memorial Scholarship

AMOUNT: None Specified
DEADLINE: None Specified
FIELDS/MAJORS: All Areas of Study

Open to full-time undergraduate students with a minimum GPA of 2.75. Based on financial need. Preference given to single mothers. Contact the address below for further information.

Alaska Pacific University
Office of Financial Aid
4101 University Dr.
Anchorage, AK   99508

399
Fleming Companies, Inc. Scholarship

AMOUNT: $2500   DEADLINE: Feb 7
FIELDS/MAJORS: Business

Awards are available at the University of Oklahoma, Norman for full-time African/Hispanic/Asian/Native American students with a minimum GPA of 3.0. Awarded for use in junior year. Two awards offered annually. Write to the address below for information.

University of Oklahoma, Norman
College of Business Administration
Undergraduate Programs, 105 Adams Hall
Norman, OK   73019

400
Flemish Community Scholarships

AMOUNT: None Specified
DEADLINE: Jan 15
FIELDS/MAJORS: Art, Music, Humanities, Sciences, Social/Political Sciences, Law, Economics,

Open to sophomores who want to spend their junior or senior year at a Flemish university, conservatory of music, or art academy affiliated with the Flemish community. Must be a U.S. citizen and have a minimum GPA of 3.2. Contact the address below for further information.

Embassy of Belgium
Attache of the Flemish Community
3330 Garfield St. NW
Washington, D.C.   20008

401
Florence Baker Bugg Scholarship

AMOUNT: $1500   DEADLINE: None Specified
FIELDS/MAJORS: Physical Education

Student must be enrolled full time and majoring in physical education or a related field. Preference is given to a female student from the Midwest. Contact the Health, Physical Education, and Recreation Department for more information.

Southwest Missouri State University
Office of Financial Aid
901 South National Ave.
Springfield, MO   65804

402
Florence Lupe Memorial Scholarships

AMOUNT: $300   DEADLINE: None Specified
FIELDS/MAJORS: Human Resources

Award open to female juniors and seniors majoring in human resource management. Contact the address below for further information.

University of Toledo—College of Business Administration
Chair, Scholarship Committee
Toledo, OH   43606

403
Florence Warnock Scholarship

AMOUNT: $1250   DEADLINE: Mar 15
FIELDS/MAJORS: All Areas of Study

Scholarship offered to a Black Hawk County High School graduate. Must be an active member in a church or synagogue. Renewable for four years. Must have a GPA of 3.0 or better. Write to the address below for details.

Florence Warnock Scholarship Committee
First Presbyterian Church
505 Franklin Street
Waterloo, IA   50703

404
Floyd Cargill Scholarship

AMOUNT: $750   DEADLINE: Jun 15
FIELDS/MAJORS: All Areas of Study

Award for an outstanding blind student enrolled in an academic, vocational, technical, or professional training program in Illinois beyond the high school level. Applicants must be legally blind, U.S. citizens from the state of Illinois. Write to the address below for more information.

Illinois Council of the Blind
PO Box 1336
Springfield, IL   62705

405
Floyd Qualls Memorial Scholarships

AMOUNT: $2500   DEADLINE: Mar 1
FIELDS/MAJORS: All Areas of Study

Scholarships are for legally blind applicants who have been admitted for vocational/technical, professional, or academic studies at post-secondary levels. Write to the address below for details.

American Council of the Blind
Scholarship Coordinator
1155 15th St., NW, Suite 720
Washington, D.C.   20005

406
Focus Scholarship

AMOUNT: None Specified   DEADLINE: May 1
FIELDS/MAJORS: Education

Scholarships available to attract minority students to the field of education. Scholarship is for junior year and renewable for senior year. Recipients receive full tuition and books. Write to the address below for information and application.

Florida International University
College of Education—ACI 140
3000 NE 145th St.
N. Miami, FL   33181

407
Ford Foundation Doctoral Fellowships for Minorities

AMOUNT: $6000-$18000   DEADLINE: Nov 4
FIELDS/MAJORS: Social and Life Sciences, Humanities, Engineering, Math, Physics

Approximately fifty predoctoral and twenty-five dissertation fellowships for doctoral students. Must be U.S. citizens or U.S. nationals, of African-American, Native American, Hispanic, Alaskan Native, or Native Pacific Islander descent. Contact your fellowship office or write to the address below for details.

National Research Council
The Fellowship Office/FFPD
2101 Constitution Avenue, NW
Washington, D.C.   20418

408
Ford Foundation Postdoctoral Fellowships for Minorities

AMOUNT: $25000   DEADLINE: Jan 3
FIELDS/MAJORS: Social and Life Sciences, Humanities, Engineering, Math, Physics

Postdoctoral fellowships are available for scholars in the fields above. Renewable. Must be U.S. citizen or U.S. national and of African-American, Native American, Hispanic, Native Alaskan, or Native Pacific Islander descent. Twenty awards offered annually. Contact your fellowship office or write to the address below for details.

National Research Council
The Fellowship Office/FFPD
2101 Constitution Avenue, NW
Washington, D.C.   20418

409
Ford Motor Hispanic Engineering Scholarship

AMOUNT: None Specified   DEADLINE: Mar 1
FIELDS/MAJORS: Electrical or Mechanical Engineering

Awards are available at the University of New Mexico for Hispanic students in electrical or mechanical engineering. Must be at the junior or senior level with at least a 3.0 GPA and active in the Hispanic engineering organization. Write to the address below for more information.

University of New Mexico, Albuquerque
Office of Financial Aid
Albuquerque, NM   87131

410
Fort Peck Tribal Higher Education Program

AMOUNT: None Specified   DEADLINE: Jul 15
FIELDS/MAJORS: All Areas of Study

Applicants must be members of the Fort Peck Assiniboine and Sioux Tribes of the Fort Peck Reservation. Must be a high school graduate or possess a GED certificate and be enrolled, or accepted for enrollment, at an accredited college or university. Must have a GPA of 2.0 or higher. Selections based on financial need. Sixty to one hundred awards offered annually. Deadlines for applications are Jul 15 for fall quarter, Dec 1 for winter quarter, Mar 1 for spring quarter, and May 1 for summer quarter (college seniors). Write to the address below for more information.

Fort Peck Tribal Education Department
PO Box 1027
Poplar, MT   59255

411
Frances Hamilton Buchholz Memorial Scholarship

AMOUNT: $400   DEADLINE: Mar 31
FIELDS/MAJORS: Elementary Education

Student must be a female elementary education major. Contact the curriculum and instruction department for more information.

Southwest Missouri State University
Office of Financial Aid
901 South National Ave.
Springfield, MO   65804

412
Frank and Cynthia McCarthy Scholarship

AMOUNT: None Specified   DEADLINE: May 1
FIELDS/MAJORS: All Areas of Study

Award open to Native American full-time undergraduate with proof of tribal enrollment. Must demonstrate leadership, extracurricular activities, and potential to contribute to the American Indian community upon graduation. Contact the address below for further information.

University of Wyoming—American Indian Studies
Professor Judith Antell, Room 109
PO Box 3431
Laramie, WY   82071

413 Frank and Loretta Thompson Indian Music Major Scholarships

AMOUNT: $400   DEADLINE: None Specified
FIELDS/MAJORS: Music

Open to Native American students who are attending school full time, majoring in music. Contact the address below for further information.

Bacone College
Financial Aid Office
99 Bacone Rd.
Muskogee, OK   74403

414 Frank E. Pilling, Sr. Minority Scholarship

AMOUNT: $1000   DEADLINE: Mar 2
FIELDS/MAJORS: Mechanical Engineering

Award open to mechanical engineering majors with a minimum GPA of 2.5. Must be able to demonstrate financial need. Preference to women and African-American students. Contact the address below for further information.

California Polytechnic State University
Financial Aid Office
212 Administration Bldg.
San Luis Obispo, CA   93407

415 Frank L. Weil and Chester M. Vernon Memorial Eagle Scout Scholarship

AMOUNT: $500-$1000   DEADLINE: Dec 31
FIELDS/MAJORS: All Areas of Study

Awards for high school seniors who are Jewish and have earned the Ner Tamid emblem and the Eagle Scout award. Must be registered active members of a Boy Scout troop, Varsity Scout team, or Explorer post. Write to the address below for more information.

National Jewish Committee on Scouting, S226
Boy Scouts of America
1325 West Walnut Hill Lane
Irving, TX   75015

416 Frank Walton Horn Memorial Scholarship

AMOUNT: $3000   DEADLINE: Mar 31
FIELDS/MAJORS: Architecture, Engineering

Open to full-time students who are legally blind. Students may be in any area of study, but architecture or engineering majors are preferred. Write to the address below for complete details.

National Federation of the Blind
Mrs. Peggy Elliott, Chairman
805 Fifth Ave.
Grinnell, IA   50112

417 Franklin Mosher Baldwin Memorial Fellowships

AMOUNT: $17000   DEADLINE: Jan 2
FIELDS/MAJORS: Anthropology

Fellowships for African students who seek an advanced degree at a major institution. Priority is given to students involved in disciplines related to human evolution. Write to the address below for more information.

L.S.B. Leaky Foundation
Grants Administration
77 Jack London Square, Ste. M
Oakland, CA   94607

418 Franklin Woman's Club Scholarship Award

AMOUNT: $300   DEADLINE: Dec 2
FIELDS/MAJORS: All Areas of Study

Award open to women who want to enroll in college and have been out of school or college at least three years. Must have a high school diploma or GED. Financial need may be considered. Contact any campus for additional information.

Paul D. Camp Community College
PO Box 737
Franklin, VA   23851

419 Fred Coffey Class of 1925 Memorial Scholarship

AMOUNT: None Specified   DEADLINE: Mar 31
FIELDS/MAJORS: All Areas of Study

Award open to graduate students who are physically or learning impaired. Must have a minimum GPA of 3.0. Contact the address below for further information.

University of North Texas
Scholarship Office
Marquis Hall #218
Denton, TX   76203

420 Fred L. McClintock Memorial Award

AMOUNT: None Specified
DEADLINE: None Specified
FIELDS/MAJORS: Baseball, Basketball, or Football

Awarded each year to a young man of Christian principle who is of sincere life purpose and has interest in athletics, especially baseball, basketball, or football. Write to the address below for more information.

Ashland University
401 College Ave.
Ashland, OH   44805

421 Fred Schleiter Scholarship

AMOUNT: None Specified   DEADLINE: Mar 1
FIELDS/MAJORS: All Areas of Study

Awards for non-resident minority students who have a high financial need. Contact the address below for further information.

Iowa State University—Special Population Unit
Office of Student Financial Aid
12 Beardshear Hall
Ames, IA   50011

422 Frederick A Downes Scholarship

AMOUNT: $2500   DEADLINE: Apr 1
FIELDS/MAJORS: Vocational/Technical

Scholarships are available to legally blind undergraduate students who are twenty-two years of age or younger, enrolled in a course of study leading to a degree or vocational credentials. Applicants must be U.S. citizens. Write to the foundation at the address below to receive information on this award and other programs they administer.

American Foundation for the Blind
Scholarship Coordinator
11 Penn Plaza, Suite 300
New York, NY   10001

423 Free Methodist Ministerial Discount

AMOUNT: None Specified   DEADLINE: Feb 15
FIELDS/MAJORS: All Areas of Study

Scholarships are available at Spring Arbor College for undergraduate students who are a) studying to be a full-time minister of the Free Methodist Church, b) dependents of FM ministers (active, retired, or deceased), c) ordained FM ministers, and d) FM missionaries or dependents of FM missionaries. Write to the address listed for more details.

Spring Arbor College
Office of Financial Aid
Spring Arbor, MI   49283

424 Freshman Awards

AMOUNT: None Specified   DEADLINE: Mar 1
FIELDS/MAJORS: All Areas of Study

Open to incoming freshmen who are members of the JACL. Several award programs are available. Applications and information may be obtained from local JACL chapters, district offices, and national headquarters at the address below. Please be certain to include a legal-sized SASE.

Japanese American Citizens League
National Scholarship and Award Program
1765 Sutter St.
San Francisco, CA   94115

425 Freshman New Mexico Native Americans Scholarship Fund

AMOUNT: None Specified   DEADLINE: Mar 1
FIELDS/MAJORS: All Areas of Study

Applicant must be a freshman Native American from New Mexico and must have a minimum GPA of 2.86. Write to the address below for details.

New Mexico State University
American Indian Program
Box 30001, Dept 5100
Las Cruces, NM   88003

426 Fritz Halbers Fellowship

AMOUNT: $3000   DEADLINE: Nov 1
FIELDS/MAJORS: Jewish Studies

Fellowships are available for research at the Leo Baeck institute for current predoctoral scholars who are studying the social, communal, and intellectual history of German-speaking Jewry. Applicants must be U.S. citizens. Write to the address below for information.

Leo Baeck Institute
Fellowship Programs
129 East 73rd Street
New York, NY   10021

427 Fund for the Advancement of Ethnic Understanding

AMOUNT: None Specified   DEADLINE: Mar 1
FIELDS/MAJORS: All Areas of Study

Awarded to underprivileged ethnic minorities in the form of scholarship aid or program aid. Contact the address listed for further information.

Elizabethtown College
M. Clarke Paine, Dir. of Financial Aid
One Alpha Dr.
Elizabethtown, PA   17022

428 GEM Fellowships

AMOUNT: Maximum: $12000
DEADLINE: Dec 1
FIELDS/MAJORS: Engineering, Sciences, Mathematics

Applicants must be engineering or science majors in their senior year or beyond. Must be U.S. citizen and one of the following minorities: Native, African, Hispanic, or Puerto Rican Americans. For graduate use only. Must have a GPA of at least 2.8 if in a master's program and a minimum GPA of 3.0 if pursuing a doctorate. Write to the address below for details. Please note if you are seeking a master's or doctoral degree.

Consortium for Graduate Degrees for Minorities
GEM Central Office
PO Box 537
Notre Dame, IN   46556

429 General Electric Fund Scholarship

AMOUNT: None Specified   DEADLINE: Mar 1
FIELDS/MAJORS: Engineering

Awards for minority students entering their sophomore, junior, or senior year studying full time in the College of Engineering. Must demonstrate academic excellence. Contact the director of the Minority Engineering Program for more information.

University of Massachusetts, Amherst
Director
Minority Engineering Program
Amherst, MA   01003

430 General Electric Minority Scholars Program

AMOUNT: None Specified
DEADLINE: None Specified
FIELDS/MAJORS: Industrial, Electrical, Mechanical Engineering

Open to minority freshmen. Must possess leadership qualities and maintain a minimum GPA of 3.0. Award may be renewed for up to two additional years provided the student continues to meet eligibility requirements. Awards made by General Electric. Write to the address listed for further information.

Georgia Institute of Technology
Financial Aid Office
225 North Ave.
Atlanta, GA   30332

431 General Motors Endowed Scholarship

AMOUNT: Maximum: $2500
DEADLINE: None Specified
FIELDS/MAJORS: All Areas of Study

Open to undergraduate minority and female students enrolled at Georgia Tech. Preference given to minority General Motors employees, spouses, and children. May be renewed for up to three years. Recipients selected by the Office of Student Financial Planning and Services. Write to the address listed for further information.

Georgia Institute of Technology
Financial Aid Office
225 North Ave.
Atlanta, GA   30332

432 General Motors Endowed Scholarships

AMOUNT: Maximum: $1000   DEADLINE: Mar 1
FIELDS/MAJORS: All Areas of Study

Open to undergraduates who are U.S. citizens with a minimum GPA of 3.0. Preference given to women or minorities who are General Motors employees or dependents. Contact the address below for further information.

New Mexico Highlands University
Financial Aid Office
201 Felix Martinez Student Svcs. Bldg.
Las Vegas, NM   87791

433 General Motors Engineering Scholarship

AMOUNT: None Specified
DEADLINE: None Specified
FIELDS/MAJORS: Electrical/Industrial/Mechanical Engineering

Open to first semester sophomores who have a minimum GPA of 3.2 and are enrolled at any of the following historically black colleges or universities: Atlanta University Center, Florida A & M, Howard University, North Carolina A & T University, Prairie View A & M University, Southern University A & M College, Tennessee State University, and Tuskegee University. Contact the financial aid office at your school for information and an application.

United Negro College Fund
Scholarship Program
PO Box 10444
Fairfax, VA   22031-4511

434 General Motors Freshmen Minority Scholarship

AMOUNT: None Specified   DEADLINE: Mar 1
FIELDS/MAJORS: Electrical, Mechanical, Computer Engineering, or Computer Science

Awards are available at the University of New Mexico for freshmen planning to enroll in one of the areas above. Applicants must be minority students in the top 25% of their class, with a high school GPA of 3.2 or better. Write to the address below for more information.

University of New Mexico, Albuquerque
Office of Financial Aid
Albuquerque, NM   87131

435
General Motors/Equal Employment Opportunity Scholarships

AMOUNT: Maximum: $1000   DEADLINE: Mar 15
FIELDS/MAJORS: All Areas of Study

Open to minority and female students who have a parent employed by G.M. Contact the address below for further information.

Muskingum College
Office of Financial Aid
New Concord, OH   43762

436
General Motors/Equal Opportunity Scholarships

AMOUNT: $1000   DEADLINE: Mar 15
FIELDS/MAJORS: All Areas of Study

Awards for female Muskingum students who have a parent employed by general motors or who are ethnic minority students. Write to the address below for more information.

Muskingum College
Office of Admission
New Concord, OH   43762

437
General Motors/League of United Latin-American Citizens Scholarships

AMOUNT: None Specified   DEADLINE: Mar 1
FIELDS/MAJORS: Engineering

Awards are available at the University of New Mexico for full-time minority students in the field of engineering. Incoming freshmen must have a GPA of at least 3.5, and college applicants must have a GPA of 3.0 or better. Contact LNESC, 500 2nd St. NW #500, Albuquerque, NM, 87102 for more information.

University of New Mexico, Albuquerque
Office of Financial Aid
Albuquerque, NM   87131

438
George & Masuo Nagatomo Memorial Scholarship

AMOUNT: None Specified   DEADLINE: None Specified
FIELDS/MAJORS: All Areas of Study, Except Theater

Awards for Mesa State sophomores, juniors, or seniors majoring in any field except theater. Must have a GPA of at least 3.0 and be of Asian descent. Must be a U.S. citizen. Contact the School of Natural Sciences and Mathematics for more information.

Mesa State College
Financial Aid Office
PO Box 2647
Grand Junction, CO   81501

439
George D. and Marion K. Roberts Scholarship Award

AMOUNT: $1250   DEADLINE: None Specified
FIELDS/MAJORS: Management

Awards for female School of Management students who have demonstrated financial need, outstanding academic achievement, and community involvement. The recipient must agree to make a donation of $1500 to the School of Management within fifteen years of graduation. For females in their sophomore, junior, or senior year. Applications for School of Management scholarships will be available in the SOM Development Office, Room 206.

University of Massachusetts, Amherst
School of Management
SOM Development Office, Room 206
Amherst, MA   01003

440
George H. Newton Christian Scholarship

AMOUNT: $1000   DEADLINE: None Specified
FIELDS/MAJORS: All Areas of Study

Recipient must exemplify Christian values and morals in his/her personal lifestyle. Must be enrolled for a minimum of 12 semester hours and demonstrate financial need. Contact the address listed for further information.

Charleston Southern University
PO Box 118087
Charleston, SC   29423

441
George J. Record School Foundation Scholarships

AMOUNT: Maximum: $3000   DEADLINE: May 20
FIELDS/MAJORS: All Areas of Study

Awards for legal residents of Ashtabula County, Ohio. Deadline date for high school seniors is May 20. Deadline date for undergraduates is Jun 20. Students will be (or are) attending a private, Protestant based school full time. Financial need must be demonstrated. Sixty-four to eighty-two awards offered annually. Contact the address below for further information.

George J. Record Foundation
Charles N. Lafferty, Executive Director
PO Box 581—365 Main St.
Conneaut, OH   44030

442
George M. Booker Scholarship for Minorities

AMOUNT: $1000-$2500   DEADLINE: Mar 15
FIELDS/MAJORS: Real Estate

Scholarships for minority students studying real estate. Must have a GPA of at least a 3.0 and be a U.S. citizen. Students should have completed at least two courses in real estate at the time of application. Two undergraduate and one graduate award offered annually. Recipients are usually announced in Jun. Write to the address below for more information.

Institute of Real Estate Management Foundation
Attn: Booker Scholarship
430 North Michigan Ave.
Chicago, IL   60611

443
George Washington Carver Project Excellence Scholarship

AMOUNT: None Specified   **DEADLINE:** None Specified
FIELDS/MAJORS: All Areas of Study

Awards for African-American seniors who reside in the Washington D.C. area. Based on academics and the ability to communicate. Must be nominated by your high school. Awards vary to pay for tuition, fees, room and board, and a stipend. Contact your high school guidance counselor for further information.

Iowa State University—Special Populations Unit
Office of Student Financial Aid
12 Beardshear Hall
Ames, IA   50011

444
Georgeanne Freudenreich Memorial Scholarships

AMOUNT: $250   **DEADLINE:** Feb 15
FIELDS/MAJORS: All Areas of Study

Awards for female students at UW-Platteville who are considered non-traditional students. One award is awarded annually. Write to the address below or contact the office at (608) 342-1125 for more information.

University of Wisconsin, Platteville
Office of Admissions and Enrollment Mgt.
Platteville, WI   53818

445
Georgia Tech Women's Forum Scholarship

AMOUNT: None Specified   **DEADLINE:** None Specified
FIELDS/MAJORS: All Areas of Study

Open to female students who have demonstrated scholastic achievement and are involved in campus and civic activities. Awards made by members of the Georgia Tech Women's Forum. Write to the address listed for further information.

Georgia Institute of Technology
Financial Aid Office
225 North Ave.
Atlanta, GA   30332

446
Geoscience Scholarships for Ethnic Minorities

AMOUNT: $4000-$10000   **DEADLINE:** Feb 1
FIELDS/MAJORS: Earth, Space, Marine Sciences, Geology, Geophysics, Hydrology

Scholarships are available at the undergraduate and graduate level in the geosciences listed above. Applicants must be U.S. citizens and underrepresented minorities. For full-time study. Based upon academic record and financial need. Approximately eighty awards offered annually. Write to the address below for details.

American Geological Institute
AGI Minority Geoscience Scholarships
4220 King Street
Alexandria, VA   22302

447
Gerald T. Wilkerson Scholarships

AMOUNT: None Specified   **DEADLINE:** Mar 1
FIELDS/MAJORS: All Areas of Study

Awards are available at the University of New Mexico for full-time Native American students with academic achievement and financial need. Write to the address below for more information.

University of New Mexico, Albuquerque
Office of Financial Aid
Albuquerque, NM   87131

448
Gerber Prize for Excellence in Pediatrics

AMOUNT: $2000   **DEADLINE:** Aug 31
FIELDS/MAJORS: Pediatric Medicine

Scholarships, fellowships, and awards for minority medical students in pediatrics. Minorities are defined here as African-American, Mexican-American, mainland Puerto Rican, and American Indian. For study at Michigan medical schools. Academics is primary consideration; need is considered. Must be a U.S. citizen. One award presented annually. Write to "Special Programs" at the address below for details.

National Medical Fellowships, Inc.
110 West 32nd St. 8th Floor
New York, NY   10001

449
Gertrude and Harry G. Fins Scholarship

AMOUNT: None Specified   **DEADLINE:** Mar 1
FIELDS/MAJORS: Law

Scholarships for Jewish men and women who are legal residents of the Chicago area. Must be attending/planning to attend DePaul University, Loyola University, IIT-Chicago/Kent, John Marshall, Southern Illinois University, or the University of Illinois at Urbana/Champaign for their law studies. Write to the address below after Dec 1 for details.

Jewish Vocational Service
Attn: Academic Scholarship Program
One South Franklin Street
Chicago, IL   60606

450 GFWC Las Vegas Woman's Club Memorial Scholarship

AMOUNT: Maximum: $1000   DEADLINE: Mar 1
FIELDS/MAJORS: All Areas of Study

Open to female, non-traditional students from San Miguel or Mora Counties. Must have a minimum GPA of 3.0 and be enrolled for 14 or more credit hours. Financial need is a significant factor in selection of recipients. Contact the address below for further information.

New Mexico Highlands University
Financial Aid Office
201 Felix Martinez Student Svcs. Bldg.
Las Vegas, NM   87791

451 Gibran, Kahlil Educational Fund

AMOUNT: None Specified   DEADLINE: Jun 1
FIELDS/MAJORS: All Areas of Study

Scholarships for Syrian and Lebanese peoples. Preference given to persons whose ancestors are from the town of Becherre or to other towns in Lebanon. Write to the address below for details.

Gibran Kahlil Educational Fund, Inc.
4 Longfellow Place, Suite 3802
Boston, MA   02114

452 Gillette Hayden Memorial Foundation Loans

AMOUNT: None Specified   DEADLINE: Aug 1
FIELDS/MAJORS: Dentistry

Loans are available to women junior, senior, or graduate level dental students. Applicants will be judged on financial need, academic ability, and current amount of indebtedness. Write to address below for details.

American Association of Women Dentists
Gilette Hayden Memorial Foundation
401 N. Michigan Ave.
Chicago, IL   60611

453 Gillian and Ellis Goodman Scholarship

AMOUNT: None Specified   DEADLINE: Mar 1
FIELDS/MAJORS: Environmental Engineering

Open to students of junior level or above who are legally domiciled in Cook County or the Chicago metro area. Preference given to career goals in engineering, focusing on environmental concerns. Contact the address below after Dec 1 for further information.

Jewish Vocational Service
Academic Scholarship Program
1 S. Franklin St.
Chicago, IL   60606

454 Ginny and Theresa Newberry Scholarship

AMOUNT: $100   DEADLINE: Feb 1
FIELDS/MAJORS: All Areas of Study

Award for single mother who is a Kentucky resident. Must have a GPA of 3.0 or higher. Must demonstrate financial need. Contact the address below for further information.

Northern Kentucky University
Financial Aid Office-Nunn Dr.
Administrative Center #416
Highland Heights, KY   41099

455 Gladys C. Anderson Memorial Scholarship

AMOUNT: $1000   DEADLINE: Apr 1
FIELDS/MAJORS: Religious Music, Classical Music

Open to legally blind women studying religious or classical music at the undergraduate level. Applicants must be U.S. citizens. One annual award. Student must submit a sample performance tape of voice or instrumental selection (not to exceed thirty minutes). Write to the address below for complete details.

American Foundation for the Blind
Scholarship Committee
11 Penn Plaza, Suite 300
New York, NY   10001

456 Gladys York Memorial Scholarship

AMOUNT: None Specified   DEADLINE: None Specified
FIELDS/MAJORS: All Areas of Study

Awards are available for full-time students at Cedarville College who attend the Calvary Baptist Church of Parkertown, New Jersey. Must have a GPA of at at least 2.0. Write to the address below for more information.

Cedarville College
Financial Aid Office
PO Box 601
Cedarville, OH   45314

457 Glamour Magazine's Top Ten College Women Competition

AMOUNT: $1000   DEADLINE: Jan 31
FIELDS/MAJORS: All Areas of Study

Open to women who are college juniors at an accredited college or university, majoring in any field of study. Each entry must include: completed application form (photo copies acceptable), an official college transcript (may be mailed separately), and a list, by year, of your activities on and off campus. Include names of activities and organizations, and briefly describe your responsibilities and contributions. A five hundred to seven hundred word essay describing your most meaningful achievements and how they relate to your field of study and your future goals is also required. Include a black and white or color photograph, no larger than 8 x 10 (for identification purposes only) and at least one letter of recommendation. Selections based on campus and community activities, leadership experience, unique and inspiring goals, and excellent academics. Winners will be notified by Jun 1, 1998. For more information, call (800) 244-GLAM.

Glamour Magazine
Top Ten College Women Competition
350 Madison Ave.
New York, NY   10017

458 Glaxo Women in Science Scholars Scholarship

AMOUNT: None Specified   DEADLINE: Sep 1
FIELDS/MAJORS: Biology, Physics, Chemistry

Award open to new, undergraduate females with an interest in a career in scientific/academic research. Contact the address below for further information.

University of North Carolina, Greensboro
Financial Aid Office
723 Kenilworth St.
Greensboro, NC   27412

459 Glen T. Simpson Scholarships

AMOUNT: None Specified   DEADLINE: Mar 1
FIELDS/MAJORS: All Areas of Study

Awards are available at the University of New Mexico for American Indian seniors who demonstrate academic achievement and financial need. Write to the address below for more information.

University of New Mexico, Albuquerque
Office of Financial Aid
Albuquerque, NM   87131

460 Gloria Fecht Memorial Scholarship

AMOUNT: $1000-$3000   DEADLINE: Mar 1
FIELDS/MAJORS: All Areas of Study

Scholarships are available for female Southern California residents enrolled at a four-year college or university, with a GPA of at least 3.0 and an interest in golf. Financial need is considered. Twenty to thirty awards are offered annually, renewable for up to four years. Write to the address below for information.

Gloria Fecht Memorial Scholarships Fund
402 West Arrow Highway, Suite 10
San Dimas, CA   91773

461 Golden Drum Scholarship

AMOUNT: None Specified   DEADLINE: Dec 15
FIELDS/MAJORS: All Areas of Study

For African-American high school seniors. Must be recommended by Achievers of Greater Miami (Dade County only) and FIU Golden Drum committee. Scholarship is renewable. Write to the address below for additional information.

Florida International University
Office of Minority Student Services
University Park
Miami, FL   33199

462 Golden Drum/Ronald A. Hammond Scholarships

AMOUNT: $17700   DEADLINE: Feb 15
FIELDS/MAJORS: All Areas of Study

Scholarships for well-qualified high school seniors of African descent. Renewable. Write to the address below for more information.

University of Miami
Office of Financial Assistance Services
PO Box 248187
Coral Gables, FL   33124

463 Golf Foundation Undergraduate Scholarships

AMOUNT: $2000   DEADLINE: Mar 1
FIELDS/MAJORS: All Areas of Study

Scholarships for graduating high school senior women who have been involved with the sport of golfing (skill or excellence in golf is not a criterion). Must be a U.S. citizen and have a minimum GPA of 3.0. Selection is made on the basis of academics, financial need, character, and an involvement with the sport of golf. Applications may be obtained by sending a request and a SASE to the address below.

Women's Western Golf Foundation
Mrs. Richard W. Willis
393 Ramsay Road
Deerfield, IL   60015

464 Gottschall-Rex Memorial Scholarship

AMOUNT: $550-$1600
DEADLINE: None Specified
FIELDS/MAJORS: Health Education, Physical Education

Award open to full-time female undergraduates who are Toledo residents. Based on financial need and academics. One to five awards offered annually. Contact the address below for further information.

University of Toledo
Dean, College of Education
301 Snyder Memorial
Toledo, OH   43606

465
Grace Foundation Scholarship Fund

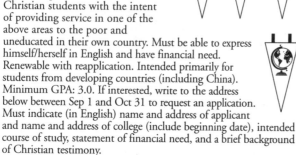

AMOUNT: Maximum: $2500
DEADLINE: Jan 31
FIELDS/MAJORS: Christian Service, Healthcare, Teaching, Theology, Welfare

Scholarships for Southeast Asian Christian students with the intent of providing service in one of the above areas to the poor and uneducated in their own country. Must be able to express himself/herself in English and have financial need. Renewable with reapplication. Intended primarily for students from developing countries (including China). Minimum GPA: 3.0. If interested, write to the address below between Sep 1 and Oct 31 to request an application. Must indicate (in English) name and address of applicant and name and address of college (include beginning date), intended course of study, statement of financial need, and a brief background of Christian testimony.

Grace Foundation Scholarship Fund
PO Box 924
Menlo Park, CA   94026

466
Grace Legendre Fellowship

AMOUNT: $1000   DEADLINE: Feb 28
FIELDS/MAJORS: All Areas of Study

Applicants must be women who are New York state residents and pursuing a full-time graduate program at an accredited New York state college or university. Must be U.S. citizens. Write to address below for details.

Business and Professional Women's Clubs of New York State
212 Mayro Building
239 Genessee Street
Utica, NY   13501

467
Graduate Awards

AMOUNT: None Specified   DEADLINE: Apr 1
FIELDS/MAJORS: All Areas of Study

Applicants must be graduate students of Japanese ancestry and members of the JACL. Several programs are available. Applications and information may be obtained from local JACL chapters, district offices, and national headquarters at the address below. Please indicate your level of study, and be certain to include a legal-sized SASE (offices in San Francisco, Seattle, L.A., Chicago, and Fresno).

Japanese American Citizens League
National Scholarship and Award Program
1765 Sutter St.
San Francisco, CA   94115

468
Graduate Dean's Multicultural Award

AMOUNT: $6600   DEADLINE: None Specified
FIELDS/MAJORS: All Areas of Study

Awards for graduate students at UW Oshkosh who are members of an underrepresented minority group. Contact the graduate school at UW Oshkosh for more details.

University of Wisconsin, Oshkosh
Financial Aid Office, Dempsey 104
800 Algoma Blvd.
Oshkosh, WI   54901

469
Graduate Fellowship Program for Native Americans

AMOUNT: $6000   DEADLINE: Nov 1
FIELDS/MAJORS: Political Science

Fellowships open to Native Americans who have received their bachelor's degree and are planning to enroll in a political science doctoral program. Must have a record of outstanding academic achievement. Contact the address below for further information.

American Political Science Association
Director of Minority Affairs
1527 New Hampshire Ave. NW
Washington, D.C.   20036

470
Graduate Fellowships for African-American Students

AMOUNT: $6000   DEADLINE: Nov 1
FIELDS/MAJORS: Political Science

Graduate fellowships for African-American doctoral students. Preference will be given to students just starting their doctoral program. Must be a U.S. citizen. Based on potential for success in graduate studies and financial needs. Fellowships will be awarded on an annual basis. Write to the address below for complete details.

American Political Science Association
1527 New Hampshire Ave., NW
Washington, D.C.   20036

471
Graduate Fellowships for Chicano and Latino Students

AMOUNT: $6000   DEADLINE: Nov 1
FIELDS/MAJORS: Political Science

Graduate fellowships for Hispanic students. APSA fellows must enroll in doctoral programs. Priority will be given to those about to enter graduate school. Must be a U.S. citizen. Based on potential for success in graduate studies and financial needs. Fellowships will be awarded on an annual basis. Write to the address below for details.

American Political Science Association
1527 New Hampshire Ave., NW
Washington, D.C.   20036

472
Graduate Fellowships for Minorities and Women in the Physical Sciences

AMOUNT: Maximum: $15000   DEADLINE: Nov 15
FIELDS/MAJORS: Physical Science or Related Fields

Six-year fellowship program for current college seniors or recent graduates not enrolled in a post-graduate program, who want to obtain a Ph.D. and are an underrepresented minority and/or female. Must be a U.S. citizen and have at least a GPA of 3.0. For study at a participating NPSC member university. Recipients must agree to work two summers at a consortium member employer. Write to L. Nan Snow, executive director, at the address below for more information.

National Physical Science Consortium
New Mexico State University
Box 30001, Dept 3 NPS
Las Cruces, NM   88003

473
Graduate Scholarship Program

AMOUNT: Maximum: $7200
DEADLINE: None Specified
FIELDS/MAJORS: All Areas of Study

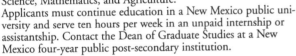

Renewable award given to New Mexico resident graduate students, with preference given to women and minorities in the fields of Business, Engineering, Computer Science, Mathematics, and Agriculture. Applicants must continue education in a New Mexico public university and serve ten hours per week in an unpaid internship or assistantship. Contact the Dean of Graduate Studies at a New Mexico four-year public post-secondary institution.

New Mexico Commission on Higher Education
Financial Aid and Student Services
PO Box 15910
Santa Fe, NM   87506

474
Graduate Student Researchers Program (Minority and Disabled Focus)

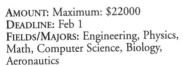

AMOUNT: Maximum: $22000
DEADLINE: Feb 1
FIELDS/MAJORS: Engineering, Physics, Math, Computer Science, Biology, Aeronautics

Applicants must be sponsored by their graduate department chair or faculty advisor; enrolled in a full-time graduate program at an accredited U.S. college or university; studying in one of the fields listed above. Student must be highly motivated to pursue their plans of study in NASA related research. Applicant must be a U.S. citizen. Write to the program manager at the address below for information. The focus of this program is to bring underrepresented racial minorities and students with disabilities into these fields of study.

NASA Graduate Student Researchers Program
NASA Headquarters
Scholarships and Fellowships
Washington, D.C.   20546

475
Grant and Programs for Theological Studies

AMOUNT: None Specified   DEADLINE: None Specified
FIELDS/MAJORS: Theology, Religion

Grants for theology students at the graduate level of study who are members of the Presbyterian Church, U.S.A. Applicants must be U.S. citizens, demonstrate financial need, and be recommended by an academic advisor or church pastor. Write to the address below for more information.

Presbyterian Church, (U.S.A.)
Office of Financial Aid
100 Witherspoon St.
Louisville, KY   40202

476
Grant M. Mack Memorial Scholarships

AMOUNT: $2000   DEADLINE: Mar 1
FIELDS/MAJORS: Business

Two scholarships for graduate and undergraduate students. Must be legally blind and majoring in business. Write to the address below for details.

American Council of the Blind
Scholarship Coordinator
1155 15th St., NW, Suite 720
Washington, D.C.   20005

477
Grant Program for Medical Studies

AMOUNT: $500-$1500
DEADLINE: None Specified
FIELDS/MAJORS: Medicine

Grants for medical students at the graduate level of study who are members of the Presbyterian Church, U.S.A. Applicants must be U.S. citizens, demonstrate financial need, and be recommended by an academic advisor or church pastor. Write to the address below for more information.

Presbyterian Church, (U.S.A.)
Office of Financial Aid
100 Witherspoon St.
Louisville, KY   40202

478
Greater Hartford Interracial Scholarship

AMOUNT: Maximum: $750   DEADLINE: Feb 24
FIELDS/MAJORS: All Areas of Study

Open to high school seniors who are residents of Hartford or contiguous suburbs. May be used at two or four-year schools. Must be in the upper third of class, be involved in community service, and be able to demonstrate financial need. This award may be renewable. Contact the address listed for further information.

Greater Hartford Interracial Scholarship Fund, Inc.
Ellis Simpson
PO Box 320644
Hartford, CT   06132

479
Green Jackets/Harris/ Howell Scholarships

AMOUNT: None Specified   DEADLINE: Mar 31
FIELDS/MAJORS: All Areas of Study

Awards open to junior and senior women who have attended the University of North Texas for at least one year. Must have a minimum GPA of 3.5. Contact the address below for further information.

University of North Texas
Scholarship Office
Marquis Hall #218
Denton, TX   76203

480
Gretchen Koo Scholarship

AMOUNT: None Specified   DEADLINE: Dec 1
FIELDS/MAJORS: All Areas of Study

Awarded to a student showing dedication to scholarship and humanitarian and Christian ideals. Write to the address listed for more information.

Spalding University
Financial Aid Office
851 S. Fourth St.
Louisville, KY   40203

481
Griffis Memorial Scholarship

AMOUNT: None Specified
DEADLINE: None Specified
FIELDS/MAJORS: Art, Drama

Awards for women studying for a bachelor's degree in art or drama at Benedictine College in Atchinson, Kansas. Applicants must have a GPA of 3.0 or above for the scholarship and 2.5 or better for an achievement award. Write to the address below for more information.

Benedictine Sisters
Mount St. Scholastica
801 South 8th St.
Atchinson, KS   66002

482
Hagop Bogigian Scholarship Fund

AMOUNT: None Specified
DEADLINE: Mar 1
FIELDS/MAJORS: Arts

Scholarships for students of Armenian descent who are enrolled in a four-year bachelor of arts degree program at Mt. Holyoke College. Must have a GPA of at least 3.0. Write to the address below for more information.

Mt. Holyoke College
Financial Aid Office
South Hadley, MA   01075

483
Hal Connolly Scholar-Athlete Award

AMOUNT: $1000   DEADLINE: Feb 28
FIELDS/MAJORS: All Areas of Study

Applicant must be a California resident, have competed in high school varsity athletics, be an incoming freshman under the age of 20, and have a disability. Write to the address below for details.

California Governor's Committee for Employment of Disabled Persons
Scholar-Athlete Awards Program
PO Box 826880, MIC 41
Sacramento, CA   94280

484
Hannah Pittis Schoenbrunn Grange Scholarship

AMOUNT: $200   DEADLINE: Apr 1
FIELDS/MAJORS: Nursing, Agriculture

Scholarships for female students at KSU pursuing a degree in nursing or for male students studying agriculture. Three awards per year. Contact the financial aid office for details.

Kent State University, Tuscarawas Campus
Financial Aid Office
University Dr., NE
New Philadelphia, OH   44663

485
Harold and Vivian Rowell Scholarship

AMOUNT: Maximum: $500   DEADLINE: None Specified
FIELDS/MAJORS: All Areas of Study

Recipient must exemplify Christian values in his/her lifestyle and commitment. First priority given to a resident of Lancaster County, South Carolina, enrolled a minimum of 12 semester hours. If other than a freshman, recipient must have at least a 2.0 GPA. Contact the address listed for further information.

Charleston Southern University
PO Box 118087
Charleston, SC   29423

486
Harold Conner African-American Scholarships

AMOUNT: None Specified   DEADLINE: Mar 1
FIELDS/MAJORS: All Areas of Study

Scholarships for incoming African-American freshmen who have a minimum GPA of 3.25. Based on high school academics, leadership record, and test scores. Renewable for four years if recipients meet pre-set standards. Contact the address below for more information.

University of Tennessee, Martin
Office of Financial Assistance
Administration Bldg. Room 210
Martin, TN   38238

487
Harriett Barnhart Wimmer Scholarship

AMOUNT: $1000   DEADLINE: Mar 31
FIELDS/MAJORS: Landscape Architecture/Design

Applicants must be female undergraduates in their last year of studying landscape architecture or design. Must demonstrate excellence in design ability and sensitivity to the environment. Contact the address below for further information.

Landscape Architecture Foundation
4401 Connecticut Ave., NW, Suite 500
Washington, D.C.   20008

488
Hartley B. Dean Medical Scholarship

AMOUNT: None Specified   DEADLINE: Mar 1
FIELDS/MAJORS: Medicine

Awards are available at the University of New Mexico for Native American medical students who are in the top half of class. Write to the address below for more information.

University of New Mexico, Albuquerque
Office of Financial Aid
Albuquerque, NM   87131

489
Hartley B. Dean Scholarship

AMOUNT: None Specified   DEADLINE: Mar 1
FIELDS/MAJORS: All Areas of Study

Awards are available at the University of New Mexico for Native American students who have financial need and satisfactory academic progress. Preference is given to students who would not be able to continue without support. Write to the address below for more information.

University of New Mexico, Albuquerque
Office of Financial Aid
Albuquerque, NM   87131

490
Hays City P.E.O. Scholarship

AMOUNT: None Specified   DEADLINE: Jan 15
FIELDS/MAJORS: All Areas of Study

Scholarship open to female residents of Hays County, Kansas, with a minimum GPA of 3.0. Write to the address below for information.

Fort Hays State University
Office of Student Financial Aid
600 Park St.
Hays, KS   67601

491
Health Professions Scholarship Program

AMOUNT: None Specified
DEADLINE: None Specified
FIELDS/MAJORS: Healthcare and Related

Scholarships are available for junior, senior, and graduate Native American and Alaskan Native students pursuing a degree in a health related field. For this program, there are payback and service obligation requirements. Must have a GPA of at least 2.0. Contact your area Indian Health Service Office or write to the Scholarships Coordinator at the address below for complete information.

Indian Health Services, U.S. Department of Health and
    Human Services
Twinbrook Metro Plaza—Suite 100
12300 Twinbrook Parkway
Rockville, MD   20852

492
Hearst Minority Fellowship

AMOUNT: $15000   DEADLINE: Feb 1
FIELDS/MAJORS: Philanthropic Research

Fellowship for minority students admitted to a master's level program in philanthropic studies at Indiana University. Non-renewable. Write to the address below for more information.

Indiana University Center on Philanthropy
550 West North Street, Suite 301
Indianapolis, IN   46202

493
Hearst Minority Scholarships

AMOUNT: None Specified   DEADLINE: Apr 30
FIELDS/MAJORS: All Areas of Study

Scholarships for minority students at the University of Wyoming. Must be an entering freshman, undergraduate transfer student, or current Hearst Minority Scholar. Must be U.S. citizens or permanent residents and have a minimum GPA of 2.5. Contact the address below for further information.

University of Wyoming
Minority Affairs Office
PO Box 3808
Laramie, WY   72071

494
Heather R. Rivas Scholarship

AMOUNT: None Specified
DEADLINE: Mar 1
FIELDS/MAJORS: Engineering

Annual award to a female graduate of a New Mexico high school who is majoring in engineering. Student must be a U.S. citizen and have a 2.5 high school GPA to qualify. Write to the address below for more information.

New Mexico State University
College of Engineering
Complex I, Box 30001, Box 3446
Las Cruces, NM   88003

495
Hebrew Immigrant Aid Society Scholarships

AMOUNT: $1000   DEADLINE: Apr 15
FIELDS/MAJORS: All Areas of Study

Scholarships for students who were, or whose parents were, assisted in immigrating to the United States (after 1985) by the Hebrew Immigrant Aid Society. All applicants must be able to demonstrate two complete semesters of attendance at a U.S. high school, college, or graduate school. Based on financial need, academics and community service. Seventy awards offered annually. Only scholarship winners will be notified. Write to the address below for details, and include a SASE.

Hebrew Immigrant Aid Society
Scholarship Awards
333 Seventh Avenue
New York, NY   10001

496
Helen Faison Scholarships

AMOUNT: $5638   DEADLINE: Jan 15
FIELDS/MAJORS: Arts and Sciences

Full tuition and fees scholarship for African-American incoming freshmen. Based on high school academics and college entrance examination. Renewable if students maintain at least a 3.0 GPA. Five awards offered annually. Write to the address below for details.

University of Pittsburgh
Office of Admissions and Financial Aid
Bruce Hall, Second Floor
Pittsburgh, PA   15260

497
Helen Harms Anderson Scholarships

AMOUNT: None Specified   DEADLINE: Feb 15
FIELDS/MAJORS: All Areas of Study

Awards for undergraduate women at UW-Platteville who demonstrate financial need. One award is offered annually. Write to the address below or contact the office at (608) 342-1125 for more information.

University of Wisconsin, Platteville
Office of Admissions and Enrollment Mgt.
Platteville, WI   53818

498
Helen James Scholarship

AMOUNT: None Specified   DEADLINE: Mar 1
FIELDS/MAJORS: Medicine

Awards are available at the University of New Mexico for female students enrolled in the UNM School of Medicine. This scholarship is only awarded every three years, and it is based on financial need. Write to the address below for more information.

University of New Mexico, Albuquerque
Office of Financial Aid
Albuquerque, NM   87131

499
Helen M. Malloch and NFPW Scholarships

AMOUNT: $500-$1000   DEADLINE: May 1
FIELDS/MAJORS: Journalism, Communications

Scholarships for undergraduate women junior, senior, or graduate students majoring in journalism/communications at an accredited institution. Applicants do not have to be NFPW members. Write for complete details.

National Federation of Press Women
4510 W. 89th St. #110
Prairie Village, KS   66207

500
Helen Mugler White Scholarship

AMOUNT: $500-$600   DEADLINE: Apr 1
FIELDS/MAJORS: All Areas of Study

The recipient must be female between the ages of twenty-four and forty-five years old, be enrolled as a classified student, have a GPA of 3.0 or higher, and have substantial financial need. Preference will be given to eligible students attending on a part-time basis, taking a minimum of nine credit hours per semester, and who show participation in some community activity or organization. Write to the address below for more information.

Christopher Newport University
Office of Financial Aid
50 Shoe Lane
Newport News, VA   23606

501
Helen Sanders Scholarship

AMOUNT: $2250-$4500   DEADLINE: Feb 1
FIELDS/MAJORS: History, Ethnohistory

Awards for entering students who are Native Americans with first priority to descendants of any of the original allottees of the Quinault reservation. Based on financial need need and academic performance. Write to the address below for more information.

Lewis and Clark College
Office of Admissions
Portland, OR   97219

502
Helen Shure Nursing Scholarship

AMOUNT: $1000-$2000   DEADLINE: Dec 15
FIELDS/MAJORS: Nursing

Awards available for full or part-time sophomores who are single mothers. Extracurricular activities and community involvement will be considered. Contact the College of Nursing, UW Oshkosh for more details.

University of Wisconsin, Oshkosh
Financial Aid Office, Dempsey 104
800 Algoma Blvd.
Oshkosh, WI   54901

503
Heltzel Memorial Scholarship

AMOUNT: None Specified
DEADLINE: None Specified
FIELDS/MAJORS: Engineering

Scholarships are available at the Catholic University of America for full-time engineering majors from the diocese of Youngstown, Ohio. Contact the financial aid office at the address below for details.

Catholic University of America
Office of Admissions and Financial Aid
Washington, D.C.   20064

504
Henry and Chiyo Kuwahara Creative Arts Scholarship

AMOUNT: None Specified   DEADLINE: Apr 1
FIELDS/MAJORS: Creative Arts

Open to students of Japanese ancestry to encourage creative projects, especially those that reflect Japanese-American culture and experience. Must also be members of the JACL. Professional artists should not apply. Applications and information may be obtained from local JACL chapters, district offices, and the national headquarters at the address below. Please indicate your level of study and be certain to include a legal-sized SASE.

Japanese American Citizens League
National Scholarship and Award Program
1765 Sutter St.
San Francisco, CA   94115

505
Henry G. Halladay Awards

AMOUNT: $760   DEADLINE: Aug 31
FIELDS/MAJORS: Medicine

Five supplemental scholarships are presented annually to African-American men enrolled in the first year of medical school who have overcome significant obstacles to obtain a medical education. Must be a U.S. citizen. Write to "special programs" at the address below for details.

National Medical Fellowships, Inc.
110 West 32nd St. 8th Floor
New York, NY   10001

506
Herbert Lehman Education Fund Scholarships

AMOUNT: $1400   DEADLINE: Apr 15
FIELDS/MAJORS: All Areas of Study

Scholarships for African-American high school seniors who will be entering a college in the South or a college that has a student population in which African-Americans are substantially underrepresented. Based on financial need and academics. Twenty to twenty-five awards offered per year. Renewable. All requests for application forms must be in writing and requested by the applicant. Write to the address below for details.

Herbert Lehman Education Fund
99 Hudson St., Suite 1600
New York, NY   10013

507
Hercules, Inc. Scholarship

AMOUNT: None Specified   DEADLINE: Mar 1
FIELDS/MAJORS: All Areas of Study

Awards are available at the University of New Mexico for minority students. Write to the address below for more information.

University of New Mexico, Albuquerque
Office of Financial Aid
Albuquerque, NM   87131

508
Heritage Scholarships

AMOUNT: $7000   DEADLINE: Jan 17
FIELDS/MAJORS: All Areas of Study

Awards for minority students in recognition of outstanding achievement in academics and extracurricular activities. Recipients must maintain a GPA of 2.5 or better in order to renew. Write to the address below for more information.

Salem College
Financial Aid Office
PO Box 10548
Winston-Salem, NC   27108

509
Herman Bernikol Scholarship Fund

AMOUNT: Maximum: $500   DEADLINE: Mar 15
FIELDS/MAJORS: All Areas of Study

Scholarships are available at ASU for full-time students of Native American heritage who are Arizona residents. Based on academic ability, character, and financial need. Preference given to past recipients. Write to the address below for information.

Arizona State University
Indian Education Department
Tempe, AZ   85281

510
Herman Oscar Schumacher Scholarship Fund

AMOUNT: $500   DEADLINE: Oct 1
FIELDS/MAJORS: All Areas of Study

Awards for male residents of Spokane County, Washington, who have completed at least one year at an accredited college and demonstrate financial need. Applicants must be Christian, loyal to the principles of democracy, and support the Constitution of the United States. Write to the address below for information. Applications will be accepted no earlier than the first day of class instruction and no later than Oct 1.

Washington Trust Bank
Trust Department
PO Box 2127
Spokane, WA   99210

511
Hermione Grant Calhoun Scholarships

AMOUNT: $3000   DEADLINE: Mar 31
FIELDS/MAJORS: All Areas of Study

Award open to female full-time students who are legally blind. Contact the address below for complete details.

National Federation of the Blind
Mrs. Peggy Elliott, Chairman
805 Fifth Ave.
Grinnell, IA   50112

512
Heublein, Avis M. Pillsbury Scholarships

AMOUNT: $400   DEADLINE: None Specified
FIELDS/MAJORS: All Areas of Study

Open to students who are Native Americans or other minorities attending school full time. Contact the address below for further information about both awards.

Bacone College
Financial Aid Office
99 Bacone Rd.
Muskogee, OK   74403

513
Higgins-Quarles Award

AMOUNT: $1000   DEADLINE: Jan 8
FIELDS/MAJORS: American History

Awards are available for minority graduate students at the dissertation stage of their Ph.D. programs. To apply, students should submit a brief two-page abstract of the dissertation project, along with a one page budget explaining the travel and research plans for the funds requested. Write to the address below for more information.

Organization of American Historians
Award and Prize Committee Coordinator
112 N. Bryan St.
Bloomington, IN   47408

514
Higher Education and Employment Assistance Programs

AMOUNT: None Specified   DEADLINE: Oct 1
FIELDS/MAJORS: All Areas of Study

Awards are available for members of the Zuni tribe who are enrolled in full-time study at a regionally accredited institution of higher learning. Applicants must have GPAs of at least 2.0. Write to the address listed for more information.

Pueblo of Zuni Tribe
Higher Education
PO Box 339
Zuni, NM   87327

515
Higher Education Incentive Scholarship Competition

AMOUNT: $1200-$4000   DEADLINE: None Specified
FIELDS/MAJORS: All Areas of Study

Scholarships are available at WMU for minority high school seniors who will be entering freshmen with a GPA of at least 3.5. Extracurricular activities will be considered. Contact the address below for further information.

Western Michigan University
Student Financial Aid
3306 Faunce Student Services Building
Kalamazoo, MI   49008

516
Hilmer G. Olson Memorial Scholarship

AMOUNT: None Specified   DEADLINE: Mar 1
FIELDS/MAJORS: Art—Painting

Scholarships are available at the University of New Mexico for full-time art students at the sophomore level and above, with a concentration in painting. Preference given to Native Americans. Write to the address below for information.

University of New Mexico, Albuquerque
College of Fine Arts
Office of the Dean
Albuquerque, NM   87131

517
Hilo Women's Club Scholarship

AMOUNT: Maximum: $550   DEADLINE: Feb 1
FIELDS/MAJORS: All Areas of Study

Scholarships are available at the University of Hawaii, Hilo for full-time female students who are graduating high school seniors at a Big Island high school. Must have a GPA of at least 3.5 or higher. Write to the address below for information.

University of Hawaii at Hilo
Financial Aid Office
200 West Kawili Street
Hilo, HI   96720

518
Hispanic Business College Fund

AMOUNT: Maximum: $1000
DEADLINE: Jan 31
FIELDS/MAJORS: Business

Ten awards for Hispanic students in the field of business. Must have GPAs of at least 3.0, be U.S. citizens, and show evidence of financial need. Write to the address listed for more information.

U.S. Hispanic Chamber of Commerce
Carmen Ortiz
1030 15th St. NW, Suite 206
Washington, D.C.   20005

519
Hispanic Civil Engineering Scholarship

AMOUNT: None Specified   DEADLINE: Mar 1
FIELDS/MAJORS: Civil Engineering

Awarded to a civil engineering major who is a U.S. citizen and a resident of Dona Ana County. Recipient must be of Hispanic descent and in good academic standing. Write to the address below for details.

New Mexico State University
College of Engineering
Box 30001, Dept. 3449
Las Cruces, NM   88003

520
Hispanic Scholarship Fund

AMOUNT: None Specified   DEADLINE: Mar 1
FIELDS/MAJORS: All Areas of Study

Scholarships are available to Hispanic students who are permanent residents of the Kansas City area who will be enrolled full time as undergraduate or graduate students Contact the LULAC Educational Center at (816) 561-0227 for further information.

Greater Kansas City Community Foundation and Affiliated Trusts
1055 Broadway
Suite 130
Kansas City, MO   64105

521
Hjordes Johnson Endowed Scholarship

AMOUNT: None Specified
DEADLINE: None Specified
FIELDS/MAJORS: Physical Education or Health

Annual award is presented to a junior or senior woman majoring in physical education or health, with at least a 3.0 GPA, and is based in professional activities relating to her major field and financial need. Write to the address below for more information.

Ashland University
401 College Ave.
Ashland, OH   44805

522
Hodson Achievement Scholarship

AMOUNT: None Specified   DEADLINE: Jan 1
FIELDS/MAJORS: All Areas of Study

Scholarship available to full-time freshmen who are members of underrepresented minority groups from mid-Atlantic states. This is a full grant to meet the student's need (minus work obligation in upperclass years). Nominations by high school guidance counselors are due Jan 1. Write to the address below for details.

Johns Hopkins University
3400 N Charles Street
Baltimore, MD   21218

523
Hoechst Celanese Engineering Scholarship

AMOUNT: None Specified   DEADLINE: None Specified
FIELDS/MAJORS: Engineering

Open to incoming freshmen minorities and women who are engineering majors. Renewable if the recipients remain in the upper 50% of an engineering program. Write to the address listed for further information.

Georgia Institute of Technology
Financial Aid Office
225 North Ave.
Atlanta, GA   30332

524
Hokkaido Scholarship

AMOUNT: None Specified   DEADLINE: Jun 1
FIELDS/MAJORS: Food and Natural Resources

Awards for UMass students in the College of Food and Natural Resources with an interest in Japan and its people and culture. For entering sophomores, juniors, or seniors. Contact the associate dean, College of Food and Natural Resources, for more information.

University of Massachusetts, Amherst
Associate Dean
College of Food and Natural Resources
Amherst, MA   01003

525
Hold the Johnson Land Scholarship

AMOUNT: None Specified
DEADLINE: Feb 15
FIELDS/MAJORS: News Communications, Broadcasting, Public Relations

Scholarships are available at the University of Oklahoma, Norman for students majoring in one of the above areas. Applicants must be juniors with a GPA of at least 3.5. Preference is given to females. One award offered annually. Write to the address below for information.

University of Oklahoma, Norman
School of Journalism and Mass Comm.
860 Van Vleet Oval
Norman, OK   73019

526
Holly A. Cornell Scholarship

AMOUNT: $5000   DEADLINE: Dec 15
FIELDS/MAJORS: Science or Engineering Relating to Water Supply and Treatment

Scholarships are available to encourage and support outstanding female and/or minority students wishing to pursue advanced training in the field of water supply and treatment. For master's degree candidates. Write to the address below for information.

American Water Works Association
Scholarship Coordinator
6666 W. Quincy Avenue
Denver, CO   80235

527 Home Congregation Grants and Matching Grants

AMOUNT: None Specified   DEADLINE: None Specified
FIELDS/MAJORS: Religion, Theology

Awards for Concordia students who intend to enter full-time church careers in the Lutheran Church—Missouri Synod. Must have GPAs of at least 2.5 and be U.S. citizens. These awards are funded by the student's home congregation. Write to the address below for more information.

Concordia University, Irvine
Financial Aid Office
1530 Concordia West
Irvine, CA   92715

528 Homeland Minorities in Banking Scholarships

AMOUNT: Maximum: $2000
DEADLINE: Apr 15
FIELDS/MAJORS: Accounting, Finance, Computer Science, Business

Open to high school seniors and college freshmen and sophomores who are Iowa residents, admitted to Loras, and are of African-American, Asian, Hispanic, or Native American descent. Must have a minimum GPA of 2.5. Contact the address listed for more information.

Loras College
Office of Financial Planning
1450 Alta Vista St., P.O. Box 178
Dubuque, IA   52004

529 Homer D. & Howard D. Olson, Martin Olson Memorial Scholarships

AMOUNT: None Specified   DEADLINE: Mar 1
FIELDS/MAJORS: Business

Scholarships are available at the University of New Mexico for full-time Native American business majors with a GPA of at least 3.0. Write to the address listed below for information.

University of New Mexico, Albuquerque
Department of Student Financial Aid
Mesa Vista Hall North
Albuquerque, NM   87131

530 Honeywell Scholarship

AMOUNT: None Specified   DEADLINE: Mar 1
FIELDS/MAJORS: Engineering

Awarded to females or ethnic minorities. Student must be a junior, senior, or graduate student and a U.S. citizen, with a 3.0 GPA. Write to the address below for more information

New Mexico State University
College of Engineering
Complex I, Box 30001, Dept. 3446
Las Cruces, NM   88003

531 Honeywell Scholarships

AMOUNT: None Specified
DEADLINE: Mar 1
FIELDS/MAJORS: Engineering, Management, or Science

Awards are available at the University of New Mexico for female or minority student athletes in the fields of engineering management, or science. Must have a minimum GPA of 2.5 and be a New Mexico high school graduate. Write to the address below for more information.

University of New Mexico, Albuquerque
Office of Financial Aid
Albuquerque, NM   87131

532 Horace B. McKenna Scholarship Fund

AMOUNT: None Specified
DEADLINE: None Specified
FIELDS/MAJORS: All Areas of Study

Scholarships are available at the Catholic University of America for full-time undergraduate minority students who reside in the district of Columbia. Contact the financial aid office at the address below for details.

Catholic University of America
Office of Admissions and Financial Aid
Washington, D.C.   20064

533 Horizons Foundation Scholarship Program

AMOUNT: $500   DEADLINE: Nov 1
FIELDS/MAJORS: Computer Science, Engineering, Physics, International Relations

Awards open to women who are at least college juniors with minimum GPAs of 3.25, who are U.S. citizens. Must be able to demonstrate financial need and an interest in pursuing a career related to national security. Contact the address listed for further information.

Wide Horizons Foundation and ADPA
Woody Lee, Scholarship Director
2101 Wilson Blvd. #400
Arlington, VA   22201

534 Howard Brown Rickard Scholarship

AMOUNT: Maximum: $1000
DEADLINE: Mar 31
FIELDS/MAJORS: Architecture, Law, Medicine, Engineering, Natural Sciences

Open to full-time students who are legally blind, working toward a career in one of the areas listed above. Write to the address below for complete details.

National Federation of the Blind
Mrs. Peggy Elliott, Chairman
805 Fifth Ave.
Grinnell, IA   50112

535 Howard Rock Foundation Scholarship Program

AMOUNT: $2500-$5000   **DEADLINE:** Mar 15
FIELDS/MAJORS: Economics, Education, Business, Public Administration

Scholarships are available for American Indian students majoring in one of the above fields. Applicants must be residents of Alaska. Four to six awards are offered annually. Write to the address below for information.

Howard Rock Foundation
1577 C Street, Suite 304
Anchorage, AK   99501

536 Howard Vollum American Indian Scholarship

AMOUNT: None Specified   **DEADLINE:** Mar 1
FIELDS/MAJORS: Science, Computer Science, Engineering, Mathematics

Open to Native American residents of: Clackamas, Multnomah, or Washington Counties in Oregon or Clark County, Washington. Must submit certification of tribal enrollment or photocopy of the Johnson O'Malley student eligibility form or a letter from your tribe stating blood quantum and/or enrollment number of parent or grandparent. Awards may be received for a maximum of fifteen quarters. Contact the address below for further information.

Oregon State Scholarship Commission
Private Awards
1500 Valley River Dr. #100
Eugene, OR   97401-2130

541
Incentive Scholarship and Grant Program for Native Americans

AMOUNT: None Specified   DEADLINE: Mar 1
FIELDS/MAJORS: All Areas of Study

Award is open to undergraduate students through doctoral candidates. For Native American students who are residents of North Carolina. Contact the address below for further information.

University of North Carolina, Greensboro
Financial Aid Office
723 Kenilworth St.
Greensboro, NC   27412

542
Indian Fellowship and American Indian Graduate Center Fellowship Program

AMOUNT: None Specified   DEADLINE: Dec 3
FIELDS/MAJORS: All Areas of Study

Open to Native Americans in a post-baccalaureate program. Must be enrolled full time, demonstrate financial need, and be certified as Indian by tribe. The Federal Government funds both programs, selects the eligible students, and determines amount of each student's fellowship. Contact the address below for further information about both fellowships.

Marquette University
Office of Admissions
1217 W. Wisconsin Ave.
Milwaukee, WI   53233

543
Indian Health Service Scholarships

AMOUNT: None Specified
DEADLINE: None Specified
FIELDS/MAJORS: Dentistry

Open to full-time students certified as Indian by tribe. These fellowships include tuition, books, instruments, and stipend. For information and application materials, contact the Indian Health Scholarship Programs Office.

Marquette University
Office of Admissions
1217 W. Wisconsin Ave.
Milwaukee, WI   53233

544
Indian Leadership Award

AMOUNT: $1565   DEADLINE: None Specified
FIELDS/MAJORS: All Areas of Study

Open to Native American students who are attending classes full time. Contact the address below for further information.

Bacone College
Financial Aid Office
99 Bacone Rd.
Muskogee, OK   74403

545
Indian Nurse Scholarship

AMOUNT: $500-$1000
DEADLINE: None Specified
FIELDS/MAJORS: Nursing

Scholarships are available for Native American nursing students who are within two years of completing their nursing programs. Must be in good academic standing and enrolled in an accredited program. Write to the address below for information.

National Society of the Colonial Dames of America
Ms. H. Eugene Trotter, Consultant
3064 Luvan Blvd.—Debordieu Colony
Georgetown, SC   29440

546
Indian Student Assistance Program Grant

AMOUNT: Maximum: $1100   DEADLINE: None Specified
FIELDS/MAJORS: All Areas of Study

Open to an enrolled member of a federally recognized tribe and/or certified as having one-fourth Indian blood. Must be a resident of Wisconsin and enrolled for at least 6 credits each semester. Must demonstrate financial need. Contact your tribal office for an Indian Certification form and application instructions.

Marquette University
Office of Admissions
1217 W. Wisconsin Ave.
Milwaukee, WI   53233

547
Institute for International Public Policy

AMOUNT: None Specified   DEADLINE: Mar 1
FIELDS/MAJORS: International Policy

This program prepares minorities for careers in international affairs through sophomore and junior year summer institutes, a junior year abroad, internships, a senior language institute, and graduate studies leading to a master's degree. Students must apply during their sophomore year of study. Write to the address below for more information.

Woodrow Wilson National Fellowship Foundation
Attn: IIPP
CN 5281
Princeton, NJ   08543

548
Institute of American Indian Arts Scholarships

AMOUNT: $300-$10000   DEADLINE: Apr 15
FIELDS/MAJORS: Art, Museum Studies

Scholarships are available for undergraduate Native American students at the Institute of American Indian Art. Based on financial need. Must be from a federally recognized Native American tribe and members of Alaskan Native Corps. Write to the address below for information.

Institute of American Indian Art
PO Box 20007
Santa Fe, NM   87504

549 Instructional Materials Fund for Ethnic Students

AMOUNT: Maximum: $200   DEADLINE: None Specified
FIELDS/MAJORS: All Areas of Study

Awards are available at Portland State University for minority students who have an unusually high book, lab, or other costs for a particular term. Must be enrolled in full-time study and in good academic standing. For undergraduate study. At least five awards offered annually. Write to the address below for more information.

Portland State University
Educational Equity Programs and Services
120 Smith Memorial Center
Portland, OR   97207

550 International Fellowships

AMOUNT: $15160   DEADLINE: Dec 2
FIELDS/MAJORS: All Areas of Study

Fellowships for one year of graduate study or advanced research in the U.S. To women of outstanding ability who are citizens of countries other than the U.S.A.. Applicants must hold the equivalent of a U.S. bachelor's degree. Forty-three awards offered annually. Write to the address below for details. Previous and current recipients of AAUW fellowships are ineligible. Also six fellowships are available for members of the International Federation of University Women to study in any country except their home country.

American Association of University Women Educational
   Foundation
2201 N. Dodge Street
Iowa City, IA   52243

551 International Scholarship Program for Community Service

AMOUNT: None Specified   DEADLINE: Nov 30
FIELDS/MAJORS: Jewish Studies, Religious Studies, Social Work, Theology

Scholarships for persons who intend to pursue careers in the above fields. Recipients should agree to work for two to three years in a community with a shortage of persons in the recipients area of study. For study in any recognized Yeshiva, school of social work, college, university, or seminary. Renewable. Write to the address below for details.

Memorial Foundation for Jewish Culture
15 E. 26th St., Room 1901
New York, NY   10010

552 Ione Hendrick Roche Memorial Endowed Scholarship

AMOUNT: $1000   DEADLINE: Feb 15
FIELDS/MAJORS: Communications

Renewable $1000 scholarship given to minority women pursuing a degree in the College of Communications at the University of Alabama. Applicants will demonstrate academic excellence and an interest in social concerns. Write to the address below for further information and an application.

University of Alabama
Dr. J.E. Roche, College of Communications
PO Box 870172
Tuscaloosa, AL   35487

553 Iowa College Foundation Minority Scholarship

AMOUNT: Maximum: $5000   DEADLINE: Mar 14
FIELDS/MAJORS: All Areas of Study

Open to minority high school seniors who are enrolling into/accepted by Loras College. Write to the address below for details.

Loras College
Office of Financial Planning
1450 Alta Vista St., P.O. Box 178
Dubuque, IA   52004

554 Iowa Pharmacists Association Women's Auxiliary Scholarship

AMOUNT: $500   DEADLINE: None Specified
FIELDS/MAJORS: Pharmacy and Related Fields

Scholarships are available at the University of Iowa for full-time female undergraduates who are pharmacy majors and residents of Iowa. One award per year. Write to the address below for information.

University of Iowa
College of Pharmacy
127 Pharmacy Building
Iowa City, IA   52240

555 Iowa State University Images Grant

AMOUNT: None Specified   DEADLINE: Mar 1
FIELDS/MAJORS: All Areas of Study

Awards for incoming minority students who are Iowa residents. Must demonstrate high financial need. Contact the address below for further information.

Iowa State University—Special Population Unit
Office of Student Financial Aid
12 Beardshear Hall
Ames, IA   50011

556
Irene Stambler Vocational Opportunities Grant Program

AMOUNT: Maximum: $2500   DEADLINE: None Specified
FIELDS/MAJORS: All Areas of Study

One-time grant for a female resident of the Metropolitan Washington area who has recently undergone a separation, divorce, death, or serious illness of her spouse. To assist with realization of career plan. Write to the address below or call (301) 881-3700 for details.

Jewish Social Service Agency of Metropolitan Washington
6123 Montrose Road
Rockville, MD   20852

557
Irvington Women's Club Scholarships

AMOUNT: $500   DEADLINE: None Specified
FIELDS/MAJORS: All Areas of Studies

Award for junior or senior level woman with demonstrated professional goals and financial need. Must be a full-time student with minimum cumulative GPA of at least 3.0. For use at Portland State University only. One to two awards offered annually. Contact the office of women's studies for more information.

Portland State University
Department of Women's Studies
PO Box 751
Portland, OR   97207

558
Isla Mils Eckert Memorial Scholarship

AMOUNT: Maximum: $500   DEADLINE: Nov 1
FIELDS/MAJORS: Business

Open to female students in the field of business. Second deadline is Jun 1. Contact the Business Administration Department for further information.

Angelo State University
Financial Aid Office
PO Box 11015
San Angelo, TX   76909

559
Italian American Chamber of Commerce Scholarships

AMOUNT: $1000   DEADLINE: May 31
FIELDS/MAJORS: All Areas of Study

Scholarships available to students of Italian ancestry who are residents of the following Illinois counties: Cook, DuPage, Kane, Lake, Will, and McHenry. Applicants may be high school seniors planning to attend a four-year school or current undergraduates. Must have a minimum GPA of 3.5. Write to the address below for details.

Italian American Chamber of Commerce of Chicago
30 S. Michigan Ave.
Chicago, IL   60603

560
Italian-American Cultural Society Scholarships

AMOUNT: $750-$1000   DEADLINE: Feb 1
FIELDS/MAJORS: All Fields of Study

Scholarships offered to Ocean County senior high students of Italian descent. Applicants must submit an essay on Italian culture. Five awards given. Amount of the award depends upon the parents standing in the society. Write to the address below for details.

Italian-American Cultural Society of Ocean County, Inc.
PO Box 1602
Toms River, NJ   08754

561
Ives Memorial Scholarship

AMOUNT: None Specified   DEADLINE: Mar 1
FIELDS/MAJORS: Teacher Education

Available for junior and senior female students enrolled in a teacher education program in the College of Education. Must demonstrate financial need and scholastic merit. Write to the address below for more information.

University of New Mexico, Albuquerque
Office of Financial Aid
Albuquerque, NM   87131

562
J. A. Knowles Memorial Scholarship

AMOUNT: None Specified   DEADLINE: None Specified
FIELDS/MAJORS: All Areas of Study

Awards are available for active members of the Methodist church who are enrolled in a United Methodist related school in Texas. Applicant must be a full-time degree candidate and a U.S. citizen or permanent resident. Write to the address below for more information.

General Board of Higher Education and Ministry
Office of Loans and Scholarships
PO Box 871
Nashville, TN   37202

563
J.R. Weber Scholarship

AMOUNT: None Specified
DEADLINE: None Specified
FIELDS/MAJORS: Ministry

Awarded to students from South Carolina who are Baptist. Awarded to those preparing for a career in Christian Ministry with Pastoral Ministry. Consideration is given to financial need. Contact the address listed for further information.

Charleston Southern University
PO Box 118087
Charleston, SC   29423

564
Jack and Estelle Rapaport '37 Scholarship

AMOUNT: Maximum: $2500   DEADLINE: Mar 1
FIELDS/MAJORS: All Areas of Study

Open to a meritorious minority student. Contact the address listed for further information.

Brooklyn College
Office of the V.P. for Student Life
2113 Boylan Hall
Brooklyn, NY   11210

565
Jackie Robinson Foundation Scholarship

AMOUNT: Maximum: $5000   DEADLINE: Apr 1
FIELDS/MAJORS: All Areas of Study

Scholarships for minority high school seniors who have been accepted into a four-year college or university. Based on academic achievement, leadership, and financial need. Must be a U.S. citizen. Check with your high school guidance counselor to see if he or she has details on this program. Otherwise, write to the address below for details.

Jackie Robinson Foundation Scholarship Fund
Attn: Scholarship Program
3 West 35th St.
New York, NY   10011

566
Jackie Robinson Memorial Scholarship

AMOUNT: $500   DEADLINE: Feb 3
FIELDS/MAJORS: All Areas of Study

Offered to a currently enrolled junior or senior student of color (Asian, Black, Hispanic, Native American) attending Evergreen full time. This scholarship seeks to recognize a student for academic achievement and outstanding commitment to community involvement and social justice. Contact the address listed for further information.

Evergreen State College
Office of the Dean of Enrollment Service
2700 Evergreen Parkway
Olympia, WA   98505-0002

567
James Carlson Memorial Scholarship

AMOUNT: None Specified   DEADLINE: Mar 1
FIELDS/MAJORS: Elementary, Secondary Education

Open to students pursuing a baccalaureate degree or in the fifth year of a five year teaching certificate program. Priority for awards is as follows: 1. African, Asian, Hispanic, or Native Americans. 2. dependents of Oregon Education Association members. 3. students with a demonstrated commitment to teach autistic children. Must be U.S. citizens or permanent residents and residents of Oregon to apply. Contact the address below for further information.

Oregon State Scholarship Commission
Private Awards
1500 Valley River Dr. #100
Eugene, OR   97401-2130

568
James Family Scholarships

AMOUNT: $500-$1000
DEADLINE: Apr 1
FIELDS/MAJORS: International Business/Relations, Political Science

Award open to students who have completed one full year at Whitworth. Must have a minimum GPA of 3.0 and possess a solid Christian commitment. Contact the address below for further information.

Whitworth College
Office of Financial Aid
300 W. Hawthorne Rd.
Spokane, WA   99251

569
James L. Kunkel Scholarship

AMOUNT: Maximum: $1000
DEADLINE: Mar 15
FIELDS/MAJORS: Accounting

Open to full-time undergraduates who are Arizona residents and enrolled in an Arizona Native American tribe. Must have a minimum GPA of 2.5 and be able to demonstrate financial need. Write to the address below for more information.

Arizona State University
Scholarship Office
Main Campus, P.O. Box 870412
Tempe, AZ   85287

570
James T. and Joanne Lynagh Endowed Minority Scholarship

AMOUNT: $1000   DEADLINE: Feb 15
FIELDS/MAJORS: Communications

Renewable $1000 scholarship given to minority full-time students, freshmen through juniors, who are enrolled in the College of Communication at the University of Alabama. Write to the address below for further information and an application.

James T. and Joanne Lynagh / Fiesta Bowl
College of Comm., University of Alabama
PO Box 870172
Tuscaloosa, AL   35487

571
James W. Keller Memorial Scholarship

AMOUNT: Maximum: $500   DEADLINE: Nov 1
FIELDS/MAJORS: All Areas of Study

Open to Hispanic males who are enrolled in/accepted to ASU. Second deadline is Jun 1. Contact the address below for further information.

Angelo State University
Financial Aid Office
PO Box 11015
San Angelo, TX   76909

572
Jan Walling Memorial Scholarship

AMOUNT: $1410   DEADLINE: Feb 1
FIELDS/MAJORS: All Areas of Study

Awards for freshmen graduates of Highlands high school. Priority will be given to handicapped applicants. Contact the address below for further information.

Northern Kentucky University
Office of Financial Aid-Nunn Dr.
Administrative Center #416
Highland Heights, KY   41099

573
Janet M. Glasgow Essay Award

AMOUNT: $1500   DEADLINE: May 31
FIELDS/MAJORS: Medicine

This award is presented to an AMWA student member for the best essay of approximately one thousand words identifying a woman physician who has been a significant role model. Write to the address below for details.

American Medical Women's Association
Glasgow Essay Award
801 N. Fairfax Street, Suite 400
Alexandria, VA   22314

574
Japanese American Treaty Centennial Scholarship

AMOUNT: Maximum: $1000   DEADLINE: Jul 12
FIELDS/MAJORS: All Areas of Study

Scholarships for students graduating from a southern California high school who are of Japanese descent. Approximately twenty awards offered annually. Write to the address below for details. Please include a SASE.

Japanese Chamber of Commerce of Southern California
244 S. San Pedro St., Room 504
Los Angeles, CA   90012

575
Japanese Government Scholarship

AMOUNT: None Specified   DEADLINE: Mar 1
FIELDS/MAJORS: All Areas of Study

Awards are available at the University of New Mexico for graduate students of Japanese descent who are under thirty-five years old and are U.S. citizens. Contact: Consulate General of Japan, 250 East First St., Suite 1110, Los Angeles, CA., 90012 for more details.

University of New Mexico, Albuquerque
Office of Financial Aid
Albuquerque, NM   87131

576
Jean Freeman Memorial Scholarship

AMOUNT: $3400   DEADLINE: Mar 31
FIELDS/MAJORS: All Areas of Study

Student must be a full-time entering freshman from the Ozarks region with a GPA of 2.0 or better. Preference is given to minority students. Two awards are offered annually. Write to the address below for more information.

Southwest Missouri State University
Office of Financial Aid
901 South National Ave.
Springfield, MO   65804

577
Jean Mullins Macey Scholarship

AMOUNT: None Specified   DEADLINE: Mar 1
FIELDS/MAJORS: Business

Scholarships are available at the University of New Mexico for full-time female business majors. Write to the address below for information.

University of New Mexico, Albuquerque
Department of Student Financial Aid
Mesa Vista Hall North
Albuquerque, NM   87131

578
Jean Mullins Macey Scholarship

AMOUNT: None Specified   DEADLINE: None Specified
FIELDS/MAJORS: All Areas of Study

Scholarships are available at the University of New Mexico for full-time junior and senior females with academic achievement who are involved in campus service. Write to the address below for information.

University of New Mexico, Albuquerque
Alumni Office
Mesa Vista Hall North, Room 1044
Albuquerque, NM   87131

579
Jean Thomas Scholarship

AMOUNT: None Specified
DEADLINE: Mar 1
FIELDS/MAJORS: Education

Awarded to an entering freshman woman at NMSU. Criteria include graduation from a New Mexico high school, interest in teaching at a junior high school level in the field of mathematics or science, a minimum ACT score of 22 in mathematics, and completion of three years of high school mathematics.
Continuing support will be based on high achievement. Write to the address below for details.

New Mexico State University
College of Education
Box 30001, Dept 3AC
Las Cruces, NM   88003

580 Jeanne Humphrey Block Dissertation Award

AMOUNT: $2500 **DEADLINE:** Apr 1
FIELDS/MAJORS: Psychology, Sociology, Behavioral Science

Dissertation grant for women doctoral students researching psychological development of women/girls. Must have completed coursework and be current doctoral candidate. Write to the address below for details.

Radcliffe College
Henry A. Murray Research Center
10 Garden Street
Cambridge, MA   02138

581 Jeannette Rankin Foundation Awards

AMOUNT: $1000 **DEADLINE:** Mar 1
FIELDS/MAJORS: All Areas of Study

Applicants must be women thirty-five years or older, United States citizens, and accepted or enrolled at a school to pursue an undergraduate degree or technical/vocational training course. Seven to ten awards given per year. Financial need is a primary factor. Send a SASE to the address below. In the lower, left-hand corner of the envelope, write "JRF 1997." Also, when applying, indicate your gender, age, and level of study or training. Requests for applications are only honored between Sep 1 and Jan 15.

Jeannette Rankin Foundation
PO Box 6653
Athens, GA   30604

582 Jeri Ewy Thiel Memorial Scholarship

AMOUNT: $1000 **DEADLINE:** Mar 2
FIELDS/MAJORS: History

Award open to history majors with a minimum GPA of 2.5. Preference given to women. Contact the address below for further information.

California Polytechnic State University
Financial Aid Office
212 Administration Bldg.
San Luis Obispo, CA   93407

583 Jewish Braille Institute of America Scholarships

AMOUNT: None Specified **DEADLINE:** None Specified
FIELDS/MAJORS: Religion/Theology, Community Service, Jewish Studies, Jewish Language

Scholarships for legally blind students studying toward a career in a field of Jewish endeavor (rabbi, cantor, communal service, Hebrew). Based on need. No formal application exists for this scholarship. Write to Gerald M. Kass at the address below for details.

Jewish Braille Institute of America
110 East 30th Street
New York, NY   10016

584 Jewish Community Scholarship Fund

AMOUNT: None Specified **DEADLINE:** Apr 15
FIELDS/MAJORS: All Areas of Study

Scholarships for needy Jewish residents of Los Angeles County, California, pursuing post-secondary education on a full-time basis. For sophomores and above with a GPA of at least 2.5. Must be able to demonstrate financial need and be U.S. citizens or permanent residents. This fund administers eleven separate scholarships. Write to the address below for details. Applications are available after Dec 15.

Jewish Vocational Service (L.A.)
6505 Wilshire Blvd., Suite 303
Los Angeles, CA   90048

585 Jewish Educational Loan Fund

AMOUNT: Maximum: $2000 **DEADLINE:** None Specified
FIELDS/MAJORS: All Areas of Study

Interest-free loans for residents of the Metropolitan Washington area who are within eighteen months of graduation (undergrad or graduate). Repayment begins after graduation. Must be a U.S. citizen (or permanent resident intending to apply for citizenship). For Jewish students. Write to the address below or call (301) 881-3700 for details.

Jewish Social Service Agency of Metropolitan Washington
6123 Montrose Road
Rockville, MD   20852

586 Jewish Undergraduate Scholarship Fund

AMOUNT: Maximum: $3500 **DEADLINE:** May 30
FIELDS/MAJORS: All Areas of Study

Scholarships for Jewish residents of the Metropolitan Washington area who are currently enrolled as undergraduates. Must be less than thirty years old. Special consideration given to refugees. Based primarily on need. Write to the address below or call (301) 881-3700 for details.

Jewish Social Service Agency of Metropolitan Washington
6123 Montrose Road
Rockville, MD   20852

587 JFCS Scholarships

AMOUNT: $5000 **DEADLINE:** None Specified
FIELDS/MAJORS: All Areas of Study

JFCS provides hundreds of grants and scholarships annually to help Jewish students with financial needs achieve their educational goals. Special scholarships are available for study in Israel. Eligibility requirements: acceptance to a college, vocational school, or university; residence in San Francisco, the Peninsula, Marin or Sonoma Counties; and a 3.0 GPA. Write to the address below for details.

Jewish Family and Children's Services
1600 Scott Street
San Francisco, CA   94115

588
Jim and Nancy Ferguson African-American Scholarship

AMOUNT: $1050   DEADLINE: Mar 31
FIELDS/MAJORS: All Areas of Study

Student must be a full-time entering freshman who is an African-American. Preference is given to graduates of Springfield high schools, followed by Greene and Christian County high schools, and then the remainder of southwest Missouri. Two awards are offered annually. Write to the address below for more information.

Southwest Missouri State University
Office of Financial Aid
901 South National Ave.
Springfield, MO   65804

589
Jim Crow Memorial Scholarship

AMOUNT: None Specified   DEADLINE: Mar 1
FIELDS/MAJORS: Journalism or Communication

Awards are available at the University of New Mexico for Native American students who can demonstrate commitment and promise to the fields of journalism or communications. Open to juniors and seniors only. Write to the address below for information.

University of New Mexico, Albuquerque
Office of Financial Aid
Albuquerque, NM   87131

590
Jimmie Ullery Charitable Trust

AMOUNT: Maximum: $1000   DEADLINE: Jun 1
FIELDS/MAJORS: Theology

Education for students in full-time Christian Service. Scholarships have been awarded primarily for study at Presbyterian Theological Seminaries. Five to eight awards offered annually. For complete details write to Mr. R. Garvin Barry, Jr., at the address below.

Jimmie Ullery Charitable Trust, Scholarship Committee
First Presbyterian Church
709 S. Boston Ave.
Tulsa, OK   74119

591
Jimmy A. Young Memorial Scholarship

AMOUNT: $1000   DEADLINE: Jun 30
FIELDS/MAJORS: Respiratory Therapy

One scholarship for a minority student in an AMA-accepted respiratory care program. The foundation prefers that students be nominated by their schools, but any student may initiate a request of sponsorship by the school. Must have a GPA of at least 3.0. Write to the address below for additional information.

American Respiratory Care Foundation
11030 Ables Lane
Dallas, TX   75229

592
Joe Illman Memorial Scholarship

AMOUNT: None Specified   DEADLINE: Mar 1
FIELDS/MAJORS: All Areas of Study

Award open to disabled undergraduates who are U.S. citizens and residents of North Carolina. Must have a minimum GPA of 2.0 and be registered with Disabled Student Services. Contact the address below for further information.

University of North Carolina, Greensboro
Financial Aid Office
723 Kenilworth St.
Greensboro, NC   27412

593
John Deere & Co. Minority Accounting Scholarships

AMOUNT: $2000   DEADLINE: Mar 1
FIELDS/MAJORS: Accounting

Scholarships are available at the University of Iowa for full-time minority students majoring in accounting. Write to the address below for information.

University of Iowa
College of Business Admin., Suite W160
108 Pappajohn Business Admin. Bldg.
Iowa City, IA   52245

594
John Deere Insurance Group Scholarships

AMOUNT: $3000   DEADLINE: Mar 1
FIELDS/MAJORS: Business

Scholarships are available at the University of Iowa for full-time senior minority business majors. Write to the address below for information.

University of Iowa
College of Business Admin., Suite W160
108 Pappajohn Business Admin. Bldg.
Iowa City, IA   52245

595

John Edgar Thompson Foundation Grant

AMOUNT: None Specified   DEADLINE: None Specified
FIELDS/MAJORS: All Areas of Study

Grants are available for daughters of deceased railroad workers who wish to pursue a post-secondary education. The father must have been an active employee of a railroad at the time of death, although the cause need not be work related. Assistance available until student reaches twenty-two years of age. Write to the address below for information. This grant may be used to assist in funding an education, although the primary purpose is to provide a monthly grant to daughters of deceased railroad workers from infancy to age eighteen or twenty-two.

John Edgar Thompson Foundation
Sheila Cohen, Director
201 South 18th Street, Suite 318
Philadelphia, PA   19103

596

John Edmund Haggai Scholarship

AMOUNT: None Specified   DEADLINE: None Specified
FIELDS/MAJORS: All Areas of Study

Open to worthy enrolled Chinese students. Recipients named by a selection committee. Write to the address listed for further information.

Georgia Institute of Technology
Financial Aid Office
225 North Ave.
Atlanta, GA   30332

597

John Edward Hess Memorial Scholarships

AMOUNT: $1000   DEADLINE: Feb 15
FIELDS/MAJORS: All Areas of Study

Two scholarships for Native American students at Black Hills State University who are residents of a South Dakota reservation with a GPA of 2.0 or better. Students must enroll for 16 hours each semester. Write to the address below for more information.

Black Hills State University
1200 University St.
Spearfish, SD   57783

598

John Fetterman Minority Journalism Scholarship

AMOUNT: None Specified   DEADLINE: Feb 1
FIELDS/MAJORS: Journalism / Radio-TV

One scholarship will be awarded to a minority student majoring in the department of journalism/Radio-TV. A minimum GPA of 2.5 is required. An ACT score of 17 is required for consideration. Write to the address below for details.

Murray State University
Office of University Scholarships
Ordway Hall, 1 Murray St.
Murray, KY   42071

599

John Hebner Memorial Scholarship

AMOUNT: $600   DEADLINE: Mar 1
FIELDS/MAJORS: All Areas of Study

Scholarships are available to legally blind students who are employed on a full-time basis and need additional funding for school while they are working. Write to the address below for details.

American Council of the Blind
Scholarship Coordinator
1155 15th St., NW, Suite 720
Washington, D.C.   20005

600

John J. and Brette Monagle Scholarship

AMOUNT: None Specified   DEADLINE: Mar 1
FIELDS/MAJORS: All Areas of Study

Awarded to full-time undergraduate students with declared majors. Student must be eligible for federal/state grants and/or must not be receiving other scholarships. A freshman must have a minimum 3.2 high school GPA and a minimum 20 ACT score. A continuing student must have a cumulative 2.75 GPA. Student must be a U.S. citizen, with preference given to New Mexico residents. Preference is given to women and minorities. Write to the address below for more information.

New Mexico State University
Office of Student Financial Aid
Box 30001, Dept. 5100
Las Cruces, NM   88003

601

John J. Aragon Scholarship

AMOUNT: None Specified   DEADLINE: Mar 1
FIELDS/MAJORS: Journalism or Communication

Awards are available at the University of New Mexico for Hispanic students in the fields of journalism or communication who can demonstrate financial need and academic ability. Write to the address below for information.

University of New Mexico, Albuquerque
Office of Financial Aid
Albuquerque, NM   87131

602

Johanna Christine Allen Memorial Scholarship

AMOUNT: None Specified   DEADLINE: Mar 1
FIELDS/MAJORS: Accounting

Open to female students and based on academics and activity in university and community affairs. Information and applications available Jan 2 through Mar 1 in the Advising Center of the college.

New Mexico State University
College of Business Admin. and Economics
Box 30001 Dept. 3AD
Las Cruces, NM   88003-8001

603
Johnson Scholarship

AMOUNT: None Specified
DEADLINE: None Specified
FIELDS/MAJORS: Consumer Studies

For female students in the department of consumer studies who are residents of Hampden County, Massachusetts, who have a minimum GPA of 3.0. Preference given to applicants pursuing an extension career. For entering sophomores, juniors, or seniors. Contact the Chair, Scholarship Committee, consumer studies for more information.

University of Massachusetts, Amherst
Chair, Scholarship Committee
Department of Consumer Studies
Amherst, MA 01003

604
Jones & Henry Engineers Minority Scholarship

AMOUNT: None Specified   DEADLINE: None Specified
FIELDS/MAJORS: Civil Engineering

Awards open sophomore, junior, and senior minority students majoring in civil engineering. Contact the address below for further information.

University of Toledo
Department of Civil Engineering
2332 Engineering Science Building
Toledo, OH 43606

605
Jose Marti Scholarship Challenge Grant Fund

AMOUNT: $2000   DEADLINE: Apr 1
FIELDS/MAJORS: All Areas of Study

Applicant must be a U.S. citizen or legal resident, Hispanic-American, and a Florida resident enrolled as full-time undergraduate or graduate student at an eligible Florida institution. Renewable. A minimum 3.0 GPA is required. Contact the financial aid office at your college or write to the address below for details.

Florida Department of Education
Office of Student Financial Assistance
1344 Florida Education Center
Tallahassee, FL 32399

606
Joseph F. Rarick American Indian Law Scholarship

AMOUNT: $100   DEADLINE: Sep 1
FIELDS/MAJORS: Law

Scholarships are available at the University of Oklahoma, Norman for full-time Native American law students in their third year of study. One award offered annually. Write to the address below for information.

University of Oklahoma, Norman
Admissions and Records
Law Center, Room 221, 300 Timberdell Rd.
Norman, OK 73019

607
Joseph L. Boscov Scholarship

AMOUNT: None Specified   DEADLINE: Mar 1
FIELDS/MAJORS: All Areas of Study

Awards for students accepted for admission to the graduate school at UMass. Preference given to women over the age of thirty-five whose studies will equip them for increased service to the needs of people and/or the environment. Students must file a FAFSA as soon as possible after Jan 1 and before the Mar 1 financial aid priority consideration date. You will automatically be considered for this scholarship if you are enrolled at the University and apply for financial aid. Separate applications, requests, or inquiries are not required and cannot be honored.

University of Massachusetts, Amherst
Office of Financial Aid Services
255 Whitmore Admin. Bldg., Box 38230
Amherst, MA 01003

608
Joseph P. Fitzpatrick S.J. Doctoral Fellowship

AMOUNT: $14000   DEADLINE: Feb 1
FIELDS/MAJORS: All Areas of Study

Fellowships open to exceptionally qualified minority students seeking the doctoral degree. Contact the address below for further information.

Fordham University
Graduate Admissions Office—Keating 216
Fordham University
Bronx, NY 10458

609
Joseph Sumner Smith Scholarship

AMOUNT: None Specified   DEADLINE: Apr 15
FIELDS/MAJORS: All Areas of Studies

Awards for active members of the Unitarian Universalists who attend Antioch College in Yellow Springs, Ohio, or Harvard College. Write to the address below for more information.

Unitarian Universalist Association of Congregations
Treasurer's Office
25 Beacon St.
Boston, MA 02108

610
Josephine K. Messerly Memorial Scholarship

AMOUNT: None Specified
DEADLINE: None Specified
FIELDS/MAJORS: Physical Education or Recreation

Awarded annually to a woman majoring in physical education and/or recreation, and based on merit and promise. Write to the address below for more information.

Ashland University
401 College Ave.
Ashland, OH   44805

611 Joyce Elder Memorial Scholarship

AMOUNT: $200   DEADLINE: Mar 1
FIELDS/MAJORS: Mathematics

Must be a sophomore level student or above majoring in mathematics with a GPA of 3.5 or higher. Preference will be given to women who have excelled in abstract algebra or foundations of higher mathematics. One award per year. Write to the address below for more information.

Eastern New Mexico University
College of Liberal Arts and Sciences
Station 19
Portales, NM   88130

612 Judy Owens Geisler Memorial Scholarship

AMOUNT: $600   DEADLINE: None Specified
FIELDS/MAJORS: History

Student must be a full-time history major who has completed 24 hours with a GPA of 3.0 or better. Recipient must be involved in public affairs through participation in campus or community service organizations. Preference is given to a female student from a rural Missouri high school. Contact the history department for more information.

Southwest Missouri State University
Office of Financial Aid
901 South National Ave.
Springfield, MO   65804

613 Julia S. Tutwiler Scholarship

AMOUNT: $750   DEADLINE: Apr 15
FIELDS/MAJORS: Education

Renewable scholarship open to all freshmen women studying education at UWA. Write to the address below for more information.

University of West Alabama
Office of Admissions
Station 4
Livingston, AL   35470

614 Julie & Bill Reiersgaard Mechanical Engineering Scholarship

AMOUNT: $500   DEADLINE: None Specified
FIELDS/MAJORS: Mechanical Engineering

Awards are available to female students majoring in mechanical engineering and working part-time, with a GPA of 3.0 or better. Recipients must intend to remain in Oregon after graduation. One award offered annually. Write to the address below for more information.

Portland State University
Engineering and Applied Sciences
118 Science Building 2
Portland, OR   92707

615 Justinian Society of Lawyers/DuPage County Chapter

AMOUNT: $1000   DEADLINE: Apr 1
FIELDS/MAJORS: Law

Applicant must have completed one semester of law school and be of Italian heritage. Applicant will also need to include a statement indicating his/her professional objectives and any special factors that should be considered. Must be a U.S. citizen. Write to address below for information and an application.

Marsha H. Cellucci, Chairwoman-Scholarship
Cellucci, Yacobellis & Holman
1155 S. Washington St #100
Naperville, IL   60540

616 Justus Beach Scholarship

AMOUNT: None Specified
DEADLINE: None Specified
FIELDS/MAJORS: Education

Awarded to a full-time undergraduate minority student majoring in any of CCSU's teacher preparation programs. Write to the address below for complete details.

Central Connecticut State University
CCSU Foundation, Inc.
PO Box 612
New Britain, CT   06050

617 Kappa Alpha Theta Foundation Scholarship

AMOUNT: $500-$10000   DEADLINE: Feb 1
FIELDS/MAJORS: All Areas of Study

Scholarships are available for Kappa Alpha Theta members. Applications available after Oct 1. Selections based on merit. Write to the address below for information.

Kappa Alpha Theta, Sarasota Area—National Office
8740 Founders Road
Indianapolis, IN   46268

618

Kappa Beta Pi Scholarship

AMOUNT: $100-$200   DEADLINE: Sep 1
FIELDS/MAJORS: Law

Scholarship available at the University of Oklahoma, Norman for full-time second or third year female law students. Based on merit and financial need. One award offered annually. Write to the address below for information.

University of Oklahoma, Norman
Admissions and Records, Law Center
Room 22, 300 Timberdell Road
Norman, OK 73019

619

Kappa Kappa Gamma Member Scholarships and Fellowships

AMOUNT: None Specified   DEADLINE: Feb 1
FIELDS/MAJORS: All Areas of Study

Graduate and undergraduate scholarships, and grants for part-time study, are available to members of Kappa Kappa Gamma. All applicants are requested to note their chapter membership on their requests. Graduates are asked to also notate if they are full or part-time students. Send a SASE to the address below or contact your chapter for more information.

Kappa Kappa Gamma Foundation
Member Scholarships/Fellowships
PO Box 38
Columbus, OH 43216-0038

620

Karen D. Carsel Memorial Scholarship

AMOUNT: $500   DEADLINE: Apr 1
FIELDS/MAJORS: All Areas of Study

Scholarship open to full-time graduate student who presents evidence of financial need. Student must submit evidence of legal blindness, three letters of recommendation, and transcripts of grades from the college he/she is attending. Write to the address below for complete details.

American Foundation for the Blind
Scholarship Committee
11 Penn Plaza, Suite 300
New York, NY 10001

621

Karen Janice Maloney and Michael J. Keating Scholarship Funds

AMOUNT: None Specified   DEADLINE: Feb 1
FIELDS/MAJORS: Flight Operations

Awards for freshmen in the flight operations program at Daniel Webster. Based on academic promise and financial need. Maloney Scholarship gives preference to women, and the Keating Scholarship is for both entering freshmen and transfer students. Transfer students must have a minimum GPA of 2.0. Write to the address below for more details.

Daniel Webster College
Financial Assistance Office
20 University Dr.
Nashua, NH 03063

622

Karen Koch Memorial Golf Scholarship

AMOUNT: None Specified
DEADLINE: None Specified
FIELDS/MAJORS: Golf (Women)

Student must be full time and a member of the SMSU women's golf team. Contact the Women's Athletics Office for more information.

Southwest Missouri State University
Office of Financial Aid
901 South National Ave.
Springfield, MO 65804

623

Karla Scherer Foundation Scholarship

AMOUNT: None Specified   DEADLINE: Mar 1
FIELDS/MAJORS: Finance, Economics

Scholarships for women wishing to pursue careers in finance or economics. Not restricted solely to academic achievers or those with financial need. Drive, desire, and determination to succeed are important criteria as well. Write to the address below for information. Must include a SASE.

Karla Scherer Foundation
737 N. Michigan Ave. #2330
Chicago, IL 60611

624

Katherine C. Mather Memorial Pre-Law Scholarship

AMOUNT: None Specified   DEADLINE: Mar 1
FIELDS/MAJORS: Pre-Law

Award for incoming full-time female freshmen. Must be ranked in the top 5% of their high school classes. Preference to a student with more than one sibling. One award offered annually. Contact the address below for further information.

Iowa State University
Office of Student Financial Aid
12 Beardshear Hall
Ames, IA 50011

625

Katherine J. Schutze Memorial Scholarship

AMOUNT: None Specified   DEADLINE: Mar 15
FIELDS/MAJORS: Theology

Applicants must be women members of the Christian Church (Disciples of Christ) who are preparing for the ordained ministry. For full-time study. Financial need is considered. Write to the address below for details.

Christian Church (Disciples of Christ)
Attn: Scholarships
PO Box 1986
Indianapolis, IN   46206

626
KATU Thomas R. Dargan Minority Scholarship

AMOUNT: Maximum: $4000   DEADLINE: May 31
FIELDS/MAJORS: Any Broadcast Curriculum

Scholarships available to minority students residing in or attending a school in Oregon or Washington. Must be enrolled in the first, second, or third year of a broadcast curriculum at a four-year college, university, or an accredited community college. Must be U.S. citizens and have a minimum GPA of 3.0. Write to the address below for more information.

KATU Thomas R. Dargan Minority Scholarship
c/o Human Resources
PO Box 2
Portland, OR   97207-0002

627
Kellie Cannon Memorial Scholarship

AMOUNT: $1200   DEADLINE: Mar 1
FIELDS/MAJORS: Computer Science, Information Science, Data Processing

Scholarships are available to legally blind students majoring in computer science or a related field. Based on academic ability. Write to the address below for details.

American Council of the Blind
Scholarship Coordinator
1155 15th St., NW, Suite 720
Washington, D.C.   20005

628
Kelly L. Darling Memorial Scholarship

AMOUNT: None Specified
DEADLINE: None Specified
FIELDS/MAJORS: Education

Awards open to female junior or senior with a disability who is enrolled in the College of Education. Contact the address below for further information.

University of Toledo
Dean, College of Education
301 Snyder Memorial
Toledo, OH   43606

629
Kentucky Tuition Waiver Program for Veterans and Their Dependents

AMOUNT: None Specified   DEADLINE: None Specified
FIELDS/MAJORS: All Areas of Study

Kentucky residents. For veterans/nat'l guardsmen/and children (under the age of twenty-three years)/ spouse/or non-remarried widow of a permanently and totally disabled war veteran who served during periods of federally recognized hostilities or was a POW or MIA. For study at a community college, vocational-technical school, or four-year college. Please contact address below for complete information.

Kentucky Division of Veterans Affairs
545 S. Third St.
Louisville, KY   40202

630
Kerr-McGee Corporation, Mobil Oil Corporation Scholarships

AMOUNT: $500-$2500   DEADLINE: Mar 1
FIELDS/MAJORS: Petroleum and Geological Engineering

Scholarships are available at the University of Oklahoma, Norman for full-time minority petroleum and geological engineering majors who are U.S. citizens. Two to five awards offered annually. Write to the address listed for information.

University of Oklahoma, Norman
Scholarship Coord., Pet. and Geol. Eng.
T301 Energy Center
Norman, OK   73019

631
Kevin Child Scholarship

AMOUNT: $500-$1000   DEADLINE: Jul 10
FIELDS/MAJORS: All Areas of Study

Awards for students with a bleeding disorder pursuing a higher education. Applicants must be affiliated with or recommended by the NHF. Two awards are given annually. Write to the address listed for more information.

National Hemophilia Foundation
110 Greene St.
Suite 303
New York, NY   10012

632
Kevin Whirlwind Horse Memorial Scholarships

AMOUNT: $250   DEADLINE: Apr 10
FIELDS/MAJORS: All Areas of Study

Two scholarships for sophomore Native American students at BHSU who have maintained a GPA of 2.0 or better. Write to the address below for more information.

Black Hills State University
S. Hemmingson, Student Support Services
University Station, Box 9510
Spearfish, SD   57799-9510

633
Ki Hoon Kim Scholarship

AMOUNT: None Specified   DEADLINE: None Specified
FIELDS/MAJORS: All Areas of Study

Awarded to Korean students attending Central Connecticut State University and University faculty and students who want to study or do research in Korea. Write to the address below for additional information.

Central Connecticut State University
CCSU Foundation, Inc.
PO Box 612
New Britain, CT   06050

634
Kimber Richter Family Scholarship

AMOUNT: None Specified   DEADLINE: Mar 15
FIELDS/MAJORS: All Areas of Study

Open to students of western Massachusetts who are of the Baha'i faith and are planning to/are attending college. Contact the address below for further information.

Community Foundation of Western Massachusetts
PO Box 15769
1500 Main St.
Springfield, MA   01115

635
King Olav V Norwegian-American Heritage Fund

AMOUNT: $250-$3000   DEADLINE: Mar 1
FIELDS/MAJORS: Norwegian Studies/American Studies

Open to American or Norwegian students who are interested in the study of Norwegian heritage and/or American heritage at a recognized institution. The foundation decides the number and value of scholarships from year to year. Write to the address below for details.

Sons of Norway Foundation
1455 W. Lake St.
Minneapolis, MN   55408

636
King-Chavez-Parks Fellowship Program

AMOUNT: $6250   DEADLINE: Jun 2
FIELDS/MAJORS: All Areas of Study

Scholarships for African-American, Native American, or Hispanic students studying at the doctoral level at Wayne State University. Must be a U.S. citizen or permanent resident. Recipients should have the intention of teaching in a Michigan post-secondary institution within one year of receiving a degree. Information and application may be obtained through the scholarship and fellowship office at the address below.

Wayne State University
Graduate Scholarship/Fellowship Office
4302 Faculty Administration Bldg.
Detroit, MI   48202

637
Knezevitch Grants

AMOUNT: $200   DEADLINE: Nov 30
FIELDS/MAJORS: All Areas of Study

Grants for students of Serbian descent. For both undergraduate or graduate study. Write to the address below for details. Be certain to enclose a SASE. Personal interview may be required.

Steven Knezevitch Trust
100 E. Wisconsin Ave., Suite 1020
Milwaukee, WI   53202

638
Knowlton Scholarship

AMOUNT: None Specified
DEADLINE: None Specified
FIELDS/MAJORS: Consumer Studies

Awards for female students in the department of consumer studies who have a cumulative GPA of 3.0 or higher. For entering sophomores, juniors, or seniors. Contact the Chair, Scholarship Committee, Department of Consumer Studies for more information.

University of Massachusetts, Amherst
Chair, Scholarship Committee
Department of Consumer Studies
Amherst, MA   01003

639
Kodak Scholarship

AMOUNT: Maximum: $10000
DEADLINE: Apr 3
FIELDS/MAJORS: Engineering, Computer Science, Chemistry, Quantitative Business

Open to Latino students seeking engineering degrees with a GPA of 3.0 or better. Must be U.S. citizens majoring in computer science, quantitative business, chemistry, or engineering (chemical, electrical, industrial, or mechanical). Must be residents of Los Angeles City, Montebello, Commerce, Bell Gardens, or Monterey Park. One award is offered annually. Write to the address listed for more information.

Telacu Education Foundation
5400 East Olympic Blvd., Ste. 300
Los Angeles, CA   90022

640
Koh Scholarship

AMOUNT: None Specified
DEADLINE: None Specified
FIELDS/MAJORS: Korean Studies

Scholarship for students of Korean descent or United States citizens studying in the Republic of Korea. Write to the address below for additional information.

Central Connecticut State University
CCSU Foundation, Inc.
PO Box 612
New Britain, CT   06050

---

641 Korean-American Scholarship Foundation

AMOUNT: None Specified DEADLINE: Mar 1
FIELDS/MAJORS: All Areas of Study

Awards are available at the University of New Mexico for sophomores or graduate students of Korean heritage who are enrolled for full-time study. Contact: Chairman of Scholarship Committee, Western Region Office, Korean American Scholarship Foundation, 20281 Running Springs Lane, Huntington Beach, CA., 92646 for more details.

University of New Mexico, Albuquerque
Office of Financial Aid
Albuquerque, NM   87131

642 Kuchler-Killian Memorial Scholarship

AMOUNT: $3000 DEADLINE: Mar 31
FIELDS/MAJORS: All Areas of Study

Open to full-time students who are legally blind from Connecticut or attending school in Connecticut. Write to the address below for details.

National Federation of the Blind
Mrs. Peggy Elliott, Chairman
805 Fifth Ave.
Grinnell, IA   50112

643 Kurt T. Chambers Award

AMOUNT: None Specified
DEADLINE: None Specified
FIELDS/MAJORS: Arboriculture

Awarded to Stockbridge School students majoring in arboriculture and park management who have need of services for learning disabilities. Contact the director of the Stockbridge School for more information.

University of Massachusetts, Amherst
Director
Stockbridge School
Amherst, MA   01003

644 Kyutaro and Yasuo Abiko Memorial Scholarships

AMOUNT: None Specified DEADLINE: Apr 1
FIELDS/MAJORS: Journalism, Agriculture

Applicants must be undergraduates of Japanese ancestry who are majoring in journalism or agriculture and are members of the JACL. Applications and information may be obtained from local JACL chapters, district offices, and the national headquarters at the address below. Please indicate your level of study and be certain to include a legal-sized SASE.

Japanese American Citizens League
National Scholarship and Award Program
1765 Sutter St.
San Francisco, CA   94115

645 Laotian Scholarship Fund Award

AMOUNT: None Specified DEADLINE: Mar 31
FIELDS/MAJORS: All Areas of Study

Awards open to U.S. citizens or permanent residents who are of Laotian descent. Must have a minimum GPA of 3.0. Contact the address below for further information.

University of North Texas
Scholarship Office
Marquis Hall #218
Denton, TX   76203

646 Laren K. McClain Memorial Scholarship

AMOUNT: $1000 DEADLINE: None Specified
FIELDS/MAJORS: Education

Awards open to physically and/or mentally challenged sophomores, juniors, and seniors. Based on financial need. Contact the address below for further information.

University of Toledo
Dean, College of Education
301 Snyder Memorial
Toledo, OH   43606

647 Larry Ratner Scholarship

AMOUNT: $500 DEADLINE: Mar 2
FIELDS/MAJORS: Business Administration

Award open to disadvantaged minority MBA candidates. Must be active in university or community activities and be able to demonstrate financial need. Must have a minimum GPA of 2.5. Contact the address below for further information.

California Polytechnic State University
Financial Aid Office
212 Administration Bldg.
San Luis Obispo, CA   93407

648 Larry W. Staley Memorial Scholarship

AMOUNT: None Specified DEADLINE: Mar 15
FIELDS/MAJORS: Business, Accounting

First preference of this award given to handicapped students in financial need. Second preference given to business or accounting majors with financial need. Selection made by the office of financial aid. (When applicable, in conjunction with the School of Business). Contact the address below for further information.

Barton College
Financial Aid Office
Wilson, NC   27893

649
Las Cruces Junior Women's Club

AMOUNT: $500   DEADLINE: Mar 1
FIELDS/MAJORS: All Areas of Study

$500 awarded to any female attending the main campus or Dona Ana Branch Community College. The recipient must show financial need and desire to further her education. Applications available in the financial aid office. Write to the address below for details.

New Mexico State University
Student Financial Aid Office
Box 30001, Dept 5100
Las Cruces, NM   88003

650
Las Mujeres De Lulac Scholarships

AMOUNT: None Specified   DEADLINE: Jun 1
FIELDS/MAJORS: All Areas of Study

Awards for Hispanics continuing education after interruption or single parents who can demonstrate financial need. Must submit most current transcript, proof of enrollment, letter of recommendation, and current financial verification. For undergraduate or graduate study. New Mexico residents only. Write to the address below for more details.

Las Mujeres De Lulac
Las Mujeres
PO Box 2203
Albuquerque, NM   87103

651
Las Mujeres De Lulac Scholarships

AMOUNT: None Specified   DEADLINE: Mar 1
FIELDS/MAJORS: All Areas of Study

Awards are available at the University of New Mexico for Hispanic women at any level of study. Write to the address below for more information.

University of New Mexico, Albuquerque
Office of Financial Aid
Albuquerque, NM   87131

652
Last Dollar Program

AMOUNT: None Specified   DEADLINE: None Specified
FIELDS/MAJORS: All Areas of Study

Awards are available for minority Virginia residents who can be classified as first-time freshmen students and are enrolled at least half time in a degree program at a Virginia public institution. Must demonstrate financial need as determined by the institution. Awards range from $400 to the cost of full-time tuition and fees. Write to the address below for more information.

Virginia Council of Higher Education
James Monroe Building
101 North 14th St.
Richmond, VA   23219

653
Latin American and Caribbean Fellowship Program

AMOUNT: Maximum: $30000   DEADLINE: Mar 28
FIELDS/MAJORS: Social Sciences/Humanities

Fellowships for Latin American and Caribbean practitioners and researchers whose work in grassroots development would benefit from advanced academic experience in the USA. Fellowships are awarded to master's candidates and higher. Must demonstrate interest in the problems of poverty and development and be nominated by home institution. Up to forty fellowships are offered per year. Write to the address below for details.

Inter-American Foundation
IAF Fellowship Programs, Dept. 555
901 N. Stuart St., 10th Floor
Arlington, VA   22203

654
Laura Hamilton Billingsley Memorial Scholarship

AMOUNT: None Specified   DEADLINE: Mar 15
FIELDS/MAJORS: Journalism, Mass Communications

Scholarships are available at the University of Oklahoma, Norman for students at master's level in journalism and mass communications, with minimum GPAs of 3.0. Preference is given to students of Native American descent. Four awards offered annually. Write to the address below for information.

University of Oklahoma, Norman
School of Journalism and Mass Comm.
860 Van Vleet Oval
Norman, OK   73019

655
Lavinia Laible Scholarship

AMOUNT: $500-$2500   DEADLINE: Apr 15
FIELDS/MAJORS: All Areas of Study

Scholarships for female residents of Kent County who are transferring from Grand Rapids Community College to the University of Michigan for their junior year. Applicants must have a GPA of at least 3.0. Contact the financial aid office at Grand Rapids Community College for information.

Grand Rapids Foundation
209-C Waters Bldg.
161 Ottawa Avenue, NW
Grand Rapids, MI   49503

656 Law Scholarships

AMOUNT: None Specified   DEADLINE: Apr 1
FIELDS/MAJORS: Law

Applicants must be of Japanese ancestry and entering or enrolled at an accredited law school. Must also be members of the JACL. Applications and information may be obtained from local JACL chapters, district offices, and the national headquarters at the address below. Please indicate your level of study, and be certain to include a legal-sized SASE.

Japanese American Citizens League
National Scholarship and Award Program
1765 Sutter St.
San Francisco, CA   94115

657 Layser Scholarship

AMOUNT: None Specified   DEADLINE: Mar 1
FIELDS/MAJORS: Christian Ministry

Awarded to a deserving student demonstrating academic ability, citizenship, and financial need, and planning a career in Christian ministry. Contact the address listed for further information.

Elizabethtown College
M. Clarke Paine, Dir. of Financial Aid
One Alpha Dr.
Elizabethtown, PA   17022

658 Leadership Award

AMOUNT: Maximum: $4000   DEADLINE: Mar 15
FIELDS/MAJORS: All Areas of Study

For incoming undergraduates who scored 20 to 24 on the ACT and 820 to 1020 on the SAT and have fewer than 25 credit hours. Must be affiliated with the Churches of Christ and a resident of campus owned housing. Write to the address below for more information.

Abilene Christian University
Leadership Scholarship Committee
Box 6000
Abilene, TX   79699

659 Lee H. Morris Memorial Scholarships

AMOUNT: $1000   DEADLINE: Mar 31
FIELDS/MAJORS: English Education

Three awards for full-time sophomores or above interested in a teaching career. Must have a GPA of 3.0 or better. Preference is given to female students from Southwest Missouri. Financial need is considered. Contact the English Department for more information.

Southwest Missouri State University
Office of Financial Aid
901 South National Ave.
Springfield, MO   65804

660 Leonard M. Perryman Communications for Scholarship Minority Students

AMOUNT: $2500   DEADLINE: Feb 15
FIELDS/MAJORS: Religious Communications/ Journalism

Applicants must be junior or senior communications minority students who intend to pursue a career in religious communications. Write to the scholarship committee at the address below for details.

United Methodist Communications
Scholarship Committee, Public Media Div.
PO Box 320
Nashville, TN   37202

661 Lettie Pate Whitehead Foundation Nursing Scholarship

AMOUNT: None Specified   DEADLINE: Apr 1
FIELDS/MAJORS: Nursing

Awarded to Christian women who reside in Virginia, are nursing majors, and demonstrate financial need. Write to the address below for more information.

Christopher Newport University
Office of Financial Aid
50 Shoe Lane
Newport News, VA   23606

662 Leveo V. Sanchez Family Endowed Scholarship

AMOUNT: Maximum: $900   DEADLINE: Mar 1
FIELDS/MAJORS: All Areas of Study

Open to students who are Native American New Mexico residents, preferably from rural communities or Pueblos, who enter as freshmen. Must have a minimum high school GPA of 2.5. Renewable if recipient maintains a 2.85 GPA and enrolls for 14 or more credit hours per semester. Contact the address below for further information.

New Mexico Highlands University
Financial Aid Office
201 Felix Martinez Student Svcs. Bldg.
Las Vegas, NM   87791

663 Lights of the Jewish Special Needs Scholarships

AMOUNT: Maximum: $1000   DEADLINE: May 31
FIELDS/MAJORS: All Areas of Study

Grants for Jewish students in the St. Louis community. For study at a two or four-year college or university in Missouri. Write to the address below for details.

Lights of the Jewish Special Needs Society
6 Sleepy Hollow Lane
St. Louis, MO   63132

664
Linda E. Jennett Endowed Fellowship

AMOUNT: None Specified   DEADLINE: Mar 1
FIELDS/MAJORS: Civil Engineering

Awards are available at the University of New Mexico for female civil engineering graduate students enrolled full time. Write to the address below for more information.

University of New Mexico, Albuquerque
Office of Financial Aid
Albuquerque, NM   87131

665
Linda J. Carter Scholarships

AMOUNT: None Specified
DEADLINE: Mar 31
FIELDS/MAJORS: All Areas of Study

Award open to members of the women's varsity basketball program. Must have a minimum GPA of 3.0. Contact the address below for further information.

University of North Texas
Scholarship Office
Marquis Hall #218
Denton, TX   76203

666
Linda M. Lampe Memorial Scholarship

AMOUNT: None Specified   DEADLINE: Feb 1
FIELDS/MAJORS: Law

Awards for female law students who are employed full time and entering their fourth year of study. Academic promise and financial need are considered. Contact the assistant dean, Chase College of Law, for further information.

Northern Kentucky University
Chase College of Law
Office of Admissions
Highland Heights, KY   41099

667
Linda Weddle Memorial Scholarships

AMOUNT: $1000   DEADLINE: Feb 7
FIELDS/MAJORS: Accounting

Scholarships are available at the University of Oklahoma, Norman for full-time female accounting majors. Based on academic ability. Applicant must be a U.S. citizen. Three awards offered annually. Write to the address below for information.

University of Oklahoma, Norman
School of Accounting
200 Adams Hall
Norman, OK   73019

668
Link Program Scholarship

AMOUNT: $2000   DEADLINE: Apr 1
FIELDS/MAJORS: Business, Engineering, or Computer and Information Sciences

Awarded to an incoming minority freshman student interested in the field of business, engineering, or computer and information sciences. Must have a minimum high school GPA of 2.5 or higher. Contact the Career Services Center for further information.

Cleveland State University
Office of Student Financial Assistance
2344 Euclid Ave.
Cleveland, OH   44115

669
Links Scholarship

AMOUNT: $750   DEADLINE: Feb 1
FIELDS/MAJORS: All Areas of Study

Awards for female minorities who are entering freshmen. Must be a U.S. citizen or permanent resident. Also must be a resident of Cincinnati, Ohio. Contact the address below for further information.

Northern Kentucky University
Financial Aid Office-Nunn Dr.
Administrative Center #416
Highland Heights, KY   41099

670
Lionel Rocha Holmes and Edward A. Dutra Scholarships

AMOUNT: $500-$1000   DEADLINE: Apr 15
FIELDS/MAJORS: All Areas of Study

Open to students with a Portuguese heritage, (within five generations). Must reside or attend school in any of the following six counties: El Dorado, Placer, Sacramento, San Joaquin, Solano, or Yolo. Must also have a minimum GPA of 3.0. Contact the address below for further information.

Portuguese Historical and Cultural Society
PHCS Scholarships
PO Box 161990
Sacramento, CA   95816

671
Lisa M. Plotkin Scholarships

AMOUNT: None Specified   DEADLINE: Apr 15
FIELDS/MAJORS: All Areas of Study

Award open to sophomores and juniors who are handicapped or majoring in a field to benefit the developmentally disabled. May be renewed. Contact the address below for further information.

Whitworth College
Office of Financial Aid
300 W. Hawthorne Rd.
Spokane, WA   99251

672 LITA/OCLC and LITA/LSSI Minority Scholarships

AMOUNT: $2500   **DEADLINE:** Apr 1
FIELDS/MAJORS: Information Science

Applicants must be Native American, Asian-American, African-American, or Hispanic graduate students who are entering or enrolled in an ALA-accredited master's program with an emphasis on library automation. Previous experience is considered, and U.S. or Canadian citizenship is required. Two awards per year. Write to the address shown for details.

American Library Association
Library and Information Technology Assn.
50 E. Huron Street
Chicago, IL   60611

673 Lorena Jonas Memorial Scholarship

AMOUNT: $200   **DEADLINE:** Apr 1
FIELDS/MAJORS: All Areas of Study

One award is available to a female student of junior status by fall semester, who evidences appropriate growth toward professional character, and who can demonstrate financial need. Contact the Office of Financial Aid or Career Services for the special application that is required.

Black Hills State University
1200 University St.
Spearfish, SD   57783

674 Los Endowment

AMOUNT: Maximum: $700   **DEADLINE:** Mar 15
FIELDS/MAJORS: All Areas of Study

Open to full-time undergraduates who are African-American, Native American, or Hispanic. Contact the address below for further information

Arizona State University
Scholarship Office Main Campus
PO Box 870412
Tempe, AZ   85287

675 Lottie Conlan Scholarship

AMOUNT: $1000-$2000   **DEADLINE:** Mar 1
FIELDS/MAJORS: All Areas of Study

Awards open to sophomores or above of Native American heritage. Four to five scholarships awarded annually. Contact the address below for further information.

University of Oklahoma, Norman
Prospective Student Services
Boyd House 407 W. Boyd
Norman, OK   73019

676 Louise Giles Minority Scholarships

AMOUNT: $3000   **DEADLINE:** Apr 1
FIELDS/MAJORS: Library Science

Applicants must be Native American, Asian-American, African-American, or Hispanic graduate students entering or enrolled in an ALA-accredited master's program. United States or Canadian citizenship is required. Must not have completed more than 12 semester hours toward master's degree. Write to the address shown for details.

American Library Association
Staff Liaison, ALA Scholarship Juries
50 E. Huron Street
Chicago, IL   60611

677 Lt. William J. Scott Scholarship

AMOUNT: $1000   **DEADLINE:** May 1
FIELDS/MAJORS: All Areas of Study

Scholarships are available at the University of Oklahoma, Norman for full-time Native American students of Osage Indian descent. Applicants must be single male students. 100–125 awards offered annually. Write to the address below for information.

University of Oklahoma, Norman
Office of Financial Aid
731 Elm, Robertson Hall
Norman, OK   73019

678 Luce Fellowship

AMOUNT: None Specified   **DEADLINE:** Feb 1
FIELDS/MAJORS: Biological Sciences

Fellowship open to female graduates. Fellowship includes a stipend and tuition remission. Contact the address below for further information.

Fordham University
Graduate Admissions Office—Keating 216
Fordham University
Bronx, NY   10458

679 Lucile B. Kaufman Women's Scholarship Fund Award

AMOUNT: $1000   **DEADLINE:** Mar 1
FIELDS/MAJORS: Manufacturing Engineering or Manufacturing Engineering Technology

Scholarships for full-time female undergraduate students who have at least 30 credit hours and are enrolled in a degree program in manufacturing engineering or manufacturing engineering technology. Must have at least a 3.5 GPA. Write to the address below for more information.

Society of Manufacturing Engineers Education Foundation
One SME Drive
PO Box 930
Dearborn, MI   48121-0930

680
Luise Meyer-Schutzmeister Award

AMOUNT: $500   DEADLINE: Jan 15
FIELDS/MAJORS: Physics

Scholarship for female doctoral student in physics. For U.S. citizens to study in U.S. or abroad, or for foreign students to study in U.S. (the AWIS also publishes a directory of financial aid) Write to the address below for details.

Association for Women in Science Educational Foundation
National Headquarters
1200 New York Ave. NW #650
Washington, D.C.   20005

681
Lulac Scholarship Programs

AMOUNT: $100-$1000   DEADLINE: Mar 31
FIELDS/MAJORS: All Areas of Study

The Lulac National Scholarship Fund is a community based scholarship program that awards over a half a million dollars each year to outstanding Hispanic students in communities served by participating councils of Lulac. To qualify, an applicant must be a U.S. citizen or legal resident and enrolled or planning to enroll in a two or four-year college or university. Applicants must apply directly to a participating Lulac council in his/her community. A list of participating Lulac councils can be obtained by sending a SASE to the Lulac National Education Service Centers at the address below.

Lulac National Educational Service Centers, Inc.
Department of Scholarship Inquiries
1133 20th St. NW #750
Washington, D.C.   20036

682
Lutheran Church— Missouri Synod District Grants

AMOUNT: $100-$1000   DEADLINE: None Specified
FIELDS/MAJORS: Religion, Theology

Awards for Concordia students who intend to enter full-time church careers in the Lutheran Church— Missouri Synod. Must have GPAs of at least 2.5 and be U.S. citizens. Renewable. Write to the address below for more information.

Concordia University, Irvine
Financial Aid Office
1530 Concordia West
Irvine, CA   92715

683
Lyle Mamer, Julia Kiene Fellowship in Electrical Energy

AMOUNT: $1000-$2000   DEADLINE: Mar 1
FIELDS/MAJORS: Electrical Related Fields

Open to women who are graduating seniors or those who have a degree from an accredited institution. The applications are judged on scholarship, character, financial need, and professional interest in electrical energy. The college or university selected by the recipient for advanced study must be accredited and approved by the EWRT Fellowship Committee. One award given for each fellowship. Write to the address below for further information.

Electrical Women's Round Table, Inc.
Executive Director
PO Box 292793
Nashville, TN   37229

684
M.A. Cartland Shackford Medical Fellowship

AMOUNT: Maximum: $3500   DEADLINE: Dec 16
FIELDS/MAJORS: Medicine

Scholarship for women studying medicine (on the graduate level). Fellowships are intended to support women with a career objective in general practice, not psychiatry. Write to the address below for information.

Wellesley College
Committee on Graduate Fellowships
106 Central Street, Career Center
Wellesley, MA   02181

685
Mabel M. Wright Scholarship

AMOUNT: $500   DEADLINE: Mar 2
FIELDS/MAJORS: Physical Education

Open to female students with promising ability. GPA must be commensurate with teacher education program requirements. Contact Rip Marsten at the address below for further information.

University of Northern Iowa
Health, Physical Ed. and Leisure Services
203 W. Gym
Cedar Falls, IA   50614

686
Maddalena and Joseph Perrella Scholarship

AMOUNT: None Specified   DEADLINE: Dec 1
FIELDS/MAJORS: All Areas of Study

Scholarship awarded to an eligible student of Italian heritage. Write to the address listed for more information.

Spalding University
Financial Aid Office
851 S. Fourth St.
Louisville, KY   40203

687

Madeline P. Peterson Scholarship for American Indian Women

AMOUNT: $6050   DEADLINE: None Specified
FIELDS/MAJORS: All Areas of Study

Scholarships are available at the University of Iowa for incoming female freshman students who are Native Americans with a tribal affiliation. Must demonstrate financial need. Write to the address below for details.

University of Iowa
Office of Student Financial Aid
208 Calvin Hall
Iowa City, IA   52242

688

Mae Lasley Osage Scholarship Fund

AMOUNT: $250-$1000   DEADLINE: Jun 15
FIELDS/MAJORS: All Areas of Study

Scholarships are available for Osage Indians who are undergraduate students at any accredited university. Write to the address below for information.

Mae Lasley Osage Scholarship Fund
PO Box 2009
Tulsa, OK   74101

689

Maeltnette Aldrich Memorial Scholarship

AMOUNT: None Specified   DEADLINE: Mar 15
FIELDS/MAJORS: All Areas of Study

Scholarships are available to women in financial need. Write to the address below for more details.

Kansas Wesleyan University
Office of Financial Assistance
100 E. Claflin
Salina, KS   67401

690

Magoichi and Shizuko Kato Memorial Scholarship

AMOUNT: None Specified
DEADLINE: Apr 1
FIELDS/MAJORS: Medicine, Theology/Religion

Open to graduate students of Japanese ancestry majoring in medicine or the ministry. Must be a member of the JACL to apply. Applications and information may be obtained from local JACL chapters, district offices, and the national headquarters at the address below. Please indicate your level of study, and be certain to include a legal-sized SASE.

Japanese American Citizens League
National Scholarship and Award Program
1765 Sutter St.
San Francisco, CA   94115

691

Maine Media Women Scholarship, Lee Agger Memorial Scholarship

AMOUNT: None Specified   DEADLINE: Apr 1
FIELDS/MAJORS: Mass Comm: Journalism, Public Relations, Broadcasting, Advertising

Scholarships are available for female Maine residents enrolled in an area listed above. Preference will be given to an applicant who has already demonstrated motivation and ability in some aspect of mass communications. For more information write to the address below.

Maine Media Women Scholarship
MMW Scholarship Committee
9 Middle Street
Hallowell, ME   04347

692

Makarios Scholarship/ Theodore and Wally Lappas Award

AMOUNT: Maximum: $1000   DEADLINE: May 5
FIELDS/MAJORS: All Areas of Study

Ten scholarships for Greek Cypriots born in Cyprus and having permanent residence and citizenship there. For study in the United States. Must have financial need and high scholastic ability. Write to the address listed for details.

Cyprus Relief Fund of America, Inc.
Makarios Scholarship Fund, Inc.
13 E. 40th St.
New York, NY   10016

693

MALDEF Communications Scholarship Program

AMOUNT: None Specified   DEADLINE: Jun 30
FIELDS/MAJORS: Communications, Journalism, Media Communications, Entertainment Law

Awards are available for Latino undergraduate or graduate students who seek a career in these fields upon graduation. Write to the address below for more information.

Mexican American Legal Defense and Education Fund
634 South Spring Street
11th Floor
Los Angeles, CA   90014

694

MALDEF Law School Scholarship Program

AMOUNT: None Specified   DEADLINE: Jun 30
FIELDS/MAJORS: Law

Open to full-time law students of Hispanic descent accepted to/enrolled in an accredited law school. Varying number of awards per year. Recipients must demonstrate a commitment to serve the Hispanic community after graduation. Write to the address below for details.

Mexican American Legal Defense and Educational Fund
MALDEF Law School Scholarship Program
634 S. Spring St., 11th Floor
Los Angeles, CA   90014

695 Manuel Pino Scholarships

AMOUNT: None Specified   **DEADLINE:** Mar 1
FIELDS/MAJORS: All Areas of Study

Awards are available at the University of New Mexico for Hispanic students. Write to the address below for more information.

University of New Mexico, Albuquerque
Office of Financial Aid
Albuquerque, NM   87131

696 Manville Scholarship

AMOUNT: $200
DEADLINE: None Specified
FIELDS/MAJORS: Chemical/Industrial/Mechanical Engineering

Awards open to females and minority students majoring in any field listed above. Based on financial need and academics. Contact the address below for further information.

University of Toledo
Department of Chemical Engineering
2207 Engineering Science Building
Toledo, OH   43606

697 Marcella Roll Memorial Scholarship

AMOUNT: $300   **DEADLINE:** None Specified
FIELDS/MAJORS: Pharmacy

Award open to full-time female students in the professional pharmacy program who can demonstrate professional involvement, academics, and need. Contact the address below for further information.

University of Toledo
Pharmacy Development Officer
College of Pharmacy
Toledo, OH   43606

698 Marcus and Theresa Levie Educational Scholarship

AMOUNT: None Specified   **DEADLINE:** Mar 1
FIELDS/MAJORS: Helping Professions

Scholarships for Jewish men and women legally domiciled in Cook County, Illinois, and identified as having promise for significant contributions in their chosen careers and need of financial assistance for full-time academic programs in one of the above fields. Must have completed at least the junior level of study or have started professional training. Write to the address below after Dec 1 for details.

Jewish Vocational Service
Attn: Scholarship Secretary
One South Franklin Street
Chicago, IL   60606

699 Marcus Foster Fellowship, Fontaine Fellowship

AMOUNT: None Specified   **DEADLINE:** Feb 5
FIELDS/MAJORS: Education

Fellowships for minority Ph.D./Ed.D. students in the GSE at the University of Pennsylvania. Foster fellowship is renewable. Contact the financial aid office at the address below for details.

University of Pennsylvania, Graduate School of Education
Financial Aid Office
3700 Walnut St.
Philadelphia, PA   19104

700 Marcus Garvey Scholarship

AMOUNT: Maximum: $1000   **DEADLINE:** May 1
FIELDS/MAJORS: All Areas of Study

Open to high school seniors who are residents of Connecticut and are of West Indian parentage. Based on academics, community service, financial need, and an essay. Contact the address listed for further information.

West Indian Foundation, Inc.
Scholarship Committee
PO Box 320394
Hartford, CT   06132

701 Margaret and Charles E. Stewart Scholarship Fund

AMOUNT: $500   **DEADLINE:** Apr 30
FIELDS/MAJORS: Religion, Theology

Awards for African-American full-time seminary students enrolled as candidates for the master's of divinity degree, in preparation for the pastorate in the Black Church of any Protestant denomination. Write to the address below for more information.

Philadelphia Foundation
1234 Market St.
Suite 1900
Philadelphia, PA   19107

702 Margaret and Sidney Jaffe Scholarship

AMOUNT: None Specified   **DEADLINE:** Mar 1
FIELDS/MAJORS: Medicine

Awards are available at the University of New Mexico for medical students or juniors or seniors in a pre-med curriculum who are of American Indian descent. Applicants must have been New Mexico high school graduates. Contact the medical school for more details.

University of New Mexico, Albuquerque
Office of Financial Aid
Albuquerque, NM   87131

703 Margaret Ann Kneller Scholarship

AMOUNT: Maximum: $500   DEADLINE: Mar 1
FIELDS/MAJORS: All Areas of Study

Open to a senior with a physical disability who can demonstrate academic achievement, leadership in student affairs, and a commitment to community service. Contact the address listed for further information.

Brooklyn College
Office of the V.P. for Student Life
2113 Boylan Hall
Brooklyn, NY   11210

704 Margaret M. Prickett Scholarship

AMOUNT: $1000   DEADLINE: Mar 31
FIELDS/MAJORS: All Areas of Study

Scholarships for daughters or granddaughters of Commissioned Officers or Warrant Officers in the U.S. Army who are on active duty, died on active duty, or retired after at least twenty years of service. For undergraduate study. Renewable. Write to the address below for details. Specify the officer's name, rank, social security number, and dates of active duty when requesting an application. Enclose a SASE.

Society of Daughters of the U.S. Army
Janet B. Otto, Scholarship Chairman
7717 Rockledge Court
West Springfield, VA   22152

705 Margaret McNamara Memorial Fund Fellowships

AMOUNT: Maximum: $6000   DEADLINE: Feb 2
FIELDS/MAJORS: All Areas of Study

Fellowships are available to women from developing countries, with a record of service to women/children. Applicants must be twenty-five years of age or older and planning to return to their country of origin within two years of the grant date. Must be able to demonstrate financial need. Write to the address below for information.

Margaret McNamara Memorial Fund
1818 H Street, NW, Room G-1000
Washington, D.C.   20433

706 Margot Karle Scholarship

AMOUNT: $200-$400   DEADLINE: Aug 15
FIELDS/MAJORS: All Areas of Study

Scholarship available to full-time female students in the City University of New York undergraduate system who have demonstrated both financial need and a high degree of community involvement. Write to the address below for more information.

Astraea National Lesbian Action Foundation
Program Director
116 E. 16th Street, 7th Floor
New York, NY   10003

707 Maria Borrero Scholarship

AMOUNT: Maximum: $500   DEADLINE: None Specified
FIELDS/MAJORS: Health Related Fields

Open to Hispanic high school seniors who are residents of Hartford, Connecticut. Must be in top 1/5 of the class with demonstrated leadership ability. Contact the address listed for further information.

Hispanic Health Council
Victoria Barrera
175 Main St.
Hartford, CT   06106

708 Marie E. Schleichert Annual College of Agriculture Scholarship

AMOUNT: $100   DEADLINE: Feb 1
FIELDS/MAJORS: Agriculture, Aquaculture, Forestry

Scholarships are available at the University of Hawaii, Hilo for full-time students studying in one of the areas listed above who are of Hawaiian or Native American ancestry with a career desire to help save the land and seas in and around Hawaii. Must be Hawaii residents. Write to the address below for information.

University of Hawaii at Hilo
Financial Aid Office
200 West Kawili Street
Hilo, HI   96720

709 Marie P. Stewart Scholarship

AMOUNT: None Specified   DEADLINE: Mar 1
FIELDS/MAJORS: All Areas of Study

Award open to female residents of North Carolina who are U.S. citizens. Preference to residents of Macon County, North Carolina or Western North Carolina. Contact the address below for further information.

University of North Carolina, Greensboro
Financial Aid Office
723 Kenilworth St.
Greensboro, NC   27412

710 Marion Barr Stanfield Art Scholarship

AMOUNT: None Specified   DEADLINE: Feb 15
FIELDS/MAJORS: Painting, Drawing, Sculpture

Applicants must be active Unitarian Universalist members who are majoring in painting, drawing, and sculpture. Financial need must be demonstrated. Write to the address below for details.

Unitarian Universalist Association
Publications Department
25 Beacon St.
Boston, MA   02108

711 Marion Burke Knott Scholarships

AMOUNT: $14260   DEADLINE: Jan 15
FIELDS/MAJORS: All Areas of Study

Scholarships for freshman Catholic students residing in the archdiocese of Baltimore with a minimum 3.75 GPA and a minimum SAT score of 1350. Write to the address below for additional information.

Loyola College in Maryland
Director of Financial Aid
4501 North Charles St.
Baltimore, MD   21210

712 Marjorie Jennings Endowed Scholarship

AMOUNT: None Specified   DEADLINE: Mar 15
FIELDS/MAJORS: All Areas of Study

First preference of this scholarship is a female student who is a resident of Kansas. Second preference is for a student with a strong belief in Christian higher education values. Write to the address listed for more details.

Kansas Wesleyan University
Office of Financial Assistance
100 E. Claflin
Salina, KS   67401

713 Mark Ulmer Scholarship

AMOUNT: Maximum: $500   DEADLINE: Jun 1
FIELDS/MAJORS: All Areas of Study

Scholarship available for Native American sophomores, juniors, or seniors who attend one of the schools in the University of North Carolina system. Applicants must have a GPA of at least 2.0, be U.S. citizens, and North Carolina residents. Write to Ms. Lana T. Dial at the address below for more information.

Triangle Native American Society
PO Box 26841
Raleigh, NC   27611

714 Marsha Hannah Endowed Scholarship

AMOUNT: None Specified   DEADLINE: Mar 1
FIELDS/MAJORS: Mathematics, Computer Science

Open to full-time students who are residents of New Mexico carrying 14 or more credit hours per semester. Preference to females. Must have a minimum GPA of 3.0. Award is full-time resident tuition and fees. Contact the address below for further information.

New Mexico Highlands University
Financial Aid Office
201 Felix Martinez Student Svcs. Bldg.
Las Vegas, NM   87791

715 Martha Love Cordonnier Scholarship and Lucinda A. Love Scholarship

AMOUNT: None Specified   DEADLINE: None Specified
FIELDS/MAJORS: Women Sports

Student must be full-time and a member of a women's athletic team. Contact the Women's Athletics Office for more information.

Southwest Missouri State University
Office of Financial Aid
901 South National Ave.
Springfield, MO   65804

716 Martin Luther King Jr. Memorial Scholarship Fund

AMOUNT: None Specified   DEADLINE: Mar 15
FIELDS/MAJORS: Education

Must be a minority active or student member of the CTA, or the dependent child of an active, retired, or deceased CTA member. For study in the fields of education or teaching. Write to the address below for details.

California Teachers Association
c/o CTA Human Rights Department
1705 Murchison Drive, PO Box 921
Burlingame, CA   94011

717 Martin Luther King Scholarship

AMOUNT: $500   DEADLINE: None Specified
FIELDS/MAJORS: All Areas of Study

Scholarships for minority students at NYIT. Program is designed to increase campus representation of minority students. Based on need and academics. Twenty awards are given annually. Write to the address below for details.

New York Institute of Technology
Old Westbury Campus
Financial Aid Office
Old Westbury, NY   11568

718 Martin Luther King, Jr. Scholarship

AMOUNT: None Specified   DEADLINE: Feb 1
FIELDS/MAJORS: All Areas of Study

Awards for African-American high school seniors who are residents of North Carolina. Priority will be given to children of NCAE members, but other selection criteria include: character, personality, and scholastic achievement. Write to the address below for more details.

North Carolina Association of Educators
NCAE Minority Affairs Commission
PO Box 27347
Raleigh, NC   27611

719 Martin Luther King, Jr. Youth Foundation Scholarships

AMOUNT: Maximum: $2000   DEADLINE: Apr 15
FIELDS/MAJORS: All Areas of Study

Open to Hartford residents who are graduating high school seniors or second year students at Capitol Community College. Based on community service, academics, and financial need. For use at four-year schools. Contact the address listed for further information.

Martin Luther King, Jr. Youth Foundation, Inc.
Ms. Valerie Bolden-Barrett
Box F
Hartford, CT   06103

720 Maurice Yonover Scholarship

AMOUNT: None Specified   DEADLINE: Mar 1
FIELDS/MAJORS: Helping Professions

Open to master's and doctoral candidates with career goals in the "helping professions." Must be legally domiciled in Cook County, the Chicago metro area, or northwest Indiana. Contact the address below for further information after Dec 1.

Jewish Vocational Service
Academic Scholarship Program
1 S. Franklin St.
Chicago, IL   60606

721 Marvin D. Mills Scholarship

AMOUNT: None Specified   DEADLINE: Feb 1
FIELDS/MAJORS: All Areas of Study

Scholarship open to African-Americans living in Kentucky. Applicants must be first-time entering freshmen with full-time status or transfer students with full-time status planning to attend Murray State University. Students must submit a written essay (at least two hundred words) on a current event or public topic and a copy of high school or college transcripts plus three letters of recommendation. Applicants must achieve a minimum ACT composite of 21 and rank in the top 25% of their class; if transferring, students must have completed at least 12 semester hours with an accumulative GPA of 2.75 on a 4.0 scale. Write to the address below for details.

Murray State University
Office of University Scholarships
Ordway Hall, 1 Murray Street
Murray, KY   42071

722 Marvin S. Corwin Scholarship

AMOUNT: None Specified   DEADLINE: Mar 1
FIELDS/MAJORS: Communications

Scholarships for Jewish men and women living in the Chicago metropolitan area who are identified as having promise for significant contributions in their chosen careers and are in need of financial assistance for full-time academic programs in one of the above fields. Must be above the junior level of study at the University of Illinois, Urbana. Write to the address below after Dec 1 for details.

Jewish Vocational Service
Attn: Scholarship Secretary
One South Franklin Street
Chicago, IL   60606

723 Mary Alice Strom-Zonta Club Scholarship

AMOUNT: Maximum: $1200   DEADLINE: Apr 1
FIELDS/MAJORS: Business

Open to female students who are residents of the Grand Traverse area and are enrolled in a business program. Contact the address listed for further information.

Northwestern Michigan College
Financial Aid Office, Admin. Bldg. #142
1701 E. Front St.
Traverse City, MI   49684

724 Mary Ann Phelps Knowles Scholarship

AMOUNT: $500   DEADLINE: Apr 1
FIELDS/MAJORS: Engineering

Scholarships are available at the University of Oklahoma, Norman for full-time female engineering majors who are juniors or above. Up to five awards are offered annually. Write to the address below for information.

University of Oklahoma, Norman
College of Engineering
Room 107, CEC
Norman, OK   73019

725
Mary Arden Scholarships

AMOUNT: $200-$1000   DEADLINE: Mar 31
FIELDS/MAJORS: English

Open to women who are junior or senior level English majors. Must have a minimum GPA of 3.0. Contact the address below for further information.

University of North Texas
Scholarship Office
Marquis Hall #218
Denton, TX   76203

726
Mary Clarke Miley Scholarships

AMOUNT: $500-$1000   DEADLINE: Mar 1
FIELDS/MAJORS: Art, Dance, Drama, Music

Scholarships are available at the University of Oklahoma, Norman for fine arts majors who are of African-American or Native American heritage. Two to four awards offered annually. Write to the address below for information.

University of Oklahoma, Norman
Dean, College of Fine Arts
540 Parrington, Room 122
Norman, OK   73019

727
Mary Katona Scholarship

AMOUNT: $500-$1000   DEADLINE: Nov 30
FIELDS/MAJORS: All Areas of Study

Scholarships are available for Connecticut resident students enrolled in or planning to enroll in an accredited college or university, who are of Hungarian descent. Based on academic ability, financial need, participation in community activities, and affiliation with Hungarian-American organizations. Must be age thirty or younger. Write to the address below for information.

American Hungarian Heritage Association
Ms. Bette S. Johnson
245 Unquowa Road, #107
Fairfield, CT   06430

728
Mary Lu Hurd Marun Memorial Scholarship

AMOUNT: $500   DEADLINE: None Specified
FIELDS/MAJORS: Physical Education, Nursing

Award for a woman student majoring in physical education or nursing with a GPA of at least 2.75. Must be a western slope resident, junior, senior status, and a full-time student. Preference given to a women pursuing a P.E. teaching degree. Write to the address below for more information.

Mesa State College
Office of Financial Aid
PO Box 2647
Grand Junction, CO   81501

729
Mary Margaret Long Hickman Scholarship

AMOUNT: $450   DEADLINE: None Specified
FIELDS/MAJORS: History

Student must be enrolled half time as a history major and plan to be a teacher. Must have a GPA of 3.0 or better. Preference is given to women over thirty years of age who are returning to school. Contact the history department for more information.

Southwest Missouri State University
Office of Financial Aid
901 South National Ave.
Springfield, MO   65804

730
Mary McEwen Schimke Scholarship

AMOUNT: Maximum: $1000   DEADLINE: Dec 16
FIELDS/MAJORS: Literature, History

Scholarship for women studying on the graduate level. The purpose of the award is to provide relief from household and child care while studying. Based on scholarly expectation and identified need. Must be over thirty years of age. Preference is given to American Studies. Candidates may have graduated from any American institution. Contact the address below for further information.

Wellesley College
Sec'y, Committee on Graduate Fellowships
106 Central St., Career Center
Wellesley, MA   02181

731
Mary Rait American Association of University Women Grant (AAUW)

AMOUNT: None Specified   DEADLINE: None Specified
FIELDS/MAJORS: All Areas of Study

Award for a mature woman returning to Mesa State for her bachelor's degree after some years of absence from the academic scene. Contact the American Association of University Women for more details.

Mesa State College
Office of Financial Aid
PO Box 3692
Grand Junction, CO   81501

732
Mary S. Stotler Scholarship

AMOUNT: $1000   DEADLINE: Mar 1
FIELDS/MAJORS: All Areas of Study

Scholarships are available at the University of Oklahoma, Norman for female students of sophomore status or above. Requires a minimum GPA of at least 3.25. Two or three awards offered annually. Write to the address below for information.

University of Oklahoma, Norman
Office of Financial Aid Services
731 Elm
Norman, OK   73019

733 Mary Stewart Memorial Scholarship

AMOUNT: None Specified   DEADLINE: Feb 15
FIELDS/MAJORS: Sports, Dance, or Recreation

Awarded annually to senior undergraduate women active in sports, dance, or recreation. Write to the address below for more information.

Black Hills State University
1200 University St.
Spearfish, SD   57783

734 Mary W. Moore Scholarship

AMOUNT: $500
DEADLINE: None Specified
FIELDS/MAJORS: Mathematics

Awards for female students majoring in the field of mathematics. Must have a GPA of 3.5. Contact the School of Natural Sciences and Mathematics for more information.

Mesa State College
Financial Aid Office
PO Box 2647
Grand Junction, CO   81501

735 Masonic Scholarships

AMOUNT: None Specified   DEADLINE: Mar 1
FIELDS/MAJORS: All Areas of Study

Awards are available at the University of New Mexico for Masons who are Albuquerque residents. Contact: 3801 Osuna Blvd. NE, Albuquerque, NM, 87109 for more details.

University of New Mexico, Albuquerque
Office of Financial Aid
Albuquerque, NM   87131

736 Mathilda Goldsmith Scholarship

AMOUNT: $1000   DEADLINE: None Specified
FIELDS/MAJORS: All Areas of Studies

Award for women who are returning to college after a significant interruption in their studies. Must be Oregon residents with a GPA of at least 3.0. One award offered annually. Contact the Department of Women's Studies for more information.

Portland State University
Department of Women's Studies
PO Box 751
Portland, OR   97207

737 Maureen E. Nolan-Cahill Memorial Scholarship

AMOUNT: None Specified
DEADLINE: None Specified
FIELDS/MAJORS: Science, Biological Science, Biology, Health Science, Chemistry, Physics

Applicants must be female students majoring in science, (biological science, biology, health science, chemistry, physics) with a GPA of at least 3.0. Applicants must demonstrate financial need. Preference will first be given to applicants who are residents of Southeast Alaska and next to graduates of Alaskan high schools. Write to the address below for more information.

University of Alaska Southeast (Juneau Campus)
Financial Aid Office
11120 Glacier Highway
Juneau, AK   99801

738 May Company Scholarship

AMOUNT: None Specified
DEADLINE: None Specified
FIELDS/MAJORS: Marketing

Awards for students of color in their sophomore, junior, or senior year. Based on financial need and strong academic performance. Applications for School of Management scholarships will be available in the SOM Development Office, Room 206.

University of Massachusetts, Amherst
School of Management
SOM Development Office, Room 206
Amherst, MA   01003

739 MBA Scholarships

AMOUNT: $2500-$10000   DEADLINE: Mar 31
FIELDS/MAJORS: All Areas of Business

Awards for minority students who are enrolled in full-time graduate or doctoral business programs. Based on financial need, activities, and GPA. Write to the address below for more information.

National Black MBA Association, Inc.
180 N. Michigan Ave.
Suite 1515
Chicago, IL   60601

740
MBNA Scholarship Program

AMOUNT: $1000   DEADLINE: Jul 15
FIELDS/MAJORS: Automotive Technology

Awards for minority high school graduates who have successfully completed at least two years in the high school auto mechanic program or have aspirations to pursue a career in the automotive industry. For students in the Chicago metropolitan area with a GPA of 2.5 or greater. Write to the address below for more information.

Mercedes-Benz of North America
Ms. Gina Blake, Chicago Urban League
4510 South Michigan Ave.
Chicago, IL   60653

741
MCI Scholarship

AMOUNT: $500
DEADLINE: None Specified
FIELDS/MAJORS: Computer Science

Open to minority students who are economically disadvantaged. Must have a minimum GPA of 3.0 overall and a 3.5 in their major courses. Four awards are given annually. Contact the address below for further information.

University of Colorado—Colorado Springs
Office of Financial Aid
1420 Austin Bluffs Pkwy., PO Box 7150
Colorado Springs, CO   80907

742
McKnight Black Doctoral Fellowship Program

AMOUNT: Maximum: $5000   DEADLINE: Jan 15
FIELDS/MAJORS: See Below

Fellowships for African-American doctoral students at participating Florida universities. For areas of study except: M.D., D.B.A., D.D.S., J.D. or D.V.M. The applicant must be a U.S. citizen. Write to the address below for details, or contact the academic department heads of your school.

Florida Endowment Fund for Higher Education
201 E. Kennedy Blvd., Suite 1525
Tampa, FL   33602

743
McMurry United Methodist Scholarship

AMOUNT: $1000   DEADLINE: Mar 15
FIELDS/MAJORS: All Areas of Study

Awards for entering freshmen at McMurry who are recommended by their church in the northwest Texas or New Mexico Conferences and are in the top 50% of their graduating high school class. For full-time study. Write to the address below for more information.

McMurry University
Box 908 McMurry Station
Abilene, TX   79697

744
Mecha-Latino Student Union Scholarship

AMOUNT: Maximum: $600   DEADLINE: Apr 1
FIELDS/MAJORS: All Areas of Study

Awards open to Hispanic undergraduate students who can demonstrate financial need. Must be a resident of Ohio. Contact the address below for further information.

University of Toledo
Office of Student Financial Aid
4023 Gillham Hall
Toledo, OH   43606

745
Mechanical Engineering Minorities/Women Scholarships

AMOUNT: None Specified
DEADLINE: None Specified
FIELDS/MAJORS: Mechanical Engineering

Open to minority and women students seeking a degree in mechanical engineering. Based on financial need and merit. Write to the address listed for further information.

Georgia Institute of Technology
Financial Aid Office
225 North Ave.
Atlanta, GA   30332

746
Medgar Evers/James Chaney Scholarships

AMOUNT: None Specified   DEADLINE: Dec 1
FIELDS/MAJORS: All Areas of Study

Awarded for two years in alternating years to minority students with high academic achievement from high school. Write to the address listed for more information.

Spalding University
Financial Aid Office
851 S. Fourth St.
Louisville, KY   40203

747
Megan E. Taylor Memorial Scholarship Fund

AMOUNT: None Specified   DEADLINE: None Specified
FIELDS/MAJORS: All Areas of Study

Scholarships are available to graduating females at Shawnee Mission South High School. Must be in the top one-third of class and be able to demonstrate financial need. Contact the Shawnee Mission South High School Counselor for further information.

Greater Kansas City Community Foundation and Affiliated Trusts
1055 Broadway #130
Kansas City, MO   64105

748 Meier & Frank, May Company Scholarship

AMOUNT: $1000   DEADLINE: None Specified
FIELDS/MAJORS: Business, Liberal Arts

Awards are available at Portland State University for minority students who are majoring in business or the liberal arts. Must be a U.S. citizen or resident alien to apply. Three awards offered annually. Write to the address below for more information.

Portland State University
Educational Equity Programs and Services
120 Smith Memorial Center
Portland, OR   97207

749 Melanie Feinstein Memorial Scholarship

AMOUNT: None Specified   DEADLINE: Mar 1
FIELDS/MAJORS: Dance

Award open to U.S. citizens to increase ethnic diversity in dance. Contact the address below for further information.

University of North Carolina, Greensboro
Financial Aid Office
723 Kenilworth St.
Greensboro, NC   27412

750 Melva T. Owen Memorial Scholarship

AMOUNT: $3000   DEADLINE: Mar 1
FIELDS/MAJORS: All Areas of Study

Scholarship for an entering freshman. Must be legally blind. Three awards offered annually. Write to the address below for details.

American Council of the Blind
Scholarship Coordinator
1155 15th St., NW, Suite 720
Washington, D.C.   20005

751 Memorial Education Fellowship

AMOUNT: $2000   DEADLINE: Mar 1
FIELDS/MAJORS: Varies

Applicants must be women maintaining legal residence in Massachusetts for at least five years and must present a letter of endorsement from the sponsoring Women's Club in your community. These awards are for graduate study. Write to the address below for details, be sure to include a SASE.

General Federation of Women's Clubs of Massachusetts
Chairman of Trustees, 245 Dutton Road
PO Box 679
Sudbury, MA   01776

752 Mental Health Minority Research Fellowship Program

AMOUNT: None Specified   DEADLINE: Feb 28
FIELDS/MAJORS: Mental Health Research

Awards for minorities who have a master's degree in social work and will begin full-time study leading to a doctoral degree or are already in a doctoral social work program. Applicants must be U.S. citizens or permanent residents and be pursuing a career in mental health research. Write to the address below for more information.

National Institute of Mental Health
1600 Duke St. #300
Alexandria, VA   22314

753 Mental Retardation Scholastic Achievement Scholarship

AMOUNT: $1000   DEADLINE: Mar 15
FIELDS/MAJORS: Mental Retardation (Special Education, Mental Health)

Scholarships for juniors and seniors who are communicant members of a Lutheran congregation and working toward a career in the field of mental retardation. Must have a GPA of at least 3.0. Write to the address below for details.

Bethesda Lutheran Homes and Services, Inc.
National Christian Resource Center
700 Hoffmann Drive
Watertown, WI   53094

754 Mentor Graphics Scholarship

AMOUNT: None Specified
DEADLINE: None Specified
FIELDS/MAJORS: Computer Science, Computer Engineering, Electrical Engineering

Open to Oregon residents who are U.S. citizens and entering junior or senior year at a four-year school. Preference to a female African or Hispanic-American. Recipients may reapply and compete annually. Contact the address below for further information.

Oregon State Scholarship Commission
Private Awards
1500 Valley River Dr. #100
Eugene, OR   97401-2130

755
MESBEC and NALE Programs

AMOUNT: None Specified   DEADLINE: Sep 15
FIELDS/MAJORS: All Areas of Study

Grants, loans, or combination awards awarded competitively to students who are at least 1/4 degree Native American. GPA of at least 3.0 required. Based on goals and potential for improving the lives of Indian peoples. For undergraduate or graduate study at any accredited college or university in the United States. Must have financial need and attend school full-time. Write to the address below for details.

Native American Scholarship Fund
Scholarship Programs
8200 Mountain Rd NE, Ste 203
Albuquerque, NM   87110

756
Methodist Ministerial Scholarships

AMOUNT: $8550   DEADLINE: None Specified
FIELDS/MAJORS: All Areas of Study

Awards are available at Emory University for children of active Methodist ministers or missionaries. Write to the address below for information.

Emory University
Office of Financial Aid
300 Boisfeuillet Jones Center
Atlanta, GA   30322

757
Metropolitan Life Foundation Program for Excellence in Medicine

AMOUNT: $2500   DEADLINE: None Specified
FIELDS/MAJORS: Medicine

Awards for minority students from Los Angeles, San Francisco, CA; Denver, CO; Tampa, FL; Atlanta, GA; Chicago/Aurora, IL; Wichita, KS; New York, NY; Tulsa, OK; Pittsburgh, Scranton, PA; Warwick/Providence, RI; Greenville, SC; or Houston, TX, in their second or third year of medicine. Based on academics, leadership, and potential for contributions in medicine. Send a SASE to the address below for more information.

National Medical Fellowships, Inc.
110 West 32nd
8th Floor
New York, NY   10001

758
Mexican-American Grocers Association Scholarships

AMOUNT: None Specified   DEADLINE: Jul 31
FIELDS/MAJORS: Business

Open to sophomore or above college students of Hispanic descent studying a business related field. Must show financial need. Renewable. Must have a GPA of at least 2.5. Write to the address below for more details. You must include a SASE for a reply.

Mexican American Grocers Association
Ms. Rosemarie Vega
405 N. San Fernando Rd.
Los Angeles, CA   90031

759
Mexican-American Women's National Association Scholarships

AMOUNT: None Specified   DEADLINE: Mar 1
FIELDS/MAJORS: All Areas of Study

Awards are available at the University of New Mexico for Hispanic women at any level of study. Contact Mana DE Albuquerque, 1923 Maderia NE, Albuquerque, NM 87110.

University of New Mexico, Albuquerque
Office of Financial Aid
Albuquerque, NM   87131

760
Michael D. Coffey— Northeast Utilities Scholarship

AMOUNT: None Specified   DEADLINE: Mar 1
FIELDS/MAJORS: Engineering

Awards for female sophomores, juniors, or seniors enrolled full time. Must have a GPA of 2.5 or better (2.0 in major) and demonstrate financial need. Contact the director of recruitment, Marston Hall for more information.

University of Massachusetts, Amherst
Director, Recruitment
Marston Hall
Amherst, MA   01003

761
Michael Joseph Glad Scholarship

AMOUNT: None Specified   DEADLINE: None Specified
FIELDS/MAJORS: All Areas of Study

Open to enrolled students at Georgia Tech who are hearing impaired. Recipients selected by the Office of Student Financial Planning and Services. Write to the address listed for further information.

Georgia Institute of Technology
Financial Aid Office
225 North Ave.
Atlanta, GA   30332

762
Michael Reese Women's Board Scholarship

AMOUNT: None Specified   DEADLINE: Mar 1
FIELDS/MAJORS: Medicine

Open to women medical students who have completed at least one year of medical school, accredited by the American Medical Association, with a minimum GPA of 3.0. Must be legally domiciled in Cook County or the Chicago metro area. Information and applications available after Dec 1 from the address below.

Jewish Vocational Service
Academic Scholarship Program
1 S. Franklin St.
Chicago, IL   60606

763
Midway Scholarships and Grants

AMOUNT: None Specified   DEADLINE: None Specified
FIELDS/MAJORS: All Areas of Study

Scholarships and grants for women accepted to or enrolled at Midway College. Awards are based on merit, need or a combination of both. The forty-seven scholarships and grants will also vary in their main concern, (i.e., specific majors, specific sports, membership in organizations). Contact the financial aid office at the address listed for details.

Midway College
Financial Aid Office
512 E. Stephens St.
Midway, KY   40347-1120

764
Mike Hampton Native American Scholarship

AMOUNT: $1293   DEADLINE: Mar 1
FIELDS/MAJORS: All Areas of Study

Open to Native American adult students returning to school in both undergraduate and graduate programs. Must demonstrate financial need. Contact the address below for further information.

University of Wyoming
Office of Student Financial Aid
Box 3335 University Station
Laramie, WY   82071

765
Minister's Dependent Grant

AMOUNT: Maximum: $1000   DEADLINE: None Specified
FIELDS/MAJORS: All Areas of Study

Awards for students who are dependents of full-time Southern Baptist Ministers. Renewable for three additional years. Contact the address below for further information.

Carson-Newman College
Office of Financial Aid
Jefferson City, TN   37760

766
Minister's Kin Scholarship

AMOUNT: $500-$800   DEADLINE: None Specified
FIELDS/MAJORS: All Areas of Study

Awards for dependents or spouses of Ministers engaged in full-time service within the Southern Baptist Convention as a Pastor; Minister of Education, Music, Children, or Youth; Chaplain; Missionary appointed by the Southern Baptist Home Mission Board or Foreign Mission Board; or denominational employee engaged in a full-time vocational ministry. Write to the address below for more information. Recipients of the CRV award are ineligible to receive the Minister's Kin Scholarship.

California Baptist College
8432 Magnolia Ave.
Riverside, CA   92504

767
Ministerial Education Scholarship

AMOUNT: None Specified
DEADLINE: None Specified
FIELDS/MAJORS: Theology, Ministerial

Awards for members of a Unitarian Universalist congregation enrolled full time in a master's of divinity degree leading to ordination as a UU minister. Write to the address below for more information.

Unitarian Universalist Association of Congregations
Office of Ministerial Education
25 Beacon St.
Boston, MA   02108

768
Minna Kaufmann Ruud Fund

AMOUNT: $3500   DEADLINE: Jan 30
FIELDS/MAJORS: Vocal Music

Scholarships for promising female singers at Chatham College. One award is given annually. Contact the Dean of Admissions address below for details.

Chatham College
Office of Admissions
Woodland Rd.
Pittsburgh, PA   15232

769
Minnesota Hispanic Education Program Scholarship

AMOUNT: None Specified   DEADLINE: None Specified
FIELDS/MAJORS: All Areas of Study

Awards open to students with Hispanic heritage. Must be U.S. citizens or permanent residents, residents of Minnesota, and attending school full time. Contact the address below for further information.

University of Minnesota, Duluth
Susana Pelayo-Woodward, Stu. Svc. Coord.
138 Library
Duluth, MN   55812

770 Minnesota Indian Scholarship Program

AMOUNT: None Specified   DEADLINE: None Specified
FIELDS/MAJORS: All Areas of Study

Scholarship for Minnesota residents who are one-fourth or more Indian ancestry. Applicants must be a member of a federally recognized Indian tribe or eligible for enrollment in a tribe. For full-time study in Minnesota. Contact your tribal education office, the Minnesota Indian Scholarship Program or write to the address below for details.

Minnesota Higher Education Coordinating Board
c/o Joe Aitken, Indian Education
1819 Bemidji Avenue
Bemidji, MN   56601

771 Minnie Pearl Scholarship Program

AMOUNT: $2000-$2500   DEADLINE: Feb 15
FIELDS/MAJORS: All Areas of Study

Scholarships for current high school seniors with significant bilateral hearing loss (must be mainstreamed) who have been accepted, but not yet in attendance, at a junior college, college, university, or technical school. Must be a U.S. citizen and have a GPA of at least 3.0. Renewable with GPA of 3.0 ($500 renewal bonus with 3.5 GPA). Write to the address below for further information.

Ear Foundation at Baptist Hospital
Minnie Pearl Scholarship Program
1817 Patterson St.
Nashville, TN   37203

772 Minorities and Women Scholarship

AMOUNT: None Specified
DEADLINE: None Specified
FIELDS/MAJORS: Engineering

Open to deserving women and minority students who have good academic standing and can demonstrate financial need. Recipients chosen by the Office of Student Financial Planning and Services. Write to the address listed for further information.

Georgia Institute of Technology
Financial Aid Office
225 North Ave.
Atlanta, GA   30332

773 Minorities in Government Finance Scholarship

AMOUNT: $3500   DEADLINE: Feb 14
FIELDS/MAJORS: Business or Political Science

Scholarship for minority undergraduate or graduate students in the above areas planning to pursue a career in state or local government finance. For full or part-time study. Must be a U.S. or Canadian citizen or permanent resident. Information may be available from the head of your accounting department. If not, write to the address below.

Government Finance Officers Association
Scholarship Committee
180 N. Michigan Avenue, Suite 800
Chicago, IL   60601

774 Minority Achievement Scholarships

AMOUNT: $4000-$30000   DEADLINE: Jan 15
FIELDS/MAJORS: All Areas of Study

For high school seniors who are in the top 25% of class with a minimum GPA of 3.4, a minimum ACT of 24 or SAT of 1100. An essay and interview will be required. Contact the financial aid office at the address below for details.

Bellarmine College
Financial Aid Office
2001 Newburg Road
Louisville, KY   40205

775 Minority Affairs Graduate Program

AMOUNT: None Specified   DEADLINE: Mar 15
FIELDS/MAJORS: All Areas of Study

Awards open to minority students accepted into the graduate school of the University of Wyoming. Must be a U.S. citizen attending school full-time. Contact the address below for further information.

University of Wyoming
Director MAGP
PO Box 3808
Laramie, WY   82071

776 Minority Alumni Affiliate Scholarship

AMOUNT: $500   DEADLINE: Apr 1
FIELDS/MAJORS: All Areas of Study

Awards open to minority undergraduate students who can demonstrate financial need. For full or part-time study. Must have a minimum GPA of 2.5. Four awards offered annually. Contact the address below for further information.

University of Toledo
Office of Student Financial Aid
4023 Gillham Hall
Toledo, OH   43606

777
Minority American Science Scholarship

AMOUNT: None Specified
DEADLINE: None Specified
FIELDS/MAJORS: Natural Science, Mathematics, Statistics, Actuarial Science

Scholarships are available at the University of Iowa for entering freshmen Hispanic, African-American, Native American or Southeast Asian students who plan to major in one of the above fields. Applicant must be a U.S. citizen with a GPA of at least 3.0. Write to the address below for information.

University of Iowa
Office of Student Financial Aid
208 Calvin Hall
Iowa City, IA   52242

778
Minority Dental Laboratory Technician Scholarship

AMOUNT: $1000   DEADLINE: Aug 15
FIELDS/MAJORS: Dental Laboratory Technology

Applicants must be U.S. citizens and enrolled or planning to enroll in a dental lab technology program accredited by the Commission on Accreditation of the American Dental Association. Students must have a minimum GPA of 2.8 and demonstrate financial need. These awards are for minority students. Write to the address below for details.

ADA Endowment and Assistance Fund, Inc.
211 East Chicago Avenue
Chicago, IL   60611

779
Minority Dental Student Scholarship Program

AMOUNT: $2000   DEADLINE: Jul 1
FIELDS/MAJORS: Dentistry

Awards for African-American, Hispanic, or Native American students entering their second year of a dental school accredited by the Commission on Dental Accreditation. Must demonstrate financial need and have a GPA of at least 2.5. Must be a U.S. citizen. Contact your school's financial aid office for more information.

ADA Endowment and Assistance Fund, Inc.
211 East Chicago Ave.
Chicago, IL   60611

780
Minority Doctoral Assistance Loan-for-Service Program

AMOUNT: Maximum: $25000   DEADLINE: Jan 1
FIELDS/MAJORS: Most Areas of Study

Awards for minority doctoral students who attend a New Mexico institution and who are also New Mexico residents. Must be U.S. citizens or permanent residents and enrolled in full-time study. Women are considered a minority for this award. Contact the graduate dean of your four-year public institution in New Mexico.

New Mexico Commission on Higher Education
Financial Aid and Student Services
PO Box 15910
Santa Fe, NM   87506

781
Minority Doctoral Study Grant Program

AMOUNT: $6000   DEADLINE: None Specified
FIELDS/MAJORS: All Areas of Study

Grants are available for minority doctoral candidates studying at Oklahoma institutions. This program was created as an incentive to increase the number of minority faculty and staff in the Oklahoma state system of higher education. Recipients must agree to teach in a state system institution two years for each year of aid. Must be an Oklahoma resident. Write to the address below for information.

Oklahoma State Regents for Higher Education
State Capitol Complex
500 Education Building
Oklahoma City, OK   73105

782
Minority Educational Opportunity Housing Scholarship

AMOUNT: $1320   DEADLINE: Feb 1
FIELDS/MAJORS: All Areas of Study

Awards for entering minority freshmen and current undergraduates who are U.S. citizens or permanent residents. Based on academics, references, and rank in graduating class. Contact the address below for further information.

Northern Kentucky University
Office of Financial Aid-Nunn Dr.
Administrative Center #416
Highland Heights, KY   41099

783
Minority Educational Opportunity Tuition Scholarship

AMOUNT: $1410   DEADLINE: Feb 1
FIELDS/MAJORS: All Areas of Study

Awards for entering minority freshmen and current undergraduates who are U.S. citizens or permanent residents. Based on academics, references, and rank in graduating class. Contact the address below for further information.

Northern Kentucky University
Office of Financial Aid-Nunn Dr.
Administrative Center #416
Highland Heights, KY   41099

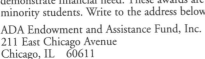

784 Minority Educator Scholarship

AMOUNT: None Specified
DEADLINE: Feb 1
FIELDS/MAJORS: Education

Awards for minority students who are U.S. citizens and Kentucky residents. Must have a minimum GPA of 2.5 and be pursuing a teaching certificate. Must agree to give one semester of teaching service for each semester scholarship was received. Contact the School of Education for further information.

Northern Kentucky University
Financial Aid Office-Nunn Dr.
Administrative Center #416
Highland Heights, KY 41099

785 Minority Engineering Program Awards

AMOUNT: $500-$8500 DEADLINE: Dec 31
FIELDS/MAJORS: Engineering

Scholarships for entering minority freshmen or minority transfer students, minority being defined as Native American, African-American, or Hispanic-American. Based on academics and professional interest. Must be a U.S. citizen. Contact the address below for further information.

University of Missouri—Rolla
106 Parker Hall
Rolla, MO 65401

786 Minority Engineering Scholarships

AMOUNT: $500-$2000
DEADLINE: None Specified
FIELDS/MAJORS: Engineering

Scholarships are available at the University of Oklahoma, Norman for full-time engineering majors who are African/Hispanic/Native Americans. Write to the address below for information.

University of Oklahoma, Norman
Director, Minority Engineering Programs
865 Asp Ave. Fh Room 221
Norman, OK 73019

787 Minority Engineering Scholarships

AMOUNT: None Specified DEADLINE: Mar 1
FIELDS/MAJORS: Engineering

Open to high school seniors who are any of the following: African-American, Native American, Mexican-American, Puerto Rican, Alaskan Native or Native Pacific Islander. Grants and research opportunities available. Financial need is considered. Contact the address below for further information.

Marquette University
Office of Admissions
1217 W. Wisconsin Ave.
Milwaukee, WI 53233

788 Minority Fellowship Program

AMOUNT: $8340-$10008 DEADLINE: Jan 15
FIELDS/MAJORS: Psychology

Fellowships for ethnic minority students pursuing doctoral degrees in APA accredited doctoral programs in psychology. Must be a U.S. citizen or a permanent resident. Applicants must be in at least their second year of training. Fellowships are from ten to twelve months with a stipend of $834 per month. Write to the address below for more information.

American Psychological Association
Minority Fellowship Program
750 First St., NE
Washington, D.C. 20002

789 Minority Fellowship Program

AMOUNT: None Specified
DEADLINE: None Specified
FIELDS/MAJORS: Psychiatry

Fellowships for psychiatric minority residents in their PGY-II year or residency. Must be U.S. citizens. Write to the address below for more information.

American Psychiatric Association
Office of Minority/National Affairs
1400 K. St., NW
Washington, D.C. 20005

790 Minority Fellowships

AMOUNT: $7800 DEADLINE: None Specified
FIELDS/MAJORS: Human Resource Management, Industrial Relations

Open to full-time minority students who are pursuing graduate degrees in Human Resource Management/Industrial Relations at one of thirteen consortium graduate schools. Must be a U.S. citizen. Write to the address below for more information.

Industrial Relations Council on Goals
PO Box 4363
East Lansing, MI 48826

791 Minority Foundation Scholarship

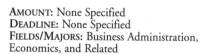

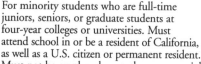

AMOUNT: None Specified
DEADLINE: None Specified
FIELDS/MAJORS: Business Administration, Economics, and Related

For minority students who are full-time juniors, seniors, or graduate students at four-year colleges or universities. Must attend school in or be a resident of California, as well as a U.S. citizen or permanent resident. Must not be employed more than twenty-eight hours per week, and must maintain GPA of at least 3.0. Contact your financial aid office or write to address below for details. If writing, please be certain to enclose a SASE with your request for information. Applications for Southern California residents are available from Feb 1 to Apr 1.

Golden State Minority Foundation
1055 Wilshire Blvd.
Suite 1115
Los Angeles, CA   90017

792
Minority Graduate Emergency Aid Fund

AMOUNT: Maximum: $1000   **DEADLINE:** None Specified
FIELDS/MAJORS: All Areas of Study

Awards are available at Portland State University for minority graduate students who find themselves in short-term straitened circumstances. Contact the Office of Graduate Studies and Research for more information.

Portland State University
Office of Graduate Studies and Research
105 Neuberger Hall
Portland, OR   97207

793
Minority Internship Program

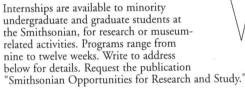

AMOUNT: $2475-$3300
DEADLINE: Feb 15
FIELDS/MAJORS: Humanities, Art Studies, Anthropology, Astrophysics, Biology, History

Internships are available to minority undergraduate and graduate students at the Smithsonian, for research or museum-related activities. Programs range from nine to twelve weeks. Write to address below for details. Request the publication "Smithsonian Opportunities for Research and Study."

Smithsonian Institution
Office of Fellowships and Grants
955 L'enfant Plaza, Suite 7000
Washington, D.C.   20560

794
Minority Leadership Awards at St. Mary of the Woods

AMOUNT: $500-$2000   **DEADLINE:** Aug 1
FIELDS/MAJORS: All Areas of Study

Grants for minority students at St. Mary of the Woods College. Need based. Minority here is defined as African, Hispanic, Asian, or Native American. Fifty to one hundred awards are offered annually. Write to the address below for details.

St. Mary of the Woods College
Office of Admissions and Financial Aid
Guerin Hall
St. Mary of the Woods, IN   47876

795
Minority Leadership Scholarship

AMOUNT: $2758   **DEADLINE:** Mar 1
FIELDS/MAJORS: All Areas of Study

Awards for entering minority SMSU students who are graduating in the upper 50% of their class and have demonstrated leadership in the minority community through involvement in various school and civic organizations. Forty awards are offered annually. Write to the address below for more details.

Southwest Missouri State University
Financial Aid Office
901 South National Ave.
Springfield, MO   65804

796
Minority Management Education Program Scholarships

AMOUNT: None Specified   **DEADLINE:** None Specified
FIELDS/MAJORS: Management

Awards for students of color for improvement, academic excellence, and leadership in the field of management. For students in their sophomore, junior or senior year. Applications for School of Management scholarships will be available in the SOM Development Office, Room 206.

University of Massachusetts, Amherst
School of Management
SOM Development Office, Room 206
Amherst, MA   01003

797
Minority Master's Fellows Loan Program

AMOUNT: $2500-$7500   **DEADLINE:** Jun 1
FIELDS/MAJORS: Mathematics, Science, Foreign Languages, Education

African-American students who are admitted to a master's program in mathematics, the sciences, or foreign languages or to African-American students in the fifth year of a teacher education program, who were recipients of the minority teacher scholarship. Students must be full time during fall/spring; can go part time for three summers. Recipients are required to teach full time in an Arkansas public school or institution for two years to receive total forgiveness of the loan. Write to the address below for more information.

Arkansas Department of Higher Education
Financial Aid Division
114 East Capitol
Little Rock, AR   72201

798
Minority Medical Faculty Development Program

AMOUNT: $75000 DEADLINE: Mar 28
FIELDS/MAJORS: Medicine/Education

Applicants must be minority physicians who are U.S. citizens, have excelled in their education, are now completing or will have completed formal clinical training, and are committed to academic careers. Minorities here are African and Mexican-Americans, Native Americans, and mainland Puerto Ricans who have completed college on the mainland. Fellowships aid research and last four years. Write to the address below for additional information.

Robert Wood Johnson Foundation
James R. Gavin III, M.D, Ph.D., Program
4733 Bethesda Ave, Ste 350
Bethesda, MD   20814

799
Minority Presence Fellowship

AMOUNT: $4000 DEADLINE: Mar 1
FIELDS/MAJORS: All Areas of Study

Award open to doctoral candidates who are African-American, U.S. citizens, North Carolina residents, and attending school full-time. Must be able to demonstrate financial need. Contact the address below for further information.

University of North Carolina, Greensboro
Financial Aid Office
723 Kenilworth St.
Greensboro, NC   27412

800
Minority Presence Fellowship

AMOUNT: $4000 DEADLINE: Mar 1
FIELDS/MAJORS: All Areas of Study

Award open to full-time graduate students who are African-American, U.S. citizens, and residents of North Carolina. Must be able to demonstrate financial need. Contact the address below for further information.

University of North Carolina, Greensboro
Financial Aid Office
723 Kenilworth St.
Greensboro, NC   27412

801
Minority Presence Grant

AMOUNT: None Specified DEADLINE: None Specified
FIELDS/MAJORS: All Areas of Study

Scholarships are available to minority North Carolina undergraduates who demonstrate financial need. For use at one of the sixteen North Carolina constituent institutions. Contact the financial aid office for information.

North Carolina State Education Assistance Authority
PO Box 2688
Chapel Hill, NC   27515

802
Minority Presence Grant Program I

AMOUNT: None Specified DEADLINE: Mar 1
FIELDS/MAJORS: All Areas of Study

Award open to incoming African-American full-time freshmen who are residents of North Carolina and can demonstrate financial need. May not have already earned a bachelor's degree. Contact the address below for further information.

University of North Carolina, Greensboro
Financial Aid Office
723 Kenilworth St.
Greensboro, NC   27412

803
Minority Presence Grant Program II

AMOUNT: None Specified DEADLINE: Mar 1
FIELDS/MAJORS: All Areas of Study

Award open to incoming full-time Freshmen who are Hispanic or Asiatic Americans. Must be North Carolina residents and be able to demonstrate financial need. May not have already earned a bachelor's degree. Contact the address below for further information.

University of North Carolina, Greensboro
Financial Aid Office
723 Kenilworth St.
Greensboro, NC   27412

804
Minority Professional Study Grant Program

AMOUNT: $4000 DEADLINE: None Specified
FIELDS/MAJORS: Medicine, Dentistry, Law, Veterinary Medicine, Optometry

Grants are available for minority students studying at Oklahoma institutions. This program was created as an incentive to increase the number of minority groups in the programs listed above. Must be a U.S. citizen. Write to the address below for information.

Oklahoma State Regents for Higher Education
State Capitol Complex
500 Education Building
Oklahoma City, OK   73105

805
Minority Scholars Program Fellowship

AMOUNT: Maximum: $13000 DEADLINE: None Specified
FIELDS/MAJORS: All Areas of Study

Programs for African-American, Hispanic-American, and Native American graduate students at Pennsylvania State. Based on academic excellence. Twenty fellowships and sixty assistantships are available. Contact the address below for further information.

Pennsylvania State University
Fellowships and Awards Office
313 Kern Graduate Building
University Park, PA   16802

806

Minority Scholars Program

AMOUNT: None Specified   DEADLINE: Feb 1
FIELDS/MAJORS: All Areas of Study

The minority scholars program is a program of career counseling, academic preparation, internships, and mentoring for selected minority students from underrepresented groups. Students must be entering as freshmen at Case Western Reserve University. Write to the address below for details.

Case Western Reserve University
Office of Financial Aid, 109 Pardee Hall
10900 Euclid Avenue
Cleveland, OH   44106

807

Minority Scholarship

AMOUNT: $1000   DEADLINE: Apr 11
FIELDS/MAJORS: Broadcasting, Journalism, Advertising, Communications (Graphic Etc.)

Applicants must be minorities and residents of the following California counties: Santa Cruz, Santa Clara, Monterey, or San Benito. Must be enrolled at or accepted into an accredited California school studying a field related to broadcasting. Write to the address below for details.

KNTV Channel 11
Scholarship Board
645 Park Ave.
San Jose, CA   95110

808

Minority Scholarship

AMOUNT: None Specified   DEADLINE: Apr 1
FIELDS/MAJORS: Dental Hygiene

Scholarships for students of underrepresented groups who have completed at least one year of a full-time accredited program in dental hygiene. Must have a GPA of at least 3.0. Based on need and career goals. Males are also considered minorities for this award. Write to the address below for more information.

American Dental Hygienists' Association Institute for Oral Health
444 N. Michigan Ave., Suite 3400
Chicago, IL   60611

809

Minority Scholarship Program

AMOUNT: $2500   DEADLINE: Oct 15
FIELDS/MAJORS: Psychology

Award for ethnic minority students accepted into a doctoral level psychology program in the state of California. Based on community involvement, leadership, knowledge of ethnic minority/cultural issues, career plans, and financial need. Scholarships are given to students in their first year of study. Write to the address below for more information.

California Psychological Association Foundation
1010 Eleventh St.
Suite 202
Sacramento, CA   95814

810

Minority Scholarship Program

AMOUNT: Maximum: $2500   DEADLINE: Oct 15
FIELDS/MAJORS: Psychology

Scholarships open to minority students who have been accepted in a first year, full-time doctoral level psychology program in a California school. Candidates must be considered a member of one or more of these established ethnic minority groups: African/Hispanic/Latino/Asian-American, Native American, Alaskan Native, or Pacific Islander. Scholarships are not made based solely on financial need, but it is taken into account. Winners will be announced in mid-December. Information and applications are sent to the financial aid offices of California graduate schools in early summer. Get the information from that source instead of writing to the address indicated.

California State Psychological Association Foundation
CSPA Scholarship Department
1022 G Street
Sacramento, CA   95814-0817

811

Minority Scholarships

AMOUNT: $1000-$1500   DEADLINE: Apr 1
FIELDS/MAJORS: All Areas of Study

Scholarships for minority students at Kent State who have a superior academic record and are returning students or new transfer students. Must be at least a sophomore. One award offered annually. Contact the financial aid office at your campus for details.

Kent State University, Tuscarawas Campus
Financial Aid Office
University Drive, NE
New Philadelphia, OH   44663

812

Minority Scholarships

AMOUNT: $300-$1500   DEADLINE: Apr 1
FIELDS/MAJORS: All Areas of Study

Scholarships for incoming minority freshmen who have a minimum GPA of at least 2.5 and score well on standardized tests. Write to the address below for more information.

Moorhead State University
Office of Scholarship and Financial Aid
107 Owens Hall
Moorhead, MN   56563

813
Minority Scholarships

AMOUNT: $500-$2500   DEADLINE: Jan 15
FIELDS/MAJORS: Architecture

Twenty-five scholarships for minority high school seniors and college freshman who are entering degree programs at schools of architecture. Write to the address listed for more details.

American Architectural Foundation
AIA/AAF Scholarship Program Director
1735 New York Ave. NW
Washington, D.C.   20006

814
Minority Scholarships

AMOUNT: None Specified   DEADLINE: None Specified
FIELDS/MAJORS: All Areas of Study

Scholarships are available for minority residents of western North Carolina who plan to attend either the University of North Carolina at Charlotte or Winston-Salem State University. Write to the address below for information.

James G.K. McClure Educational and Development Fund, Inc.
Sugar Hollow Farm
11 Sugar Hollow Lane
Fairview, NC   28730

815
Minority Student Leadership Award

AMOUNT: Maximum: $650   DEADLINE: Mar 15
FIELDS/MAJORS: All Areas of Study

Open to admitted entering freshmen who are African-American, Native American, Asian American, Alaskan Native, or Pacific Islander. Must be Kentucky residents who have a minimum high school GPA of 2.5. Must be able to demonstrate academics and/or extracurricular activities. Contact the address below for further information.

Morehead State University
Office of Admissions
306 Howell-McDowell
Morehead, KY   40351

816
Minority Teachers of Illinois and David A. Debolt Teacher Scholarships

AMOUNT: $5000   DEADLINE: None Specified
FIELDS/MAJORS: Preschool, Elementary, Secondary Education

Scholarships open to African-American, Native American, Hispanic, or Asian students who plan to become teachers. Must be full-time undergraduates at sophomore level or above. Must sign a teaching commitment to teach one year for each year assistance is received. Must be U.S. citizens or permanent residents and Illinois residents. Contact the address below for further information about both scholarships.

Illinois Student Assistance Commission
1755 Lake Cook Road
Deerfield, IL   60015

817
Minority Teachers Scholarship

AMOUNT: $5000   DEADLINE: Jun 1
FIELDS/MAJORS: Education

African-American college juniors enrolled full time and admitted to an approved program resulting in teacher certification. Must have at least a 2.5 cumulative GPA. New awards are made to juniors only; continuing awards are made to seniors only. For Arkansas residents. Write to the address below for more information.

Arkansas Department of Higher Education
Financial Aid Division
114 East Capitol
Little Rock, AR   72201

818
Minority Teaching Fellows Program

AMOUNT: $5000   DEADLINE: Apr 15
FIELDS/MAJORS: Education

For freshmen who are Tennessee residents entering teaching education programs in Tennessee. Must have a GPA of 2.5 or better and agree to teach at a K-12 level in a Tennessee public school for one year. Contact your high school guidance office or the financial aid office for more information.

Tennessee Student Assistance Corporation
Suite 1950 Parkway Towers
404 James Robertson Parkway
Nashville, TN   37243

819
Minority/Disadvantaged Scholarship Program

AMOUNT: $500-$3000   DEADLINE: Jan 17
FIELDS/MAJORS: Architecture

Applicants must be minority and/or disadvantaged high school seniors or current freshmen who are attending or plan to attend an NAAB school. Must be able to demonstrate financial need. Must be nominated by architect, counselor, pastor, dean of architectural school, etc. Nominations are due Dec 12, and the application and other paperwork is due Jan 17. Twenty awards per year. Renewable for up to three years. Students must be U.S. citizens and have a GPA of 2.0 or above. Write to "Minority/Disadvantaged Scholarship Program" at the address below for details.

American Institute of Architects
American Architectural Foundation
1735 New York Ave., NW
Washington, D.C.   20006

820
Miss Teenage America Contest

AMOUNT: Maximum: $10000   DEADLINE: Sep 15
FIELDS/MAJORS: All Areas of Study

Scholarships are available for young women under the age of nineteen with academic ability, who are involved in school and community activities. The winner receives a $10000 scholarship, a monthly column in *Teen*, and a year of travel and public appearances. Information and applications are available in the Jun and Jul issues of *Teen*.

Teen Magazine
Peterson Publishing Company
6420 Wilshire Blvd.
Los Angeles, CA   90048

824 Mobil Oil Minority Scholarships

AMOUNT: None Specified
DEADLINE: None Specified
FIELDS/MAJORS: Chemical, Electrical, Computer, Mechanical Engineering

Open to minority students majoring in areas listed. Recipients selected by the Office of Student Financial Planning and Services. Write to the address listed for further information.

Georgia Institute of Technology
Financial Aid Office
225 North Ave.
Atlanta, GA   30332

821 Missouri Minority Teacher Education Scholarship

AMOUNT: $3000   DEADLINE: Feb 15
FIELDS/MAJORS: Math Education, Science Education

Student must be a minority who has ranked in the top 25% of his/her high school class, scored at or above the 75th percentile on the ACT or SAT exam, and entered an approved math or science teacher education program. Must be a Missouri resident. Contact the DESE for more information.

Southwest Missouri State University
Office of Financial Aid
901 South National Ave.
Springfield, MO   65804

825 Modesto Bee Minority Internship

AMOUNT: None Specified   DEADLINE: Dec 31
FIELDS/MAJORS: Journalism, Photography, Graphics

Open to minority college students focusing on journalism, photography, and graphics. Write to the address below for more information.

Modesto Bee
Sanders Lamont, Executive Editor
PO Box 5256
Modesto, CA   95352

822 Missouri Minority Teacher Education Scholarship

AMOUNT: Maximum: $3000   DEADLINE: Feb 15
FIELDS/MAJORS: Education, Math, or Science

Awards for minority Missouri students (African/Asian/Hispanic/Native Americans) planning to enter one of the fields listed above. Applicants must have a GPA of 3.0 or greater if they have completed 30 or more hours of college, or be in the top 25% of their graduating class or above the 75 percentile on the SAT or ACT if a high school senior. Must commit to teach in Missouri public schools for five years. Contact your high school guidance counselor, financial aid office, or college advisor to request an application.

Missouri Department of Elementary and Secondary Education
PO Box 480
Jefferson City, MO   65102

826 Mollie Ann Peterson Scholarship

AMOUNT: None Specified   DEADLINE: Mar 1
FIELDS/MAJORS: Education

Award open to female education majors. Contact the address below for further information.

University of North Carolina, Greensboro
Financial Aid Office
723 Kenilworth St.
Greensboro, NC   27412

823 MLS Scholarship for Minority Students

AMOUNT: $2000   DEADLINE: Dec 1
FIELDS/MAJORS: Medical Librarianship

Scholarship for minority students entering or continuing graduate school in Health Science Librarianship. Must be studying in an ALA accredited school. Write to the address below for details.

Medical Library Association
Program Services
6 N. Michigan Ave., Suite 300
Chicago, IL   60602

827 Monsanto Company— Science and Mathematics Scholarship

AMOUNT: $1000   DEADLINE: None Specified
FIELDS/MAJORS: Science

Student must have completed at least 90, but not more than 110 hours, with a GPA of 3.75 in their major field of study in the College of Natural and Applied Sciences. Preference is given to a minority student. Must enroll in fifteen hours each semester. Contact the College of Natural and Applied Sciences for more information.

Southwest Missouri State University
Office of Financial Aid
901 South National Ave.
Springfield, MO   65804

828
Monsanto Company Scholarships

AMOUNT: $2574   DEADLINE: Dec 1
FIELDS/MAJORS: Chemical, Electrical, Mechanical, or Civil Engineering

Awards for incoming minority freshmen who are from Iowa, Illinois, Missouri, Kansas, or Nebraska. Must have ranked in upper 10% of their high school class and demonstrate financial need. Awards are for resident tuition, room, board, books, supplies, and computer fees. One or two awards are offered annually. Contact the address below for further information.

Iowa State University—College of Engineering
Cheryl Moller-Wong
116 Marston Hall-Engineering Student Svc
Ames, IA   50011

829
Monsanto Opportunity in Engineering Scholarship

AMOUNT: $1952   DEADLINE: Dec 31
FIELDS/MAJORS: Chemical, Civil, Electrical, or Mechanical Engineering

Scholarships are available at the University of Iowa for full-time freshman minority students majoring in one of the above fields. Based upon academic record and financial need. Applicants must reside in Iowa, Illinois, Kansas, Missouri, or Nebraska. Write to the address below for information.

University of Iowa
Student Services, College of Engineering
3100 Engineering Building
Iowa City, IA   52242

830
Monticello College Foundation Fellowship for Women

AMOUNT: $12000   DEADLINE: Jan 20
FIELDS/MAJORS: History (Western and American), Women's Studies, Literature

Open to women with Ph.D. degrees. Preference will be given to applicants who are particularly concerned with the study of women, but study may be proposed in any field appropriate to Newberry's Collections. Must be a U.S. citizen. Fellowship is for six months work in residence at the Newberry Library. Write to the address below for complete details.

Newberry Library
Committee on Awards
60 W. Walton St.
Chicago, IL   60610

831
Morris Scholarship

AMOUNT: $750-$1250   DEADLINE: Feb 1
FIELDS/MAJORS: All Areas of Study

Open to undergraduates and graduate students who are minority Iowa residents. Contact the address listed for more information.

Loras College
Office of Financial Planning
1450 Alta Vista St., PO Box 178
Dubuque, IA   52004

832
Morrison Center MSW Minority Scholarship

AMOUNT: $6000   DEADLINE: Mar 1
FIELDS/MAJORS: Social Work

Award for a graduate student in social work. Requires demonstrated interest and commitment to providing mental health services for children, youth, and families. Applicant must be in the MSW program and be a minority student entering their second year of field placement. One award offered annually. Contact the Graduate School of Social Work for more information.

Portland State University
Graduate School of Social Work
300 University Center Building
Portland, OR   97207

833
Morton A. Gibson Memorial Scholarships

AMOUNT: $2500   DEADLINE: May 30
FIELDS/MAJORS: All Areas of Study

Grants (2) for current high school seniors in the metropolitan Washington area who have performed significant volunteer service in the local Jewish community or under the auspices of a Jewish organization. For full-time undergraduate study in the U.S. Based on volunteer service, need, and academics. Write to the address below or call (301) 881-3700 for details.

Jewish Social Service Agency of Metropolitan Washington
6123 Montrose Road
Rockville, MD   20852

834
Mount Ida College—Edith Folsom Hall Scholarship

AMOUNT: $500   DEADLINE: Mar 1
FIELDS/MAJORS: All Areas of Study

Applicants must be young women high school graduates who have been accepted by Mount Ida College. Several scholarships available. Write to the address below for details, be sure to include a SASE.

General Federation of Women's Clubs of Massachusetts
777 Dedham St.
Newton Centre, MA   02159

835 Mozelle and Willard Gold Memorial Scholarship

AMOUNT: Maximum: $3000   DEADLINE: Mar 31
FIELDS/MAJORS: All Areas of Study

Scholarship open to full-time students who are legally blind. Contact the address below for further information.

National Federation of the Blind
Mrs. Peggy Elliott, Chairman
814 Fifth Ave. #200
Grinnell, IA   50112

836 Mr. and Mrs. Richard L. Leza Scholarship

AMOUNT: $1300   DEADLINE: Mar 1
FIELDS/MAJORS: Chemical, Civil, Electrical, Computer, or Mechanical Engineering

Approximately $1,300 given annually to a junior majoring in chemical, civil, electrical/computer, or mechanical engineering. Recipient must be a U.S. citizen, have at least a 3.0 GPA, be Hispanic, and be a resident of Arizona, California, or New Mexico. Write to the address below for more information.

New Mexico State University
College of Engineering
Complex I, Box 30001, Dept. 3446
Las Cruces, NM   88003

837 Multicultural Achievement Scholarships

AMOUNT: Maximum: $2000   DEADLINE: Mar 1
FIELDS/MAJORS: All Areas of Study

Scholarships are available to students who are members of an ethnic minority with GPAs of 3.0, ACT scores of 20, and SAT scores of 930. Contact the address listed for further information.

University of Arkansas
Office of Admissions
200 Silas H. Hunt Hall
Fayetteville, AR   72701

838 Multicultural Fellowships

AMOUNT: Maximum: $8000   DEADLINE: Apr 1
FIELDS/MAJORS: All Areas of Study

Awards open to African-American, Asian-American, Hispanic-American, and Native American incoming freshmen. Renewable with maintaining GPAs of 2.0 and 2.25. Based on commitment to work, service, and academics. Contact the address below for further information.

Lebanon Valley College
Office of Admissions
101 N. College Ave.
Annville, PA   17003

839 Multicultural Grants

AMOUNT: Maximum: $1500   DEADLINE: Feb 1
FIELDS/MAJORS: All Areas of Study

Awards for African-American, Native American, and Hispanic-American students who can demonstrate financial need. Write to the address below for more information.

Lewis and Clark College
Office of Admissions
Portland, OR   97219

840 Multicultural Scholars Awards

AMOUNT: $2000-$7000   DEADLINE: Feb 15
FIELDS/MAJORS: All Areas of Study

Awards for students of color applying for admission to the University of Evansville. Based on strength of academic record and leadership abilities. Renewable. Write to the address listed for more information.

University of Evansville
Office of Financial Aid
1800 Lincoln Ave.
Evansville, IN   47722

841 Multicultural Scholarship Program

AMOUNT: $1750-$3500
DEADLINE: None Specified
FIELDS/MAJORS: All Areas of Study

Scholarships are available at Washington State University for full-time minority entering freshmen or transfer students with a GPA of at least 3.0 who are U.S. citizens. Write to the address below for information.

Washington State University
Office of Scholarship Services
Pullman, WA   99164

842 Music Assistance Fund Scholarships

AMOUNT: $500-$2500   DEADLINE: Dec 16
FIELDS/MAJORS: Music, Instrumental

Scholarships for students of African-American descent (and similar heritages such as African-Caribbean, etc.) who are studying toward a career in this country's symphony orchestra. Must be a U.S. citizen. Based on auditions, recommendations, and need. Must be a student of orchestral instruments. (Note: voice, piano, saxophone, composition and conducting are not included.) Write to the address below for details.

American Symphony Orchestra League
1156 Fifteenth Street NW
Suite 800
Washington, D.C.   20005

843 Music Scholarship

AMOUNT: Maximum: $1500
DEADLINE: None Specified
FIELDS/MAJORS: Vocal, Instrumental, Piano Performance

Recipients will be selected by the music department for participation in a music performance group or as staff accompanists. Recipient must sign a contractual agreement with the college. Auditions and ability to sight read are required. Write to the address below or contact the music department for more information.

California Baptist College
8432 Magnolia Ave.
Riverside, CA   92504

844 Myrtle A. Merritt Scholarship

AMOUNT: None Specified
DEADLINE: Mar 2
FIELDS/MAJORS: Physical Education

Open to junior and senior female students with a minimum GPA of 3.0. Contact Rip Marsten at the address below for further information.

University of Northern Iowa
Health, Physical Ed.and Leisure Services
203 W. Gym
Cedar Falls, IA   50614

845 Myrtle Moore Women in Business Scholarship

AMOUNT: None Specified   DEADLINE: Mar 1
FIELDS/MAJORS: Business

Award for a full-time female undergraduate business student who has a GPA of at least 3.0 and has successfully completed 27-40 credit hours by the effective date of the award. Award is in-state tuition, fees, room, board, and books. Write to the address below for more information.

Eastern New Mexico University (Noble Foundation)
ENMU College of Business
Station 49
Portales, NM   88130

846 Myrtle Okey Scholarships

AMOUNT: None Specified   DEADLINE: Mar 1
FIELDS/MAJORS: All Areas of Study

Awards are available at the University of New Mexico for American Indian students. Write to the address below for more information.

University of New Mexico, Albuquerque
Office of Financial Aid
Albuquerque, NM 87131

847 NABWA Scholarships

AMOUNT: $5000-$10000   DEADLINE: Feb 15
FIELDS/MAJORS: Law

Scholarships for female minority law students in their first or second year of law school or those in their third year of a four-year program. Four to six awards offered annually. Write to the address below for information and an application.

National Association of Black Women Attorneys
Office of the President, Mabel D. Haden
3711 Macomb Street, NW
Washington, D.C.   20016

848 NACCC Grant

AMOUNT: $700   DEADLINE: None Specified
FIELDS/MAJORS: All Areas of Study

Awards for full-time undergraduates and graduates whose congregation is a member of the NACCC (Nebraska Association of Congregations for Concordia College). Applicant's pastor must sign the application. Renewable. Write to the address below, or contact the office of church relations for more information.

Concordia College, Nebraska
Office of Financial Aid
800 N. Columbia Ave.
Seward, NE   68434

849 NAHJ Scholarships

AMOUNT: $1000-$2000   DEADLINE: Feb 28
FIELDS/MAJORS: Journalism, Print/Broadcast

For high school seniors, undergraduates, or graduate students majoring in journalism. Based on academic excellence, financial need, and interest in journalism as a career. Contact the address below for further information.

National Association of Hispanic Journalists
529 14th Street, NW
1193 National Press Bldg.
Washington, D.C.   20045

850 Namepa National Minority Scholarship Awards

AMOUNT: Maximum: $1000   DEADLINE: Jul 21
FIELDS/MAJORS: Engineering

Awards for minorities who are incoming freshmen and undergraduate transfer students. Freshmen must have a minimum GPA of 2.0 and an ACT score of 25 or SAT of 1000. Transfer students must have a minimum GPA of 3.0. Contact the address below for further information.

Namepa National Scholarship Fund
Namepa, Inc., Scholarship Chair
1133 W Morse Blvd. #201
Winter Park, FL   32789

851

Nancy Lorraine Jensen Memorial Scholarship Fund

AMOUNT: None Specified   DEADLINE: Mar 1
FIELDS/MAJORS: Chemistry, Physics, Chemical,
Electrical, Mechanical Engineering

Awards open to women undergraduates between
seventeen and thirty-five years of age who are members
or descendants of members of at least three years.
Applicants must be full-time students who have completed at least one term. Contact the address below
for further information.

Sons of Norway Foundation
1455 W. Lake St.
Minneapolis, MN   55408

852

Nancy Ryles Scholarship

AMOUNT: $5000   DEADLINE: None Specified
FIELDS/MAJORS: All Areas of Studies

Award for women working toward an undergraduate degree who
have been unable to begin and/or complete their college education
due to financial need, family responsibility, or personal disabilities. For use at Portland State University only. One or more
awards offered annually. Contact the office of women's studies for
more information.

Portland State University
Department of Women's Studies
PO Box 751
Portland, OR   97207

853

Nancy Williams Wahl Scholarship

AMOUNT: None Specified   DEADLINE: Feb 15
FIELDS/MAJORS: Psychology

Scholarships are awarded to a woman majoring in
psychology with a minimum of 45 credit hours and a
GPA of 3.0 or above. Write to the address below for
more information.

Murray State University
Office of University Scholarships
Ordway Hall, PO Box 9
Murray, KY   42071

854

NASA Training Project

AMOUNT: None Specified
DEADLINE: Mar 1
FIELDS/MAJORS: Engineering,
Mathematics, Physics

Awards are available at the University of New
Mexico for undergraduates with a GPA of at
least 3.0 in the fields above. Must be a minority
student or a student who is physically challenged.
Recipients must indicate a willingness to invest at
least 10 hours per week for structured study and to work at a
NASA sponsored facility in a co-op education program when eligible. Write to the address below for more information.

University of New Mexico, Albuquerque
Office of Financial Aid
Albuquerque, NM   87131

855

National Association for Hispanic Elderly Association Scholarship

AMOUNT: None Specified   DEADLINE: None Specified
FIELDS/MAJORS: Physical Therapy, Human Service,
Geriatrics, Social Service, Health

Scholarships are available at the University of Oklahoma,
Norman for full-time students majoring in the above
areas. Write to the address below for information.

University of Oklahoma, Norman
Department of Physical Therapy
OUHSC, PO Box 26901
Oklahoma City, OK   73190

856

National Association of Black Journalists Scholarship Awards

AMOUNT: $2500   DEADLINE: Mar 21
FIELDS/MAJORS: Journalism

Twelve scholarships awarded to African-American
college students in or intending to pursue a career in
journalism. Must be U.S. citizens and have a minimum
GPA of 2.5. For undergraduate students at a four-year
school or graduates. Must be/become a member of NABJ
and can't have previously won this award. Nomination by school
advisor, dean, or faculty member is required. Write to the address
below for further information.

National Association of Black Journalists Program
University of Maryland
3100 Taliaferro Hall
College Park, MD   20742

857

National Black Nurses' Association—Lauranne Sams Scholarship Award

AMOUNT: None Specified   DEADLINE: None Specified
FIELDS/MAJORS: Nursing

Scholarships are available at the University of Iowa for full-time
students majoring in nursing, who are of African-American
descent, and active members of a local chapter of the National
Black Nurses' Association. Write to the address below for information.

University of Iowa
College of Nursing
101 Nursing Building
Iowa City, IA   52240

858
National City Corporate Named Scholarships

AMOUNT: None Specified DEADLINE: Jul 1
FIELDS/MAJORS: All Areas of Study. Applicants must
have an interest in Banking as a career.

National City Bank of Pennsylvania has established
a scholarship fund with the Foundation for
Independent Colleges and Universities of
Pennsylvania (FIC) for the purpose of showing
the bank's support of private higher education in
the Commonwealth, and as a means of attracting high quality
individuals to its management training program. Scholarships
available for juniors to be used in their senior year. Must be
attending school full time, have a minimum GPA of 3.2, be U.S.
citizens or legal residents, and have an interest in a career in banking. First preference is for students of color, with second preference to women. Must be attending any of the twenty-one FIC
member colleges in western Pennsylvania. If this information is
sent to you, your school is a member school. Consideration given
to academics and quality and extent of extracurricular activities.
Contact the financial aid office at your school for information
and an application.

Foundation for Independent Colleges, Inc.
800 N. Third St. #502
Harrisburg, PA   17102

859
National Federation of the Blind American Action Fund Scholarship

AMOUNT: $10000 DEADLINE: Mar 31
FIELDS/MAJORS: All Areas of Study

Award available to full-time students who are legally blind. Based
on academic ability. One award offered annually. Write to the
address below for details.

National Federation of the Blind
Mrs. Peggy Elliott, Chairman
805 Fifth Ave.
Grinnell, IA   50112

860
National Federation of the Blind Computer Science Scholarship

AMOUNT: $3000 DEADLINE: Mar 31
FIELDS/MAJORS: Computer Science

Open to legally blind full-time students studying in the computer
science field. Write to the address below for more information.

National Federation of the Blind
Mrs. Peggy Elliot, Chairwoman
805 Fifth Ave.
Grinnell, IA   50112

861
National Federation of the Blind Educator of Tomorrow Award

AMOUNT: $3000 DEADLINE: Mar 31
FIELDS/MAJORS: Education

Open to full-time students who are legally blind, working toward
a career in education at the primary, secondary, or post-secondary
level. Write to the address below for details.

National Federation of the Blind
Mrs. Peggy Elliott, Chairman
805 Fifth Ave.
Grinnell, IA   50112

862
National Federation of the Blind Humanities Scholarship

AMOUNT: $3000 DEADLINE: Mar 31
FIELDS/MAJORS: Humanities

Open to full-time students who are legally blind and majoring in
any of the traditional humanities. Write to the address below for
details.

National Federation of the Blind
Mrs. Peggy Elliott, Chairman
805 Fifth Ave.
Grinnell, IA   50112

863
National Federation of the Blind of Illinois Scholarships

AMOUNT: $1000 DEADLINE: Mar 31
FIELDS/MAJORS: All Areas of Study

Award open to legally blind students who are residents of Illinois
and enrolled full time in school. Two awards offered annually.
Contact the address below for further information.

National Federation of the Blind of Illinois
Deborah Kent Stein, Chairman
5817 N. Nina
Chicago, IL   60631

864
National Federation of the Blind Scholarships

AMOUNT: Maximum: $3000 DEADLINE: Mar 31
FIELDS/MAJORS: All Areas of Study

Scholarships for full-time students who are legally blind. Thirteen
total scholarships available. Write to the address below for complete details.

National Federation of the Blind
Mrs. Peggy Elliott, Chairman
805 Fifth Ave.
Grinnell, IA   50112

865
National Hispanic Scholar Awards

AMOUNT: $7500   DEADLINE: Feb 1
FIELDS/MAJORS: All Areas of Study

Awards for students who are named scholars in the National Hispanic Scholar Recognition Program (NHSRP). Renewable. Write to the address below for more information.

Southwestern University
Admissions Office
Georgetown, TX   78626

866
National Hispanic Scholarship Fund

AMOUNT: $500-$1000   DEADLINE: Jun 5
FIELDS/MAJORS: All Areas of Study

Scholarships are available to U.S. citizens or permanent residents of Hispanic background who have completed at least 15 units of college work prior to submission of application. Must be enrolled in college in the fall and be in attendance through the spring (every year). Write to the address below for more information.

Florida International University
Financial Aid Office
University Park, PC 125
Miami, FL   33199

867
National Hispanic Scholarship Fund

AMOUNT: None Specified
DEADLINE: Mar 1
FIELDS/MAJORS: Engineering, Computer Science

Awards are available at the University of New Mexico for sophomores, juniors, or seniors of Hispanic origin who have a GPA of at least 3.0. Must be a U.S. citizen or permanent resident. Write to the address below for more information.

University of New Mexico, Albuquerque
Office of Financial Aid
Albuquerque, NM   87131

868
National Hispanic Scholarship

AMOUNT: Maximum: $5000   DEADLINE: Feb 15
FIELDS/MAJORS: All Areas of Study

Entering freshman must be recognized as a National Hispanic Scholar, with a minimum GPA of 3.0. Award is renewable by maintaining GPA. Honorable mention recipients and semi-finalists may qualify for a partial scholarship. Write to address below for information and application.

Florida International University
Office of Admissions
PC 140 University Park
Miami, FL   33199

869
National Hispanic Scholarship Program

AMOUNT: $500-$2000   DEADLINE: Oct 1
FIELDS/MAJORS: All Areas of Study

Scholarships for Hispanic students. Undergraduates must be attending full time, have already earned at least 15 credit hours, and have a minimum GPA of 2.5. Graduates must carry a minimum of 6 units. Must be U.S. citizens or permanent residents. Applications are available Aug 15 through the deadline date. Applications must be postmarked by Oct 1. Based on academics, financial need, letter of recommendation, personal statement, and donor conditions. Consideration is also given to such factors as region, college, and major. May be used at two or four-year colleges and universities. Notifications will be mailed to students in the spring. Further information may be obtained by writing to the address listed, (be sure to include a SASE for a reply).

National Hispanic Scholarship Fund
Selection Committee
1 Sansome St. #1000
San Francisco, CA   94104

870
National Italian-American Foundation Scholarships

AMOUNT: Maximum: $5000   DEADLINE: May 25
FIELDS/MAJORS: All Areas of Study

The National Italian-American Foundation offers a wide variety of awards for qualified Italian-American students. Contact the address below for further information.

National Italian-American Foundation
Dr. Maria Lombardo, Education Director
1860 Nineteenth St. NW
Washington, D.C.   20009

871
National Methodist Foundation Scholarships at APU

AMOUNT: $2000-$3000   DEADLINE: Apr 1
FIELDS/MAJORS: All Areas of Study

Scholarship for students at Alaska Pacific University who are members of the United Methodist Church. Must meet criteria determined by their conference and have a proven record of academic accomplishment. Financial need is considered. Three to four awards offered annually. Contact the financial aid office and your department for further information.

Alaska Pacific University
APU Scholarships
4101 University Drive
Anchorage, AK   99508

872
National Ministerial Association Student Aid Fund

AMOUNT: None Specified   DEADLINE: None Specified
FIELDS/MAJORS: Ministry

Through annual offerings from the individuals and churches, the Ashland-based Brethren Church gives support of young men who are studying for the ministry. Aid is given on the basis of need and scholarship. Write to the address below for more information.

Ashland University
401 College Ave.
Ashland, OH   44805

873
National Minority Scholarship Program

AMOUNT: $1500   DEADLINE: Apr 11
FIELDS/MAJORS: Public Relations, Communications

Applicants must be minority undergraduate students in public relations attending four-year accredited schools. Must have a GPA of at least 3.0. and be a member of the Public Relations Student Society of America. Students majoring or minoring in public relations will be given preference. Students should have obtained at least junior status by the time the scholarship will be used. If your school does not offer a public relations degree, a major in communications or journalism is acceptable. Write to the address below for details.

Public Relations Society of America
Director, Educational Affairs
33 Irving Place
New York, NY   10003

874
National Presbyterian College Scholarship

AMOUNT: $500-$1400   DEADLINE: Dec 1
FIELDS/MAJORS: All Areas of Study

Scholarships for high school seniors who are members of the Presbyterian Church (U.S.A.) and are U.S. citizens or permanent residents. Applicants must take the SAT/ACT prior to Dec 15 of their senior year. Write to the address below for information and an application.

Presbyterian Church (U.S.A.)
Office of Financial Aid for Studies
100 Witherspoon Street, Room M042-A
Louisville, KY   40202

875
National Presbyterian Scholarships

AMOUNT: $500-$1500   DEADLINE: Mar 15
FIELDS/MAJORS: All Areas of Study

Open to full-time students who are members of the Presbyterian Church (U.S.A.). Based on academics and financial need. This application is available from the Church from Dec 1 through the deadline.

Muskingum College
Office of Financial Aid
New Concord, OH   43762

876
National Presbyterian Scholarships

AMOUNT: None Specified   DEADLINE: Mar 15
FIELDS/MAJORS: All Areas of Study

Awards for Muskingum students who are Presbyterian and can demonstrate financial need. Write to the address below for more information.

Muskingum College
Office of Admission
New Concord, OH   43762

877
National Science Foundation Minority Graduate Research Fellowships

AMOUNT: Maximum: $24500   DEADLINE: Nov 6
FIELDS/MAJORS: Science, Mathematics, Engineering

Open to minorities who are U.S. citizens or permanent residents for graduate study leading to research based master's or doctoral degrees in the fields listed above. Based on all available documentation of ability, including academic records, recommendations regarding the applicant's qualifications, and GRE scores. Fellowships include a stipend of $15,000 for twelve month tenure and a cost of education allowance or $9,500 per tenure year. Contact the address below for further information.

National Science Foundation
Oak Ridge Associated Universities
PO Box 3010
Oak Ridge, TN   37831

878
National Women's Missionary Society Award

AMOUNT: None Specified   DEADLINE: None Specified
FIELDS/MAJORS: Missionary

An annual stipend is given by the National Women's Missionary Society of the Ashland-based Brethren Church, to a Brethren woman at the beginning of her senior year. Write to the address below for more information.

Ashland University
401 College Ave.
Ashland, OH   44805

879
Native American Education Grants

AMOUNT: $200-$1500   DEADLINE: Jun 1
FIELDS/MAJORS: All Areas of Study

Undergraduate grants for Alaska Natives and Native Americans pursuing college educations. Must be U.S. citizens and have completed at least one semester of work at an accredited institution of higher education. Applicants must be members of the Presbyterian Church (U.S.A.) and demonstrate financial need. Write to address below for details. Specify Native American

Education Grants (NAEG).
Presbyterian Church (U.S.A.)
Office of Financial Aid for Studies
100 Witherspoon Street
Louisville, KY   40202

880 Native American Internship Program

AMOUNT: $2500-$3000
DEADLINE: None Specified
FIELDS/MAJORS: Humanities, Art, Agriculture, Archeology, Anthropology, History

Internships available for Native American undergraduate and graduate students at the Smithsonian, for research or museum activities related to Native American studies. Program lasts for ten weeks. Write to the address below for details. Request the publication "Smithsonian Opportunities for Research and Study."

Smithsonian Institution
Office of Fellowships and Grants
955 L'Enfant Plaza, Suite 7000
Washington, D.C.   20560

881 Native American Scholarships

AMOUNT: None Specified   DEADLINE: None Specified
FIELDS/MAJORS: All Areas of Study

Awards for Native American students at Colorado State University who are members of U.S. Indian tribes. Write to the address below for details, or contact the Native American student services office at 312 Student Services.

Colorado State University
Financial Aid Office
108 Student Services
Fort Collins, CO   80523

882 Native American Student Aid

AMOUNT: Maximum: $1550
DEADLINE: None Specified
FIELDS/MAJORS: All Areas of Study

Grants for Native Americans who are N.Y. residents, on an official tribal roll of a N.Y. State Tribe (or children of), and attending an approved post-secondary institution in N.Y. State. Renewable for up to four years. Write to the address below for complete details.

New York State Education Department
Attn: Native American Education Unit
478 Education Building Annex
Albany, NY   12234

883 Native American Tuition Waivers

AMOUNT: $5514   DEADLINE: None Specified
FIELDS/MAJORS: All Areas of Study

Awards for Native American students at UMass that are certified as such by the U.S. Bureau of Indian Affairs and are permanent legal residents of Massachusetts. For more information, contact the Commonwealth on Indian Affairs, John W. McCormick Bldg., One Ashburton Place, Room 1004, Boston, MA 02108.

University of Massachusetts, Amherst
Office of Financial Aid Services
255 Whitmore Admin. Bldg., Box 38230
Amherst, MA   01003

884 NCR Corporation Scholarship

AMOUNT: None Specified
DEADLINE: None Specified
FIELDS/MAJORS: Finance

Awards for outstanding finance majors and participants in the school's minority management education program. For students in their sophomore, junior, or senior year. Applications for School of Management scholarships will be available in the SOM Development Office, Room 206.

University of Massachusetts, Amherst
School of Management
SOM Development Office, Room 206
Amherst, MA   01003

885 Nearly New Foundation Scholarship

AMOUNT: None Specified   DEADLINE: May 1
FIELDS/MAJORS: All Areas of Study

Open to outstanding female students. Contact the address listed for further information.

Walker College
Financial Aid Office
1411 Indiana Ave.
Jasper, AL   35501-4967

886 Neca Navajo Engineering and Construction Authority

AMOUNT: None Specified   DEADLINE: Mar 1
FIELDS/MAJORS: Engineering

Awards are available at the University of New Mexico for American Indian engineering students. Contact the School of Engineering for more information.

University of New Mexico, Albuquerque
Office of Financial Aid
Albuquerque, NM   87131

887
Neviaser Ahana Student Achievement Award

AMOUNT: $2000 DEADLINE: Mar 15
FIELDS/MAJORS: All Areas of Study

Awards for incoming freshmen who are African-American, Asian, Hispanic, or Native American with GPAs of at least 2.5 and a class rank in the upper 50% of their graduating class. Preference will be given to Dane County residents. Renewable. Write to the address below for details.

Edgewood College
Office of Admissions
855 Woodrow Street
Madison, WI 53711

888
New Mexico Space Grant Undergraduate Scholarship

AMOUNT: $2000 DEADLINE: Mar 1
FIELDS/MAJORS: Astronomy, Biology, Chemistry, Physics, Computer Science, or Math

Up to $2000 awarded to approximately five undergraduates in the College of Engineering or in the College of Arts and Sciences majoring in astronomy, biology, chemistry, physics, computer science, or math. Students must have a GPA of 3.0 and be U.S. citizens. Women and minority students are greatly preferred. Applications available from the Financial Aid or the Space Grant Office, or write to the address below for details.

New Mexico State University
Student Financial Aid Office
Box 30001, Dept 5100
Las Cruces, NM 88003

889
New York Life Foundation Scholarships for Women in Health Professions

AMOUNT: $500-$1000 DEADLINE: Apr 15
FIELDS/MAJORS: Healthcare

Undergraduate women, twenty-five or older, seeking the necessary education for a career in a healthcare field and within twenty-four months of graduation. Must demonstrate need. Must be a U.S. citizen. The pre-application screening form is only available between Oct 1 and Apr 1. Up to one hundred scholarships are available. Not for graduate study, correspondence programs, or non-degreed programs. Relatives of officers of New York Life Insurance Company are ineligible. Write to address below for details.

Business and Professional Women's Foundation
Scholarships
2012 Massachusetts Avenue, NW
Washington, D.C. 20036

890
NEWH Chicago Chapter Scholarships

AMOUNT: $1000 DEADLINE: JUN 1
FIELDS/MAJORS: Hospitality, Food Services, Hotel Management

Awards are available for female students over halfway through an accredited hospitality/food services related program. Applicants must demonstrate financial need, have good grades, and reside in the Chicago area. Write to the address below or email jgoldsberry@tjbc.com for more information.

Network of Executive Women in Hospitality, Chicago Chapter
Jill Goldsberry
PO Box 3835
Chicago, IL 60654

891
Newhouse Scholarship/ Internship Program

AMOUNT: $5000 DEADLINE: Feb 28
FIELDS/MAJORS: Print Journalism

For Hispanic college juniors and seniors majoring in print journalism. Recipients will have an opportunity to participate in a summer intern program following their junior year. Write to the address below for more information.

National Association of Hispanic Journalists
529 14th Street, NW
1193 National Press Building
Washington, D.C. 20045

892
Nicaraguan and Haitian Scholarship Program

AMOUNT: $4000-$5000 DEADLINE: Jul 1
FIELDS/MAJORS: All Areas of Study

Scholarships for residents of Florida who were born in Nicaragua or Haiti or hold citizenship in either country. Applicant needs a cumulative high school GPA of 3.0 on a 4.0 scale and needs to have demonstrated community service. Write to the address below for details.

Florida Department of Education
Office of Student Financial Assistance
1344 Florida Education Center
Tallahassee, FL 32399

893
Nicholas & Elizabeth Melnick Instructional Leadership Scholarship

AMOUNT: None Specified DEADLINE: Feb 1
FIELDS/MAJORS: Education Administration

Awards for students who have been admitted to the education administration graduate program in the School of Education. Preference will be given to minority students. Must be a resident of Kentucky. Contact the School of Education for further information.

Northern Kentucky University
Financial Aid Office-Nunn Dr.
Administrative Center #416
Highland Heights, KY 41099

894
NIGMS Predoctoral Fellowships

AMOUNT: Maximum: $1500
DEADLINE: Nov 15
FIELDS/MAJORS: Medical Science

Awards are available for minority graduate students working toward their Ph.D. in medical science. Must be U.S. citizens. Write to the address below for additional information.

National Institute of General Medical Sciences
National Institute of Health
45 Center Dr. MSC 6200, Room 2AS.43
Bethesda, MD   20892

895
NMSU Minority Presidential Scholarship

AMOUNT: $400   DEADLINE: Mar 1
FIELDS/MAJORS: All Areas of Study

Scholarships for entering freshmen at New Mexico State University who are minority group members. Fifteen awards per year. Must have a high school GPA of at least 2.5. Returning students with a GPA of 3.0 or better are also eligible. Renewable. Contact the Associate Vice President's Office, Dept. 3445 for more information.

New Mexico State University
Office of Student Financial Aid
Box 30001, Dept. 3445
Las Cruces, NM   88003

896
Non-Resident Tuition Waiver Scholarships for Minority Students

AMOUNT: $1000   DEADLINE: Mar 1
FIELDS/MAJORS: All Areas of Study

Scholarships are available at the University of Oklahoma, Norman for full-time graduate minority students who are residents of a state other than Oklahoma. Write to the address below for information.

University of Oklahoma, Norman
Graduate College
1000 Asp Ave., Room 313
Norman, OK   73019

897
Nordstrom Scholarships

AMOUNT: $2000   DEADLINE: May 8
FIELDS/MAJORS: Business

Scholarships are available for undergraduate students with disabilities enrolled in or planning to enroll in a business program. Requires a four-part essay of not more than fifteen pages and documentation of your handicap. Five awards are given annually. Write to the address below for information.

President's Committee on Employment of People with
    Disabilities
Scholarship Program
1331 F Street, NW
Washington, D.C.   20004

898
North American Indian Department Scholarships

AMOUNT: None Specified   DEADLINE: Apr 15
FIELDS/MAJORS: All Areas of Study

Scholarships are available for undergraduate Native American students. Must be able to demonstrate tribal affiliation. Write to the address below for information and be sure to enclose a SASE.

International Order of the King's Daughters and Sons, Inc.
PO Box 1017
34 Vincent Ave.
Chautauqua, NY   14722

899
North American Student Fund

AMOUNT: None Specified   DEADLINE: Mar 1
FIELDS/MAJORS: Medicine

Awards are available at the University of New Mexico for Native American students who are unable to finance his or her own education. Write to the address below for more information.

University of New Mexico, Albuquerque
Office of Financial Aid
Albuquerque, NM   87131

900
North Port Business and Professional Women's Organization Scholarships

AMOUNT: $500-$1000   DEADLINE: Apr 15
FIELDS/MAJORS: All Areas of Study

Scholarships are available for female residents of North Port, Florida. Based on academic ability and financial need. Write to the address below for information.

North Port Area Business and Professional Women's Organization
c/o Arline Q. Reeves
PO Box 7085
North Port, FL   34287

901
Northwest Danish Foundation Scholarships

AMOUNT: $250-$1000   DEADLINE: Mar 15
FIELDS/MAJORS: All Areas of Study

Open to students who are of Danish descent and are residents of Washington or Oregon. The scholarship may be used for study in Denmark. Preference given to applicants who can demonstrate active participation in their Danish communities. Contact the address below for further information.

Northwest Danish Foundation
1833 N. 105th St. #203
Seattle, WA   98133

902
NSA Undergraduate Training Program

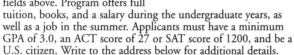

AMOUNT: None Specified
DEADLINE: Nov 10
FIELDS/MAJORS: Computer Science, Electrical or Computer Engineering, Languages, Math

Program for high school seniors, (particularly minorities) who are interested in studying one of the fields above. Program offers full tuition, books, and a salary during the undergraduate years, as well as a job in the summer. Applicants must have a minimum GPA of 3.0, an ACT score of 27 or SAT score of 1200, and be a U.S. citizen. Write to the address below for additional details.

National Security Agency
Manager, Undergraduate Training Program
9800 Savage Rd. #68640 Attn: S232R (UT)
Ft. Meade, MD   20755

903
Nursing Grants for Persons of Color

AMOUNT: $2000-$4000
DEADLINE: None Specified
FIELDS/MAJORS: Nursing

Awards are available for Minnesota students of color in a nursing program in the state of Minnesota. Must be a U.S. citizen or permanent resident. Write to the address below for more information.

Minnesota Higher Education Services Office
400 Capital Square
550 Cedar St.
Saint Paul, MN   55101

904
Nursing Scholastic Achievement Scholarships

AMOUNT: $1000   DEADLINE: Mar 15
FIELDS/MAJORS: Nursing

Scholarships for communicant members of Lutheran congregations who are juniors or seniors in a school of nursing. Must have a GPA of at least 3.0 and be able to demonstrate past or present involvement (a minimum of 100 hours) in a community or church activity that benefits people who are mentally retarded. Write to the address below for details.

Bethesda Lutheran Homes and Services, Inc.
National Christian Resource Center
700 Hoffmann Drive
Watertown, WI   53094

905
Oakville, Ind., Brethren Church Scholarship

AMOUNT: $500   DEADLINE: None Specified
FIELDS/MAJORS: Ministry, Christian Work

Given to a student from the Oakville Brethren Church preparing for the ministry or full time Christian work. Write to the address below for more information.

Ashland University
401 College Ave.
Ashland, OH   44805

906
Ojai First Christian Church Scholarship

AMOUNT: None Specified
DEADLINE: None Specified
FIELDS/MAJORS: Theology (Ministry)

Scholarships are awarded to Disciple students planning to enter the ministry. Contact the address listed for further information.

Chapman University
333 N. Glassell
Orange, CA   92866

907
Oklahoma Area Higher Education Grant Program

AMOUNT: None Specified   DEADLINE: None Specified
FIELDS/MAJORS: All Areas of Study

Open to members of the Seneca-Cayuga, Ottawa, Eastern Shawnee, Miami, Quapaw, Modoc, and Iowa of KS, and NE Indian tribes that are recognized federally. All students must be full time and have a GPA of at least a 2.0. Submit applications for the fall qtr. by Jun 1, winter qtr. Oct 15, spring qtr. Jan 15, and summer qtr. Apr 15. For more information write to the address below.

Bureau of Indian Affairs
Oklahoma Area Education Office
4149 Highline Blvd., Ste. 380
Oklahoma City, OK   73108

908
Oncology Nursing Ethnic Minority Bachelor's Scholarships

AMOUNT: $2000   DEADLINE: Feb 1
FIELDS/MAJORS: Oncology Nursing

Scholarships available to minority bachelor's students in the field of oncology nursing. All applicants must be currently licensed registered nurses. For full or part-time students in an NLN-accredited School of Nursing. Write to the address listed for more information.

Oncology Nursing Foundation
501 Holiday Dr.
Pittsburgh, PA   15220

909
Oncology Nursing Ethnic Minority Master's Scholarships

AMOUNT: $3000   DEADLINE: Feb 1
FIELDS/MAJORS: Oncology Nursing

Scholarships available to ethnic minority master's students enrolled in the field of oncology nursing. All applicants must be currently licensed registered nurses. For full-time or part-time students. Write to the address listed for more information.

Oncology Nursing Foundation
501 Holiday Dr.
Pittsburgh, PA   15220

910 One Accord Gospel Choir Scholarship

AMOUNT: Maximum: $500
DEADLINE: None Specified
FIELDS/MAJORS: All Areas of Study

Recipient must exemplify Christian values in his/her lifestyle and commitment. Must be a sophomore, junior, or senior with a cumulative GPA of at least 2.5 or above. Contact the address listed for further information.

Charleston Southern University
PO Box 118087
Charleston, SC   29423

911 Opha Auxiliary Scholarship

AMOUNT: $250   DEADLINE: Feb 1
FIELDS/MAJORS: Pharmacy

Scholarships are available at the University of Oklahoma, Norman for full-time female third or fourth year pharmacy majors. Based on academic excellence. Write to the address below for information.

University of Oklahoma, Norman
College of Pharmacy
PO Box 26901
Oklahoma City, OK   73190

912 Opportunity at Iowa Scholarships

AMOUNT: $3000   DEADLINE: None Specified
FIELDS/MAJORS: All Areas of Study

Scholarships are available at the University of Iowa for entering freshmen minority students who have a minimum GPA of at least 3.5. Contact your high school guidance counselor or write to the address below for more information.

University of Iowa
Office of Admissions
107 Calvin Hall
Iowa City, IA   52242

913 Order Sons of Italy in America, Grand Lodge of Illinois Scholarships

AMOUNT: None Specified   DEADLINE: Aug 1
FIELDS/MAJORS: All Areas of Study

Scholarships for high school seniors who are residents of Illinois and are of Italian descent. Based on need, transcripts, and recommendation of principal or faculty advisor. Write to the scholarship committee at the address below for details.

George J. Spatuzza Scholarship Award Foundation
Order Sons of Italy in America, Illinois
7222 W. Cermack Rd, Suite 409
North Riverside, IL   60546

914 Oryx Scholarship Fund

AMOUNT: $1000   DEADLINE: Mar 1
FIELDS/MAJORS: Geophysics

Scholarships are available at the University of Oklahoma, Norman for full-time geophysics majors, who are female, members of a minority group, or handicapped and show academic potential. Write to the address below for information.

University of Oklahoma, Norman
Director, School of Geology and Geophysics
100 East Boyd Street, Room 810
Norman, OK   73019

915 Osage Tribal Education Committee Program

AMOUNT: None Specified   DEADLINE: None Specified
FIELDS/MAJORS: All Areas of Study

Open to Osage Indians enrolled in accredited post-secondary educational institutions, including college, university, and technical and vocational schools. Submit applications by the fall semester Jul 1, spring semester Dec 31, and summer term May 1. For more information write to the address below.

Osage Tribal Education Committee
Oklahoma Area Education Office
4149 Highline Blvd., Ste. 380
Oklahoma City, OK   73108

916 Otto M. Stanfield Legal Scholarship

AMOUNT: None Specified   DEADLINE: Feb 15
FIELDS/MAJORS: Law

Open to active Unitarian Universalists who are entering law school and have financial need. Write to the address below for details.

Unitarian Universalist Association
Publication Department
25 Beacon St.
Boston, MA   02108

917
P.E.O. Educational Fund

AMOUNT: Maximum: $1500   DEADLINE: None Specified
FIELDS/MAJORS: All Areas of Study

Scholarships for young women with the recommendation of the local P.E.O. Sisterhood. Applicant must be within two years of completing her course of study and have had at least twelve consecutive months as a non-student. Requests for information and applications must be sent to your local P.E.O. Chapter

P.E.O. Educational Fund
Mrs. Ruth Melton
3806 Marie Cook Dr.
Montgomery, AL   36109

918
Paducah Sun Minority Scholarships

AMOUNT: None Specified   DEADLINE: Feb 15
FIELDS/MAJORS: Newspaper Journalism

Scholarships are awarded to minority students who are full-time students preparing for a career in the field of newspaper journalism with a GPA of 2.75 or above. Write to the address below for more information.

Murray State University
Office of University Scholarships
Ordway Hall, PO Box 9
Murray, KY   42071

919
Palm Aire Women's Club Scholarship

AMOUNT: $1200   DEADLINE: Apr 1
FIELDS/MAJORS: All Areas of Study

Scholarships are available for female Sarasota or Manatee County residents who demonstrate academic excellence, participation in extracurricular activities, show financial need, and have a minimum GPA of at least 3.0. Applicants must have attended Manatee Community College for at least 60 hours and plan to transfer to a university to pursue a bachelor's degree. Write to the address below for information.

Palm Aire Women's Club
c/o Florence White, Co-Chair
5849 Clubside Dr
Sarasota, FL   34243

920
Pan American Round Table II Endowed Scholarships

AMOUNT: None Specified   DEADLINE: Mar 1
FIELDS/MAJORS: Latin-American Studies

Awards are available at the University of New Mexico for female students in a Latin-American studies program. Applicant must exhibit financial need and be enrolled in one of the dual degree graduate programs. Must be a legal resident of New Mexico. Write to the address below for more information.

University of New Mexico
Latin American Studies Graduate Program
525 Buena Vista SE
Albuquerque, NM   87131

921
Panasonic and Itzhak Perlman Young Soloists Award

AMOUNT: None Specified   DEADLINE: Nov 3
FIELDS/MAJORS: Vocal Music, Instrumental Music

Scholarship is available to applicants who are vocalist or instrumentalist and are twenty-five years of age and under and disabled. Write to the address below for more information.

Very Special Arts
Education Office
J.F. Kennedy Ctr. for the Performing Art
Washington, D.C.   20566

922
Parajon, Hla Scholarships

AMOUNT: None Specified   DEADLINE: Jan 1
FIELDS/MAJORS: All Areas of Study

Scholarships for Hispanic, Asian, and Native American freshmen at Denison University. Strong academic performance and potential is required. Based on academics, extracurricular achievements, and recommendations from counselors and teachers. Renewable if recipients maintain pre-set standards. Thirty awards offered annually from each of the two sponsors. Awards are one half tuition. Contact the office of admissions or the financial aid office at the address listed for details.

Denison University
Financial Aid Office
Box M
Granville, OH   43023

923
Parkersburg Zonta Club Scholarship

AMOUNT: $500   DEADLINE: May 9
FIELDS/MAJORS: All Areas of Study

Scholarships for graduates of high schools in, or current residents of, Wood County, West Virginia or Belpre, Ohio. Must have GPA of at least 3.0 and be a full-time female student who is a junior or senior. Based on application, need, and a well-defined career objective. Write to the address below for details.

Zonta Club of Parkersburg
PO Box 184
Parkersburg, WV   26102

924
Pastor's Scholarships

AMOUNT: $500-$4000   DEADLINE: Jan 1
FIELDS/MAJORS: All Areas of Study

Awards for students who live in the Wheeling-Charleston diocese and have demonstrated academic achievement. The College sends nomination forms to the pastors in this district each fall, and those interested in this scholarship should contact their pastors. Write to the address below for more information.

Wheeling Jesuit College
Student Financial Planning
316 Washington Ave.
Wheeling, WV   26003

925
Patricia A. Doyle Scholarships

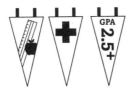

AMOUNT: None Specified
DEADLINE: Feb 15
FIELDS/MAJORS: Physical Education, Health

Awards for continuing female students at UW-Platteville who are of traditional age and have a GPA of 2.5 or greater. Also based on participation in student activities and financial need. Two awards are offered annually. Write to the address below or contact the office at (608) 342-1125 for more information.

University of Wisconsin, Platteville
Office of Admissions and Enrollment Mgt.
Platteville, WI 53818

926
Patricia Lange Memorial Scholarship

AMOUNT: $500   DEADLINE: None Specified
FIELDS/MAJORS: Mathematics

Open to mathematics majors of at least junior standing. Preference given to female students. Scholarship is a $250 award per semester. Contact the address below for further information.

University of Northern Iowa
Russell Campbell
220 Wright Hall
Cedar Falls, IA 50614

927
Paul A. and Velma Wimmer Carl Endowed Scholarship

AMOUNT: None Specified   DEADLINE: None Specified
FIELDS/MAJORS: Elementary Education or Business

Awards made annually to two students as follows: 50% to a woman full-time student entering her junior year and majoring in elementary education, and 50% to a full-time student majoring in business. The award is made on the basis of need, academic promise, and attitude, with preference given to residents of Ashland County. Write to the address below for more information.

Ashland University
401 College Ave.
Ashland, OH 44805

928
Paul Cuffe Memorial Fellowship

AMOUNT: $2400   DEADLINE: None Specified
FIELDS/MAJORS: Naval History

Fellowships are available for scholars researching the participation of Native and African-Americans in maritime activities, using the scholarly resources of New England. Write to the address below for information.

Munson Institute of American Maritime Studies
Director
Box 6000, Mystic Seaport Museum
Mystic, CT 06355

929
Paul E. Morgan Scholarships

AMOUNT: None Specified
DEADLINE: Dec 1
FIELDS/MAJORS: Engineering

Awards for incoming freshmen who are women, Native Americans, or Hispanic or African-Americans. Based on academic achievement. Contact the address below for further information.

Iowa State University—College of Engineering
Cheryl Moller-Wong
116 Marston Hall-Engineering Student Svc
Ames, IA 50011

930
Paul W. Klipsch Scholarship Fund, in Honor of Dr. Clark S. Defandorf

AMOUNT: None Specified   DEADLINE: Sep 1
FIELDS/MAJORS: All Areas of Study

Scholarship for young men and women of the Tewa tribe of San Juan Pueblo, New Mexico. Recipients should use their knowledge and skills to improve the life of the tribe. Applicants must be full-time students at NMSU or one of the branch campuses. The recipient is to be a person who actively participates in a religion consistent with the belief in a supreme being. Write to the address below for details.

New Mexico State University
American Indian Program
Box 30001, Dept 4188
Las Cruces, NM 88003

931
Pauline M. Alt Re-entry Scholarship

AMOUNT: None Specified   DEADLINE: None Specified
FIELDS/MAJORS: All Areas of Study

Awarded to matriculated undergraduates with preference given to women who have returned to higher education following an absence of three or more years. Write to the address below for additional information.

Central Connecticut State University
CCSU Foundation, Inc.
PO Box 612
New Britain, CT 06050

932
Pauly D'Orlando Memorial Art Scholarship

AMOUNT: None Specified **DEADLINE:** Mar 31
FIELDS/MAJORS: Enameling, Drawing, Painting, or Printmaking

Award for members of a Unitarian Universalist congregation studying in the areas listed above. Write to the address below for more information.

Unitarian Universalist Association of Congregations
Anti-Oppression Education/Resources Dept
25 Beacon St.
Boston, MA   02108

933
Paumanauke Native American Indian Scholarship

AMOUNT: $500 **DEADLINE:** Jul 1
FIELDS/MAJORS: All Areas of Study

Scholarships are available for tribally enrolled Native Americans attending colleges, universities, or accredited post-secondary institutions on a full-time basis. Write to the address below for information.

Paumanauke Pow-Wow and Native American Living Arts Festival, Inc.
333 Lagoon Drive South
Copiague, NY   11726

934
Payne Family Scholarship

AMOUNT: Maximum: $500 **DEADLINE:** None Specified
FIELDS/MAJORS: All Areas of Study

Recipient must be a professing Christian and have financial need. Contact the address listed for further information.

Charleston Southern University
PO Box 118087
Charleston, SC   29423

935
Pearl Dutton Crafts Award

AMOUNT: None Specified
DEADLINE: None Specified
FIELDS/MAJORS: Ministry

Awarded to a student who is a member of the Williamstown, Ohio, Brethren Church, provided that he or she maintains satisfactory scholarship and is certified by the pastor or other official of the Williamstown church. In the event of no qualified candidates, it will be awarded to a pre-seminary student preparing for ministry in the Ashland-based Brethren Church on the basis of financial need, scholarship, and spiritual promise. Write to the address below for more information.

Ashland University
401 College Ave.
Ashland, OH   44805

936
Pearl H. Falk Scholarships

AMOUNT: $400 **DEADLINE:** Mar 31
FIELDS/MAJORS: All Areas of Study

Scholarships are available at the University of Iowa for undergraduate students who are Protestant. Preference is given to incoming freshmen. Applicants must be Iowa residents. Write to the address below for information.

University of Iowa
Iowa State Bank & Trust, Trust Dept.
PO Box 1700
Iowa City, IA   52244

937
Pearl Hull Falk Scholarship

AMOUNT: $400 **DEADLINE:** None Specified
FIELDS/MAJORS: All Areas of Study

Awards open to Iowa residents who are of the Protestant faith and attending the University of Iowa full time. Based on character and scholastic record. Eighty to ninety awards are offered annually. Contact the address below for further information.

Pearl Hull Falk Scholarship Committee
Iowa State Bank and Trust Company
PO Box 1700—Trust Department
Iowa City, IA   52244

938
Pennsylvania District Women's Missionary Society Award

AMOUNT: $200 **DEADLINE:** None Specified
FIELDS/MAJORS: Missionary

Award given to a woman who is a member of the Ashland-based Brethren Church. Write to the address below for more information.

Ashland University
401 College Ave.
Ashland, OH   44805

939
PEO Chapter D Ethel Montgomery Memorial Scholarship

AMOUNT: None Specified **DEADLINE:** None Specified
FIELDS/MAJORS: All Areas of Study

Applicants must be full-time female students who are admitted to any degree program on the Juneau campus of UAS and who demonstrate financial need, motivation, and scholastic achievement. Write to the address below for more information.

University of Alaska Southeast (Juneau Campus)
Financial Aid Office
11120 Glacier Highway
Juneau, AK   99801

940
PEO Chapter G Scholarships

AMOUNT: None Specified
DEADLINE: None Specified
FIELDS/MAJORS: Education

Applicants must be full-time female students who demonstrate motivation, academic achievement, leadership potential, and financial need. One scholarship will be awarded to an Education major on the UAS Juneau campus; one scholarship is open to female students who are admitted to any degree program at UAS Juneau. Write to the address below for more information.

University of Alaska Southeast (Juneau Campus)
Financial Aid Office
11120 Glacier Highway
Juneau, AK   99801

941
Pergamon-NWSA Graduate Scholarship in Women's Studies

AMOUNT: $500-$1000   DEADLINE: Feb 15
FIELDS/MAJORS: Women's Studies

Award available for a woman researching for a master's thesis or Ph.D. dissertation in women's studies. Preference will be given to NWSA members and to those whose research projects focus on "color" or "class." Two awards per year. Write to the address below for details.

National Women's Studies Association
7100 Baltimore Avenue, Suite 301
University of Maryland
College Park, MD   20740

942
Peter and Alice Koomruian Armenian Education Fund

AMOUNT: None Specified   DEADLINE: None Specified
FIELDS/MAJORS: All Areas of Study

Awards for undergraduate and graduate students of Armenian descent who are enrolled in an accredited U.S. College or university. Based on financial need and academic ability. Send a SASE to the address below for more information.

Peter and Alice Koomruian Fund
PO Box 0268
Moorpark, CA, 93020

943
Peter Doctor Memorial Indian Scholarship Foundation

AMOUNT: None Specified   DEADLINE: May 31
FIELDS/MAJORS: All Areas of Study

Open to students who are enrolled members of New York State Indian tribes after one full year of college. Applicants must contact their representative according to what Reservation they are enrolled with. Write to the address below for more information.

Peter Doctor Memorial Indian Scholarship Foundation, Inc.
Clara Hill, Treasurer
PO Box 731
Basom, NY   14013

944
Peter Grunwald Scholarship

AMOUNT: $1500   DEADLINE: Mar 31
FIELDS/MAJORS: All Areas of Study

Award open to legally blind students who are residents of Illinois and enrolled full time in school. Contact the address below for further information.

National Federation of the Blind of Illinois
Deborah Kent Stein, Chairman
5817 N. Nina
Chicago, IL   60631

945
Philip Pearlman Scholarship Fund

AMOUNT: $500   DEADLINE: Jun 15
FIELDS/MAJORS: Social Service, Rabbinics, Education, Jewish Studies

Scholarships for Jewish residents of New Jersey who are studying toward a career in the Jewish field, whether in the Rabbinate, Cantorate, Education, Administration, or Social Work fields. For undergraduate or graduate studies in the U.S. or Israel. Recipients or a family member must be present at the Jewish Festival (on Sep 7th) to accept the award. Write to the address below for details.

Jewish Festival of the Arts
Ms. Simi Pearlman, Committee Chairman
34 Wellington Rd.
East Brunswick, NJ   08816

946
Phillips Petroleum and Sun Refining and Marketing Scholarships

AMOUNT: None Specified   DEADLINE: None Specified
FIELDS/MAJORS: Chemical Engineering

Open to female students pursuing a degree in chemical engineering. Selection made by the School of Chemical Engineering for both awards. Write to the address listed for further information.

Georgia Institute of Technology
Financial Aid Office
225 North Ave.
Atlanta, GA   30332

947
Phillips Petroleum Minority/Female Accounting Scholarship

AMOUNT: $500   DEADLINE: Feb 7
FIELDS/MAJORS: Accounting

Minority/female student must be a full-time junior or senior accounting major who has completed or is currently enrolled in Intermediate Accounting I with a minimum 2.75 GPA. Contact the COBA office for more information.

Southwest Missouri State University
Office of Financial Aid
901 South National Ave.
Springfield, MO   65804

948
Phillips Petroleum Scholarship

AMOUNT: $1500   DEADLINE: Mar 1
FIELDS/MAJORS: Petroleum Engineering

Scholarships available at the University of Oklahoma, Norman for new full-time minority petroleum engineering majors, with a minimum GPA of 3.0 who are U.S. citizens. One to two awards offered annually. Write to the address below for information.

University of Oklahoma, Norman
Scholarship Coord., Pet. and Geol. Eng.
T301 Energy Center
Norman, OK   73019

949
Phillips Petroleum Scholarship

AMOUNT: $2500   DEADLINE: Sep 1
FIELDS/MAJORS: Law

Scholarship available at the University of Oklahoma, Norman for full-time second-year female law students. Based on merit. One award offered annually. Individual award requirements will vary. Write to the address below for information.

University of Oklahoma, Norman
Admissions and Records, Law Center
Room 22, 300 Timberdell Road
Norman, OK   73019

950
Philo Bennett Scholarship

AMOUNT: None Specified   DEADLINE: Mar 1
FIELDS/MAJORS: All Areas of Study

Awards are available at the University of New Mexico for freshmen women who are from New Mexico. Awards are only given in the spring. Write to the address below for more information.

University of New Mexico, Albuquerque
Office of Financial Aid
Albuquerque, NM   87131

951
Pi Alpha Gamma Award

AMOUNT: $200   DEADLINE: None Specified
FIELDS/MAJORS: All Areas of Study

Awarded to a woman at the end of her junior year. Write to the address below for more information.

Ashland University
401 College Ave.
Ashland, OH   44805

952
Pilot Club of Tulsa Scholarship

AMOUNT: None Specified   DEADLINE: Mar 1
FIELDS/MAJORS: Dentistry

Scholarships are available at the University of Oklahoma, Norman for full-time female graduate dentistry or dental hygiene students who are in their fourth year of study. One award offered annually. Write to the address below for information.

University of Oklahoma, Norman
College of Dentistry
1001 Stanton L. Young Blvd.
Oklahoma City, OK   73190

953
Pimalco/Gila River Indian Community Scholarship

AMOUNT: None Specified   DEADLINE: Jul 30
FIELDS/MAJORS: All Areas of Study

Open to residents of the Gila River Indian Community and/or on the tribal registry of the Maricopa or Pima Indian tribes. Must be admitted to ASU as full-time students. Renewable up to five years so long as academic standards are met. Contact the address below for further information.

Arizona State University
Scholarship Office Main Campus
PO Box 870412
Tempe, AZ   85287

954
Pleasant View Baptist Church of Wren, Ohio Endowed Scholarship Fund

AMOUNT: None Specified   DEADLINE: None Specified
FIELDS/MAJORS: All Areas of Study

Awards available for Baptist students at Cedarville College from the Pleasant View Church. Must have a GPA of at least 2.0 and demonstrated financial need. Write to the address below for more information.

Cedarville College
Financial Aid Office
PO Box 601
Cedarville, OH   45314

955 Plocieniak Scholarships

AMOUNT: None Specified   DEADLINE: Mar 1
FIELDS/MAJORS: All Areas of Study

Scholarships offered to incoming, full-time freshmen at Loyola University who are of Polish descent and are fluent in the Polish language. Applicants must pass a language proficiency test. Renewable for up to three years. Write to the address below for details.

Loyola University
Undergraduate Admissions Office
820 North Michigan Avenue
Chicago, IL   60611

956 PNM Native American Scholarship

AMOUNT: None Specified   DEADLINE: Mar 1
FIELDS/MAJORS: All Areas of Study

Open to Native Americans who are residents of New Mexico. Must be affiliated with a recognized New Mexico Pueblo tribe. Each level of school has its own minimum GPA requirement: freshmen must have at least a 2.0; sophomores a minimum of 2.3; juniors and seniors at least a 2.5, and graduate students must have a minimum of 3.0. Preference given to undergraduates. Contact the address below for further information.

Eastern New Mexico University
Vice President for Student Affairs
Station 34
Portales, NM   88130

957 Polingaysi Qoyawayma Teaching Program

AMOUNT: None Specified
DEADLINE: None Specified
FIELDS/MAJORS: Math/Science Education

Scholarships for student members of the American Indian Science and Engineering Society. Must be able to prove tribal enrollment. For graduate studies toward teaching certificate. Program is designed to support teachers who will work in teaching math and sciences to Native American students. Write to the address below for details.

American Indian Science and Engineering Society
Scholarship Coordinator
5661 Airport Blvd.
Boulder, CO   80301-2339

958 Polish Heritage Scholarship

AMOUNT: $500   DEADLINE: Mar 15
FIELDS/MAJORS: All Areas of Study

Scholarships for students of Polish descent attending Grand Rapids Junior College. Write to the address below for details.

Grand Rapids Community College Foundation Scholarships
Director of Financial Aid
143 Bostwick, NE
Grand Rapids, MI   49503

959 Porter McDonnell Memorial Award

AMOUNT: Maximum: $1000
DEADLINE: Nov 10
FIELDS/MAJORS: Surveying

Open to women students pursuing a bachelor's degree, who have the potential for leadership in the surveying and mapping profession. Contact the address below for further information.

American Cartographic Association
Lilly Matheson, ACSM Awards Program
5410 Grosvenor Lane #100
Beghesda, MD   20814-2144

960 Portuguese Foundation, Inc. Scholarships

AMOUNT: $500-$2000   DEADLINE: Mar 1
FIELDS/MAJORS: All Areas of Study

Awards are available for high school seniors of Portuguese ancestry. Must be a resident of Connecticut, demonstrate academic success, community service, and financial need, and be a U.S. citizen or permanent resident. Five to seven awards offered annually. Write to the address below for more details.

Portuguese Foundation, Inc.
Mr. Fernando Rosa
86 New Park Ave.
Hartford, CT   06106

961 Postgraduate Scholarship Program

AMOUNT: None Specified   DEADLINE: Feb 15
FIELDS/MAJORS: All Areas of Study

Must be nominated by the faculty athletic representative or director of athletics of an NCAA member institution. Eligibility is restricted to student athletes attending NCAA member institutions. 125 awards per year. Must be U.S. citizens and ethnic minorities. Selections are made in the academic year in which the student completes his or her final season of eligibility for intercollegiate athletics under NCAA legislation. Write to the address below for details.

National Collegiate Athletic Association
6201 College Blvd.
Overland Park, KS   66211

962 Predicanda Degeer Scholarship

AMOUNT: None Specified   DEADLINE: Mar 1
FIELDS/MAJORS: All Areas of Study

Awards are available at the University of New Mexico for full-time students who have financial need. First preference is given to native New Mexican students of Hispanic descent. Write to the address below for more information.

University of New Mexico, Albuquerque
Office of Financial Aid
Albuquerque, NM   87131

963 Prepharmacy Scholarship

AMOUNT: None Specified   DEADLINE: May 1
FIELDS/MAJORS: Pharmacy

Scholarship for African-American students from the state of Washington who are studying to become a pharmacist. Based on academics, an essay, and an interview with the coalition scholarship committee in the Seattle area. Write to the address below for more information.

Northwest Pharmacists Coalition
PO Box 22975
Seattle, WA   96122

964 Presbyterian Ethnic Leadership Supplemental Grant

AMOUNT: $500-$1000   DEADLINE: None Specified
FIELDS/MAJORS: Ministry

Open to full-time students who are African, Asian, Hispanic, Native Americans or Alaskan Natives. Must be enrolled in a Presbyterian Church seminary or theological institution approved by the students' Committee on Preparation for Ministry. Must be studying for the first professional degree for a church occupation or a position within one of the ecumenical agencies in which the Presbyterian Church participates. Contact the address below for further information.

Presbyterian Church (U.S.A.)
Office of Financial Aid for Studies
100 Witherspoon St.
Louisville, KY   40202-1396

965 Presbyterian Grants

AMOUNT: Maximum: $1000   DEADLINE: Mar 15
FIELDS/MAJORS: All Areas of Study

Awards open to full-time students who are communicant members of the Presbyterian Church, U.S.A. Contact the address below for further information.

Muskingum College
Office of Financial Aid
New Concord, OH 43762

966 Presbyterian Study Grant

AMOUNT: $500-$2000
DEADLINE: None Specified
FIELDS/MAJORS: Preparation for Ministry

Open to full-time students in a Presbyterian Church seminary or theological institution approved by the students' Committee on Preparation for Ministry. Must be studying for the first professional degree for a church occupation or a position within one of the ecumenical agencies in which the Presbyteria Church participates. Contact the address below for further information.

Presbyterian Church (U.S.A.)
Office of Financial Aid for Studies
100 Witherspoon St.
Louisville, KY   40202-1396

967 President's Outstanding Minority and Morton S. Katz Scholarships

AMOUNT: $1000-$3000   DEADLINE: Mar 1
FIELDS/MAJORS: All Areas of Study

Awards open to minority high school seniors who have demonstrated high academic potential. Based on rank, ACT scores and community involvement. Must be enrolled/accepted into University of Minnesota, Duluth. Contact the address below for further information.

University of Minnesota, Duluth
Admissions Office
20 Campus Center
Duluth, MN   55812

968 President's Postdoctoral Fellowship Program

AMOUNT: Maximum: $27000
DEADLINE: Dec 1
FIELDS/MAJORS: Mathematics, Computer Science, Engineering, Physics

Twenty fellowships are available at Oakland for minority and female postdoctoral scholars committed to careers in university teaching or research. Applicants must be U.S. citizens or permanent residents, and hold, or have acquired the Ph.D by the year of the award. Write to the address listed for information on these and other programs that are available.

University of California, Oakland
Office of the President
300 Lakeside Drive, 18th Floor
Oakland, CA   94612

969 President's Scholar Program Minority Scholarships

AMOUNT: None Specified   DEADLINE: None Specified
FIELDS/MAJORS: All Areas of Study

Scholarships available to African, Hispanic, Asian, and Native American graduate students. Must be able to demonstrate high achievement or unusual potential as artists, designers, or educators. Must be U.S. citizens or permanent residents. Financial need is a critical priority. Two awards offered annually. Contact the address below for further information.

Rhode Island School of Design
Financial Aid Office
2 College St.
Providence, RI   02903

970 Presidential Merit Scholars Program

AMOUNT: $8370 DEADLINE: Mar 2
FIELDS/MAJORS: All Areas of Study

Program for incoming freshmen with a GPA of at least 3.5 and a minimum SAT score of 1100 or ACT score of 23. Renewable with a GPA of 3.3 during the first year and a 3.5 each year thereafter. Write to the address below for more information.

California Baptist College
8432 Magnolia Ave.
Riverside, CA 92504

971 Presidential Scholarship

AMOUNT: None Specified DEADLINE: Feb 1
FIELDS/MAJORS: Psychology

Scholarships open to minority students enrolled in a psychology degree program. These awards may be given in concert with other awards or separately. Contact the address below for further information.

Fordham University
Graduate Admissions Office—Keating 216
Fordham University
Bronx, NY 10458

972 Presidents Achievement Award for Freshmen and Aggie Spirit Awards

AMOUNT: $1000-$3000 DEADLINE: Jan 8
FIELDS/MAJORS: All Areas of Study

Scholarships are available for African-American and Hispanic-American high school seniors. Based on academic achievement, test scores, leadership skills, and class rank. Applicants must be U.S. citizens and have a minimum GPA of 3.0. Write to the address below for details.

Texas A & M University
Department of Student Financial Aid
College Station, TX 77843

973 Pride Scholarship

AMOUNT: None Specified
DEADLINE: None Specified
FIELDS/MAJORS: All Areas of Study

Awards for minority students at Wheeling Jesuit College based on academics and leadership. Write to the address below for more information.

Wheeling Jesuit College
Student Financial Planning
316 Washington Ave.
Wheeling, WV 26003

974 Priscilla Maxwell Endicott Scholarship Fund

AMOUNT: $500-$1000 DEADLINE: Apr 20
FIELDS/MAJORS: All Areas of Study

Award for female high school seniors or women enrolled in college. Must have a standing as an amateur woman golfer, demonstrate financial need and scholastic achievement, and provide letters of recommendation from a teacher and a golf pro or coach. Must also be a resident of Connecticut. May be used for two or four-year schools Contact your high school guidance counselor for further information and an application, or write to the address listed.

Connecticut Women's Golf Association
Ms. Julie Keggi, Scholarship Chairwoman
1321 Whittemore Rd.
Middlebury, CT 06762

975 Priscilla R. Morton Scholarship

AMOUNT: None Specified DEADLINE: Jun 1
FIELDS/MAJORS: All Areas of Study

Scholarships are available for Methodist students who are U.S. citizens and enrolled in an accredited institution. Preference is given to students with a GPA of 3.5 or higher attending United Methodist schools. Write to the address below for information.

General Board of Higher Education and Ministry
Office of Loans and Scholarships
PO Box 871
Nashville, TN 37202

976 Proctor & Gamble Minority Scholarships

AMOUNT: None Specified
DEADLINE: None Specified
FIELDS/MAJORS: Chemical Engineering

Open to worthy minority students majoring in chemical engineering. Applicants must be U.S. citizens or permanent residents. Selections made by the School of Chemical Engineering. Write to the address below for further information.

Georgia Institute of Technology
Financial Aid Office
225 North Ave.
Atlanta, GA 30332

977 Professional Church Work Grant

AMOUNT: Maximum: $4500
DEADLINE: None Specified
FIELDS/MAJORS: Christian Service,
Education, Social Work

Awards for students at Concordia University, Oregon, who indicate an intent to serve the Lord Jesus Christ in a Lutheran Church—Missouri Synod ministry, i.e., pastor, teacher, Director of Christian Education, or social worker. You will receive guaranteed $4500 per year as part of your financial assistance. Write to the address listed for more information.

Concordia University, Oregon
Office of Admissions
2811 NE Holman St.
Portland, OR   97211

978 Professional Churchwork Grant

AMOUNT: $750
DEADLINE: None Specified
FIELDS/MAJORS: Religious Work

Awards for full-time undergraduates who are members of the Lutheran Church—Missouri Synod, who declare their intent and commitment to enter full-time professional church work. Renewable upon conditions set by the dean. Write to the address below for more information.

Concordia College, Nebraska
Office of Financial Aid
800 N. Columbia Ave.
Seward, NE   68434

979 Professional Education Scholarship for Graduate Study

AMOUNT: Maximum: $1000   DEADLINE: May 1
FIELDS/MAJORS: Journalism

Must be women members of NFPW with a B.A. or B.S. and two years membership. Based on academic and professional performance, career potential, and financial need. Write to the address below for details.

National Federation of Press Women
4510 W 89th St #110
Prairie Village, KS   66207

980 Professional Opportunities for African-American Students and Graduates

AMOUNT: $1300   DEADLINE: Apr 15
FIELDS/MAJORS: All Areas of Study

Students must be admitted to graduate school for the first time, in the spring or summer semester. Must be U.S. citizens or permanent residents. This is a one time award for students of African-American descent. Write to the address below for more information.

Florida International University
Division of Graduate Studies, PC 520
University Park
Miami, FL   33199

981 Program in Public Policy and International Affairs

AMOUNT: $1500-$15000   DEADLINE: Mar 14
FIELDS/MAJORS: Public Policy/International Affairs

Minority program for undergraduate and graduate students interested in careers in public policy and international affairs. Must be a U.S. citizen or permanent resident. Awards start at $1500 for freshmen, $3000 for seniors, and $15000 for graduates. Write to the address below for details.

Woodrow Wilson National Fellowship Foundation
Dr. Richard O. Hope, VP, WWNFF
CN 5281
Princeton, NJ   08543

982 Project Succeed Displaced Homemaker Scholarship

AMOUNT: Maximum: $400   DEADLINE: Apr 1
FIELDS/MAJORS: All Areas of Study

Awards open to women who are twenty-seven years of age or above and are Ohio residents. Must have lost primary means of support through separation, divorce, widowhood, or the disability of a spouse. Contact the address below for further information.

University of Toledo
Office of Student Financial Aid
4023 Gillham Hall
Toledo, OH   43606

983 Provost Scholars

AMOUNT: None Specified   DEADLINE: Feb 20
FIELDS/MAJORS: All Areas of Study

A limited number of scholarships are designated in the name of the Provost of the University of San Diego. They are generally reserved for underrepresented students of high achievement who have financial need. Write to the address below for information.

University of San Diego
Office of Financial Aid
5998 Alcala Park
San Diego, CA   92110

984
Prunty Scholarship

AMOUNT: $500-$1500   DEADLINE: Jun 16
FIELDS/MAJORS: Nursing

Scholarships are available at the University of Oklahoma, Norman for full-time students who are at least 1/4 Native American and have a minimum GPA of 2.0. Write to the address below for information.

University of Oklahoma, Norman
College of Nursing
PO Box 26901
Oklahoma City, OK   73190

985
Puerto Rican Legal Defense and Education Fund Scholarship

AMOUNT: $1000-$5000   DEADLINE: Jan 31
FIELDS/MAJORS: Law

Open to Puerto Rican or other Hispanic law students. Based on need, academic promise, and Latino community involvement. Generally, must be already enrolled into a J.D. program. Also offered is a summer law internship program. Please contact the address below for complete information.

Puerto Rican Legal Defense and Education Fund, Inc.
99 Hudson St.
New York, NY   10013

986
Q-1 Scholarship

AMOUNT: None Specified
DEADLINE: None Specified
FIELDS/MAJORS: All Areas of Study

Open to full-time undergraduate minority students with a minimum GPA of 2.5. Based on financial need. Preference given to first generation college students, women, and transfer students. Contact the address below for further information.

Alaska Pacific University
Office of Financial Aid
4101 University Dr.
Anchorage, AK   99508

987
Quota International of Springfield Scholarship

AMOUNT: $1000   DEADLINE: Feb 1
FIELDS/MAJORS: Hearing Impaired

Scholarship available to a resident of the greater Springfield area who is either 1) hearing impaired or 2) studying a field pertaining to working with the hearing impaired. Write to the address below for details.

Quota Club of Springfield
219 North Main Street
East Longmeadow, MA   01028

988
Racial Minority Group Assistance

AMOUNT: Maximum: $500   DEADLINE: Feb 15
FIELDS/MAJORS: All Areas of Study

Scholarships are available at Spring Arbor College for minority undergraduate students, with preference given to African-Americans. Write to the address listed for more details.

Spring Arbor College
Office of Financial Aid
Spring Arbor, MI   49283

989
Ralph H. Woods Memorial Scholarships

AMOUNT: None Specified   DEADLINE: Feb 1
FIELDS/MAJORS: All Areas of Study

This scholarship provides three awards for physically disabled graduating high school seniors who have demonstrated academic achievement, community service, and financial need. Applicants should describe disabling condition on application. Must be a resident of Kentucky. Write to the address below for details.

Murray State University
Office of University Scholarships
Ordway Hall, 1 Murray St.
Murray, KY   42071

990
Ramona's Mexican Food Products Scholarship

AMOUNT: None Specified
DEADLINE: Jun 1
FIELDS/MAJORS: Medicine, Law, Business, Engineering, or Journalism

The Ramona's Mexican Food Products Scholarship is available to students of Hispanic descent, wishing to pursue a career in one of the fields listed above. Student must have a 3.5 GPA or better, be planning to attend a school in the state of California, and be currently enrolled in Lincoln, Garfield, or Roosevelt high school. Student must remain single while on scholarship. No student is allowed to change their major field of study without first notifying the foundation. Any change outside the fields specified by the foundation would result in the loss of the scholarship. Write to the address below for details.

Ramona's Mexican Food Products, Inc.
Scholarship Foundation
13633 South Western Avenue
Gardena, CA   90249

991 Ray Marshall Memorial Scholarship

AMOUNT: None Specified   DEADLINE: Mar 2
FIELDS/MAJORS: Hotel/Restaurant Management, Travel, Tourism

Open to full-time degree seeking undergraduates of Latino descent. Must be U.S. citizens or permanent residents. The amount of this award varies, up to 60% of tuition. Contact the address below for further information.

United States International University
Financial Aid Office
10455 Pomerado Rd.
San Diego, CA   92131

992 Ray Marshall Tuition Assistance Scholarships

AMOUNT: None Specified   DEADLINE: Mar 2
FIELDS/MAJORS: Hotel/Restaurant Management, Travel, Tourism

Open to undergraduates who are of Latino descent. Must be employees of hotels or restaurants that have formal programs of monetary support for employee continuing education. This award is for tuition credit only. Amount varies, up to 60% of tuition. Renewable if recipients meet the University's academic standards. Contact the address below for further information.

United States International University
Financial Aid Office
10455 Pomerado Rd.
San Diego, CA   92131

993 Rebecca Beaty Kennedy Scholarship

AMOUNT: None Specified
DEADLINE: None Specified
FIELDS/MAJORS: Liberal Arts

Awarded annually to a female liberal arts student demonstrating academic promise. Write to the address below for more information.

Ashland University
401 College Ave.
Ashland, OH   44805

994 Recognition Scholars Program

AMOUNT: $500   DEADLINE: Feb 1
FIELDS/MAJORS: All Areas of Study

Scholarships are available at the University of New Mexico for entering minority freshmen who have demonstrated outstanding leadership and involvement in high school or community activities. Must be a resident of New Mexico and have a GPA of 2.8 or greater. Approximately four hundred awards offered annually. Write to the address below for information.

University of New Mexico, Albuquerque
Student Financial Aid Office
Mesa Vista Hall North, Student Services
Albuquerque, NM   87131

995 Regents Healthcare Scholarships for Medicine or Dentistry

AMOUNT: $1000-$10000   DEADLINE: None Specified
FIELDS/MAJORS: Medicine/Dentistry

Program for minority residents of New York for at least one year preceding date of award. Students must be enrolled in/accepted to an approved medical/dental school in New York. Must agree to practice in a designated shortage area for at least twenty-four months. Renewable. Must be a U.S. citizen or legal resident. One hundred awards per year. Eighty awards for medicine, and twenty awards for dentistry. Write to the address below for complete details.

New York State Education Department
Bureau of Post-Secondary Grants Admin.
Cultural Education Center
Albany, NY   12230

996 Regents Professional Opportunity Scholarships

AMOUNT: $1000-$5000   DEADLINE: None Specified
FIELDS/MAJORS: All Areas of Approved Study

Minority U.S. citizen or permanent resident. New York resident (at least one year), enrolled in a New York institution in program requiring state license. Typical fields are Veterinary Medicine, Medicine, Pharmacy, Engineering, Dental Hygiene, Physical Therapy, etc. For undergraduate or graduate-level study. Must agree to practice in New York State for at least one year. 220 awards per year. Write to the address below for details.

New York State Education Department
Bureau of Post-Secondary Grants Admin.
Cultural Education Center
Albany, NY   12230

997 Regional Scholarships

AMOUNT: $5000   DEADLINE: Feb 15
FIELDS/MAJORS: All Areas of Study

Awards for first-year women who have demonstrated superior scholastic achievement and distinguished themselves in their extracurricular activities or personal interests. Must have a GPA of 3.2 from high school and an SAT score of at least 1100. Based on both merit and financial need. Ten awards offered annually. Write to the address below for additional information.

Mills College
Office of Financial Aid
5000 MacArthur Blvd.
Oakland, CA   94613

998 Rehabilitation Assistance for Visually Handicapped Scholarship

AMOUNT: None Specified   DEADLINE: None Specified
FIELDS/MAJORS: All Areas of Study

Awards for North Carolina residents enrolled in a full-time undergraduate or graduate programs in a North Carolina school. Student must be legally blind or have a progressive eye condition that may result in blindness. Awards are need based. Contact the address below for further information.

Services for the Blind
Chief of Rehabilitation Services
309 Ashe Ave.
Raleigh, NC   27606

999 Renate W. Chasman Scholarship for Women

AMOUNT: $2000   DEADLINE: May 1
FIELDS/MAJORS: Natural Sciences, Engineering, Mathematics

Scholarships are available for women who are continuing their education after an interruption. Applicant must be a resident of Long Island and be enrolled as a junior, senior, or graduate student in one of the fields listed above. Must be a U.S. citizen or permanent resident. Write to the address below for information.

Brookhaven Women in Science
PO Box 183
Upton, NY 11973

1000 Research Resident Scholar-Katrin H. Lamon Native American Fellowship

AMOUNT: None Specified   DEADLINE: Dec 1
FIELDS/MAJORS: Human Behavior, Culture, Humanities, Anthropology

Fellowships for pre and postdoctoral Native Americans whose field work or basic research is complete. Applications will be evaluated on the basis of overall excellence and the significance of the proposed project. Predoctoral applicants must be nominated by their degree granting department. Contact the address below for further information.

School of American Research
660 Garcia Street
PO Box 2188
Santa Fe, NM   87504

1001 Rev. R.G. and Elizabeth Trent Endowed Scholarship

AMOUNT: None Specified   DEADLINE: Mar 15
FIELDS/MAJORS: Music, Art

Scholarships are available to a female student studying music and art. Write to the address below for more details.

Kansas Wesleyan University
Office of Financial Assistance
100 E. Claflin
Salina, KS   67401

1002 Reverend Joseph B. Rognlien Scholarship

AMOUNT: $4750   DEADLINE: Mar 15
FIELDS/MAJORS: All Areas of Study

Award open to full-time undergraduate students who are children or grandchildren of Christian Ministers. One award offered annually. Contact the address below for further information.

Iowa State University
Office of Student Financial Aid
12 Beardshear Hall
Ames, IA   50011

1003 Reverend Uvaldo Martinez Memorial Scholarship

AMOUNT: None Specified   DEADLINE: Mar 1
FIELDS/MAJORS: Nursing

Awards are available at the University of New Mexico for full-time female nursing students with a minimum GPA of 2.5 and financial need. Applicants must be Spanish speaking and desire to enter the field of public health nursing in New Mexico. Write to the address below or contact the School of Nursing for more details.

University of New Mexico, Albuquerque
Office of Financial Aid
Albuquerque, NM 87131

1004 Rhode Island Polonia Undergraduate Scholarships

AMOUNT: $500   DEADLINE: Feb 15
FIELDS/MAJORS: All Areas of Study

Awards for high school seniors who are Rhode Island students of Polish-American descent accepted in a two or four-year post-secondary school. Must be a U.S. citizen, have a minimum GPA of "B", and be able to demonstrate financial need. Write to the address below for more information.

Rhode Island Polonia Scholarship Foundation
Foundation Office
866 Atwells Ave.
Providence, RI   02909

1005
Richard G. Lane Memorial History Scholarship

AMOUNT: None Specified   DEADLINE: None Specified
FIELDS/MAJORS: History

Award open to students majoring in history. Preference given to Asian students or students studying military history. Contact the address below for further information.

University of North Carolina, Greensboro
Financial Aid Office
723 Kenilworth St.
Greensboro, NC   27412

1006
Richard Klutznick Scholarship Fund

AMOUNT: Maximum: $2500   DEADLINE: Apr 1
FIELDS/MAJORS: Social Work

Applicants must be Jewish graduate students attending accredited schools, studying social work, and having records of good scholarship. Award recipients must agree to accept a two-year position with BBYO upon graduation. Write to the address below for details.

B'nai Brith Youth Organization
1640 Rhode Island Ave., NW
Washington, D.C.   20036

1007
Rita G. Sanchez Scholarships

AMOUNT: None Specified   DEADLINE: Mar 1
FIELDS/MAJORS: All Areas of Study

Awards are available at the University of New Mexico for full-time Hispanic undergraduates with academic ability and financial need. Must be a resident of New Mexico. Write to the address below for more information.

University of New Mexico, Albuquerque
Office of Financial Aid
Albuquerque, NM   87131

1008
Robert and Rosemary Low Memorial Scholarships

AMOUNT: None Specified   DEADLINE: Apr 15
FIELDS/MAJORS: All Areas of Study

Award is available at Portland State University for full-time graduate students with disabilities. Award is merit-based, but financial need may be considered. One award is offered. Contact the Office of Graduate Studies and Research for more information.

Portland State University
Office of Graduate Studies and Research
105 Neuberger Hall
Portland, OR   97207

1009
Robert "Aqqaluk" Newlin, Sr. Memorial Trust Scholarship

AMOUNT: None Specified   DEADLINE: Sep 1
FIELDS/MAJORS: All Areas of Study

Scholarships available to Alaskan Natives who are residents of or associated with the Northwest Arctic Borough of the state of Alaska. Based on academics, financial need, and Inupiaq cultural activities. For students in vocational training through post-graduate level. Contact the address below for further information.

Robert "Aqqaluk" Newlin, Sr. Memorial Trust
Martha Siikauraq, Executive Director
PO Box 509
Kotzebue, AK   99752

1010
Robert B. Bailey III Minority Student Scholarships

AMOUNT: $250-$1000   DEADLINE: Nov 1
FIELDS/MAJORS: Foreign Studies

Awards are available for minority students interested in study abroad. The stipend is intended for use in the cost of travel or the program fee. Must be U.S. citizens or permanent residents and be able to demonstrate financial need. Nov 1 is the deadline for the Winter/Spring program, and Apr 1 is the deadline for the Summer/Fall program. Notification is about three weeks after the deadlines. Write to the address below for more information.

Council on International Educational Exchange
Scholarship Committee
205 East 42nd St.
New York, NY   10017

1011
Robert D. Watkins Minority Graduate Fellowship

AMOUNT: $12000   DEADLINE: May 1
FIELDS/MAJORS: Microbiological Sciences

One year fellowship for students who are African-American, Hispanic-American, Native American, or Native Pacific Islander. Must have completed first year of doctoral studies in microbiological science, be ASM student member, and be U.S. citizen or permanent resident. Project's mentor must also be an ASM member. Write to the address below for additional information.

American Society for Microbiology
Office of Education and Training
1325 Massachusetts Ave., NW
Washington, D.C.   20005

1012
Robert L. Quimby Memorial Fund

AMOUNT: $100
DEADLINE: None Specified
FIELDS/MAJORS: All Areas of Study

Awards for female athletes at Mesa State College. Must be enrolled full-time and have a GPA of at least 3.5. Contact the athletic department for more details.

Mesa State College
Office of Financial Aid
PO Box 3692
Grand Junction, CO   81501

1013
Rockwell International Scholarship

AMOUNT: $1000   DEADLINE: Mar 1
FIELDS/MAJORS: Chemical Engineering, Electrical Engineering, Mechanical Engineering

$1000 annually for a female or minority student of junior standing majoring in chemical, electrical, or mechanical engineering. Recipient is chosen by the company based on career potential, scholastic achievement, and need. Write to the address below for more information.

New Mexico State University
College of Engineering
Complex I, Box 30001, Dept. 3449
Las Cruces, NM   88003

1014
Rockwell International Scholarships

AMOUNT: None Specified   DEADLINE: Mar 1
FIELDS/MAJORS: Electrical, Mechanical Engineering

Awards are available at the University of New Mexico for undergraduate female or minority students in electrical or mechanical engineering. Selection based on academic achievement. Must be a U.S. citizen. Write to the address below for more information.

University of New Mexico, Albuquerque
Office of Financial Aid
Albuquerque, NM   87131

1015
Roger Lang Memorial Scholarship

AMOUNT: None Specified
DEADLINE: None Specified
FIELDS/MAJORS: All Areas of Study

Applicants must be Native Alaskan residents of southeast Alaska and must demonstrate motivation, academic achievement, and leadership potential. Undergraduate applicants must have a minimum GPA of 2.5; graduate applicants must have a minimum GPA of 3.0. Write to the address below for more information.

University of Alaska Southeast (Juneau Campus)
Financial Aid Office
11120 Glacier Highway
Juneau, AK   99801

1016
Roland P. Dodds and Bob Dole Endowed Scholarships

AMOUNT: None Specified   DEADLINE: Mar 15
FIELDS/MAJORS: All Areas of Study

Scholarships are available to students with disabilities. Write to the address below for more details about both awards.

Kansas Wesleyan University
Office of Financial Assistance
100 E. Claflin
Salina, KS   67401

1017
Roman Catholic High School Scholarship

AMOUNT: None Specified   DEADLINE: None Specified
FIELDS/MAJORS: All Areas of Study

Scholarships are available at the Catholic University of America for full-time students who are graduates of the Roman Catholic High School of Philadelphia. This award is not offered every year. Contact the financial aid office at the address below for details.

Catholic University of America
Office of Admissions and Financial Aid
Washington, D.C.   20064

1018
Ronald H. Brown Commercial Service Fellowship Program

AMOUNT: None Specified   DEADLINE: Feb 14
FIELDS/MAJORS: Political Science, International Affairs/Trade, Government

Program designed for handicapped upper undergraduates who are U.S. citizens. This award provides for tuition, fees, books, and room and board. Contact the address below for further information.

Woodrow Wilson National Fellowship Foundation
Dr. Richard O. Hope, Director
Box 2434
Princeton, NJ   08543

1019
Ronald McDonald Children's Charities Health and Medical Scholars Program

AMOUNT: $1000   DEADLINE: Jan 31
FIELDS/MAJORS: Pre-Medical or Healthcare

Awards for African-American college sophomores in one of the fields above. Applicants must have a GPA of at least 3.0, have unmet financial need, and be involved in community service in the area of healthcare. Sixty awards are given annually. Write to the address below for more information.

United Negro Scholarship Fund
8260 Willow Oaks Corporate Drive
PO Box 10444
Fairfax, VA   22031

1020

Rosa Parks Scholarship

AMOUNT: None Specified   DEADLINE: Mar 1
FIELDS/MAJORS: All Areas of Study

Awards for students demonstrating financial need and academic achievement. Students must file a FAFSA as soon as possible after Jan 1 and before the Mar 1 financial aid priority consideration date. You will automatically be considered for this scholarship if you are enrolled at the University and apply for financial aid. Separate applications, requests, or inquiries are not required and cannot be honored.

University of Massachusetts, Amherst
255 Whitmore Administration Building
Box 38230
Amherst, MA   01003

1021

Rose & Joseph Sokol Scholarship Fund

AMOUNT: $500   DEADLINE: None Specified
FIELDS/MAJORS: All Areas of Study

The Rose and Joseph Sokol scholarship fund was established in memory of Rose and Joseph Sokol by their children. It is dedicated to helping South Carolina residents of the Jewish faith in need of financial aid to attend any college of their choosing. For undergraduate study. Write to the address below between Sep 1 and Nov 1 for details.

Rose & Joseph Sokol Scholarship Fund
Mrs. Dorothy S. Kipnis
118 Chadwick Dr.
Charleston, SC   29407

1022

Rose Garreau Memorial Endowment Scholarships

AMOUNT: Maximum: $1000   DEADLINE: Mar 15
FIELDS/MAJORS: All Areas of Study

Open to sophomores through graduate students who are enrolled full time and are of Native American descent. Must be able to demonstrate financial need. Based on academics and financial need. Contact the address below for further information.

Arizona State University
Scholarship Office Main Campus
PO Box 870412
Tempe, AZ   85287

1023

Rowley/Ministerial Education Scholarship

AMOUNT: None Specified   DEADLINE: Mar 15
FIELDS/MAJORS: Theology

Applicants must be members of the Christian Church (Disciples of Christ) who are preparing for the ordained ministry. Must be a full-time student. Financial need is considered. Write to the address below for details.

Christian Church (Disciples of Christ)
Attn: Scholarships
PO Box 1986
Indianapolis, IN   46206

1024

Roxie Armfield King Scholarship

AMOUNT: $1492   DEADLINE: Mar 1
FIELDS/MAJORS: All Areas of Study

Award open to female residents of Guilford County, North Carolina. Must be U.S. citizens. Contact the address below for further information.

University of North Carolina, Greensboro
Financial Aid Office
723 Kenilworth St.
Greensboro, NC   27412

1025

Roy E. Jones Memorial Scholarship

AMOUNT: $750   DEADLINE: Mar 1
FIELDS/MAJORS: Business, Accounting

Scholarship open to Native Americans majoring in any business discipline who are at least a sophomore with a minimum GPA of 2.75. Native American applicants must be able to prove Indian descent by using the form BIA 4432 "verification of Indian preference". Financial need is not a factor for selection. Two awards offered annually. Write to the address below for details.

University of Wyoming
College of Business
c/o Jacquelin Buchanan
Laramie, WY   82071

1026

Roy Wilkins Scholarship

AMOUNT: $1000   DEADLINE: Apr 30
FIELDS/MAJORS: All Areas of Study

Applicant must be an African-American high school senior and be a member of the NAACP. Student must have a GPA of 2.5. Write to the address below for more details.

NAACP Special Contribution Fund
Education Department
4805 Mount Hope Drive
Baltimore, MD   21215

1027

Rozenwaig Single Mothers Scholarship Fund

AMOUNT: $2000   DEADLINE: Mar 5
FIELDS/MAJORS: Social Work

Scholarship is available to a graduate student in good academic standing in the School of Social Work. The student must be a single mother, over the age of thirty-five, and demonstrate financial need. Essay on family life required. Write to the address below for more information.

Florida International University
College of Urban and Public Affairs
Office of the Dean—AC1 200
North Miami, FL   33181

1028

RPCNA Grants at Geneva

AMOUNT: None Specified   DEADLINE: None Specified
FIELDS/MAJORS: All Areas of Study

Renewable scholarships for students at Geneva College who are communicant members of the reformed Presbyterian Church of North America (RPCNA). For full-time study. Contact the Office of Admissions for further information.

Geneva College
Office of Admissions
Beaver Falls, PA   15010

1029

RTNDF Summer and Entry-Level Internships

AMOUNT: None Specified   DEADLINE: Mar 1
FIELDS/MAJORS: News Management, Electronic Journalism

Internship program juniors, seniors, or graduate minority students who are interested in news management or electronic journalism. Write to the address below for more information.

Radio and Television News Directors Foundation
1000 Connecticut Ave., NW
Suite 615
Washington, D.C.   20036

1030

Rudolph Dillman Memorial Scholarship

AMOUNT: $2500   DEADLINE: Apr 1
FIELDS/MAJORS: Rehabilitation, Education of Visually Impaired and Blind Persons

Open to legally blind graduates and undergraduates who are studying in the field of rehabilitation and/or education of visually impaired and blind persons. Must be U.S. citizens. Write to the address below for complete details.

American Foundation for the Blind
Scholarship Committee
11 Penn Plaza, Suite 300
New York, NY   10001

1031

Ruth Baty Jones & Maurice Barnett Jones, Dorothy Pownall Scholarships

AMOUNT: $1500-$2000   DEADLINE: None Specified
FIELDS/MAJORS: Journalism

Scholarships are available at the University of Iowa for full-time female senior journalism majors who have been active in the area of investigative and explanatory journalism. Three awards per year. Write to the address below for information.

University of Iowa
School of Journalism and Mass Comm.
205 Communications Center
Iowa City, IA   52242

1032

Ruth Lewis Petit Memorial Award

AMOUNT: None Specified   DEADLINE: None Specified
FIELDS/MAJORS: All Areas of Study

Available annually to an upperclass woman on the basis of general promise, financial need, and scholarship. Write to the address below for more information.

Ashland University
401 College Ave.
Ashland, OH   44805

1033

Ruth M. Jessie Collings Scholarship

AMOUNT: None Specified   DEADLINE: Mar 1
FIELDS/MAJORS: Pre-Med

Award open to female students who are U.S. citizens. Contact the address below for further information.

University of North Carolina, Greensboro
Financial Aid Office
723 Kenilworth St.
Greensboro, NC   27412

1034

Ruth McKaughan and W. Bryan Carter Scholarship

AMOUNT: None Specified   DEADLINE: Mar 1
FIELDS/MAJORS: English

Award open to female undergraduates who are U.S. citizens and residents of Guilford, Rowan, or Buncombe Counties, North Carolina. Applicants must be single and without a car. Contact the address below for further information.

University of North Carolina, Greensboro
Financial Aid Office
723 Kenilworth St.
Greensboro, NC   27412

1035
Ruth N. Ely Endowed Scholarship

AMOUNT: None Specified
DEADLINE: None Specified
FIELDS/MAJORS: Education or Religion

Awarded annually to an undergraduate student(s) majoring in education or religion. Preference is given to qualified students who are active members of the Brethren Church. Write to the address below for more information.

Ashland University
401 College Ave.
Ashland, OH   44805

1036
Ruth Patton Grady Scholarship

AMOUNT: None Specified
DEADLINE: Mar 15
FIELDS/MAJORS: Elementary Education

Open to entering freshmen who will be majoring in elementary education. First preference given to minorities, second preference to all other entering freshmen, and third preference to transfer students. Must have a minimum GPA of 3.0 and at least a score of 920 on the SAT. Renewable if recipient maintains a minimum GPA of 2.75 and continues as an elementary education major. Contact the address below for further information.

Barton College
Financial Aid Office
Wilson, NC   27893

1037
Ruth Satter Memorial Award

AMOUNT: $500-$1000   DEADLINE: Jan 15
FIELDS/MAJORS: All Areas of Study

Scholarship for women pursuing their doctorate who have taken at least three years off to raise children. Applications available after Oct 1. Write to the address below for more details.

Association for Women in Science Educational Foundation
National Headquarters
1200 New York Ave. NW #650
Washington, D.C.   20005

1038
Sachs Foundation Scholarship

AMOUNT: $3500-$4500   DEADLINE: Mar 1
FIELDS/MAJORS: All Areas of Study

Scholarships are available for African-American students who are residents of Colorado. Applicant must demonstrate financial need. Undergraduates must have a GPA of at least 3.5, and graduate students must have a GPA of at least 3.8. Community involvement is also an important aspect of evaluation. Write to the address below for information.

Sachs Foundation
90 S. Cascade Avenue, Suite 1410
Colorado Springs, CO   80903

1039
Sallie and Beulah Alexander Scholarship

AMOUNT: $1000   DEADLINE: Apr 1
FIELDS/MAJORS: All Areas of Study

Scholarships are available at the University of Oklahoma, Norman for students who are of Comanche Indian heritage. Four to seven awards offered annually. Write to the address below for information.

University of Oklahoma, Norman
Office of Financial Aid Services
731 Elm
Norman, OK   73019

1040
Sam Eschenbach Minority Scholarship

AMOUNT: None Specified
DEADLINE: None Specified
FIELDS/MAJORS: Mechanical Engineering

Open to minority students who are majoring in mechanical engineering. Recipients selected by the School of Mechanical Engineering. Write to the address listed for further information.

Georgia Institute of Technology
Financial Aid Office
225 North Ave.
Atlanta, GA   30332

1041
Sam S. Kuwahara Memorial Scholarship

AMOUNT: None Specified   DEADLINE: Apr 1
FIELDS/MAJORS: Agriculture

Awards for undergraduate students of Japanese ancestry who are studying agriculture and are members of the JACL. Write to the address below for more details. Please be sure to include a SASE with your request.

Japanese American Citizens League
National Headquarters
1765 Sutter St.
San Francisco, CA   94115

1042
Samuel Robinson Award

AMOUNT: $1000   DEADLINE: Apr 1
FIELDS/MAJORS: All Areas of Study

Scholarships for juniors or seniors at a Presbyterian college. Applicants must be U.S. citizens and members of the Presbyterian Church (U.S.A.). Must be a full-time student. Write to the address below for information and an application.

Presbyterian Church (U.S.A.)
Office of Financial Aid for Studies
100 Witherspoon Street
Louisville, KY   40202

1043
San Jose GI Forum Scholarships

AMOUNT: $500-$2000   DEADLINE: Mar 21
FIELDS/MAJORS: All Areas of Study

Scholarships for Hispanic students who are graduating from Santa Clara County (CA) high schools. Must have a GPA of at least 2.5 and plan to enroll in an accredited college or university in an associate's or bachelor's degree program. Write to address below for details.

San Jose GI Forum Scholarship Foundation Inc.
1680 Alum Rock Ave.
San Jose, CA   95116

1044
Santa Fe Pacific Hispanic-American Scholarships

AMOUNT: None Specified   DEADLINE: None Specified
FIELDS/MAJORS: All Areas of Study

High school graduates of Hispanic origin must be accepted or enrolled into a college or university. Three award programs, each with an unspecified number of awards, one based on academics, one on potential as a student, and one on need. All applicants must be U.S. citizens or permanent residents. Contact your high school guidance counselor or write to the address below for details.

Lulac National Educational Service Centers, Inc.
Program Director
2100 M Street, NW, Ste. 602
Washington, D.C.   20037

1045
Sato Memorial Scholarship

AMOUNT: $500
DEADLINE: None Specified
FIELDS/MAJORS: Engineering, Mathematics, Natural Sciences

Awards are available at Portland State University for Asian students in the fields of math, engineering, or natural science. A GPA of 3.0, as well as enrollment in at least 12 credits is required to apply. Renewable. One to two awards offered annually. Write to the address below for more information.

Portland State University
Educational Equity Programs and Services
120 Smith Memorial Center
Portland, OR   97207

1046
Scholars in Residence Program Fellowships

AMOUNT: Maximum: $30000
DEADLINE: Jan 13
FIELDS/MAJORS: Black Culture, History, Museum Administration

To assist scholars and professionals whose research in the black experience will benefit from extended access to the center's collections. Allows fellows to spend six months to a year in residence and includes seminars, forums, and conferences. Candidates for advanced degrees must have received the degree or completed all the requirements for it by the center's deadline. Contact the address below for further information and application.

Schomburg Center for Research in Black Culture
515 Malcolm X Boulevard
New York, NY   10037

1047
Scholarships for Children of Missionaries

AMOUNT: None Specified   DEADLINE: Jun 1
FIELDS/MAJORS: All Areas of Study

Scholarships for children of missionaries (active, retired, or deceased) from the Episcopal Church. Available for undergraduate or graduate level study. Write to the address below for more details.

Episcopal Church Center
815 Second Ave.
New York, NY   10017

1048
Scholarships for Foreign Students

AMOUNT: None Specified   DEADLINE: Jun 1
FIELDS/MAJORS: Church Related Studies, Theology

Scholarships for students from developing countries who are in some type of theological training within the Anglican Communion. Preference is given to students pursuing a master's degree, but it is open for all levels of study. Write to the address below for more details. Applications must be authorized or approved by the diocesan Bishop, the Archbishop, or another provincial authority.

Episcopal Church Center
815 Second Ave.
New York, NY   10017

1049
Scholarships for Minority Ministries

AMOUNT: None Specified   DEADLINE: Jun 1
FIELDS/MAJORS: Church Related Studies, Theology

Scholarships for Asian-American, African-American, Hispanic, and Native American students for assistance in pursuing theological education or a graduate-level degree at a church approved seminary or in an Episcopal studies program. Write to the address below for more details.

Episcopal Church Center
815 Second Ave.
New York, NY   10017

1050
Scholarships for Minority Students

AMOUNT: $2500   DEADLINE: Mar 15
FIELDS/MAJORS: All Areas of Study

Open to African-American, Hispanic-American, and Native American students. Based on academics, leadership, and demonstrated financial need. Contact the coordinator of minority student admissions at the address below for details.

Rochester Institute of Technology
Bausch & Lomb Center, Financial Aid Office
60 Lomb Memorial Drive
Rochester, NY   14623

1051
Schuyler M. Meyer, Jr. Scholarship Fund

AMOUNT: $1000   DEADLINE: Jun 15
FIELDS/MAJORS: All Areas of Study

Scholarships are available for Native Americans who demonstrate financial need, academic ability, and potential for success. Applicants must be single parents, full-time students, and have a GPA of 2.0 or better. Write to the address below for information.

American Indian Science and Engineering Society
Scholarship Coordinator
5661 Airport Blvd.
Boulder, CO   80301-2339

1052
Science and Technology Fellowships

AMOUNT: $5000-$9500   DEADLINE: Dec 15
FIELDS/MAJORS: Architecture, Computer Science, Engineering, Mathematics, Statistics

Open to women who are citizens or permanent residents of the United States preparing to enter designated fields with low female participation. Available to candidates for the final year of a master's degree program. Write for complete details.

American Association of University Women Educational Foundation
2201 N. Dodge Street
Iowa City, IA   52243

1053
Science Application International Corporation Awards

AMOUNT: None Specified   DEADLINE: Mar 1
FIELDS/MAJORS: Electrical Engineering, Computer Science

Awards are available at the University of New Mexico for minority juniors or seniors studying electrical engineering or computer science students who are willing to participate in the minority engineering program. Recipients must be willing to work as interns with the SAIC in the summer. Write to the address below for more information.

University of New Mexico, Albuquerque
Office of Financial Aid
Albuquerque, NM   87131

1054
Scottish Gardening Scholarship

AMOUNT: None Specified   DEADLINE: Dec 31
FIELDS/MAJORS: Horticulture

Awards for students who have completed two years in a horticulture program. Must be hard working and have a strong interest in horticulture as a career. This scholarship covers the cost to and from Scotland, one year's tuition at Threave School of Gardening, and a monthly stipend. Write to the address below for more information.

Scottish Heritage U.S.A.-National Junior Horticulture Association
Project Coordinator, Mr. Tom Clark
253 Bachelor St.
Granby, MA   01033

1055
Sealaska Scholarship Program

AMOUNT: None Specified   DEADLINE: Apr 1
FIELDS/MAJORS: All Areas of Study

Scholarships for either Alaskan Natives (as defined by the Alaskan Native Claims Settlement Act (43USCA,1602(b)) who are (or are dependents of) shareholders or stockholders of Sealaska Corporation or Native Americans who reside in southeastern Alaska. Write to the address below for details.

Sealaska Heritage Foundation
Scholarship Program
One Sealaska Plaza, Suite 201
Juneau, AK   99802

1056
Seix-Dow Fellowship

AMOUNT: None Specified   DEADLINE: Feb 1
FIELDS/MAJORS: Economics, International Development, International Economics

Fellowships open to Hispanic students enrolled in any of the above listed areas. Contact the address below for further information.

Fordham University
Graduate Admissions Office—Keating 216
Fordham University
Bronx, NY   10458

1057
Selected Professions Fellowship

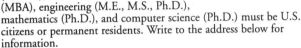

AMOUNT: $5000-$9500   DEADLINE: Dec 17
FIELDS/MAJORS: Architecture, Business Admin., Engineering, Math, Computer Science

Fellowships are available for women who are in the final year of an advanced degree in the fields of architecture (master's), business administration (MBA), engineering (M.E., M.S., Ph.D.), mathematics (Ph.D.), and computer science (Ph.D.) must be U.S. citizens or permanent residents. Write to the address below for information.

American Association of University Women
Fellowship Programs
2201 N. Dodge St. Department 67
Iowa City, IA   52243

1058
Seminole/Miccosukee Indian Scholarships

AMOUNT: None Specified   DEADLINE: None Specified
FIELDS/MAJORS: All Areas of Study

Applicants must be Florida residents and members of the Seminole or the Miccosukee tribes. Can be either full or part-time undergraduate or graduate student. Must demonstrate financial need. Write for further information. Details and application forms are available from your tribal office.

Florida Department of Education
Office of Student Financial Assistance
1344 Florida Education Center
Tallahassee, FL   32399

1059
Sequoyah Graduate Fellowships

AMOUNT: None Specified   DEADLINE: Oct 1
FIELDS/MAJORS: All Areas of Study

Fellowships are available for American Indian or Native Alaskan graduate students. Ten awards are offered for study in all areas. Write to the address below for details.

Association on American Indian Affairs, Inc.
Box 268
Sisseton, SD   57262

1060
Sequoyah Heritage Award

AMOUNT: None Specified
DEADLINE: None Specified
FIELDS/MAJORS: Arts and Sciences

University of Oklahoma-Norman offers the Sequoyah heritage award to full-time Native American students with (60-90 hrs.) completed. Applicant must show potential for significant contributions to the Indian community. One to two awards offered annually. Write to the address below for information.

University of Oklahoma, Norman
College of Arts and Sciences
601 Elm, Room 429
Norman, OK   73019

1061
Sertoma Scholarships for Students with Hearing Loss

AMOUNT: $1000   DEADLINE: May 2
FIELDS/MAJORS: All Areas of Study

Scholarships are available for full-time students enrolled in or planning to enroll in any accredited four-year program. Applicants must have a documented hearing loss and a GPA of at least 3.2. Based on academic ability. Thirteen scholarships are offered annually. Write to the address below for information.

Sertoma International
Sertoma Scholarship
1912 East Meyer Blvd.
Kansas City, MO   64132

1062
Service Loan

AMOUNT: $1500   DEADLINE: Apr 1
FIELDS/MAJORS: All Areas of Study

Provides undergraduate students with an opportunity to pay a portion of their educational debt through service in various school, church, and community projects. Applicants must be full-time sophomore or junior students and must serve 300 hours in a campus-related project, Church-related project, community organization, or as a volunteer in a mission. Contact the financial aid office at your school for information and forms. If applications are not available there, write to address below.

Presbyterian Church (U.S.A.)
Office of Financial Aid for Studies
100 Witherspoon Street
Louisville, KY   40202

1063
SETAC Program for Minority Students and Mentors in Environmental Chemistry

AMOUNT: None Specified   DEADLINE: Sep 8
FIELDS/MAJORS: Environmental Chemistry and Toxicology

Awards are available for minority students and faculty mentors in the areas of environmental chemistry or toxicology. Selected individuals will receive a one-year membership to the Society of Environmental Toxicology and Chemistry and funds to travel and attend the SETAC world conference in Canada. Write to the address below for more information.

Society of Environmental Toxicology and Chemistry
Mr. Rodney Parrish, Executive Director
1010 North 12th Avenue
Pensacola, FL   32501

1064

Shauna May Memorial Scholarship

AMOUNT: $1000   DEADLINE: Feb 3
FIELDS/MAJORS: Humanities, Literature, History, Philosophy, Anthropology, Psychology, or Religion

Offered to a new or currently enrolled student with junior or senior standing attending Evergreen full time, who is pursuing studies in the humanities: literature, history, philosophy, anthropology, psychology, and religion. Contact the address listed for further information.

Evergreen State College
Office of the Dean of Enrollment Service
2700 Evergreen Parkway
Olympia, WA   98505-0002

1065

Sheryl McCormick Asian Studies Scholarship

AMOUNT: None Specified   DEADLINE: None Specified
FIELDS/MAJORS: Chinese, Asian Studies

Awards for students at UMass given in order of priority: 1) a Chinese major participating in the Tunghai University program, 2) a Chinese major with the best all-around academic record, 3) a student concentrating in Asian studies. Contact the Chair of the Asian Studies Dept., not the address below, for additional information.

University of Massachusetts, Amherst
Office of Financial Aid Services
255 Whitmore Admin. Bldg., Box 38230
Amherst, MA   01003

1066

Shirley Mewborn Perseverance Scholarship

AMOUNT: None Specified   DEADLINE: None Specified
FIELDS/MAJORS: All Areas of Study

Open to female students who have a minimum GPA of 3.0 and can demonstrate financial need. Awarded by the Office of Student Financial Planning and Services. Write to the address below for further information.

Georgia Institute of Technology
Financial Aid Office
225 North Ave.
Atlanta, GA   30332

1067

SHPE Engineering and Science Scholarships

AMOUNT: $500-$7000   DEADLINE: Apr 15
FIELDS/MAJORS: Engineering, Science

Scholarships for Hispanic students seeking careers in science or engineering. For undergraduate or graduate study. Based on potential, character, need, involvement, and scholastic aptitude. Must be attending school full time. Write to the address below for details.

Society of Hispanic Professional Engineers Foundation
SHPE Scholarships, Kathy Borunda
5400 E. Olympic Blvd., Suite 210
Los Angeles, CA   90022

1068

Sisterhood of Mary and Martha Award

AMOUNT: $200   DEADLINE: None Specified
FIELDS/MAJORS: All Areas of Study

Given to a woman in her freshman year. Write to the address below for more information.

Ashland University
401 College Ave.
Ashland, OH 44805

1069

Six Month Internships

AMOUNT: $8000   DEADLINE: Jan 31
FIELDS/MAJORS: Art History, Art Conservation

Internships for African-American, Hispanic, or other minority students who are studying art history or a related field. For seniors, recent graduates, or graduate students. For study at the museum. Write to the address below for additional information.

Metropolitan Museum of Art
Office of Academic Programs
1000 Fifth Ave.
New York, NY   10028

1070

SNPA Foundation Adopt-A-Student Minority Scholarship Program

AMOUNT: $1000-$2000   DEADLINE: Apr 1
FIELDS/MAJORS: Journalism, Business, Advertising, Graphics, Computer Science

Open to high school seniors or graduates who are minorities, have at least a "C" average, and have been nominated by SNPA members. Contact a member newspaper of the SNPA Foundation for more information on nomination procedures and application.

Southern Newspaper Publishers Association
PO Box 28875
Atlanta, GA 30358

1071

Solis Family Fellowship

AMOUNT: $600   DEADLINE: Jan 6
FIELDS/MAJORS: Public Services

Open to full-time Latino master's degree students planning a career to serve Latino people and communities in the U.S. Must be U.S. citizens or permanent residents. Contact the address below for further information.

University of California, Berkeley
Office of Financial Aid Graduate Unit
201 Sproul Hall #1960
Berkeley, CA   94720

1072
Sophie S. Laval Memorial Scholarship

AMOUNT: None Specified   DEADLINE: Apr 1
FIELDS/MAJORS: Business Administration, Economics, Social Science, Religion

Open to junior and senior women who are residents of Florida. Must have a minimum GPA of 2.4 and be able to demonstrate financial need. Contact the address below for details.

Flagler College
Director of Financial Aid
PO Box 1027
St. Augustine, FL   32085

1073
Soroptimist International of Olympia Endowment Scholarship

AMOUNT: $500   DEADLINE: Feb 1
FIELDS/MAJORS: All Areas of Study

Offered to a new or currently enrolled Evergreen female student who has completed a minimum of 45 credits at the time of application, with demonstrated involvement in community activities/services. The successful applicant must enroll as a full-time student. Contact the address listed for further information.

Evergreen State College
Office of the Dean of Enrollment Service
2700 Evergreen Parkway
Olympia, WA   98505-0002

1074
Soroptimists International of Yreka

AMOUNT: $575   DEADLINE: May 1
FIELDS/MAJORS: All Areas of Study

Scholarships are open to female freshman who are enrolled full time at the College of the Siskiyous. Applicant must be a resident of Siskiyou County, be able to demonstrate financial need, and be twenty-five years of age or older. This scholarship is renewable for a maximum of two years. Write to the address below for details.

College of the Siskiyous
Financial Aid Office
800 College Ave.
Weed, CA   96094

1075
Soroptimist International of Hays Training Award

AMOUNT: None Specified   DEADLINE: Jan 15
FIELDS/MAJORS: All Areas of Study

Scholarships open to women completing undergraduate programs or entering vocational or technical training programs. Must be head of a household. Write to the address below for information.

Soroptimist International of Hays
Jolene Moore
1921 Whittier
Hays, KS   67601

1076
Soroptimist International of Hays Youth Citizenship Award

AMOUNT: None Specified   DEADLINE: Jan 15
FIELDS/MAJORS: All Areas of Study

Scholarships open to high school seniors who have made outstanding contributions to home, school, or community. Write to the address below for information.

Soroptimist International of Hays
Jolene Moore
1921 Whittier
Hays, KS   67601

1077
South Carolina Graduate Incentive Fellowship Program

AMOUNT: Maximum: $10000   DEADLINE: None Specified
FIELDS/MAJORS: All Areas of Study

Fellowships for South Carolina residents who are members of a minority group attending a South Carolina public college or university. For graduate and doctoral study. Write to the address below for additional information.

South Carolina Commission on Higher Education
1333 Main Street, Suite 200
Columbia, SC   29201

1078
South Carolina "Other Race" Program

AMOUNT: Maximum: $1000   DEADLINE: None Specified
FIELDS/MAJORS: All Areas of Study

Scholarships for South Carolina residents who are members of a minority group attending a South Carolina public college or university. Write to the address below for additional information.

South Carolina Commission on Higher Education
1333 Main Street, Suite 200
Columbia, SC   29201

1079
Southeast Laymen's Scholarship

AMOUNT: $200   DEADLINE: None Specified
FIELDS/MAJORS: All Areas of Study

The scholarship is awarded each year to a seminary or pre-seminary student of the Southeast District of the Ashland-based Brethren Church. If there are no eligible candidates, the scholarship is given to a worthy student of the Brethren Church. Write to the address below for more information.

Ashland University
401 College Ave.
Ashland, OH   44805

1080
Spencer T. Olin Fellowships for Women in Graduate Study

AMOUNT: $20000-$33000
DEADLINE: Feb 1
FIELDS/MAJORS: See Listing of Fields Below

Fellowships are available at Washington University for female scholars in one of the following fields: Biology, Biomedicine, Humanities, Physics, Math, Social Science, Behavioral Science, Architecture, Business Administration, Engineering, Fine Arts, Law, Medicine, and Social Work. For master's and doctoral level study. Write to the address below for information.

Monticello College Foundation / Washington University
Margaret Watkins, Olin Fellowship Prog.
Campus Box 1187, One Brookings Drive
St. Louis, MO   63130

1081
Spirit of Freedom Foundation Scholarship Fund

AMOUNT: None Specified
DEADLINE: None Specified
FIELDS/MAJORS: Fine/Performing Arts, Museum Studies

Scholarships are available to African-American undergraduates and graduate students pursuing or enhancing careers in the fine and performing arts or in museum studies. Graduates must have a bachelor's degree and at least one year of professional experience in the arts or museum studies. Must be living in the greater Kansas City area. Undergraduates must be in a four-year institution planning to work in the greater Kansas City area. Contact the address listed for further information.

Greater Kansas City Community Foundation and Affiliated Trusts
1055 Broadway #130
Kansas City, MO   64105

1082
Springfield Business and Professional Women's Club Scholarship

AMOUNT: $400   DEADLINE: Mar 31
FIELDS/MAJORS: All Areas of Study

Student must be a full-time junior or senior with a GPA of 3.0 or better. Preference is given to women who demonstrate financial need. Write to the address below for more information.

Southwest Missouri State University
Office of Financial Aid
901 South National Ave.
Springfield, MO   65804

1083
SREB Doctoral Scholars Program

AMOUNT: $12000   DEADLINE: Apr 1
FIELDS/MAJORS: All Areas of Study

Awards are available for the purpose of encouraging ethnic minority students to pursue doctoral degrees and become college level teachers. Preference is given to Science, Engineering and Mathematics students. For residents of Alabama, Arkansas, Florida, Georgia, Kentucky, Louisiana, Maryland, Virginia, Mississippi, North/South Carolina, Oklahoma, Texas, Tennessee, and West Virginia. Write to the address below for information.

Southern Regional Education Board
592 Tenth Street, NW
Atlanta, GA   30318

1084
Stanley Mark Thomson Endowed Memorial Scholarship

AMOUNT: None Specified   DEADLINE: None Specified
FIELDS/MAJORS: All Areas of Study

Open to enrolled students who are Alaskan Natives, with preference given to residents of Unalakleet. Based on financial need. Contact the address below for further information.

Alaska Pacific University
Office of Financial Aid
4101 University Dr.
Anchorage, AK   99508

1085
Stanley Schiff Memorial Scholarship

AMOUNT: Maximum: $250   DEADLINE: Mar 1
FIELDS/MAJORS: Judaic Studies

Open to a graduating senior who plans to continue Judaic studies in graduate school. Contact the address below for further information.

Brooklyn College
Office of the V.P. for Student Life
2113 Boylan Hall
Brooklyn, NY   11210

1086
Star Supporter Scholarship/Loan

AMOUNT: None Specified   DEADLINE: Mar 15
FIELDS/MAJORS: Theology, Church Related Studies

Applicants must be African-American members of the Christian Church who are preparing to enter the Ordained Ministry and can demonstrate financial need. Full-time enrollment is mandatory. Write to the address below for details.

Christian Church (Disciples of Christ)
Attn: Scholarships
PO Box 1986
Indianapolis, IN   46206

1087
State Farm Insurance Companies Scholarship

AMOUNT: None Specified   DEADLINE: Nov 1
FIELDS/MAJORS: Insurance

Open to minority and female students interested in careers in the insurance industry. Second deadline date is Jun 1. Contact the Business Administration Department for further information.

Angelo State University
Financial Aid Office
PO Box 11015
San Angelo, TX   76909

1088
State Scholarship for Ethnic Recruitment

AMOUNT: None Specified
DEADLINE: None Specified
FIELDS/MAJORS: All Areas of Study

For Texas minority residents who are incoming freshmen with at least 830 on the SAT or 17 on the ACT. Undergraduates and incoming transfer students must have a minimum GPA of 2.5. Graduates must have a GPA of at least 3.0. Must be able to demonstrate financial need. Write to the address below for details.

Texas A & M University
Student Financial Aid Department
College Station, TX   77843

1089
State Scholarship Program for Ethnic Minorities in Nursing

AMOUNT: Maximum: $3000   DEADLINE: None Specified
FIELDS/MAJORS: Nursing

Scholarships for Texas residents who are minorities attending a Texas four-year public college. Must be enrolled in an accredited nursing program. Write to the address below for details.

Texas Higher Education Coordinating Board
PO Box 12788
Austin, TX   78711

1090
State Scholarship Program for Ethnic Recruitment

AMOUNT: None Specified   DEADLINE: None Specified
FIELDS/MAJORS: All Areas of Study

Scholarships are available to Texas residents attending a Texas four-year public college, who are minority students. Undergraduates must have a minimum GPA of 2.5. Graduate students must have a minimum GPA of 3.0. Write to the address below for details.

Texas Higher Education Coordinating Board
PO Box 12788
Austin, TX   78711

1091
Steinsick/Egly Scholarship Fund and Women's Golf Scholarship

AMOUNT: None Specified   DEADLINE: Mar 31
FIELDS/MAJORS: All Areas of Study

Awards open to participants in the women's golf program. Must have a minimum GPA of 3.0. Contact the address below for further information about both awards.

University of North Texas
Scholarship Office
Marquis Hall #218
Denton, TX   76203

1092
Stoody-West Fellowship

AMOUNT: $6000   DEADLINE: Feb 15
FIELDS/MAJORS: Journalism (religious)

Awards for Christian graduate students enrolled in journalism at accredited schools who plan a career in religious journalism. Write to the fellowship committee at the address below for details.

United Methodist Communications
Fellowship Committee, Public Media Div.
PO Box 320
Nashville, TN   37202

1093
Storer Scholarships

AMOUNT: $2192   DEADLINE: None Specified
FIELDS/MAJORS: All Areas of Study

Scholarships for African-American high school seniors planning to attend WVU. Based on academic achievement. State residency not required. Must have a minimum GPA of at least 3.0. Twenty awards per year. Contact the financial aid office at the address below for details.

West Virginia University
Financial Aid Office
PO Box 6004
Morgantown, WV   26506

1094
Student Aid Award for Physically Disabled Students

AMOUNT: $1500   DEADLINE: Dec 31
FIELDS/MAJORS: All Areas of Study

Scholarships for physically handicapped students. Applicants must be between the ages of fifteen and thirty-five and be able to demonstrate financial need. Contact your local Venture Club or write to the address below for details.

Venture Clubs of the Americas
Two Penn Center Plaza, Suite 100
Philadelphia, PA   19102

1095
Student Opportunity Scholarships

AMOUNT: $100-$1400   DEADLINE: Apr 1
FIELDS/MAJORS: All Areas of Study

Open to high school seniors who are African-American, Hispanic-American, Asian-American, Native American, and Alaskan Natives and are Presbyterian Church members and U.S. citizens or permanent residents. Must be able to demonstrate financial need. Write to the address below for details. Specify Student Opportunity Scholarships (SOS).

Presbyterian Church (U.S.A.)
Office of Financial Aid for Students
100 Witherspoon Street
Louisville, KY   40202

1096
Sub-Saharan Africa Dissertation Internship Awards

AMOUNT: $20000   DEADLINE: Mar 2
FIELDS/MAJORS: All Areas of Study

Fellowships are available to African scholars who have completed all the Ph.D. requirements except the dissertation. Award is to increase the quality of overseas advanced studies for outstanding African scholars and to enhance the relevance of their training to the process of economic development in Africa. Priority is given to agricultural and environmental majors. Write to the address below for information.

Rockefeller Foundation
African Dissertation Internships
420 Fifth Avenue
New York, NY   10018

1097
Successor Grant

AMOUNT: Maximum: $1000
DEADLINE: None Specified
FIELDS/MAJORS: Religion, Theology

Awards for Concordia students who are eligible Lutheran Church—Missouri Synod young men named by their pastor. Applicants must plan to enter the seminary after graduation from Concordia. Must be U.S. citizens and have GPAs of at least 2.5. Renewable. Write to the address below for more information.

Concordia University, Irvine
Financial Aid Office
1530 Concordia West
Irvine, CA   92715

1098
Sumitomo Bank of California Scholarships

AMOUNT: None Specified   DEADLINE: Apr 1
FIELDS/MAJORS: Business, Banking, Accounting, Economics, International Trade

Applicants must be of Japanese ancestry, California residents attending California schools, and majoring in the above fields. Must also be members of the JACL. Applications and information may be obtained from local JACL chapters, district offices, and the national headquarters at the address below. Please indicate your level of study and be certain to include a legal-sized SASE.

Japanese American Citizens League
National Scholarship and Award Program
1765 Sutter St.
San Francisco, CA   94115

1099
Summer Internship Program

AMOUNT: None Specified   DEADLINE: Apr 1
FIELDS/MAJORS: All Areas of Study

Ten-week summer internship program to provide valuable work experience for a blind post-secondary student. Duties include activities in the areas of public information and education, membership assistance, communications, legislative monitoring, and publications. Write to the address below for details.

American Council of the Blind
Oral Miller, Executive Director
1155 15th St., NW, Suite 720
Washington, D.C.   20005

1100
Summer Research Fellowships in Law and Social Science

AMOUNT: $3500   DEADLINE: Mar 3
FIELDS/MAJORS: Social Science, Humanities

Fellowships available for minority students who have completed their sophomore year. Applicants must have a minimum GPA of 3.0 and intend to pursue graduate studies in the above fields. Must be U.S. citizens or permanent residents. The program lasts ten weeks, and the recipients will work at the ABF offices for thirty-five hours per week. Awards will be announced by Apr 15. Write to the address below for information.

American Bar Foundation
Assistant Director
750 N. Lake Shore Drive
Chicago, IL   60611

1101
Summer Research Program for Minorities and Women

AMOUNT: None Specified   DEADLINE: Dec 1
FIELDS/MAJORS: Engineering, Math, Science, Physics

Program offers minority and women students technical employment experience at Bell Laboratories. Students should have completed their third year of college. Must be U.S. citizens or permanent residents. Write to the address below or call (908) 582-6461 for complete details.

AT&T Bell Laboratories
University Relations, Srp Manager
101 Crawfords Corner Rd, Rm 1B-222
Holmdel, NJ   07733

1102
SUNY Empire State Honors Awards for African, Latino, and Native Americans

AMOUNT: None Specified   DEADLINE: None Specified
FIELDS/MAJORS: All Areas of Study

Awards are available for freshmen at SUNY, Potsdam based on academic achievement. Must be an African-American, Latino, or Native American student to apply. Write to the address below for more information.

SUNY, Potsdam
Office of Admissions
44 Pierrepont Ave
Potsdam, NY   13676

1103
Susan E. Terry Scholarship for "Returning Women"

AMOUNT: $150   DEADLINE: Dec 2
FIELDS/MAJORS: All Areas of Study

Award open to women who are twenty-one years of age or above. Must be enrolled in one or more courses and be a resident of Franklin County, Virginia. Contact any campus for additional information.

Paul D. Camp Community College
PO Box 737
Franklin, VA   23851

1104
Susan Given State Farm Insurance Annual Award

AMOUNT: None Specified   DEADLINE: None Specified
FIELDS/MAJORS: Business

Awarded to young women with a major in the business field. Susan Given's gift matched through the State Farm Insurance Matching Gift Program. Write to the address below for more information.

Ashland University
401 College Ave.
Ashland, OH   44805

1105
Susan James McDonald Memorial Scholarship

AMOUNT: $1000   DEADLINE: None Specified
FIELDS/MAJORS: Management

Awards for juniors in the School of Management. Recipient will be selected on the basis of scholarship, financial need, and commitment to the highest ideals of the management profession. Female students will be given preference. Applications for School of Management scholarships will be available in the SOM Development Office, Room 206.

University of Massachusetts, Amherst
School of Management
SOM Development Office, Room 206
Amherst, MA   01003

1106
Susan Reynard Dedischew Memorial Scholarship

AMOUNT: None Specified   DEADLINE: None Specified
FIELDS/MAJORS: Counseling Psychology

Scholarships are awarded to re-entry women students majoring in counseling psychology. Contact the address listed for further information.

Chapman University
333 N. Glassell
Orange, CA   92866

1107
Susan Zisselman Memorial Scholarship

AMOUNT: Maximum: $1000   DEADLINE: Mar 1
FIELDS/MAJORS: Arts, Humanities

Open to a deserving disabled student. Must be able to demonstrate financial need and a commitment to the arts or humanities. Contact the address listed for further information.

Brooklyn College
Office of the V.P. for Student Life
2113 Boylan Hall
Brooklyn, NY   11210

1108
Swiss Benevolent Society of Chicago Scholarships

AMOUNT: Maximum: $2500   DEADLINE: Feb 28
FIELDS/MAJORS: All Areas of Study

Scholarships for residents of Illinois and southern Wisconsin who are Swiss nationals or of Swiss descent. Applicants may be high school seniors with exam scores of 26 ACT and 1050 SAT. If applicant is an undergraduate, must have a minimum GPA of 3.5. Must be U.S. citizens or permanent residents. Write to the address below for details.

Swiss Benevolent Society of Chicago
Scholarship Committee
6440 N. Bosworth Avenue
Chicago, IL   60626

1109
Sybil Weaver Scholarship

AMOUNT: $1000   DEADLINE: Mar 1
FIELDS/MAJORS: All Areas of Study

Scholarships are available at the University of Oklahoma, Norman for female students who have a GPA of 3.25 or above. Two to three awards per year. Write to the address below for information.

University of Oklahoma, Norman
Office of Financial Aid Services
731 Elm
Norman, OK   73019

1110
Sylvia Lewis General Scholarship Fund Award

AMOUNT: $1000   DEADLINE: Mar 1
FIELDS/MAJORS: All Areas of Study

Scholarships are available at the University of Oklahoma, Norman for full-time minority students, who have a GPA of at least 2.0 (undergraduate) or 3.0 (graduate). Based on academic, leadership, and citizenship qualities. Write to the address below for information.

University of Oklahoma, Norman
Assoc. Director, Student Support Service
Hester Hall, Room 200
Norman, OK   73019

1111
T. Eliot Weier Undergraduate Scholarship

AMOUNT: $1000   DEADLINE: None Specified
FIELDS/MAJORS: Botany, Plant Pathology, Plant Science

Open to minority high school seniors. Must have a minimum combined SAT score of 1000 and rank in the top 10% of graduating class. Renewable through school with satisfactory grades. Contact the address below for further information.

Purdue University—Dept. of Botany and Plant Pathology
Professor R.C. Coolbaugh
Lilly Hall of Life Sciences #I—420
West Lafayette, IN   47907

1112
Talented Minority Scholarship Program

AMOUNT: $5000   DEADLINE: None Specified
FIELDS/MAJORS: All Areas of Study

Incoming students are considered for this award during the admissions process; no separate application needed. Returning UMass students must complete an application during Feb to be considered. Returning UMass students can receive additional information from the office of enrollment services at the University of Massachusetts, Amherst.

University of Massachusetts, Amherst
Office of Financial Aid Services
255 Whitmore Admin. Bldg., Box 38230
Amherst, MA   01003

1113
Teachers for Catholic Schools Program Scholarship

AMOUNT: None Specified   DEADLINE: Apr 1
FIELDS/MAJORS: Education

Open to students of the Catholic faith. Must provide a letter of support from your pastor or clergyman capable of judging your potential for teaching in a Catholic school and a statement of why you wish to teach in a Catholic school. Contact the address listed for more information.

Loras College
Office of Financial Planning
1450 Alta Vista St., P.O. Box 178
Dubuque, IA   52004

1114
Teachers' Loan-for-Service Program

AMOUNT: Maximum: $4000   DEADLINE: Jul 1
FIELDS/MAJORS: Education

Loans for minority or physically disabled students from New Mexico who attend a New Mexico institution and are studying to be teachers of grades K through 12. Open to undergraduate or graduate students. Loan will be forgiven if recipient agrees to serve at a public institution in Lea, Otero, Eddy, Chaves, or Roosevelt Counties in New Mexico following graduation. Write to the address below for more information.

New Mexico Commission on Higher Education
Financial Aid and Student Services
PO Box 15910
Santa Fe, NM   87506

1115
Telesensory Scholarship

AMOUNT: $1000   DEADLINE: Apr 1
FIELDS/MAJORS: All Areas of Study

Open to legally blind full-time undergraduates who are U.S. citizens. Must provide official transcript of grades, proof of acceptance at a college or university, and evidence of legal blindness. Write to the foundation at the address below to receive information on this award and other programs they administer.

American Foundation for the Blind
Scholarship Coordinator
11 Penn Plaza, Suite 300
New York, NY   10001

1116 Texas Minority Leaders in Education Scholarship Program

AMOUNT: $1000-$2000   DEADLINE: None Specified
FIELDS/MAJORS: Education

Minority students must be planning to pursue a career in education in Texas upon graduation. Must be accepted or enrolled as full-time students in one of the public universities affiliated with this program. Must have a GPA of at least a 3.0. Write to the address listed for more information.

Southwestern Bell Foundation
Pearl Garza Fracchia, Area Manager
One Bell Plaza, Room 3040
Dallas, TX   75202

1117 Thaddeus John Bell, II Memorial Scholarship

AMOUNT: $500   DEADLINE: None Specified
FIELDS/MAJORS: Sports

Awarded to a African-American student athlete enrolled full time, participating in varsity football, basketball, or track, and having the highest GPA of all candidates applying, with a minimum GPA of 2.5. Contact the address listed for further information.

Charleston Southern University
PO Box 118087
Charleston, SC   29423

1118 Thanks Be to Grandmother Winifred Foundation

AMOUNT: Maximum: $5000   DEADLINE: Mar 21
FIELDS/MAJORS: All Areas of Study

Grants are available to women who are least fifty-four years of age and U.S. citizens with a social security number. Applicants must submit a grant proposal that benefits adult women. (Those who are twenty-one years of age or above.) A second deadline date for these awards is Sep 21. Write to the address below for more information.

Thanks Be to Grandmother Winifred Foundation
PO Box 1449
Wainscott, NY   11975

1119 The Ralph J. Bunche Scholars Program

AMOUNT: None Specified   DEADLINE: None Specified
FIELDS/MAJORS: All Areas of Study

Awards for minority students at Colby College who have demonstrated scholastic strength and leadership potential and are involved in extracurricular activities. Candidates are nominated by guidance counselors, alumni, community leaders, and organizations across the country. Must be U.S. citizens or permanent residents. Write to the address below for additional information.

Colby College
Director of Financial Aid
Lunder House
Waterville, ME   04901

1120 Theo Dykes Memorial Scholarship

AMOUNT: None Specified   DEADLINE: Apr 1
FIELDS/MAJORS: All Areas of Study

Award for an African-American male with demonstrated economic need, as verified by parent's tax return for prior year or other suitable documents. Must be a graduating high school senior or college student with a GPA of 2.5 or better. Also based on three letters of reference, an essay on the challenge to American families today, and involvement in school and community activities. This award is available for students in the metropolitan Washington D.C. area. Contact Nylcare customer service at (800) 635-3121 for more information.

Nylcare/Mid-Atlantic Scholarship Foundation, Inc.
7617 Ora Glen Drive
Greenbelt, MD 20770

1121 Theresa E. Beneke Memorial Pre-Med Scholarship

AMOUNT: None Specified   DEADLINE: Mar 1
FIELDS/MAJORS: Pre-Med

Award for incoming full-time women freshmen. Must be in top 5% of their high school classes. Preference given to students with more than one sibling. One award offered annually. Contact the address below for further information.

Iowa State University
Office of Student Financial Aid
12 Beardshear Hall
Ames, IA   50011

1122 Thomas F. Zimmerman Ministerial Grant

AMOUNT: $730   DEADLINE: Feb 15
FIELDS/MAJORS: All Areas of Study

Scholarships are available at Evangel for full-time students who are legal dependents of nationally appointed full-time Assemblies of God ministers who can demonstrate great financial need. Write to the address below for information.

Evangel College
Office of Enrollment
1111 N. Glenstone
Springfield, MO   65802

1123
Thomas H. Kean Minority Student Scholarships

AMOUNT: $1000-$10000 DEADLINE: Mar 1
FIELDS/MAJORS: All Areas of Study

Scholarships available at Drew for first-year minority students who do not qualify for the Drew Scholars Program. Write to the address below for information or contact your school guidance counselor.

Drew University
Office of Financial Assistance
Madison, NJ   07940

1124
Thomas P. Papandrew Scholarship

AMOUNT: $1000 DEADLINE: Mar 31
FIELDS/MAJORS: Landscape Architecture/Design

Applicants must be minority students enrolled at Arizona State University in a landscape architecture or design program. Applicant must be an Arizona resident and a full-time student. Renewable. Write to the address below for additional information.

Landscape Architecture Foundation
4401 Connecticut Ave., NW, Suite 500
Washington, D.C.   20008

1125
Thomas R. Williams Scholarship

AMOUNT: None Specified DEADLINE: None Specified
FIELDS/MAJORS: All Areas of Study

Open to ethnic minority students who are residents of Georgia. Financial need is a second priority. Write to the address listed for further information.

Georgia Institute of Technology
Financial Aid Office
225 North Ave.
Atlanta, GA   30332

1126
Thurgood Marshall Scholarships

AMOUNT: None Specified
DEADLINE: None Specified
FIELDS/MAJORS: All Areas of Study

Awards for entering freshman who are pursuing a bachelor's degree full time at one of the thirty-seven historically black public colleges and universities. Applicants must be U.S. citizens, have a GPA of at least 3.0, and have a score of 1000 or more on the SAT or a 24 or higher on the ACT. Renewable for four years. Write to the address below or contact the on-campus TMSF coordinator for more information.

Thurgood Marshall Scholarship Fund
Scholarship Coordinator
100 Park Ave.
New York, NY   10017

1127
Thurmond E. Williamson Scholarship Fund

AMOUNT: None Specified DEADLINE: Mar 1
FIELDS/MAJORS: Latin-American Studies

Awards are available at the University of New Mexico for graduate students in a Latin-American studies program. Applicant must exhibit outstanding academic achievement. Write to the address below for more information.

University of New Mexico, Albuquerque
Office of Financial Aid
Albuquerque, NM   87131

1128
Tina Guimaraes Memorial Scholarship and American Indian Funding

AMOUNT: $2000 DEADLINE: None Specified
FIELDS/MAJORS: Biology

Awards open to undergraduates who are Native American or Native Alaskan, enrolled in a federally recognized tribe. Contact the address below for further information.

University of Minnesota, Duluth
Nick Whelihan, Director of Financial Aid
Duluth, MN   55812

1129
Tony Orlando Yellow Ribbon Scholarship

AMOUNT: $500 DEADLINE: Mar 14
FIELDS/MAJORS: Travel and Tourism, Hotel/Motel Management

Awards for students with disabilities who are residents of North America and enrolled in a college in North America. High school seniors must have a GPA of 3.0 or better and continuing students must have a GPA of at least 2.5. Write to the address below for more information.

National Tour Foundation
546 East Main St.
PO Box 3071
Lexington, KY   40596

1130
Touch the Face of God Scholarship

AMOUNT: None Specified DEADLINE: May 30
FIELDS/MAJORS: Aviation

Award for young female pilots, at least eighteen years of age, who demonstrate a true love of flying and the field of aviation. Applicants must have a GPA of 3.0 or greater and submit a letter describing her feelings about aviation and her motives for desiring to become a professional pilot. Write to the address below for more information.

Nancy Horton Scholarship Fund, Inc.
234 Jay Hakes Road
Cropseyville, NY   12052

1131

Tracy Harrington Dickinson Scholarship

AMOUNT: $3500   DEADLINE: Mar 1
FIELDS/MAJORS: Liberal Arts

Awards for freshmen females at Lake Erie College who are in a non-scientific discipline within the liberal arts. Applicant must have a high school GPA of at least 3.0. Write to the address below for more information.

Lake Erie College
Financial Aid Office
391 W. Washington St.
Painesville, OH   44077

1132

Training Awards Program

AMOUNT: $3000-$5000   DEADLINE: Dec 15
FIELDS/MAJORS: All Areas of Study

Scholarships for mature women. For technical or vocational training or for completion of undergraduate degree. Regional and national awards are also available ($3000-regional, $5000-national). Applicants must be considered the head of a household. Application is made through participating Soroptimist Clubs. Club addresses can be found in your local telephone directory, chamber of commerce, or city hall.

Soroptimist International of the Americas, Inc.
Two Penn Center Plaza
Suite 1000
Philadelphia, PA   19102

1133

Training Fellowship for Minorities in Substance Abuse Research

AMOUNT: $5000   DEADLINE: None Specified
FIELDS/MAJORS: Substance Abuse and Treatment, Epidemiology, Health Policy

Awards for minority students in the second or third year of study in any of the fields listed above. Must be a U.S. citizen. Ten awards presented annually. Send a SASE to the address below for more information.

National Medical Fellowships, Inc.
110 West 32nd
8th Floor
New York, NY   10001

1134

Training in the Neurosciences for Minorities

AMOUNT: $10000-$18000   DEADLINE: Jan 15
FIELDS/MAJORS: Neurosciences

Fellowships for ethnic minority students pursuing doctoral degrees in APA accredited doctoral programs in psychology or neuroscience. Must be a U.S. citizen or permanent resident. Write to the address below or call (202) 336-6027 for more information.

American Psychological Association
Minority Fellowship Program/Neuroscience
750 First St., NE
Washington, D.C.   20002

1135

Transportation Planning Division Minority Scholarship

AMOUNT: $2500   DEADLINE: May 15
FIELDS/MAJORS: Planning—Traffic/Transportation

Scholarships for minority (African-American, Hispanic, Asian-American, and Native American) undergraduate or graduate students specializing in transportation planning. Applications may be available in planning departments (or programs). If not available there, details and forms may be obtained by writing to "Planning Division Minority Scholarship in Transportation Planning" at the below address.

American Planning Association
479-A Oro Dam Blvd.
Oroville, CA   95965

1136

Tribute Endowment Scholarship

AMOUNT: Maximum: $500   DEADLINE: Mar 15
FIELDS/MAJORS: All Areas of Study

Open to African-American full-time graduate and undergraduate students who can demonstrate financial need. Undergrads must have a minimum GPA of 2.5, and graduates must have at least a 3.0 GPA to apply. Contact the address below for further information.

Arizona State University
Scholarship Office Main Campus
PO Box 870412
Tempe, AZ   85287

1137

Truman D. Picard Scholarship Program

AMOUNT: $1500   DEADLINE: Feb 28
FIELDS/MAJORS: Natural Resources

Awards for high school seniors and undergraduates who are Native American or Alaskan students. Must be able to show academic merit, financial need, and be a member of a federally recognized tribe or Native Alaska corporation. Four awards offered annually. Contact the address below for further information.

Intertribal Timber Council
Attn: Education Committee
4370 NE Halsey St.
Portland, OR   97213

1138
Trustee Scholarships

AMOUNT: Maximum: $10000
DEADLINE: Feb 15
FIELDS/MAJORS: All Areas of Study

Awards for first-year women who have demonstrated superior scholastic achievement and distinguished themselves in their extracurricular activities or personal interests. Must have a GPA of 3.5 from high school and an SAT score of at least 1200. Based on merit and financial need. Write to the address below for additional information.

Mills College
Office of Financial Aid
5000 MacArthur Blvd.
Oakland, CA   94613

1139
Trustees' Award

AMOUNT: None Specified
DEADLINE: None Specified
FIELDS/MAJORS: All Areas of Study

Awards for Concordia students from underrepresented ethnic backgrounds. Must have a GPA of at least 2.5 and be a U.S. citizen. Write to the address below for more information.

Concordia University, Irvine
Financial Aid Office
1530 Concordia West
Irvine, CA   92715

1140
Tuition Waiver Program for North American Indians

AMOUNT: None Specified   DEADLINE: None Specified
FIELDS/MAJORS: All Areas of Study

Open to any Michigan resident who is at least 1/4 North American Indian (certified by their Tribal Nation) and willing to attend any public Michigan college, university, or community college. Award is for all levels of study. Renewable. Write to the address below for further information (including procedures for certification of ancestry, if necessary). Bureau of Indian Affairs also provides funds for persons who are at least 1/8 American Indian. Information on BIA awards may also be obtained from the address below.

Michigan Commission on Indian Affairs
611 West Ottawa Street
Lansing, MI   48913

1141
Tull Metals Company Scholarship

AMOUNT: None Specified
DEADLINE: None Specified
FIELDS/MAJORS: Industrial, Systems Engineering

Open to minority students who are beginning their junior year. Preference given to residents of the Midwest. Awards made by the School with approval from the Tull Metals Company. Write to the address listed for further information.

Georgia Institute of Technology
Financial Aid Office
225 North Ave.
Atlanta, GA   30332

1142
Tyree, Fisher & Meredith, and Bob & Nancy Good Scholarships

AMOUNT: None Specified   DEADLINE: Jan 1
FIELDS/MAJORS: All Areas of Study

Scholarships for African-American students at Denison University. Based on strong academic performance and potential. The Tyree and Fisher/Meredith awards are renewable if recipients maintain pre-set standards. Awards range from one third to one half tuition. Contact the office of admissions or the financial aid office at the address listed for details.

Denison University
Financial Aid Office
Box M
Granville, OH   43023

1143
U Foundation Scholarships

AMOUNT: None Specified
DEADLINE: Mar 1
FIELDS/MAJORS: Marketing, Electrical Engineering

Awards are available at the University of New Mexico for handicapped students studying in the fields of marketing or electrical engineering. Write to the address below for more information.

University of New Mexico, Albuquerque
Office of Financial Aid
Albuquerque, NM   87131

1144
U.S. Environmental Protection Agency Scholarship

AMOUNT: $4000   DEADLINE: Jun 15
FIELDS/MAJORS: Chemistry, Chem. Eng., Environmental Sciences, Biology, and Related

Scholarship for students with junior status or higher enrolled full time. Must agree to work at the Environmental Protection Agency, a tribal location, or an environmental facility during the summers, if a job is offered. Students may reapply every year. Write to the address below for details.

American Indian Science and Engineering Society
Scholarship Coordinator
5661 Airport Blvd.
Boulder, CO   80301-2339

1145
UCC Ministerial Discount

AMOUNT: $1000   DEADLINE: Feb 15
FIELDS/MAJORS: All Areas of Study

Awards are available to full-time Elon College students who are dependent children of full-time ministers in the United Church of Christ. Write to the address below for details.

Elon College
Office of Financial Planning
2700 Campus Box
Elon College, NC   27244

1146

UNCF/Merck Science Initiative

AMOUNT: None Specified
DEADLINE: None Specified
FIELDS/MAJORS: Biomedical Research

Awards for outstanding African-American students pursuing a career in the field of biomedical research. Fifteen awards offered to undergraduates, twelve awards to graduate students, and ten awards at the postdoctoral level. Contact the address listed for further information.

United Negro College Fund
Scholarship Program
PO Box 10444
Fairfax, VA   22031

1147

Undergraduate/Graduate Loans

AMOUNT: $200-$1500   DEADLINE: None Specified
FIELDS/MAJORS: All Areas of Study

Loans for full-time undergraduate or graduate students who are U.S. citizens and members of the Presbyterian Church (U.S.A.). Based upon academic ability and demonstrated financial need. Write to the address below for details.

Presbyterian Church (U.S.A.)
Office for Financial Aid for Studies
100 Witherspoon Street
Louisville, KY   40202

1148

Undergraduate and Graduate Scholarships

AMOUNT: $350-$1000   DEADLINE: Apr 1
FIELDS/MAJORS: All Areas of Study

Applicants must be students of Armenian ancestry enrolled at an accredited college or university. Based on financial need. Involvement with the Armenian community is considered. Renewable once. Scholarships available for both undergraduates and graduate students. Write to the address below for details.

Armenian Relief Society of North America, Inc.
Ms. Seda Aghamianz
80 Bigelow Ave.
Watertown, MA   02172

1149

Undergraduate Awards

AMOUNT: None Specified   DEADLINE: Apr 1
FIELDS/MAJORS: All Areas of Study

For members of the JACL who are undergraduates and have a minimum of a year for completion of their education. Applications and information may be obtained from local JACL chapters, district offices, and national headquarters at the address below. Please indicate your level of study and be certain to include a legal-sized SASE. (offices are in San Francisco, Seattle, L.A., Chicago, and Fresno)

Japanese American Citizens League
National Scholarship and Award Program
1765 Sutter St.
San Francisco, CA   94115

1150

Undergraduate Disabled Student Scholarship Program

AMOUNT: $1000-$2000   DEADLINE: Mar 15
FIELDS/MAJORS: All Areas of Study

Scholarships are offered to disabled students who are U.S. citizens and residents of California or Hawaii. Scholarships are for undergraduate work at an accredited community college, university, or licensed vocational school only. Individuals applying must be in second semester of senior year in high school or have completed high school or passed the GED. Write to the address below for more information.

California-Hawaii Elks Major Project, Inc.
Scholarship Committee
5450 East Lamona Ave.
Fresno, CA   93727

1151

Undergraduate Minority Scholarship Program

AMOUNT: $2500   DEADLINE: May 15
FIELDS/MAJORS: Planning and Urban Development, Public Admin., Environmental Science

Scholarships for minority (African-American, Hispanic, and Native American) undergraduates in planning programs in the U.S. Based on academics and leadership potential. Must be U.S. citizens. For sophomores, juniors, and seniors. Applications may be available in planning departments (or programs). If not available there, details and forms may be obtained by writing to "Planning and the Black Community Division Scholarship" in care of the address below.

American Planning Association
Fellowships and Scholarships in Planning
1776 Massachusetts Ave., NW
Washington, D.C.   20036

1152

Underrepresented Minority Achievement Scholarships for Juniors

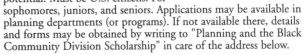

AMOUNT: None Specified   DEADLINE: May 1
FIELDS/MAJORS: All Areas of Study

Awards are available at Portland State University for African-American, Hispanic, or Native American juniors. Must maintain a GPA of at least 2.5 (GPA of 2.7 or better in major) and be enrolled in at least 12 credits per term. Approximately thirty-two awards offered annually. Contact the Educational Equity Programs and Services for more information.

Portland State University
Office of Admissions
104 Neuberger Hall
Portland, OR 97207

1153

Union Bank Scholarships

AMOUNT: None Specified
DEADLINE: Apr 1
FIELDS/MAJORS: Business, Accounting, Economics, International Trade

Applicants must be of Japanese ancestry and California residents majoring in the above fields. Must also be members of the JACL. Applications and information may be obtained from local JACL chapters, district offices, and the national headquarters at the address below. Please indicate your level of study, and be certain to include a legal-sized SASE.

Japanese American Citizens League
National Scholarship and Award Program
1765 Sutter St.
San Francisco, CA 94115

1154

Union Pacific Railroad Scholarship

AMOUNT: None Specified   DEADLINE: Mar 1
FIELDS/MAJORS: Civil, Electrical, or Mechanical Engineering

Awards are available at the University of New Mexico for minority or female juniors in the areas of study listed above. Must have a GPA of at least 3.0. Write to the address below for more information.

University of New Mexico, Albuquerque
Office of Financial Aid
Albuquerque, NM 87131

1155

Union Pacific, Gilcrease Foundations Scholarships

AMOUNT: $400   DEADLINE: None Specified
FIELDS/MAJORS: All Areas of Study

Open to students who are Native Americans and attending school full time. Contact the address below for further information about both awards.

Bacone College
Financial Aid Office
99 Bacone Rd.
Muskogee, OK 74403

1156

United Methodist Student Grant

AMOUNT: Maximum: $1000
DEADLINE: None Specified
FIELDS/MAJORS: All Areas of Study

Awards available at Central Methodist for full-time undergraduate students who are active members of a United Methodist Church. Applicants must be residents of Missouri. Renewable with a 2.5 GPA. Write to the address listed for details.

Central Methodist College
Financial Aid Office
411 Central Methodist Square
Fayette, MO 65248

1157

United Technologies/ Pratt and Whitney Scholarship in Business

AMOUNT: None Specified   DEADLINE: None Specified
FIELDS/MAJORS: Management

Awards for School of Management juniors or seniors who are from an underrepresented population in greater Hartford or western Massachusetts. Applications for School of Management scholarships will be available in the SOM Development Office, Room 206.

University of Massachusetts, Amherst
School of Management
SOM Development Office, Room 206
Amherst, MA 01003

1158

University African-American Graduate Fellowships

AMOUNT: None Specified   DEADLINE: Mar 1
FIELDS/MAJORS: All Areas of Study

Six fellowships for African-American graduate students enrolled full time at Syracuse University. Must enroll in at least one course in African-American studies (3 credit hours). Contact the graduate admissions office for details.

Syracuse University
Office of Financial Aid
200 Archbold
Syracuse, NY 13244

1159

University of Evansville United Methodist Scholarships

AMOUNT: Maximum: $2500   DEADLINE: Feb 15
FIELDS/MAJORS: All Areas of Study

Awards for students who are members of United Methodist Churches and are recommended by their ministers. Renewable. Write to the address listed for more information.

University of Evansville
Office of Financial Aid
1800 Lincoln Ave.
Evansville, IN 47722

1160
University Women's Association Scholarship

AMOUNT: $500 **DEADLINE:** Mar 1
FIELDS/MAJORS: All Areas of Study

Scholarships are available at the University of Oklahoma, Norman for junior or senior students who are Oklahoma residents, with a GPA of at least 3.5. Must be able to demonstrate financial need. Write to the address below for information.

University of Oklahoma, Norman
Office of Financial Aid Services
731 Elm
Norman, OK   73019

1161
University Women's Association Scholarship

AMOUNT: None Specified   **DEADLINE:** Jan 15
FIELDS/MAJORS: All Areas of Study

Scholarships open to women students attending Fort Hays State. Based on academics and financial need. Write to the address below for information.

Fort Hays State University
Office of Student Financial Aid
600 Park St.
Hays, KS   67601

1162
University Women's Club Scholarship

AMOUNT: None Specified   **DEADLINE:** Mar 1
FIELDS/MAJORS: All Areas of Study

Award open to incoming female freshmen who are U.S. citizens. Contact the address below for further information.

University of North Carolina, Greensboro
Financial Aid Office
723 Kenilworth St.
Greensboro, NC   27412

1163
University Women's Club Scholarships

AMOUNT: $500-$1000   **DEADLINE:** Apr 1
FIELDS/MAJORS: All Areas of Study

Awards open to women undergraduates based on academics and financial need. Two of the three awards are for non-traditional students. Contact the address below for further information.

University of Toledo
Office of Student Financial Aid
4023 Gillham Hall
Toledo, OH   43606

1164
Unocal Corporation Scholarship

AMOUNT: $1000-$2000
DEADLINE: Mar 1
FIELDS/MAJORS: Petroleum or Geological Engineering

Scholarships are available at the University of Oklahoma, Norman for full-time minority or female petroleum or geological engineering majors who are U.S. citizens. One to two awards offered annually. Write to the address below for information.

University of Oklahoma, Norman
Scholarship Coord., Pet. and Geol. Eng.
T301 Energy Center
Norman, OK   73019

1165
Upper Iowa Church Scholarships

AMOUNT: None Specified   **DEADLINE:** None Specified
FIELDS/MAJORS: All Areas of Study

Since Upper Iowa University is a non-denominational private institution and therefore interdenominational in nature, it recognizes the significant contribution religion makes to our society. To qualify for consideration for these scholarships, students must have an application signed by their priest, pastor, rabbi, minister, or other recognized officer within the church community, attesting to the student's membership status within that church's organization. Write to the address below for more information.

Upper Iowa University
Financial Aid Office
PO Box 1857
Fayette, IA   52142-1857

1166
Upperclass Minority Scholarship

AMOUNT: None Specified   **DEADLINE:** Apr 1
FIELDS/MAJORS: All Areas of Study

Applicants must be currently enrolled MSU minority students who have a minimum GPA of 2.5. Must be enrolled for at least 12 credits per term. Write to the address below for more information.

Moorhead State University
Office of Scholarship and Financial Aid
107 Owens Hall, Campus Box 327
Moorhead, MN   56563

1167
UPS Scholarships for Female and Minority Students

AMOUNT: $2500   **DEADLINE:** Nov 15
FIELDS/MAJORS: Industrial Engineering

Scholarships are available for undergraduate industrial engineering majors who are enrolled on a full-time basis, members of the institute, have a GPA of at least 3.4, and are of junior standing or below. Applicants must be minority or female students and be nominated by their school's

IIE department head. Contact your school's industrial engineering department head for information.

Institute of Industrial Engineers
Scholarship Program
25 Technology Park/Atlanta
Norcross, GA   30092

1168

Uranga Loan

AMOUNT: None Specified   **DEADLINE:** Jan 12
FIELDS/MAJORS: Foreign Studies

Open to currently enrolled students of Mexican descent who can demonstrate financial need. Contact the address below for further information.

University of Washington
Center for Chicano Studies B 521
Padelford Hall Box 354380
Seattle, WA   98195

1169

Urban League of Greater Hartford Scholarships for African-Americans

AMOUNT: Maximum: $1000   **DEADLINE:** May 10
FIELDS/MAJORS: All Areas of Study

Open to African-American high school graduates or GED recipients who are residents of the greater Hartford area. Must be enrolled or accepted to an accredited college or university. Based on community involvement, grades, SAT scores, and financial need. Contact the address below for further information.

Urban League of Greater Hartford Scholarship
Ms. Beverly LeConche
1229 Albany Ave.
Hartford, CT   06112

1170

Ventura County Minority Business Group Scholarships

AMOUNT: Maximum: $4000   **DEADLINE:** Apr 8
FIELDS/MAJORS: Business

Applicants must be high school graduating seniors. They must be minority students who are enrolled, or intending to enroll, as a candidate for a business-related degree at a fully accredited college, university, vocation, trade, or business school. Must have a GPA of 3.0 or better and be a resident of Ventura County, California. Write to the address below for more information.

Ventura County Community Foundation
1355 Del Norte Rd.
Camarillo, CA   93010

1171

Vera Almon Sampley Scholarships

AMOUNT: None Specified   **DEADLINE:** Mar 31
FIELDS/MAJORS: All Areas of Study

Awards open to women juniors and seniors. Based on academics. Contact the address below for further information.

University of North Texas
Scholarship Office
Marquis Hall #218
Denton, TX   76203

1172

Vermell Pattillo Keeslar Memorial Scholarship

AMOUNT: None Specified
DEADLINE: None Specified
FIELDS/MAJORS: Women Sports

Student must be full-time and a member of a women's athletic team. Must have a GPA of 3.0 or better. Contact the Women's Athletics Office for more information.

Southwest Missouri State University
Office of Financial Aid
901 South National Ave.
Springfield, MO   65804

1173

Verne Catt McDowell Corporation Scholarship

AMOUNT: None Specified   **DEADLINE:** None Specified
FIELDS/MAJORS: Theology/Religion

Applicants must be members of the Christian Church (Disciples of Christ) seeking to become ministers and accepted into a graduate program at an approved institution of theological education. Preference given to students from Oregon. Four students are supported at a time. Write to the address shown below for details.

Verne Catt McDowell Corporation
PO Box 1336
Albany, OR   97321-0440

1174

Vicki Carr Scholarship Fund for California Students

AMOUNT: None Specified   **DEADLINE:** Apr 15
FIELDS/MAJORS: All Areas of Study

Awards for California residents of Latino heritage. Must be between the ages of seventeen and twenty-two. Must be a legal U.S. resident. Send a SASE to the address below for an official application. Applications will only be accepted between Feb 1 and Apr 15.

Vikki Carr Scholarship Foundation
PO Box 5126
Beverly Hills, CA   90210

1175

Vicki Carr Scholarship Fund for Texas Students

AMOUNT: None Specified   **DEADLINE:** Mar 1
FIELDS/MAJORS: All Areas of Study

Awards for Texas residents of Latino heritage. Must be between the ages of seventeen and twenty-two. Must be a U.S. citizen or permanent resident. Send a SASE to the address below for an official application. Applications will only be accepted between Jan 1 and Mar 1.

Vikki Carr Scholarship Foundation
PO Box 780968
San Antonio, TX   78278

1176
Victor Sikevitz and The Janet and Samuel A. Goldsmith Scholarships

AMOUNT: None Specified   DEADLINE: Mar 1
FIELDS/MAJORS: Communal Service

Open to juniors or above who are legally domiciled in Cook County or the Chicago metro area. For students with career goals in Jewish communal service. Contact the address below for further information after Dec 1.

Jewish Vocational Service
Academic Scholarship Program
1 S. Franklin St.
Chicago, IL   60606

1177
Viola Jones Collins Scholarship

AMOUNT: None Specified
DEADLINE: None Specified
FIELDS/MAJORS: Ministry

The scholarship will be awarded to a student who is studying for the ministry in the Ashland-based Brethren Church. Write to the address below for more information.

Ashland University
401 College Ave.
Ashland, OH   44805

1178
Virginia Transfer Grant Program

AMOUNT: None Specified   DEADLINE: None Specified
FIELDS/MAJORS: All Areas of Study

For a minority Virginia resident in undergraduate study at a public Virginia college or university. Transferring student must have at least a 2.0 GPA. All students who transfer to Virginia State University or Norfolk State University are eligible. Must demonstrate financial need. May be renewed up to two years if recipients meet satisfactory academic program standards, (as defined for financial aid recipients at the institution attended.) Awards may be up to full tuition and fees. Write to the address below for complete details.

Virginia Council of Higher Education
James Monroe Bldg.
101 N. 14th St.
Richmond, VA   23219

1179
Virmond-Heyl Scholarship

AMOUNT: None Specified   DEADLINE: Jan 15
FIELDS/MAJORS: All Areas of Study

Scholarships open to junior and senior women students who are residents of Ellis or Gove County, Kansas. Write to the address below for information.

Fort Hays State University
Office of Student Financial Aid
600 Park St.
Hays, KS   67601

1180
Vocational Rehabilitation Benefits

AMOUNT: Maximum: $2000
DEADLINE: None Specified
FIELDS/MAJORS: All Areas of Study

Grants for physically or mentally handicapped South Carolina residents who are attending a South Carolina college or university. Based on financial need. Contact the nearest Vocational Rehabilitation Office or the Vocational Rehabilitation Dept., 1410 Boston Ave., P.O. Box 15, W. Columbia, SC 29171.

South Carolina Commission on Higher Education
1333 Main Street, Suite 200
Columbia, SC   29201

1181
Vocational Rehabilitation Grants

AMOUNT: None Specified   DEADLINE: Nov 1
FIELDS/MAJORS: All Areas of Study

Grants are available to students with any type of impairment/disability (speech, hearing, sight, rheumatic heart, missing limbs, crippling disabilities. etc.) Contact the local Vocational Rehabilitation Center for counseling, evaluation, and determination of their eligibility for these grants. There are three deadline dates: Jun 1 (academic year), Nov 1 (spring semester), and Apr 1 (summer).

Elizabeth City State University
Financial Aid Office
Parkview Drive
Elizabeth City, NC   27909

1182
Vocational Rehabilitation Program

AMOUNT: None Specified   DEADLINE: None Specified
FIELDS/MAJORS: All Areas of Study

Program for North Carolina residents who have a mental or physical disability which is a handicap to employment. Contact the local Vocational Rehabilitation Office for further information.

University of North Carolina, Greensboro
Financial Aid Office
723 Kenilworth St.
Greensboro, NC   27412

1183
Vollum American Indian Scholarships

AMOUNT: $500-$1000
DEADLINE: None Specified
FIELDS/MAJORS: All Areas of Study

Awards are available at Portland State University for undergraduates of Native American descent. Must have a GPA of 2.75 or better and show evidence of financial need. One to two awards offered annually. Contact the educational equity programs and services for more information.

Portland State University
Office of Admissions
104 Neuberger Hall
Portland, OR 97207

1184
Walter O. Mason Jr. Scholarship

AMOUNT: $1000   DEADLINE: May 1
FIELDS/MAJORS: Health Science

Scholarships are available at the University of Oklahoma, Norman for full-time minority health science majors. Four awards offered annually. Write to the address below for information.

University of Oklahoma, Norman
Director, Office of Financial Aid
OUHSC, P.O. Box 26901
Oklahoma City, OK 73190

1185
Walter Reed Smith Scholarship

AMOUNT: None Specified
DEADLINE: None Specified
FIELDS/MAJORS: Home Economics, Nutrition, Nursing

Scholarships for students in Home Economics who are direct descendants of worthy confederates. Must be able to prove lineage. For women over the age of thirty. Contact the UDC nearest you. If the address is not known, write to the below address for further information and address.

United Daughters of the Confederacy
Scholarship Coordinator
328 North Boulevard
Richmond, VA 23220

1186
War Veterans Scholarship

AMOUNT: None Specified
DEADLINE: Mar 2
FIELDS/MAJORS: Crop Science, Animal Science, Agribusiness

Award open to sophomores, juniors, and seniors with a minimum GPA of 2.5. Preference given disadvantaged minority students. Contact the address below for further information.

California Polytechnic State University
Financial Aid Office
212 Administration Bldg.
San Luis Obispo, CA 93407

1187
Warner-Hall, Presbyterian Women of the Church, and P.I.E. Scholarships

AMOUNT: $600-$2000   DEADLINE: Mar 15
FIELDS/MAJORS: All Areas of Study

Scholarships for St. Andrew's students who are members of the Presbyterian Church. Must be nominated by your pastor or youth minister for Warner-Hall Award or by the women of the Church for the Presbytery award. The P.I.E. Award is a matching contribution for students from a local congregation. Write to the address listed or contact your local church for more complete details.

St. Andrews College
Office of Financial Aid
1700 Dogwood Mile
Laurinburg, NC 28352

1188
Warren M. Anderson Scholarship

AMOUNT: $1200   DEADLINE: Feb 1
FIELDS/MAJORS: All Areas of Study

Scholarships are available at the Indiana State University for full-time students who rank in the top 10% of their graduating class or have a GPA of at least 3.0. Must be of African-American descent. Based on school and community service activities. Write to the address below for details.

Indiana State University
Office of Admissions
Terre Haute, IN 47809

1189
Welfare Training Stipend

AMOUNT: $6000   DEADLINE: Mar 1
FIELDS/MAJORS: Social Work

Award for graduate minority students who are interested in a career in child welfare services and are entering the second year of field placement. One or more awards offered annually. Contact the Graduate School of Social Work for more information.

Portland State University
Graduate School of Social Work
300 University Center Building
Portland, OR 97207

1190
West Indian Migrant Farm Workers Memorial Scholarship

AMOUNT: Maximum: $1000   DEADLINE: Mar 31
FIELDS/MAJORS: All Areas of Study

Open to high school seniors of West Indian heritage. Selections based on academics and financial need. Contact the address listed for further information.

West Indian Foundation, Inc.
Scholarship Committee
PO Box 320394
Hartford, CT   06132-0394

1191 Westinghouse/CBS Career Horizons Scholarship

AMOUNT: None Specified
DEADLINE: None Specified
FIELDS/MAJORS: Electrical/Industrial/
Mechanical Engineering, Computer
Science, Accounting, Business, Finance,
Marketing, Communications, Journalism

Open to sophomores and juniors who have
a minimum GPA of 3.0 and are enrolled at
any of the following historically black colleges or universities:
Atlanta University Center, Florida A & M, Howard University,
North Carolina A & T University, Prairie View A & M
University, Southern University A & M College, Tennessee State
University, and Tuskegee University. Contact the financial aid
office at your school for information and an application.

United Negro College Fund
Scholarship Program
PO Box 10444
Fairfax, VA   22031-4511

1192 Wexner Graduate Fellowship Program

AMOUNT: None Specified   **DEADLINE:** Feb 1
FIELDS/MAJORS: Jewish Studies

Awards for North American students who are college graduates
and plan to enter a graduate program in preparation for a career
in Jewish Education, communal service, the Rabbinate, the
Cantorate, or Jewish Studies. Write to the address below for more
information.

Wexner Foundation
158 W. Main St.
PO Box 668
New Albany, OH   43054

1193 Whitney M. Young Memorial Scholarship

AMOUNT: $500-$800   **DEADLINE:** Jul 15
FIELDS/MAJORS: All Areas of Study

Available for male or female minority students who are currently
enrolled in a post-secondary institution. Students must maintain a
GPA of 2.5 or better. Must demonstrate financial need and live in
the Chicago area. Write to the address below for more information.

Chicago Urban League
Gina Blake, Scholarship Specialist
4510 South Michigan Ave.
Chicago, IL   60653

1194 Whittier Scholarship

AMOUNT: None Specified   **DEADLINE:** None Specified
FIELDS/MAJORS: Consumer Studies

Awards for female seniors in the department of consumer studies
who have a cumulative GPA of 3.0 or higher and demonstrated
financial need. Contact the Chair, Scholarship Committee,
Department of Consumer Studies for more information.

University of Massachusetts, Amherst
Chair, Scholarship Committee
Department of Consumer Studies
Amherst, MA   01003

1195 WICHE Doctoral Scholars Program

AMOUNT: None Specified
DEADLINE: None Specified
FIELDS/MAJORS: All Areas of Study

Awards are available for the purpose of encouraging
ethnic minority students to pursue doctoral degrees
and become college level teachers. Preference is given
to science, engineering, and mathematics students. For
residents of Alaska, Arizona, Colorado, Hawaii, Idaho, Montana,
Nevada, Oregon, Utah, North/South Dakota, New Mexico,
Washington, and Wyoming. Write to the address below for information.

Western Interstate Commission for Higher Education
PO Drawer P
Boulder, CO   80301

1196 WICI, Seattle Professional Chapter Communications Scholarships

AMOUNT: None Specified   **DEADLINE:** Mar 3
FIELDS/MAJORS: Communications

Awards for Washington residents and/or students at a four-year
institution in the state of Washington. For female juniors, seniors,
or graduate students. Three awards offered annually. Applications
are available at many financial aid offices and schools or departments of communication, or write to the address below for details
and an application.

Women in Communications, Inc., Seattle Professional Chapter
WICI Scholarship Chair
8310 Southeast 61st Street
Mercer Island, WA   98040

1197
WICPA Minority Accounting Program

AMOUNT: $4000 DEADLINE: Nov 29
FIELDS/MAJORS: Accounting

Scholarships are available for high school seniors who are residents of Wisconsin and are planning to enroll in an accredited accounting program at an accredited Wisconsin college or university. Applicant must have a GPA of at least 3.0 and be of Hispanic, African-American, Native American, or Asian descent. Write to the address below for information.

WICPA Educational Foundation, Inc.
235 N. Executive Drive, Ste. 200
PO Box 1010
Brookfield, WI   53008

1198
Will Rogers Scholarship

AMOUNT: $1000 DEADLINE: Mar 1
FIELDS/MAJORS: All Areas of Study

Scholarships are available at the University of Oklahoma, Norman for students who are handicapped. Ten to twenty awards are offered each year. Write to the address below for information.

University of Oklahoma, Norman
Office of Financial Aid Services
731 Elm
Norman, OK   73019

1199
William C. Stokoe Scholarship

AMOUNT: $1000 DEADLINE: Mar 15
FIELDS/MAJORS: Deaf Education, Sign Language

Must be a deaf student who is pursuing part-time or full-time graduate studies in a field related to sign language or the deaf community, or is developing a special project on one of these topics. Write to the address below for details.

National Association of the Deaf
Stokoe Scholarship Secretary
814 Thayer Ave.
Silver Spring, MD   20910

1200
William G. Corey Memorial Scholarship

AMOUNT: $3000 DEADLINE: Mar 1
FIELDS/MAJORS: All Areas of Study

Scholarship awarded to the top applicant from Pennsylvania. Must be legally blind. Write to the address below for details.

American Council of the Blind
Scholarship Coordinator
1155 15th St., NW, Suite 720
Washington, D.C.   20005

1201
William Randolph Hearst Endowed Scholarship for Minority Students

AMOUNT: None Specified DEADLINE: None Specified
FIELDS/MAJORS: All Areas of Study

Awarded annually to an outstanding minority student on the basis of scholarship, promise, and financial need. Write to the address below for more information.

Ashland University
401 College Ave.
Ashland, OH   44805

1202
Willie P. Morrow Memorial Scholarship

AMOUNT: $500 DEADLINE: Apr 1
FIELDS/MAJORS: All Areas of Study

Scholarships for African-American students at Kent State who are residents of Tuscarawas County. Based on financial need and academic potential. One award per year. Contact the financial aid office at your campus for details.

Kent State University, Tuscarawas Campus
Financial Aid Office
University Drive, NE
New Philadelphia, OH   44663

1203
Wilson Sertoma Club Scholarship

AMOUNT: Maximum: $500 DEADLINE: Mar 15
FIELDS/MAJORS: Education of the Deaf and Hard of Hearing

Open to students who are deaf or hard of hearing or students majoring in the education of the deaf and hard of hearing. First preference given to residents of Wilson County. Selection made by the School of Education. Contact the address below for further information.

Barton College
Financial Aid Office
Wilson, NC   27893

1204
Wisconsin Electric Scholarship

AMOUNT: None Specified
DEADLINE: Feb 15
FIELDS/MAJORS: Electrical Engineering

Awards for electrical engineering majors with a GPA of 2.9 or greater who have an intended emphasis in power/energy area. Must be female or minority students of sophomore or junior standing to apply. One award is given annually. Write to the address below for more information.

University of Wisconsin, Platteville
Office of Enrollment and Admissions
Platteville, WI   53818

1205

Wisconsin Public Service Corporation Scholarships

AMOUNT: None Specified   DEADLINE: Feb 15
FIELDS/MAJORS: Electrical or Mechanical Engineering

Awards are available at UW-Platteville for female and/or minority sophomore electrical or mechanical engineering majors. Must have a GPA of 2.0 or better and financial need. Renewable. One award is given annually. Write to the address below for more information.

University of Wisconsin, Platteville
Office of Enrollment and Admissions
Platteville, WI   53818

1206

Women in Construction Scholarship

AMOUNT: None Specified   DEADLINE: Feb 15
FIELDS/MAJORS: Civil Engineering, Construction Engineering

Scholarships are awarded annually to a full-time Murray State student pursuing a degree in civil or construction engineering technology. Write to the address below for more information.

Murray State University
Office of University Scholarships
Ordway Hall, P.O. Box 9
Murray, KY   42071

1207

Women in Engineering Program

AMOUNT: $500   DEADLINE: Jan 15
FIELDS/MAJORS: Engineering, Computer Science

Scholarships for women who are either freshmen or transfer students at the University of Missouri, Rolla pursuing an engineering degree. Approximately thirty awards per year. Not renewable. Contact Mr. Floyd Harris, director, women in engineering program, at the address below for details.

University of Missouri—Rolla
106 Parker Hall
Rolla, MO   65401

1208

Women in Engineering/ Catharine S. Eberly Center

AMOUNT: $400   DEADLINE: None Specified
FIELDS/MAJORS: Engineering

Awards open to females enrolled in the College of Engineering. Must have a minimum GPA of 2.0. Contact the address below for further information.

University of Toledo
Dianne Mills/Lora Beckwith
Tucker Hall 0168
Toledo, OH   43606

1209

Women in Management Scholarship

AMOUNT: $1000   DEADLINE: Feb 15
FIELDS/MAJORS: All Areas of Study

Candidate must be a woman, at least twenty-six years old, and within two years of completing a bachelor's degree or pursuing a graduate degree. Must live or attend college in Kane, Kendall, or DeKalb Counties, or west of Route 53 in DuPage County, and have a GPA of at least 3.0. Write to the address below for more information.

Women in Management—Aurora Chapter
PO Box 2632
Aurora, IL   60507

1210

Women in Science and Engineering Scholarship

AMOUNT: $1000   DEADLINE: Dec 31
FIELDS/MAJORS: Agriculture/Biological/Physical/ Computer Sciences, Math, Engineering

Awards for entering women freshmen who are/were in the top 5% of their graduating classes or have an ACT composite score of 30 or higher. Contact the address below for further information.

Iowa State University—Women in Science and
    Engineering Program
Krishna S. Athreya
210 Lab of Mechanics
Ames, IA   50011

1211

Women in Science Scholarship

AMOUNT: $250
DEADLINE: None Specified
FIELDS/MAJORS: Science

Student must be a full-time sophomore with a major in the College of Natural and Applied Sciences with a GPA of 3.0 or better. Preference is given to women. Contact the College of Natural and Applied Sciences for more information.

Southwest Missouri State University
Office of Financial Aid
901 South National Ave.
Springfield, MO   65804

1212

Women in Management Scholarship

AMOUNT: None Specified   DEADLINE: Apr 1
FIELDS/MAJORS: Management, Business

Open to students enrolled in a degree program planning to pursue a management or business career. One undergraduate award and one award for graduates. Contact the address listed for further information.

Women in Management, Inc.
Scholarship Chairperson
PO Box 1334
Dubuque, IA   52004-1334

1213
Women of the ELCA— Lay Women Scholarships

AMOUNT: $500-$2000   DEADLINE: Apr 1
FIELDS/MAJORS: All Areas of Study (except Church-certified professions)

Open to laywomen, twenty-one years of age or above, who are members of an ELCA congregation and have experienced an interruption in their schooling of at least two years since high school. Cannot be studying for ordination, the Diaconate, or Church-certified professions. Based on academics, need, educational goals, and Christian commitment. Must be a U.S. citizen. Write to the address below for details.

Women of the Evangelical Lutheran Church in America
8765 W. Higgins Road
Chicago, IL   60631

1214
Women of Wayne Alumni Association Scholarships

AMOUNT: None Specified   DEADLINE: None Specified
FIELDS/MAJORS: All Areas of Study

Scholarships for women students at Wayne State University studying part time on the undergraduate, graduate, or post-graduate level. Write to the address below for details.

Wayne State University
Women's Resource Center
573 Student Center Bldg.
Detroit, MI   48202

1215
Women on Books Scholarship

AMOUNT: Maximum: $1000
DEADLINE: Jun 12
FIELDS/MAJORS: English, Journalism, Creative Writing

Open to African-American students who have a minimum GPA of 2.5. Must be currently attending a four-year school, pursuing a writing career (creative or journalism). Must also be able to demonstrate financial need. Contact the address below for further information.

Women on Books
Scholarship Committee
879 Rainier Ave. N #A105
Renton, WA   98055

1216
Women's Advertising Club of Toledo

AMOUNT: $500   DEADLINE: None Specified
FIELDS/MAJORS: Communications

Award open to full-time female juniors and seniors who are residents of Toledo. Contact the address below for further information.

University of Toledo
Coordinator of Student Services-J. Green
403 Libbey Hall
Toledo, OH   43606

1217
Women's Endowment Program Scholarship

AMOUNT: None Specified   DEADLINE: Apr 15
FIELDS/MAJORS: All Areas of Study

Open to women pursuing degrees who are twenty-five years of age or older. Must have a minimum GPA of 3.0 and be enrolled for at least 12 hours per semester, (9 hours if employed full time). Contact the address below for further information.

University of Colorado—Colorado Springs
Office of Financial Aid
1420 Austin Bluffs Pkwy., P.O. Box 7150
Colorado Springs, CO   80907

1218
Women's Research and Education Institute Congressional Fellowship

AMOUNT: None Specified   DEADLINE: Feb 15
FIELDS/MAJORS: Women and Public Policy Issues

Annual fellowship program that places women graduate students in congressional offices and on strategic committee staffs. Encouraging more effective participation by women in the formation of policy at all levels. Must be currently enrolled in a graduate degree program. Award is tuition and a living stipend for an academic year. Write to the address below for details and enclose a SASE.

Women's Research and Education Institute
Shari Miles, Director
1750 New York Ave. NW # 350
Washington, D.C.   20006

1219
World Relief Foundation/E. Phillip Kirschner/Roy & Alice Spinks Awards

AMOUNT: $400-$600   DEADLINE: None Specified
FIELDS/MAJORS: All Areas of Study

Open to Native American students who are attending school full time. Contact the address below for further information about all three awards.

Bacone College
Financial Aid Office
99 Bacone Rd.
Muskogee, OK   74403

1220
WTOL-TV Broadcast and Communications Scholarship

AMOUNT: $3000   DEADLINE: None Specified
FIELDS/MAJORS: Broadcast Communications

Awards open to African-American and Hispanic-American undergraduates. Must be at least a junior with a minimum GPA of 3.0. Contact the address below for further information.

Fifty Men and Women of Toledo and Image, NW Ohio Chapter
J.C. Caldwell
PO Box 3557
Toledo, OH   43608

1221 Wyeth-Ayerst Scholarships

AMOUNT: $2000   DEADLINE: Apr 15
FIELDS/MAJORS: Bio/Medical Research and Technology, Pharmaceuticals, Public Health

Scholarships are open to women, twenty-five years of age or older, who are U.S. citizens studying in one of the fields above. Applicants must be graduating within twelve to twenty-four months from Sep 1, demonstrate need for financial assistance, and be accepted into an accredited program of course study at a U.S. institution. Student must have a plan to use the training to upgrade skills for career advancement, pursue a new career field, or enter or re-enter the job market. Write to the address below for details.

Business and Professional Women's Foundation
Scholarships
2012 Massachusetts Avenue NW
Washington, D.C.   20036

1222 Wynonna G. Hubbard Scholarship

AMOUNT: $1000   DEADLINE: None Specified
FIELDS/MAJORS: All Areas of Study

Scholarships are available at the University of Iowa for African-American women who are full-time students of at least junior status. Applicant must have a GPA of at least 3.0 and be able to demonstrate financial need. Students must be nominated by their college.

University of Iowa
Office of the Provost
111 Jessup Hall
Iowa City, IA   52242

1223 Xerox Scholarship

AMOUNT: None Specified
DEADLINE: Mar 1
FIELDS/MAJORS: Engineering

Must be a Hispanic student majoring in engineering, a U.S. citizen, and have a 3.0 GPA. Write to the address below for more information.

New Mexico State University
College of Engineering
Complex I, Box 30001, Dept. 3449
Las Cruces, NM   88003

1224 Xerox Technical Minority Scholarship Program

AMOUNT: None Specified   DEADLINE: Sep 15
FIELDS/MAJORS: Engineering and Science

Scholarships for full-time minority students enrolled in one of the following fields: chemical, computer, electrical, materials, mechanical, optical, or civil engineering; computer science; physics; or imaging. Must be U.S. citizens or permanent residents. Write to Eleanor J. Krieger, college relations manager, at the address below for details.

Xerox Corporation, Staffing Strategies and Solutions
Technical Minority Scholarship Fund
800 Phillips Road—205-99E
Webster, NY   14580

1225 Yale New Haven Hospital Minority Nursing/Allied Health Scholarship

AMOUNT: Maximum: $1500   DEADLINE: Feb 16
FIELDS/MAJORS: Nursing, Allied Health

Open to high school seniors who are Connecticut residents and enrolled or accepted into a four-year school with an accredited nursing or allied health program. Based on financial need and academics. Contact the address below for further information.

Yale New Haven Hospital
Human Resources
20 York St.
New Haven, CT   06504

1226 Yearlings Scholarship

AMOUNT: None Specified   DEADLINE: Feb 1
FIELDS/MAJORS: All Areas of Study

Applicants must be female, age twenty-five or above, who are residents of Boone, Campbell, or Kenton Counties. Must maintain a minimum 3.0 GPA and demonstrate financial need. Contact the address below for further information.

Northern Kentucky University
Financial Aid Office-Nunn Dr.
Administrative Center #416
Highland Heights, KY   41099

1227
Yellow Jacket Foundation/Green and Gold Scholarship

AMOUNT: None Specified   DEADLINE: None Specified
FIELDS/MAJORS: Sports

These are available to male and female first-, second-, third-, or fourth-year student athletes who are sport team members. The Lady Jackets may receive awards in volleyball, and/or basketball, cross country, and/or track. The men may receive awards in football, basketball, cross country, and/or track. Contact the Athletic Director for more information.

Black Hills State University
Athletic Director
University Station, Box 9924
Spearfish, SD   57799-9924

1228
Yoshiko Tanaka Memorial Scholarship

AMOUNT: None Specified   DEADLINE: Apr 1
FIELDS/MAJORS: Japanese Language and Culture

Awards for undergraduate students of Japanese ancestry who have an interest in Japanese language, culture, or enhancing U.S.-Japan relations. Applicants must be members of the JACL. Write to the address below for more details. Please be sure to include a SASE with your request.

Japanese American Citizens League
National Headquarters
1765 Sutter St.
San Francisco, CA   94115

1229
Yutaka Nakazawa Memorial Scholarship

AMOUNT: None Specified   DEADLINE: Apr 1
FIELDS/MAJORS: Judo

Applicants must be of Japanese ancestry and studying judo at the college level. Must also be members of the JACL. Applications and information may be obtained from local JACL chapters, district offices, and the national headquarters at the address below. Please indicate your level of study and be certain to include a legal-sized SASE.

Japanese American Citizens League
National Scholarship and Award Program
1765 Sutter St.
San Francisco, CA   94115

1230
Zell Boseman Memorial/ Alaska Black Caucus Scholarship

AMOUNT: None Specified   DEADLINE: None Specified
FIELDS/MAJORS: All Areas of Study

Scholarships are available to racial minority students (Black, Hispanic, Alaska Native, American Indian, Asian, American/Pacific Islander). Must be Alaska residents. Preference will be given to first-time students and persons returning to formal study after a period of absence. Write to the address below for more information.

University of Alaska Southeast (Juneau Campus)
Financial Aid Office
11120 Glacier Highway
Juneau, AK   99801

1231
Zia Transfer Scholarships

AMOUNT: $1000   DEADLINE: May 15
FIELDS/MAJORS: All Areas of Study

Scholarships are available at the University of New Mexico for minority transfer students who have completed 30 credit hours with a GPA of at least 3.25. Must be involved in school/community activities. Write to the address below for information.

University of New Mexico, Albuquerque
Student Financial Aid Office
Mesa Vista Hall North, Room 1044
Albuquerque, NM   87131

1232
Zonta Club of Olympia Scholarship

AMOUNT: $500   DEADLINE: Feb 3
FIELDS/MAJORS: All Areas of Study

Offered to a currently enrolled female Evergreen student attending at least half time, who is twenty-three years or older as of Mar 15, 1997, and who has at that date been a resident of Thurston County for at least twelve consecutive months. Applicants should demonstrate an interest in business or the professions (legal, medical, etc.) and personal commitment to improving the legal, political, economic, and professional status of women. Contact the address listed for further information.

Evergreen State College
Office of the Dean of Enrollment Service
2700 Evergreen Parkway
Olympia, WA   98505-0002

1233
Zonta Scholarship

AMOUNT: Maximum: $1000   DEADLINE: May 15
FIELDS/MAJORS: All Areas of Study

Scholarships for area women who are returning to school after an interruption, with the intention of returning to the work force afterwards. Award(s) will be one for $1000 or two awards for $500 each. Awards dependent on number and types of applications received. Write to the address below for details.

Zonta Club of Green Bay
Scholarship Program
PO Box 97
Green Bay, WI   54305

Major/Career Objective Index

 FINE ARTS

HUMANITIES

MEDICINE

728, 857, 903, 904, 908, 909, 984, 1003, 1089, 1185, 1225

Optometry, 804

Pharmacy/Pharmacology/ Pharmaceutical, 3, 554, 697, 911, 963, 996, 1221

Public Health, 69, 1221

Therapy (General), 329, 591, 855, 996, 1030

Veterinary Medicine, 110, 742, 804, 996

SCIENCE

Agriculture/Agricultural Engineering, 22, 26, 50, 178, 228, 243, 312, 314, 358, 473, 484, 644, 708, 880, 1041, 1186, 1210

Animal Science, 1186

Aquaculture, 708

Arboriculture, 643

Astronomy, 888

Atmospheric Science, 76

Biochemistry, 63

Biology, 64, 458, 474, 678, 737, 793, 888, 1080, 1128, 1144, 1210

Botany, 1111

Chemistry, 63, 64, 351, 458, 639, 851, 888, 1063, 1144

Conservation, 194

Earth Science, 446

Ecology/Environmental Science, 193, 194, 453, 1056, 1144, 1151

Energy-Related Studies, 193, 194

Forestry, 233, 708

Geology, 64, 446

Geophysics, 446, 914

Geoscience, 225, 446

Horticulture, 50, 1054

Hydrology, 76, 446

Life Sciences, 122, 407, 408

Marine/Oceanic Sciences, 76, 446

Mathematics, 18, 122, 270, 369, 407, 408, 428, 473, 474, 536, 611, 714, 734, 777, 797, 822, 854, 877, 888, 902, 926, 968, 999, 1045, 1052, 1057, 1080, 1083, 1101, 1195, 1210

Math/Science Secondary Education, 1, 579, 821, 957

Meteorology, 76

Microbiological Sciences, 106, 1011

Natural Resources, 1, 233, 524, 1137

Natural Sciences, 534, 777, 999, 1045

Physical Sciences, 122, 472, 1210

Physics, 64, 93, 407, 408, 458, 474, 533, 680, 737, 793, 854, 888, 968, 1080, 1101, 1224

Science (General), 1, 18, 27, 32, 40, 55, 58, 78, 101, 167, 176, 193, 201, 270, 340, 394, 400, 428, 496, 526, 531, 536, 737, 797, 822, 827, 877, 968, 1060, 1067, 1080, 1083, 1101, 1191, 1195, 1211, 1224

Soil/Water Conservation, 178

Space Science, 446

Statistics, 777, 1052

Wildlife, 126

SOCIAL SCIENCES

American History, 41, 513, 635

Anthropology, 417, 793, 880, 1000, 1064

Archaeology, 73, 127, 880

Armenian Studies, 25, 98

Behavioral Sciences, 122, 377, 580, 1080

Community Service, 583

Counseling, 175, 1106

Criminal Justice, 49

Ethnic Studies, 1046, 1065, 1228

Foreign Studies, 191, 635, 640, 1010, 1168

Geriatrics, 855

Government, 981, 1018

History, 501, 582, 612, 729, 730, 793, 830, 880, 928, 1005, 1046, 1064

Home Economics, 243, 1185

International Relations, 25, 533, 547, 568, 981, 1018

Jewish Studies, 269, 282, 426, 551, 583, 945, 1085, 1192

Latin-American Studies, 920, 1127

Law, 25, 81, 82, 141, 209, 246, 283, 331, 373, 400, 449, 534, 606, 615, 618, 624, 656, 666, 693, 694, 742, 804, 847, 916, 949, 985, 990, 1080

Law Enforcement, 49

Leisure Studies, 171

Philanthropic Studies, 492

Planning, 1135, 1151

Special Criteria Index

Swiss, 237, 1108

Syrian, 451

West Indian, 700, 1190

 GRADE POINT AVERAGE

Minimum GPA 2.5
44, 71, 193, 197, 208, 222, 228, 251, 267, 276, 305, 310, 337, 362, 370, 398, 425, 428, 493, 494, 508, 527, 531, 537, 569, 582, 584, 598, 647, 662, 668, 721, 728, 740, 758, 760, 776, 778, 779, 784, 812, 815, 817, 818, 856, 869, 887, 895, 910, 918, 925, 947, 986, 994, 1003, 1015, 1025, 1026, 1043, 1088, 1090, 1097, 1117, 1120, 1136, 1139, 1152, 1156, 1166, 1183, 1186, 1193, 1204, 1215

Minimum GPA 3.0
2, 7, 14, 24, 29, 45, 47, 84, 86, 98, 113, 114, 116, 117, 127, 140, 143, 145, 157, 182, 189, 199, 202, 206, 211, 243, 262, 279, 290, 294, 295, 326, 335, 349, 350, 351, 365, 375, 400, 403, 409, 419, 430, 432, 433, 434, 438, 442, 450, 454, 460, 463, 465, 481, 482, 486, 490, 496, 500, 518, 521, 530, 533, 538, 557, 568, 587, 591, 600, 603, 605, 612, 614, 626, 638, 639, 645, 654, 655, 659, 665, 670, 714, 725, 729, 732, 736, 741, 753, 755, 762, 771, 774, 777, 791, 822, 837, 841, 844, 845, 853, 854, 858, 867, 868, 873, 888, 892, 902, 904, 919, 923, 948, 972, 997, 1004, 1019, 1036, 1045, 1061, 1066, 1082, 1091, 1093, 1100, 1109, 1116, 1126, 1129,

1130, 1131, 1167, 1170, 1172, 1188, 1194, 1209, 1211, 1217, 1222, 1223, 1226, 1231

Minimum GPA 3.5
15, 25, 40, 139, 192, 263, 437, 479, 515, 517, 525, 611, 679, 711, 734, 827, 912, 970, 975, 990, 1012, 1038, 1108, 1138, 1160

 MILITARY

74, 248, 280, 379, 629, 704, 1185

RELIGION

Assembly of God, 107, 1122

Baha'i, 634

Baptist, 15, 118, 222, 227, 324, 393, 456, 563, 765, 766, 843, 954, 970

Catholic, 10, 95, 129, 146, 147, 169, 186, 272, 358, 503, 532, 711, 924, 1017, 1113

Christian, 97, 163, 174, 192, 420, 440, 465, 480, 485, 510, 568, 657, 661, 712, 743, 910, 934, 973, 1002

Christian Science, 36

Church of Christ, 658

Church of the Brethren, 158, 162, 268, 309, 872, 878, 905, 935, 938, 1035, 1079, 1177

Disciples of Christ, 133, 172, 221, 285, 302, 303, 342, 625, 906, 1023, 1086, 1173

Eastern Orthodox, 332

Episcopal, 135, 148, 1047, 1048, 1049

Free Methodist, 423

Jewish, 12, 18, 123, 202, 203, 269, 282, 415, 426, 449, 453, 551, 583, 584, 585, 586, 587, 663, 698, 720, 722, 833, 945, 1006, 1021, 1085, 1176, 1192

Lutheran, 125, 173, 220, 345, 362, 383, 527, 682, 753, 848, 904, 977, 978, 1097, 1139, 1213

Methodist, 52, 378, 756, 975

Presbyterian, 91, 226, 239, 475, 477, 590, 874, 875, 876, 879, 964, 965, 966, 1028, 1042, 1062, 1095, 1147, 1187

Protestant, 334, 441, 701, 936, 937

Religion (Any), 46, 403, 1072, 1165

Unitarian, 213, 609, 710, 767, 916, 932

United Church of Christ, 1145

United Methodist, 43, 52, 54, 136, 367, 387, 562, 660, 871, 1092, 1156, 1159

WOMEN

4, 5, 6, 7, 10, 13, 21, 26, 41, 42, 42, 44, 45, 47, 48, 55, 56, 57, 58, 59, 60, 61, 64, 66, 75, 84, 85, 88, 89, 94, 96, 103, 108, 110, 113, 114, 121, 122, 124, 126, 127, 128, 134, 139, 143, 144, 145, 153, 159, 160, 170, 171, 176, 177, 178, 179, 180, 182, 183, 184, 185, 189, 190, 197, 199, 200, 207, 211, 225, 229, 238, 248, 253, 256, 258, 266, 268, 270, 277, 278, 279, 280, 281, 284, 287, 288, 292, 293, 294, 295,

OTHER

School Index